Accounting Princ[iples for] Tax Purposes

Fourth Edition

Accounting Principles for Tax Purposes

Fourth Edition

Lynne Oats B.Bus, PGDip, PhD
Reader in Accounting and Taxation, University of Warwick

and

Paul Tuck B.Sc, FCA
Lecturer in Accounting and Auditing, University of Buckingham

Bloomsbury Professional

Bloomsbury Professional Ltd, Maxwelton House, 41–43 Boltro Road, Haywards Heath, West Sussex, RH16 1BJ

© Bloomsbury Professional Ltd 2010

Previously published by Tottel Publishing Ltd

All rights reserved. No part of this publication may be reproduced in any material form (including photocopying or storing it in any medium by electronic means and whether or not transiently or incidentally to some other use of this publication) without the written permission of the copyright owner except in accordance with the provisions of the Copyright, Designs and Patents Act 1988 or under the terms of a licence issued by the Copyright Licensing Agency Ltd, Saffron House, 6–10 Kirby Street, London EC1N 8TS. Applications for the copyright owner's written permission to reproduce any part of this publication should be addressed to the publisher.

Warning: The doing of an unauthorised act in relation to a copyright work may result in both a civil claim for damages and criminal prosecution.

Crown copyright material is reproduced with the permission of the Controller of HMSO and the Queen's Printer for Scotland. Any European material in this work which has been reproduced from EUR-lex, the official European Communities legislation website, is European Communities copyright.

A CIP Catalogue record for this book is available from the British Library.

ISBN: 978 1 84766 380 1

Typeset by Phoenix Photosetting, Chatham, Kent
Printed and bound in Great Britain by Martins the Printers, Berwick-upon-Tweed, Northumberland

Preface to the Fourth Edition

The preface to the third edition of this book, by F. Michael Cochrane, observed that:

> 'the pace of change does not seem to slacken... Since the second edition, there has been relatively little relevant change on the accounting side, but there has been a significant movement in relation to tax which further aligns the tax with the accounting rules whilst at the same time preserving some time-honoured differences.'

At that time, the new issues of concern included discussions about the applicability of accounting standards for tax purposes and the increasing reference to accounting principles in tax cases.

In the ten years or so since the publication of the third edition, the pace of change has arguably quickened, and on both sides of the fence – the accounting rules and the tax law; and new developments in the intervening years include:

- Increased use of accounting rules and principles by specific design within the tax legislation such as the rules for goodwill and intangibles and loan relationships;
- The output from the Tax Law Rewrite process, which has seen both income tax and corporation tax legislation restructured and re-written, albeit keeping the underlying principles intact;
- A new Companies Act in 2006, partly a re-write but also containing significant simplification; and
- Significant changes to accounting standards, most notably the increased convergence between UK GAAP and international standards.

What appeared at first to be a straightforward task, to bring the third edition up to date, soon became an enormous endeavour, not only in tracking and explaining changes to existing rules and practices, but also introducing the new developments in the international arena. In the course of producing this fourth edition, we have also taken the opportunity to re-structure the book and introduce some new topic areas.

It is hoped that this volume will serve a useful purpose for tax practitioners whose knowledge of accounting is either limited or even just a bit rusty. As the overlap between tax and accounting rules continues to grow, it is even more important now than it was ten years ago, for tax practitioners to have a sound grasp of how the world of accounting works and is changing.

Lynne Oats

Paul Tuck

Contents

Preface to the Fourth Edition	*v*
Table of Examples	*xiii*
Table of Statutes	*xv*
Table of Statutory Instruments	*xviii*
Table of UK Accounting Standards	*xix*
Table of International Accounting Standards	*xxii*
Table of International Financial Reporting Standards	*xxiii*
Table of Cases	*xxv*
Abbreviations and References	*xxix*
Chapter 1 Introduction	**1**
Part I Accounting Principles and Financial Statements	**5**
Chapter 2 The Legal and Institutional Framework	**7**
Limited liability companies – the legalities	7
Limited liability companies – the institutions	20
The accounts of non-limited companies	22
Summary	23
Chapter 3 An Accounting Overview	**25**
The 'entity' convention	25
The balance sheet	26
The profit and loss account	32
Accounting ratios and jargon	35
Chapter 4 Financial Statements – Which Version of Accounting Standards?	**40**
Chapter 5 Back to Basics: Accounting Principles	**43**
Legal requirements	44
Accounting bases	45
Historical cost accounting rules	45
Alternative accounting rules	45
Financial Reporting Standard 18 (FRS 18)	55
Developments in fundamental accounting concepts	56
Difficult issues	57
Capital or revenue	58
Revenue (income and expenditure) – timing	60

Contents

Chapter 6 Substance Over Form	63
Financial Reporting Standard 5 (FRS 5)	63
Application of FRS 5	64
Methodology	65
Profit recognition	67
Distributable profits	67
International standards	68
Taxation	68

Chapter 7 The Presentational Standards	71
Segmental reporting	71
Statement of Standard Accounting Practice 25 (SSAP 25)	72
Comparison with International Accounting Standards	73
Taxation considerations	73
Reporting financial performance	74
Financial Reporting Standard 3 (FRS 3)	74
Comparison with International Accounting Standards	88
Taxation considerations	88
Earnings per share	88
Taxation considerations	91

Chapter 8 Post-Balance Sheet Events	92
Financial Reporting Statement 21 (FRS 21)	92
International Accounting Standard 10 (IAS 10)	93
Taxation	94
Extended debates	96

Chapter 9 Related Parties	97
Financial Reporting Standard 8 (FRS 8)	97
International Accounting Standard 24 (IAS 24)	100
Taxation	100

Chapter 10 Smaller Entities	101
Financial Reporting Standard for Smaller Entities (FRSSE)	101
The IASB view	102

Chapter 11 Cash Flow Statements	104
Financial Reporting Standard 1 (Revised 1996) (FRS 1)	104
International Accounting Standards	108
Taxation consequences	109

Part II Basic Accounting Issues	111

Chapter 12 Revenue Recognition	113
FRS 5: Application Note G	113
Urgent Issues Task Force (UITF 40)	115
International Accounting Standard 18 (IAS 18)	116
Taxation considerations	116

Chapter 13 Stocks and Work in Progress	118
Statement of Standard Accounting Practice 9 (SSAP 9)	119
Stocks	119

Costs	119
Methods of costing	122
Net realisable value	123
Disclosures	124
Company law requirements	124
Comparison with International Accounting Standards	125
Taxation considerations	125

Chapter 14 Long-term Contracts — 127
Attributable profit	127
Foreseeable losses	128
Payments on account	128
Comparison with International Accounting Standards	131
Taxation	131

Chapter 15 Tangible Fixed Assets — 132
Initial measurement	132
Start-up costs	133
Finance costs	133
Subsequent expenditure	133
Alternative valuation bases	134
Impairment	135
Gains and losses other than through impairment	136
Investment properties	136
International Accounting Standard 16 (IAS 16)	137

Chapter 16 Depreciation — 138
Financial Reporting Standard 15 (FRS 15)	138
Methods of computing depreciation	139
'Complex assets'	141
Revaluations	141
Permanent diminution in value	142
Disclosures	143
Statement of Standard Accounting Practice 19 (SSAP 19)	144
Taxation	146

Chapter 17 Acquiring Assets on Finance — 147
Statement of Standard Accounting Practice 21 (SSAP 21)	148
Operation of the standard – lessees	150
Operation of the standard – lessors	153
Disclosures	154
Problem areas	154
Comparison with International Accounting Standards	155
Taxation	155

Chapter 18 Provisions and Contingencies — 158
Financial Reporting Standard 12 (FRS 12)	158
International Accounting Standards	162
Taxation considerations	162

Contents

Chapter 19	**Pensions**	**164**
	Statement of Standard Accounting Practice 24 (SSAP 24)	164
	Financial Reporting Statement 17 (FRS 17)	165
	International Accounting Standard 19 (IAS 19)	165
	Taxation	166
Chapter 20	**Employee Share Ownership Plans**	**167**
	UK GAAP	167
	International Standards	169
	Taxation considerations	169
Chapter 21	**Government Grants**	**170**
	UK GAAP	170
	International Standards	171
	Taxation considerations	172
Chapter 22	**Accounting for Tax**	**176**
	Accounting for VAT	176
	Accounting for corporate income tax	177
	International Accounting Standards	184
	Taxation considerations	185
Part III	**Advanced Accounting Issues**	**187**
Chapter 23	**Groups**	**189**
	Corporate law	190
	Accounting principles	194
	Comparison with International Accounting Standards	211
	Taxation	212
Chapter 24	**Foreign Currency Translation**	**215**
	Statement of Standard Accounting Practice 20 (SSAP 20)	215
	Individual companies	216
	Group consolidated accounts	218
	FRS 23 and IAS 21	220
	Comparison with International Accounting Standards	220
	Taxation	221
	The old system	222
	Examples	224
Chapter 25	**Goodwill and Intangible Assets**	**229**
	Financial Reporting Standard 10 (FRS 10)	229
	Financial Reporting Standard 7 (FRS 7)	231
	Valuation basis	232
	Cost of acquisition	233
	Business bought for resale	233
	Determination of fair value	233
	Comparison with International Accounting Standards	238
	Taxation	239
	The intangibles regime	239

Contents

Chapter 26 Research and Development Expenditure — **242**
Statement of Standard Accounting Practice 13 (SSAP 13) — 242
Definitions — 242
Accounting treatment — 243
Disclosures — 244
Companies Act requirements — 244
Comparison with International Accounting Standards — 245
Taxation — 245

Chapter 27 Financial Instruments — **246**
Financial Reporting Standard 25 (FRS 25) — 247
Financial Reporting Standard 4 (FRS 4) — 248
Financial Reporting Standard 13 (FRS 13) — 249
Financial Reporting Standard 26 (FRS 26) — 249
Financial Reporting Standard 29 (FRS 29) — 250
International Standards — 251
Taxation considerations — 251
Recent tax developments — 252
Summary — 256

Chapter 28 Corporate Transactions – The Theory — **257**
The price of limited liability — 257
Reserves — 258
Distributable profits — 262
Acquisition accounting — 263
Merger accounting — 264
Group accounts — 266
Purchase of own shares — 267
Demergers — 269
Financial assistance — 269

Chapter 29 Corporate Transactions – The Practice — **271**
Reorganisation — 271
Acquisition of assets — 273
Incorporation of a sole trader business — 274
Acquisition of a subsidiary — 275
Acquisition of a 'hive down' company — 278
Dividend out of pre-acquisition profits — 280
Purchase of own shares — 281
Merger — 286
Demerger of two companies — 287
Comparison with International Accounting Standards — 291

Chapter 30 Limited Liability Partnerships — **292**
Legal requirements — 292
UK GAAP — 293
Payments to members — 294
Retirement benefits — 294
Taxation — 295
Revenue recognition and provisions — 295

Contents

	Related parties	295
	Taxation considerations	295

Part IV Conceptual Developments — 297

Chapter 31 Accounting and Tax Profit – Background and Present Position — 299
Basic tax principles	299
The problems	300
The analysis	302

Chapter 32 Future Developments — 305
IFRS adoption	305
Convergence	305
eXtensible Business Reporting Language (XBRL)	308
Common Consolidated Corporate Tax Base (CCCTB)	309
Speculation on future developments in Accounting and Financial Reporting Standards	309

Appendices — 311

Appendix A   A Summary and Commentary on the Main Cases — 313

Appendix B   Further Reading — 330

Index   *333*

Table of Examples

Example 3.1	26	Example 23.5	199
Example 3.2	27	Example 23.6	201
Example 3.3	30	Example 23.7	202
Example 3.4	33	Example 23.8	204
Example 3.5	33	Example 23.9	206
Example 5.1	47	Example 23.10	208
Example 7.1	76	Example 24.1	224
Example 7.2	78	Example 24.2	225
Example 7.3	80	Example 24.3	225
Example 7.4	81	Example 24.4	226
Example 7.5	84	Example 24.5	226
Example 7.6	90	Example 24.6	227
Example 8.1	95	Example 25.1	234
Example 11.1	105	Example 25.2	236
Example 13.1	120	Example 25.3	237
Example 13.2	124	Example 28.1	265
Example 14.1	129	Example 28.2	269
Example 16.1	140	Example 29.1	271
Example 16.2	140	Example 29.2	272
Example 16.3	142	Example 29.3	273
Example 17.1	150	Example 29.4	274
Example 17.2	152	Example 29.5	275
Example 21.1	172	Example 29.6	276
Example 21.2	173	Example 29.7	278
Example 21.3	174	Example 29.8	280
Example 21.4	174	Example 29.9	282
Example 22.1	178	Example 29.10	282
Example 22.2	179	Example 29.11	284
Example 22.3	180	Example 29.12	285
Example 23.1	190	Example 29.13	286
Example 23.2	195	Example 29.14	287
Example 23.3	197	Example 29.15	289
Example 23.4	198		

Table of Statutes

[*All references are to paragraph number and appendices*]

A

Administration of Estates
   Act 1925 . . . . 10.1
   s 55(1)(x) 11.39

B

Bills of Exchange
   Act 1882 . . . . 11.68, 11.70

C

Capital Allowances Act 1990
   s 150 . . . . 25.21

Capital Allowances Act 2001
   s 67 . . . . 17.2, 17.29

Companies Act 1890

Companies Act 1948 . . . . 2.15

Companies Act 1981 . . . . 5.3

Companies Act 1985 . . . . 5.3, 9.1, 21.5, 26.10
   s 130 . . . . 29.12
   155–158 . . . . 28.49
   227 . . . . 23.2
   228 . . . . 23.8
   229 . . . . 23.7
   230 . . . . 23.8
   231 . . . . 23.7
   244 . . . . 2.10
   248 . . . . 23.8
   256 . . . . 2.20
   258 . . . . 23.4
   262(3) . . . . App A
   383 . . . . 23.8
   466 . . . . 23.8
   Sch 4A 23.6
   Sch 5 . . . . 23.7
      para 10(1)(d) . . . . App A

Companies Act 1989 . . 23.3, 23.4, 23.10

Companies Act 2006 . . 2.2, 2.10, 2.12, 2.25, 5.3, 5.22, 5.24, 5.26, 7.3, 8.1, 9.1, 10.1, 10.5, 15.2, 15.4, 15.7, 15.8, 15.10, 16.14, 16.15, 23.2, 23.3, 23.10, 23.40, 20.4, 26.1, 27.1, 27.6, 28.36, 30.2, 30.4
   s 15, 16 . . . . 2.3
   Pt 7 . . . . 10.2
   269 . . . . 28.22
   382 . . . . 2.7, 11.2
   386, 387 . . . . 2.10, 2.11
   388, 389 . . . . 2.10
   390 . . . . 2.14
   392 . . . . 2.14
   393, 394 . . . . 2.10
   395 . . . . 2.10, 2.15
   415 . . . . 2.10, 2.16
   417 . . . . 2.16
   423–425 . . . . 2.10
   426, 427 . . . . 2.18
   437 . . . . 2.10, 2.18
   441 . . . . 2.18
   442 . . . . 2.10
   444(3) 2.7
   451, 452 . . . . 2.18
   465 . . . . 2.7
   477 . . . . 2.7, 10.3
   480 . . . . 2.9
   485 . . . . 2.10, 2.17
   489 . . . . 2.10, 2.17
   498 . . . . 2.17
   610 . . . . 28.9, 28.33, 29.43
      (3) 28.9
   611 . . . . 28.9, 28.34
   612 . . . . 28.9, 28.32, 28.34, 29.3, 29.36, 29.37

Table of Statutes

Companies Act 2006 – *contd*
s 613	28.9
622	28.12
628	28.12
645	28.7, 28.9
656	28.18
678	28.49
687	28.42, 29.28
688	28.44
Pt 18 Ch 4 (ss 690–708)	28.7, 28.40
s 690	28.40
694	28.42
709	28.45
733	28.13, 28.44
(3)	29.28
761	2.4
830	5.16, 28.19, 28.21
831	5.16, 28.19
833	2.9
836	28.20, 28.24
844	26.11
845	26.24
846	26.24, 29.40

Companies (Audit, Investigations and Community Enterprise) Act 2004 ... 1.9

Corporation Tax Act 2009 .... 27.14
s 9	2.14
35	1.2, 31.2
46	1.2, 1.9, 4.12, 12.7, 31.9
53	5.28, 27.14
54	27.14
Pt 5 (ss 292–475)	27.13
s 295(1)	27.14
297(2)–(4)	27.14
301(1)	27.14
(4)–(7)	27.14
302	27.16
(1)	27.14
303(1)	27.14
307(2)–(4)	27.15
308(2)	27.15
313(1)	27.15
320, 321	27.15
Pt 5 Ch 16 (ss 456–463)	27.14
Pt 6 (ss 477–569)	27.13, 27.16
s 483	27.16
Pt 6 Ch 6 (ss 501–521)	27.16
Pt 7 (ss 570–710)	27.13, 27.17
577	27.17

Corporation Tax Act 2009 – *contd*
s 579	27.17
589	27.17
Pt 8 (ss 711–906)	25.22
s 715	25.22
727	25.22
729	25.23
730	25.23
Pt 8 Ch 4 (ss 733–741)	25.23
s 734	25.23
737	25.23
740	25.23
Pt 8 Ch 6 (ss 745–753)	25.23
s 751	25.23
Pt 8 Ch 7 (ss 754–763)	25.23
s 765	28.4
866	8.11
1218	2.9
1219	2.9
1316(1)	2.9

Corporation Tax Act 2010
s 37	2.14
138	2.14
439	2.6
466	2.6

F

Finance Act 1986
s 75	29.38
77	29.3, 29.38

Finance Act 1993 ..... 19.1, 24.21, 27.12
s 139	24.26

Finance Act 1994 .... 16.19, 27.12

Finance Act 1996 .... 24.24, 27.12
s 100	27.16
Sch 9 para 14	16.19

Finance Act 1997
s 82	23.36

Finance (No 2) Act 1997
s 47	23.36

Finance Act 1998 .... 2.24, 2.25
s 42	12.7, 13.17, 31.8
s 42(2)	31.8
s 46	5.20

Table of Statutes

Finance Act 2002
s 64	5.21
103	31.8
(5)	2.24

Finance Act 2002 – *contd*
Sch 22	5.21
Sch 29	25.22

Finance Act 2003
Sch 23	20.8

Finance Act 2004
s 50	2.24, 31.8
196, 197	19.9

Finance Act 2006
Sch 8	17.33
Sch 15	12.7

Finance Act 2008 | 26.13
s 34	13.17
Sch 15	13.17

Finance Act 2009 | 17.32
Sch 46	2.19

Financial Services Act 1986 | 23.9

I

Income and Corporation Taxes Act 1988
s 13	2.8
s 18	2.8
Sch D	31.9
Case I	31.2, 31.8
Case II	31.8
60	31.2
100	29.20
160	8.11
209	27.11
(2)(b)	29.26
(4)	29.41
213(2)	29.41
(3)(b)(ii)	29.44
219	29.26
343	29.20
(4)	29.20
402	23.38
409, 410	23.24
413	27.11
416	23.39, 27.11
417	27.11
419	8.11

Income and Corporation Taxes Act 1988 – *contd*
707	29.3
768	23.23, 29.20
832(1)	27.11
836A	31.8
Sch 18	27.11

Income Tax Act 2007
s 682	5.18

Income Tax (Trading and Other Income) Act 2005
s 5	1.2, 31.2
25	1.2, 1.9, 4.12, 12.7, 24.22, 31.9
58	27.10
236, 237	5.21

J

Joint Stock Companies Act 1844 | 2.15

L

Limited Liability Partnerships Act 2000 | 30.1

T

Taxation of Chargeable Gains Act 1992
s 117	29.17
126	29.41, 29.44
135	29.16, 29.38
138	29.3, 29.16
139	29.44
162	6.21, 29.10
171	23.38, 29.20
179	29.20
192	29.41

Taxes Management Act 1970
s 20	2.11
20B	2.11
99	2.11

V

Value Added Tax Act 1994
s 43	23.40
Sch 8	2.9
Sch 9	2.9
Sch 11	
para 6	2.11

Table of Statutory Instruments

[*All references to paragraph numbers*]

Accounting Standards (Prescribed Body) Regulations 1990, SI 1990/1667 .... 2.20

Companies (Summary Financial Statement) Regulations 2008, SI 2008/374 .... 2.12

Income Tax (Pay As You Earn) Regulations 2003, SI 2003/2682 reg 97(1) 2.11

Large and Medium-sized Companies and Groups (Accounts and Reports) Regulations 2008, SI 2008/410 .... 2.12, 5.4, 5.8, 5.9, 5.11, 6.13, 9.1, 10.2, 13.12, 15.6, 16.1, 16.8, 16.12, 16.15, 23.2, 26.11, 28.3, 28.9, 28.11, 28.35

Limited Liability Partnerships (Accounts and Audit) (Application of Companies Act 2006) Regulations 2008, SI 2008/1911 .... 30.1, 30.2, 30.4

Limited Liability Partnerships Regulations 2001, SI 2001/1090 .... 30.1

Small Companies and Groups (Accounts and Directors' Report) Regulations 2008, SI 2008/409............ 2.12, 5.4, 5.8, 5,9, 5.11, 6.13, 10.2, 13.12, 15.6, 16.1, 16.8, 16.12, 16.15, 23.2, 26.11, 28.3, 28.9, 28.11, 28.35

Table of UK Accounting Standards

[*All references are to paragraph numbers and appendices*]

**Financial Reporting
Standard 1** 2.12,
11.1, 11.2, 11.3,
11.4, 11.6, 11.7,
11.8, 30.6, 30.8

**Financial Reporting
Standard 2** 23.6,
23.10, 23.33

**Financial Reporting
Standard 3** 5.12,
7.2, 7.12, 7.13,
7.15, 7.16, 7.18,
7.19, 7.20, 7.21,
7.23, 7.26, 10.6,
15.10, 16.11, 16.14,
21.12, 25.20, 30.6,
App A

**Financial Reporting
Standard 4** 15.4,
24.14, 25.12, 27.1,
27.4, 27.10, 27.11
para 8 .... 27.4

**Financial Reporting
Standard 5** 6.2,
6.9, 6.10, 6.11,
6.14, 6.15, 6.16,
6.17, 6.18, 6.22,
10.6, 12.1, 12.4,
17.27, 20.2, 30.11,
31.6
para 23, 24 .... 6.10
para 27 .... 6.11
para 29 .... 6.12
Application Note A 6.9
Application Note B 6.9, 6.15
Application Note C 6.9, 6.10
Application Note D 6.9
Application Note E 6.9
Application Note F 6.9

Application Note G 5.12, 6.9,
6.15, 12.2,
12.3, 12.4,
12.5, 30.11

**Financial Reporting
Standard 6** 28.36,
28.37, 29.3, 29.21,
29.23, 29.36, 29.37,
29.46
App 1
para 16 .... 29.22

**Financial Reporting
Standard 7** 25.8,
25.9, 25.10, 25.11,
25.20, 28.27, 29.6

**Financial Reporting
Standard 8** 9.1,
9.2, 9.8, 9.9,
9.10, 9.11, 9.12,
9.13, 30.12

**Financial Reporting
Standard 9** 11.1,
23.25, 23.26, 23.28,
23.29, 23.31, 23.32,
23.34, 23.35

**Financial Reporting
Standard 10** 18.2,
25.1, 25.2, 25.3,
25.4, 25.8, 25.9,
25.16, 25.17, 25.18,
25.19, 25.20, 23.17,
28.27, 29.6, 29.7,
29.10, 29.12

**Financial Reporting
Standard 11** 15.2,
15.8, 15.9, 15.11
para 10 .... 15.9

Table of UK Accounting Standards

Financial Reporting Standard 12 .... 5.31, 5.36, 5.37, 15.2, 18.1, 18.5, 18.6, 18.8, 18.9, 18.10, 18.11, 18.13, 18.18, 18.20, 30.9, 30.11, App A

Financial Reporting Standard 13 .... 27.1, 27.5

Financial Reporting Standard 14 .... 7.2, 7.28

Financial Reporting Standard 15 .... 5.12, 15.1, 15.2, 15.3, 15.4, 15.6, 15.9, 15.10, 15.11, 15.12, 16.1, 16.2, 16.3, 16.8, 16.9, 16.12, 16.17, 26.7, 28.11

Financial Reporting Standard 16 .... 22.5, 22.6

Financial Reporting Standard 17 .... 19.1, 19.2, 19.5, 19.6, 19.7, 19.8, 30.9

Financial Reporting Standard 18 .... 5.3, 5.22, 5.23, 13.17, 27.5

Financial Reporting Standard 19 .... 22.5, 22.7, 22.11, 22.12, 22.13, 22.14, 22.15, 22.17, 22.20, 22.21
para 25 .... 22.16

Financial Reporting Standard 20 .... 20.4, 20.5, 20.6, 20.7, 24.1

Financial Reporting Standard 21 .... 8.1, 8.2, 8.7, 8.8, 8.9, 8.10

para 9 .... 8.3
para 21 .... 8.5

Financial Reporting Standard 22 .... 7.2, 7.28, 7.29, 7.34

Financial Reporting Standard 23 .... 24.1, 24.16, 24.17, 24.24, 27.6

Financial Reporting Standard 24 .... 27.6

Financial Reporting Standard 25 .... 27.1, 27.2, 27.3, 27.4, 27.7, 27.8, 30.7, 30.8, 30.9
para 20 .... 27.2

Financial Reporting Standard 26 .... 27.1, 27.4, 27.5, 27.6, 27.7, 27.8

Financial Reporting Standard 29 .... 27.3, 27.6, 27.7, 27.8

Statement of Standard Accounting Practice 1 .... 5.3, 23.25, 23.39

Statement of Standard Accounting Practice 2 .... 5.3, 5.5, 5.22, 5.24, 5.26, App A

Statement of Standard Accounting Practice 3 .... 7.2

Statement of Standard Accounting Practice 4 .... 21.2, 21.3, 21.4, 21.5, 21.7

Statement of Standard Accounting Practice 5 ..... 22.2

Table of UK Accounting Standards

Statement of Standard
    Accounting Practice 6 .... 7.2,
                   7.12, 7.20, App A

Statement of Standard
    Accounting Practice 8 ..... 22.6

Statement of Standard
    Accounting Practice 9 ..... 12.3,
                 13.1, 13.2, 13.3,
                 13.4, 13.9, 13.10,
              13.11, 13.14, 13.16,
              13.17, 14.1, 14.3,
             14.9, 14.10, 30.11,
                        App A
App 3 .... 14.6

Statement of Standard
    Accounting Practice 10 ... 11.1

Statement of Standard
    Accounting Practice 13 .... 26.2,
                   26.3, 26.9,
                26.10, 26.12

Statement of Standard
    Accounting Practice 14 .... 23.10

Statement of Standard
    Accounting Practice 15 ... 22.7,
                         22.11

Statement of Standard
    Accounting Practice 17 .... 8.1

Statement of Standard
    Accounting Practice 18 .... 18.20

Statement of Standard
    Accounting Practice 19 .... 15.1,
                15.11, 16.12, 16.14,
              16.15, 16.16, 16.18,
                         22.7

Statement of Standard
    Accounting Practice 20 .... 24.1,
               24.2, 24.4, 24.6,
               24.7, 24.8, 24.9,
            24.10, 24.11, 24.12,
            24.13, 24.14, 24.16,
            24.18, 24.20, 24.22,
                24.24, 24.26

Statement of Standard
    Accounting Practice 21 .... 1.4,
                  1.5, 1.6, 1.7,
              17.3, 17.4, 17.8,
            17.16, 17.20, 17.22,
            17.23, 17.24, 17.27,
            17.28, 17.31, 27.4,
                        App A

Statement of Standard
    Accounting Practice 22 .... 25.1,
               25.8, 25.17, 25.18
App 3 .... 25.14

Statement of Standard
    Accounting Practice 23 .... 28.36

Statement of Standard
    Accounting Practice 24 .... 19.1,
                     19.4, 19.6

Statement of Standard
    Accounting Practice 25 ... 7.2,
               7.3, 7.4, 7.6, 7.7,
                  7.8, 7.10
Para 43 .... 7.7

Table of International Accounting Standards

[*All references are to paragraph numbers*]

International Accounting Standard 1	7.26, 9.9
International Accounting Standard 2	13.16
International Accounting Standard 7	11.8
International Accounting Standard 8	7.26
International Accounting Standards 10	8.1, 8.9
International Accounting Standards 11	14.9
International Accounting Standard 12	13.17, 22.20, 22.21
para 5....................	22.20
International Accounting Standard 14	7.8
International Accounting Standard 16	15.12
International Accounting Standard 17	17.28
International Accounting Standard 18	12.5, 12.7, 22.19
International Accounting Standard 19	19.7, 19.8, 20.7
International Accounting Standard 20	21.7
International Accounting Standard 21	24.1, 24.16, 24.17, 24.18, 24.24
International Accounting Standard 24	9.1, 9.4, 9.10
International Accounting Standard 27	23.33, 29.45
International Accounting Standard 28	23.34
International Accounting Standard 31	23.35
International Accounting Standard 32	27.8
International Accounting Standard 33	7.28
International Accounting Standard 36	25.20
International Accounting Standard 37	18.1, 18.18
International Accounting Standard 38	25.20, 26.12
International Accounting Standard 39	4.4, 27.8
International Accounting Standard 41	21.7

Table of International Financial Reporting Standards

[All references are to paragraph numbers]

**International Financial
    Reporting Standard 2** 20.7

**International Financial
    Reporting Standard 3** 25.20, 29.46

**International Financial
    Reporting Standard 7** 27.8

Table of Cases

[All references are to paragraph numbers and appendices]

A

Astall v Revenue and Customs Commissioners [2008] EWHC 1471 (Ch), [2008] STC 2920, [2008] BTC 713, [2008] STI 1646, Ch D.................... 6.22

B

BSC Footwear Ltd v Ridgway [1972] AC 544, [1971] 2 WLR 1313, [1971] 2 All ER 534, 47 TC 495, (1971) 50 ATC 153, [1971] TR 121, (1971) 115 SJ 408, HL.. App A

Barclays Mercantile Business Finance Ltd v Mawson (Inspector of Taxes); sub nom ABC Ltd v M (Inspector of Taxes) [2004] UKHL 51, [2005] 1 AC 684, [2004] 3 WLR 1383, [2005] 1 All ER 97, [2005] STC 1, 76 TC 446, [2004] BTC 414, 7 ITL Rep 383, [2004] STI 2435, (2004) 154 NLJ 1830, (2004) 148 SJLB 1403, HL.. 6.22

Briggenshaw v Crabb (1948) 41 R & IT 518, 30 TC 331 .... 23.42

D

Duomatic Ltd, Re [1969] 2 Ch 365, [1969] 2 WLR 114, [1969] 1 All ER 161, (1968) 112 SJ 922, Ch D... 8.11

Duple Motor Bodies v Ostime. *See* Ostime (Inspector of Taxes) v Duple Motor Bodies Ltd

E

ECC Quarries Ltd v Watkis (Inspector of Taxes) [1977] 1 WLR 1386, [1975] 3 All ER 843, [1975] STC 578, 51 TC 153, [1975] TR 185, (1975) 119 SJ 562, Ch D.. App A

Edward Collins & Sons v IRC; sub nom Collins & Sons v IRC (1924) 12 TC 773, 1925 SC 151, 1925 SLT 51, IH.. App A

F

Furniss (Inspector of Taxes) v Dawson [1984] AC 474, [1984] 2 WLR 226, [1984] 1 All ER 530, [1984] STC 153, 55 TC 324, (1984) 15 ATR 255, (1984) 81 LSG 739, (1985) 82 LSG 2782, (1984) 134 NLJ 341, (1984) 128 SJ 132, HL 6.18, 6.22

G

Gallagher v Jones (Inspector of Taxes). *See* Threlfall v Jones (Inspector of Taxes)

Gresham Life Assurance Society v Styles (Surveyor of Taxes) [1892] AC 309, (1890) 3 TC 185, HL.. App A

H

Heather (Inspector of taxes) v PE Consulting Group Ltd [1973] Ch 189, [1972] 3 WLR 833, [1973] 1 All ER 8, 48 TC 293, [1972] TR 237, (1972) 116 SJ 824, CA.. App A

Table of Cases

Herbert Smith (A Firm) v Honour (Inspector of Taxes) [1999] STC 173, 72 TC 130, [1999] BTC 44, [1999] EG 23 (CS), (1999) 96(11) LSG 70, (1999) 149 NLJ 250, (1999) 143 SJLB 72, [1999] NPC 24, Ch D .... 31.7, App A

I

IRC v James Spencer & Co; sub nom Spencer & Co v IRC, 1950 SC 345, 1950 SLT 266, 32 TC 111, [1950] TR 153, IH.. 18.20
IRC v McGuckian; McGuckian v IRC [1997] 1 WLR 991, [1997] 3 All ER 817, [1997] STC 908, [1997] NI 157, 69 TC 1, [1997] BTC 346, (1997) 94(27) LSG 23, (1997) 141 SJLB 153, HL.. 6.22
IRC v Secan Ltd; IRC v Ranon Ltd. 74 TC 1, 3 ITL Rep 496, CFA (HK) .... 13.17, App A

J

JP Hall & Co Ltd v IRC [1921] 3 KB 152, CA; reversing [1921] 1 KB 213, 12 TC 382, KBD.. App A
Johnston (Inspector of Taxes) v Britannia Airways [1994] STC 763, 67 TC 99, Ch D .... 1.8, 31.14, 31.17, 31.19, App A

M

Meat Traders Ltd v Cushing [1997] SCD 245, SpC .... 31.7, App A

O

Odeon Associated Theatres Ltd v Jones; sub nom Odeon Associated Cinemas v Jones [1973] Ch 288, [1972] 2 WLR 331, [1972] 1 All ER 681, 48 TC 257, [1971] TR 373, (1971) 115 SJ 850, CA .... App A
Ostime (Inspector of Taxes) v Duple Motor Bodies Ltd; Duple Motor Bodies v IRC [1961] 1 WLR 739, [1961] 2 All ER 167, 39 TC 537, (1961) 40 ATC 21, [1961] TR 29, (1961) 105 SJ 346, HL .... 13.17, App A
Owen (Inspector of Taxes) v Southern Railway of Peru Ltd. *See* Southern Railway of Peru Ltd v Owen (Inspector of Taxes)

P

Patrick (Inspector of Taxes) v Broadstone Mills Ltd [1954] 1 WLR 158, [1954] 1 All ER 163, 47 R & IT 41, 35 TC 44, (1953) 32 ATC 464, [1953] TR 441, (1954) 98 SJ 43, CA.. App A
Pearce (Inspector of Taxes) v Woodall Duckham Ltd [1978] 1 WLR 832, [1978] 2 All ER 793, [1978] STC 372, 51 TC 271, [1978] TR 87, (1978) 122 SJ 299, CA... App A
Pepper (Inspector of Taxes) v Hart [1993] AC 593, [1992] 3 WLR 1032, [1993] 1 All ER 42, [1992] STC 898, [1993] ICR 291, [1993] IRLR 33, [1993] RVR 127, (1993) 143 NLJ 17, [1992] NPC 154, HL 24.21

R

R v IRC, ex p SG Warburg & Co Ltd [1994] STC 518, (1995) 7 Admin LR 517, 68 TC 300, QBD.. App A
RTZ Oil and Gas Ltd v Elliss (Inspector of Taxes) [1987] 1 WLR 1442, [1987] STC 512, 61 TC 132, (1987) 131 SJ 1188, Ch D .... App A
Revenue and Customs Commissioners v William Grant & Sons Distillers Ltd (Scotland); sub nom William Grant & Sons Distillers Ltd v IRC; IRC v William Grant & Sons Distillers Ltd; Small (Inspector of Taxes) v Mars UK Ltd [2007] UKHL 15, [2007] 1 WLR 1448, [2007] 2 All ER 440,

Table of Cases

[2007] STC 680, 2007 SC (HL) 105, 2007 SLT 522, 2007 SCLR 468, 78 TC 442, [2007] BTC 315, [2007] STI 1165, (2007) 151 SJLB 470, 2007 GWD 17-306, HL .... 13.17, 31.11, App A
Ryan v Asia Mill; Heather v Asia Mill, 44 R & IT 698, 32 TC 275, (1951) 30 ATC 110, [1951] TR 181, [1951] WN 390, (1951) 95 SJ 544, HL .... App A

S

Secan. *See* IRC v Secan Ltd
Seaham Harbour Dock Co v Crook (Inspector of Taxes) (1931) 41 Ll L Rep 95, HL 21.8
Sharkey (Inspector of Taxes) v Wernher; sub nom Wernher v Sharkey (Inspector of Taxes) [1956] AC 58, [1955] 3 WLR 671, [1955] 3 All ER 493, 48 R & IT 739, 36 TC 275, (1955) 34 ATC 263, [1955] TR 277, (1955) 99 SJ 793, HL 13.17
Shearer v Bercain Ltd [1980] 3 All ER 295, [1980] STC 359, 63 TC 698, [1980] TR 93, (1980) 124 SJ 292, Ch D 5.18
Southern Railway of Peru Ltd v Owen (Inspector of Taxes); sub nom Peru v Owen (Inspector of Taxes); Owen (Inspector of Taxes) v Southern Railway of Peru Ltd [1957] AC 334, [1956] 3 WLR 389, [1956] 2 All ER 728, 49 R & IT 468, 36 TC 634, (1953) 32 ATC 147, [1956] TR 197, (1956) 100 SJ 527, HL .... 18.20, App A
Spencer & Co v IRC. *See* IRC v James Spencer & Co
Sun Insurance Office v Clark [1912] AC 443, 6 TC 59, HL .... App A
Symons (Inspector of Taxes) v Weeks; sub nom Symons (Inspector of Taxes) v Lord Llewelyn Davies Personal Representative [1983] STC 195, 56 TC 630, [1983] BTC 18, Ch D .... 12.6, 31.13, 31.15, App A

T

Tapemaze Ltd v Melluish (Inspector of Taxes) [2000] STC 189, 73 TC 167, [2000] BTC 50. [2000] STI 160, (2000) 97(8) LSG 37, Ch D .... App A
Threlfall v Jones (Inspector of Taxes); Gallagher v Jones (Inspector of Taxes) [1994] Ch 107, [1994] 2 WLR 160, [1993] STC 537, 66 TC 77, (1993) 90(32) LSG 40, (1993) 137 SJLB 174, CA .... 1.7, 27.10, 31.13, App A

V

Vallambrosa Rubber Co Ltd v IRC; sub nom Vallambrosa Rubber Co Ltd v Farmer (Surveyor of Taxes), 1910 SC 519, 1910 1 SLT 307, IH .... 1.7, App A

W

WT Ramsay Ltd v IRC; Eilbeck (Inspector of Taxes) v Rawling [1982] AC 300, [1981] 2 WLR 449, [1981] 1 All ER 865, [1981] STC 174, 54 TC 101, [1982] TR 123, (1981) 11 ATR 752, (1981) 125 SJ 220, HL 6.19
Whimster & Co v IRC; sub nom Whimster & Co v IRC (1925) 23 Ll L Rep 79, 1926 SC 20, 1925 SLT 623, 12 TC 813, IH .... App A
Willingale (Inspector of Taxes) v International Commercial Bank Ltd [1978] AC 834, [1978] 2 WLR 452, [1978] 1 All ER 754, [1978] STC 75, 52 TC 242, [1978] TR 5, (1978) 122 SJ 129, HL .... 31.17, App A

Abbreviations and References

ABBREVIATIONS

Accounting Regulations	=	Small Companies and Groups (Accounts and Directors' Report) Regulations 2008 (SI 2008/409) and Large and Medium-sized Companies and Groups (Accounts and Reports) Regulations 2008 (SI 2008/410)
ACT	=	Advance Corporation Tax
AIM	=	Alternative Investment Market
APB	=	Auditing Practices Board
ASB	=	Accounting Standards Board
ASC	=	Accounting Standards Committee
BIM	=	Business Income Manual
CA	=	Companies Act
CAA 1990	=	Capital Allowances Act 1990
cl	=	clause
CTA 2009	=	Corporation Tax Act 2009
CTA 2010	=	Corporation Tax Act 2010
FA	=	Finance Act
ED	=	Exposure Draft
EIS	=	Enterprise Investment Scheme
EPS	=	Earnings Per Share
EC	=	European Community
EU	=	European Union
FASB	=	Financial Accounting Standards Board (US)
FB	=	Finance Bill
FRED	=	Financial Reporting Exposure Draft
FRRP	=	Financial Reporting Review Panel
FRS	=	Financial Reporting Standard
FRSSE	=	Financial Reporting Standard For Small Entities
GAAP	=	Generally Accepted Accounting Practice
HMRC	=	Her Majesty's Revenue and Customs
ICAEW	=	Institute of Chartered Accountants in England and Wales
IAS	=	International Accounting Standard (International Standard issued before 2001)
IAS Regulation	=	Regulation (EC) 1606/2002
IASB	=	International Accounting Standards Board

Abbreviations and References

ICTA 1988	=	Income and Corporation Taxes Act 1988
IFRS	=	International Financial Reporting Standard (International Standard issued after 2001)
IHTA 1984	=	Inheritance Tax Act 1984
IIMR	=	Institute of Investment Management and Research
ISA	=	International Auditing Standard
ITA 2007	=	Income Tax Act 2007
ITEPA 2005	=	Income Tax, Earnings and Pensions Act 2005
ITTOIA 2007	=	Income Tax, Trading and Other Income Act 2007
para	=	paragraph
PE	=	Price Earnings Ratio
s	=	section
Sch	=	Schedule
SI	=	Statutory Instrument
SME	=	small or medium-sized enterprise
SP	=	HMRC Statement of Practice
SSAP	=	Statement of Standard Accounting Practice
STRGL	=	Statement of Recognised Gains and Losses
TMA 1970	=	Taxes Management Act 1970
TCGA 1992	=	Taxation of Chargeable Gains Act 1992
UITF	=	Urgent Issues Task Force
VATA 1994	=	Value Added Tax Act 1994

REFERENCES

TC	=	Official Reports of Tax Cases
STC	=	Simon's Tax Cases
ATC	=	Annotated Tax Cases
All ER	=	All England Law Reports
SCD	=	Special Commissioner's Decision

Chapter 1

Introduction

1.1 'Profit per accounts'. Every tax practitioner must have reproduced this three-word phrase numerous times, but how well does he understand how that figure – which he has just extracted from the 'accounts' handed to him by his accounting colleagues – has been arrived at? This applies even to those practitioners with an accounting background, because the world of accounting standards, principles and practices has changed, and continues to change, so fast that anyone who departs from the mainline of accounting and financial reporting soon loses touch. This book sets out to explain what is meant by the word 'profit' and how it fits into the world of accounting and tax.

1.2 But why should this be of importance? Business profits are charged to income tax by *ITTOIA 2005, s 5*, and corporation tax by *CTA 2009, s 35*, which state that tax shall be charged in respect of the 'profits of a trade'. *ITTOIA 2005, s 25* and *CTA 2009, s 46* both state that the profits of a trade must be calculated in accordance with generally accepted accounting practice. There are specific rules governing types of income or expense which are to be taxed or tax deductible, but nowhere in the statute is there to be found any definition of 'full amount of profits'. Therein lies the problem.

1.3 In the early days of taxation, this absence of definition caused problems. Disputes arose and cases were taken to court. At that time, the accountancy profession was not yet fully organised and there was no regulatory framework to give assistance in interpreting the phrases 'annual profits' or 'full amount of profits'. So, judges were left very much to their own devices. It was universally recognised that the phrases should mean the 'profits of an enterprise as determined on proper commercial principles'. It was the task of the courts to discover what these principles were.

1.4 It is not necessary at this stage of the book to follow all the twists and turns in the history of judicial interpretation (Chapter 31 gives a more detailed tracing of the development of thinking in this regard). It does help to know where we stand at present. This may perhaps best be illustrated in relation to *SSAP 21* (which sets out the accounting rules for dealing with leased assets and is dealt with in detail in Chapter 17).

1.5 Introduction

1.5 As will be seen, *SSAP 21* provides that assets held on certain types of lease are treated as though owned by the lessee for the purpose of preparing accounts. In arriving at the measure of the lessee's trading profits, the lessee should not deduct the lease rentals payable, but there is a calculation to be made which results in them charging depreciation and a finance charge in their profit and loss account.

1.6 In 1991, the Revenue decided (*SP 3/91*) that, in future, accounts prepared under *SSAP 21* principles would be acceptable without adjustment for tax purposes. This was really quite revolutionary. Accounting rules derived from an accounting standard, which effectively elevated substance over form (by treating as 'owned' that which was legally only 'leased') and gave rise to a 'depreciation' charge, would be regarded as acceptable for tax purposes.

1.7 The matter went even further in 1992 and 1993 when two taxpayers decided to challenge the Inland Revenue. Two cases, with virtually identical facts, were heard before the courts simultaneously (*Threlfall v Jones, Gallagher v Jones* [1993] STC 537). The Inland Revenue argued that *SSAP 21* principles should apply and produced expert accountants as witnesses in support. The taxpayers sought to exclude *SSAP 21* and relied on certain very old cases (principally *Vallambrosa Rubber Co Ltd v Inland Revenue Commissioners* 1910 SC 519). Despite a slight setback in the High Court, the Inland Revenue won a comprehensive victory in the Court of Appeal. The cases did not proceed to the House of Lords.

1.8 In 1994, the case of *Johnston v Britannia Airways* [1994] STC 763 confirmed the trend. Discussions with the Inland Revenue resulted in the issue of a series of Questions and Answers (Tax 10/95) which confirmed the latest Revenue thinking.

1.9 This shift in policy then manifested itself in numerous ways. The codification of the true and fair view, and subsequent clarification of generally accepted accounting practice as being UK GAAP or, more recently, IFRS has been an important change. The new rules for the taxation of income from property, foreign exchange profits and losses and corporate loan relationships all closely follow accounting principles. *ITTOIA 2005, s 25* and *CTA 2009, s 46* state that the 'profits of a trade must be calculated in accordance with generally accepted accounting principles subject to any adjustment required or authorised by law'. Since 1998, further changes in HMRC (or Inland Revenue as it then was) include the appointment of financial reporting specialists to provide advice to tax inspectors on accountancy issues, and the creation of a 'gateway' between HMRC and the Financial Reporting Review Panel (FRRP). The legal gateway was formally enacted by the *Companies (Audit, Investigations and Community Enterprise) Act 2004* and a Memorandum of Understanding (MOU) between the Revenue and the FRRP, and allows HMRC to inform the FRRP when it detects irregularities in the accounts of companies submitted as part of the corporation tax self-assessment process.

1.10 In a nutshell, nearly 200 years of tax history can be summarised thus:

- business taxation is based on profits as determined on a proper commercial basis;
- early judicial decisions laid down principles;
- more recently, judges have placed greater reliance on accountancy rules and evidence; and
- the recent trend has been for HMRC to elevate accountancy rules and evidence to a pre-eminent position.

1.11 What this means is that it is crucial for tax practitioners to be completely comfortable with what their accounting colleagues are up to. This book sets out to help the reader understand the general principles underlying financial accounts. At appropriate points in each chapter, the particular tax relevance of the accountancy principle being described will be flagged.

1.12 But, finally, a word of warning. Just as the tax system is catching up with 'conventional' accounting, recent trends from accounting standard setters (in the UK and overseas) have progressed down new paths, in which economic substance is to be preferred to legal form, and where even the continuing relevance and retention of the profit and loss account is called into question. Also, in Europe there is currently a debate about adopting a common consolidated corporation tax base. This gives a whole new set of problems for the future – and these are addressed in Chapter 32.

1.13 Furthermore, in 2002, the European Union issued a Regulation *requiring* certain company financial statements, and *permitting* others, to be prepared in accordance with international accounting standards.

This book has been organised into three distinct parts. Part I deals with fundamental accounting concepts and the legal and accounting requirements for basic financial statements. In Part II, more detail is provided in relation to specific issues covered by accounting standards. In each of these, the discussion deals only with the accounts of an individual company. The complexities of consolidated accounts for groups of companies are left until Part III, where some more problematic areas are also introduced. Finally, Part IV deals with some conceptual issues, relating to the current and prospective interweaving of notions of accounting and tax profits.

PART I

ACCOUNTING PRINCIPLES AND FINANCIAL STATEMENTS

The aim of this Part is to describe the background legal and institutional framework within which accounting operates, and also to introduce some fundamental accounting concepts and principles. The development of accounting standards is a relatively recent phenomenon, but nonetheless has moved at an alarmingly rapid rate, particularly over the past 20 years, as has its interrelationship with income and corporation tax.

The chapters in this Part seek to guide the reader through some basic concepts in order to develop an understanding of the setting in which accounting developments take place, as well as the way accountants 'think'. They also introduce the standards that are relevant for presenting the totality of various financial statements (Part II will then deal with the individual components on a topic-by-topic basis). Both Parts I and II deal only with the financial statements of individual companies, not groups of companies.

In Chapter 2, the legal and institutional framework is described. Since the primary focus of the book is incorporated entities, an initial explanation of the legal environment for companies is provided, including the requirements for producing accounts and a description of the various public and private regulatory bodies that have an interest in accountancy practice.

Chapters 3 to 6 present an overview of accounting, with an introduction to the basic financial statements, specifically the balance sheet and the profit and loss account, as well as some fundamental concepts that guide the development of financial reporting practices.

Chapters 7 to 11 inclusive then deal with specific accounting standards. In each of these chapters, following a brief introduction to the background to current practice, the UK GAAP is discussed before considering the international standards and the tax implications.

Chapter 2

The Legal and Institutional Framework

2.1 The principal types of trading entity considered in this book will be: the sole trader, the partnership, and the limited liability company.

There are very few legal or institutional rules governing the preparation of accounts of unincorporated businesses – in general, accounts for these enterprises tend to be modelled on those prepared for their limited company counterparts, albeit without all the 'frills'. Additionally, a number of ad hoc practices have developed.

This chapter considers in detail the position as regards the limited liability company, with a final commentary on the differences in practice encountered with accounts of sole traders and partnerships.

LIMITED LIABILITY COMPANIES – THE LEGALITIES

2.2 Such entities form the major part of business organisation in the western world. Because of their crucial significance, it is important to be familiar, in outline at least, with some of the fundamental legal concepts. (Many business enterprises trade through a number of related companies, generally known as 'groups'. Chapter 23 deals exclusively with group issues, and this chapter excludes further reference to groups of companies.) Almost all companies encountered in the commercial context have the proprietors' interests in them represented by 'shares'. These companies are formed by reference to the *Companies Acts*. The latest *Companies Act* (*CA 2006*) received Royal Assent on 8 November 2006 and has been progressively implemented between that date and the full implementation date of 1 October 2009. One stated aim of *CA 2006* is to make it easier to set up and run a company.

Formation

2.3 A company limited by reference to 'shares' comes into existence, or is 'formed', when the Registrar of Companies (at Companies House) issues a Certificate of Incorporation (*CA 2006, ss 15* and *16*).

This is only done when certain formalities have been complied with, including the lodging with him of the proposed company's 'rule book' which is called

2.4 *The Legal and Institutional Framework*

the 'Memorandum and Articles of Association'. The Memorandum describes the relationship between the company and the outside world, and the Articles describe the relationship between the members (or shareholders) of the company. The Memorandum tends to be a short and fairly general document whilst the Articles are much longer and more precise; *CA 2006* significantly reduced the content of the Memorandum. In practice, the Articles are frequently studied, particularly where there are shareholder disputes.

The Memorandum and Articles can be tailor-made but, to make things easier, model sets of Memoranda and Articles are available and usually adopted. This is the equivalent of buying an off-the-peg suit and having it altered to fit. So common and easy is this procedure that company formation agents frequently form companies with no particular objective in mind, and then retain them 'on the shelf'. When a customer approaches 'to form a company', they merely take a pre-formed company 'from the shelf' and make any necessary alterations before transferring the shares in the company to the customer.

Classification of companies by status

2.4 In forming a company, a decision needs to be made as to whether the company is to be a private company (in which case, its name will end with the word 'Limited' or 'Ltd') or a public company (in which case, its name will end with 'public limited company' or 'plc'). These notations are not universally used, however, and you can find different ways of referring to public and private companies in other parts of the world.

A private company may start trading immediately on the issue of its Certificate of Incorporation but it may not issue its shares to the general public. Most companies in the UK are private.

A public company cannot start trading until it has been issued with a trading certificate under *CA 2006, s 761* by the Registrar of Companies. The Registrar will only do this if the company's authorised share capital is a minimum of £50,000, of which at least 25% by value of shares in the company have been issued for cash. A public company may issue its shares to the public. A person dealing with a public company should draw comfort from the fact that the shareholders have committed at least £12,500, so if things go wrong there is a buffer of at least that much that can be lost without creditors or customers suffering. In an extreme case, the buffer in a private company may only be £1.

It is possible for private companies to re-register as public, and vice versa, providing the relevant conditions are satisfied.

2.5 Because of its inability to offer shares to the general public, a private company may not be 'quoted' on the Stock Exchange 'full market', or the Alternative Investment Market (AIM). A public company may be quoted but is not necessarily so. Indeed, these days many larger private companies are re-registering as public companies – a relatively cheap and painless exercise – simply for the kudos attaching to the 'plc' suffix.

2.6 Tax law generally does not recognise the distinction between public and private companies.

The closest counterpart lies in the distinction between close and non-close companies as defined in *CTA 2010, s 439*, which has quite widespread application throughout the *Taxes Acts*, and the transactions in securities rules which are currently under review.

There is no reason why a private company cannot be non-close; conversely, a public company may itself be close. Frequently, this is just the position. Indeed, even quoted companies can be – and many are – close companies. This is a point frequently overlooked. However, quoted companies have an additional 'get-out' clause from being close under *CTA 2010, s 466*. Broadly, this applies where 35 per cent or more of the equity is held by the public and the company is quoted (subject to other restrictions).

Classification of companies by size

2.7 *CA 2006, ss 382* and *465* distinguish small, medium and large companies.

All public companies are 'large' for these purposes. Financial parameters are set to classify private companies into one or other of the categories. The figures (for periods on or after 6 April 2008) are listed below.

Small companies

Must satisfy at least two of the three following criteria:

- Turnover   not more than £6.5 million
- Balance sheet total   not more than £3.26 million
- Number of employees   not more than 50

Balance sheet total broadly means the total of all assets (including fixed and current).

Medium-sized companies

Must satisfy at least two of the three following criteria:

- Turnover   not more than £25.9 million
- Balance sheet total   not more than £12.9 million
- Number of employees   not more than 250

2.8 *The Legal and Institutional Framework*

Large companies

All other companies.

With only a very minor exception (relating exclusively to small companies), all companies of whatever size must produce full accounts, but small companies may also prepare abbreviated accounts with much reduced disclosures, and they are permitted to lodge only the abbreviated accounts with the Registrar of Companies should they wish. (This relaxation does not, however, apply to certain companies operating in the financial sector or to public companies.) The previous *Companies Act* allowed medium-sized companies to also lodge abbreviated accounts. HMRC require full and not abbreviated accounts to be submitted to them unless the turnover is less than £30,000.

If a small company uses abbreviated accounts, a special auditor's opinion is required (*CA 2006, s 444(3)*), but not if the company is exempt from audit. The audit exemption applies where the company is small, and has turnover not exceeding £6.5 million and a balance sheet total not exceeding £3.26 million (*CA 2006, s 477*).

The audit relaxation has no effect in relation to whether accounts should comply with accounting standards (see **2.20** below). However, in this respect *CA 2006* does recognise a distinction between small/medium companies on one hand and large/public companies on the other.

A company's accounts must state whether the accounts are in accordance with applicable accounting standards and, if not, to give particulars and reasons. If accounts are prepared in accordance with FRSSE, the balance sheet must include a statement to that effect, but no profit and loss statement or directors' report will be required.

2.8 The nearest the corporation tax legislation gets to recognising a distinction between companies on the basis of size is in *ICTA 1988, s 13*, which introduces the concept of 'small companies relief'. More accurately, it should be described as small profit relief because its effect (for the financial year 2009/10) is to charge the first £300,000 of company profits at 21%, the next £1,200,000 at 29.75%, with the excess being taxed at 28% (these limits are reduced proportionally where the accounting period is less than 12 months and/or where there are active associated companies, wherever resident). This same size criterion is used to determine whether a company falls into the proposed system of quarterly corporation tax payments.

For VAT, a size distinction is recognised in (at least) five principal areas:

- turnover below £68,000 – no compulsory registration;
- turnover anticipated over £68,000 in next 30 days – compulsory immediate registration, if not exempt supplies;
- turnover under £1,350,000 p.a. – may use annual accounting scheme and/or cash accounting scheme;
- turnover under £150,000 p.a. – may use flat rate scheme; and

The Legal and Institutional Framework **2.10**

- VAT payable exceeds £2 million – must make monthly payments to HMRC.

The above limits are changed periodically.

Classification of companies by activity

2.9 The *Companies Acts* and the various *Taxes Acts* are littered with 'special case' companies. These include banks, building societies, insurance companies etc. It is not the intention to analyse such individual exceptions to the general rules. There are, however, some general principles:

- **Dormant companies**

    CA 2006, s 480 defines a dormant company as one in which, during a financial period, no significant accounting transaction occurs. A significant accounting transaction is any transaction except the issuing of shares to the subscribers to the Memorandum and Articles.

    No audit is needed for a company which is in a period of dormancy.

- **Investment companies**

    CA 2006, s 833 defines an investment company for this purpose. Specifically, only public limited companies are included. The principal consequence of being such a company is that it will be subject to restrictions on the amounts which may be distributed.

    For corporation tax purposes, the definition is substantially different (*CTA 2009, s 1218*). This is relevant to the deductibility of management expenses (*CTA 2009, s 1219*) and possibly the higher rate of corporation tax (*CTA 2009, s 1316(1)*).

- **Nature of supplies**

    Most relevant for VAT purposes, in establishing if the supplies are zero-rated (*VATA 1994, Sch 8*) or exempt (*VATA 1994, Sch 9*).

Directors' accounting responsibilities

2.10 A company is managed by its directors. The Articles will contain provisions regarding the appointment and removal of directors, but in the final analysis it is the shareholders who determine the composition of the board (of directors). *CA 2006* introduced a minimum age for directors of 16, and also removed the maximum age of 70 that used to apply to directors of PLCs.

Directors' responsibilities, particularly in relation to accounts and accounting, are increasingly onerous, and the policing of their discharging thereof is being tightened up year by year. *CA 2006* states that the primary duty of the directors is to act in a way that promotes the success of the company for the benefit of shareholders as a whole.

2.11 *The Legal and Institutional Framework*

Some of the more important and relevant responsibilities are to:

(*a*) ensure that full accounting records are kept (*CA 2006, ss 386, 387*);

(*b*) ensure that accounting records are retained for three years (private companies) and six years (public companies) (*CA 2006, ss 388, 389*);

(*c*) prepare a balance sheet and profit and loss account for each financial year (the 'accounts') (*CA 2006, ss 394, 395*);

(*d*) ensure the accounts show a 'true and fair view' (*CA 2006, s 393*);

(*e*) append a directors' report (*CA 2006, s 415*);

(*f*) appoint the first auditors (*CA 2006, ss 485, 489*);

(*g*) distribute accounts, directors' report and auditors' report to members and others (*CA 2006, ss 423–425*);

(*h*) lay accounts, directors' and auditors' reports for each financial year before the company in general meeting (*CA 2006, s 437*); and

(*i*) deliver to the Registrar of Companies a copy of the accounts, directors' and auditors' report within nine months of the end of the accounting period for private companies, and within seven months for public companies (*CA 2006, s 442*; previously, 10 months and seven months respectively under *CA 1985, s 244*).

Keeping and maintaining accounting records

2.11 *CA 2006, ss 386* and *387* provide that a company must keep such accounting records as are sufficient to disclose with reasonable accuracy the financial position of the company at any time. Any officer (eg a director) knowingly authorising or permitting the company to keep inadequate records commits an offence.

Accounting records must be preserved for three years from the date on which they were made for private companies, and for six years in the case of public companies. The Act is very specific on the question of what the accounting records should comprise: in particular, there must be kept:

- receipts and payments details; and
- a record of assets and liabilities;

and, if the company's business involves dealing in goods:

- statements of stock at the end of each financial year;
- stock-taking records from which the year-end figures are derived; and
- statements of all goods sold other than by ordinary retail trade and of all goods purchased in sufficient detail to enable the goods, the buyers and sellers to be identified.

The Legal and Institutional Framework 2.11

Under corporation tax self-assessment, companies must retain their records and supporting documentation for corporation tax purposes until the latest of:

- the sixth anniversary of the end of the accounting period;
- the date any enquiry into the return is completed; and
- the day on which the enquiry window for the return closes.

A company must also keep records for PAYE purposes for three years after the end of the tax year to which they relate, and the records must be available for inspection by officers of HMRC. Penalties for non-compliance are imposed. Almost identical provisions exist in relation to records and availability for National Insurance purposes (*SI 2003/2682, reg 97(1)*).

For VAT purposes, *VATA 1994, Sch 11, para 6* leads to extremely detailed records being required. HMRC have the power to inspect and remove (or, to use their own rather quaint jargon, 'lift') the records. The necessary paperwork must be maintained for six years unless HMRC agree otherwise. As would be expected, there is a battery of penalty procedures to encourage compliance.

The requirement to have PAYE/NIC records (for three years) and VAT records (for six years) is often overlooked when there is a change of company ownership.

A particularly interesting but difficult area relates to 'records' maintained by an accountant and forming part of his working papers. It is important to distinguish between an 'accountant', who assists (typically small) companies to prepare their annual statutory accounts, and the 'auditor', who performs a challenge process (or audit) on the statutory accounts and expresses an audit opinion on those statutory accounts.

In the case of many smaller companies, the accountant's working papers may well comprise part of the client company's accounting records required to be kept under *CA 2006*. If so, those records should be retained for at least the period of three years (private company) or six years (public company). There is no other specific provision requiring retention of accounting and auditing working papers, but common sense suggests that the papers should be kept for at least as long as any legal actions in which the papers may be relevant could be instigated. This is generally six years.

Under *TMA 1970, s 20B*, audit working papers and a tax adviser's 'relevant communications' are privileged and therefore may not be required for production by HMRC. The larger firms of auditors, in particular, generally specify in their engagement letters that their audit working papers remain their property at all times and do not form part of the company's accounting records, nor absolve the company's directors from their statutory duty to maintain adequate accounting records. However, particularly in the case of proprietorship companies, what are loosely described as 'audit' papers frequently encompass, in strict terms, part of the company's accounting records. This is a difficult and sensitive area. Under *TMA 1970, s 20*, a tax accountant convicted of a tax offence or suffering a penalty (under *TMA 1970, s 99*) loses this privilege. To the surprise of many practitioners, the

2.12 *The Legal and Institutional Framework*

Government's 1994 *Finance Bill* at *clause 241* introduced provisions to widen the Revenue's powers to gain access to accountants' working papers. Subject to the agreement of a Special Commissioner, privilege would have been lost where there were reasonable grounds for believing that an accountant had knowingly assisted in the preparation of a false return. After much protest from relevant professionals and professional bodies, the clause was dropped.

Format of accounts

2.12 *CA 2006* provides for standardised formats for accounts to be required by regulation. *SI 2008/410* sets out the requirements for accounts and reports for large and medium-sized companies and groups and came into force on 6 April 2008. The requirements for small companies and groups are contained in *SI 2008/409*. The rules relating to summary financial statements are contained in *SI 2008/374*.

For large and medium-sized companies, no fewer than two balance sheets and four profit and loss account formats are set out in pro-forma form. Additionally, certain other information must be set out, if not in the balance sheet or profit and loss account themselves, then in the 'Notes to the Accounts'. The Notes thereby become an integral part of the accounts. Accounts formatted or set out in any other way do not conform with the legal requirement. Consequently, virtually all company accounts adopt one or other of the formats. There is no real fundamental difference, other than presentational, in the various formats.

The balance sheet formats require the assets to be grouped into fixed and current, and the liabilities to be grouped into current (becoming due within 12 months) and long term. Shareholders' funds are to be analysed into constituent parts (share capital, share premium and reserves).

The profit and loss accounts require disclosure of turnover and some of the major cost components enabling the pre-tax profit on mainline activity to be quantified. Other income is separately identified, as is interest payable, which leads to the calculation of the profit after interest and tax on ordinary activities. Extraordinary items and the tax thereon are separately shown. All four profit and loss formats end with the 'bottom line' – 'profit or loss for the financial year'.

There is no requirement for the preparation of a 'cash flow' statement in the *Companies Acts*. This matter is more fully discussed in Chapter 11, but for public, large and medium-sized private companies (as defined in **2.7** above), the accountancy standard *FRS 1* (see **2.20** below) provides that a cash flow statement should form part of the accounts. Virtually all such companies therefore do produce such statements as part of their accounts. As this is not a specific requirement of *CA 2006*, there is no strict format to adopt although most companies follow the layout suggested in *FRS 1*. Failure to prepare a cash flow statement, when required, generally leads to an audit qualification (see **2.17** below).

Format of accounts under international accounting standards

2.13 There are a number of differences between accounts prepared under UK GAAP and international accounting standards. In general, the international requirements are less prescriptive than their UK equivalent, with only the major categories that should be used being specified. However, there are a number of differences of detail that are worth noting:

- The profit and loss account is normally referred to as the 'Income Statement'.

- Rather than distinguishing between 'fixed' and 'current' items in the balance sheet, the distinction under international standards is between 'current' and 'non-current'. For most purposes, the difference is merely one of terminology, but differences can arise with, for example, debtors payable in more than 12 months. Under international standards, such debtors would be classified as 'non-current'.

- International standards classify preference shares as quasi-debt, rather than as part of the share capital of the company. The result is that they are shown under liabilities (generally long-term), rather than as part of shareholders' funds in the balance sheet. Similarly, dividends on preference shares are shown as part of finance costs in the Income Statement, rather than as distributions of profits.

- Proposed dividends on ordinary shares are not considered to be a 'liability' under international standards until such time as they are approved by the shareholders at the AGM, on the grounds that the liability does not crystallise until such approval is given (even though instances of shareholders declining the dividend proposed by the directors are remarkably rare). Instead of showing proposed dividends on ordinary shares as distributions of profits in the profit and loss account/ Income Statement and an accrual in current liabilities, the financial statements would disclose the proposed dividend on ordinary shares as a Note. Dividends actually paid in the year (normally, last year's final dividend and this year's interim dividend) are generally shown as reserve movements. This treatment only applies to dividends on *ordinary* shares – dividends on preference shares are considered to be 'liabilities' on the due date under the terms on which the shares were issued.

Financial year

2.14 A company's financial year is determined under *CA 2006, s 390*. The Act uses the concept of 'accounting reference period'. The financial year is co-terminous with the accounting reference period except that, at the directors' discretion, the financial year may end up to seven days before or after the end of accounting reference period. This provision is clearly intended to permit accounts to run up to a convenient annual date, eg the last Friday in March.

A company's first accounting reference period must be for at least six months but no more than 18 months. Failure by the directors to notify the Registrar of

2.15 *The Legal and Institutional Framework*

Companies within nine months of incorporation of the company's accounting reference date causes that date to fall by default on the last day of the month in which the anniversary of incorporation falls. Subsequent accounting reference dates end on the 12-month anniversary of the preceding period, subject to the company's capacity to change. A change can usually only be effected for the current and future periods under *CA 2006, s 392*, but no period may exceed 18 months. Generally, a company cannot extend its accounting reference period more than once in any five-year period.

Corporation tax is due on the profits of each 'accounting period'. An accounting period frequently corresponds to a company's financial year, but there is no necessity for this to be the case, for the tax definition (in *CTA 2009, s 9*) is very different from the company law definition. In particular, there will be a difference for companies newly beginning or ceasing to trade, or for companies which have changed their accounting reference dates. This may well require the activities of a company during a particular financial year to be allocated or apportioned to the separate (tax) accounting periods falling within that year. This can have consequences for such diverse purposes as group relief (corresponding accounting periods – *CTA 2010, s 37*) and carry back of losses (*CTA 2010, s 138*).

True and fair view

2.15 The accounts prepared by the directors must show a 'true and fair' view of the state of affairs of the company at the end of the financial year, and the profit and loss account must give a true and fair view of the profit and loss of the company for the financial year (*CA 2006, s 395*). This is an overriding requirement, and may in exceptional circumstances permit directors to depart from fundamental accounting principles and applicable accounting standards (subject to the disclosure of the fact).

There is no definition in corporate law of the expression 'true and fair'. *CA 2006* specifies five fundamental principles to be applied in determining figures to be included in accounts (these are considered in detail in Chapter 5). If there are special reasons for disapplying any of these principles in a particular instance, this fact and the reasons for it must be disclosed in the accounts.

SI 2008/410, reg 10 specifies that the 'Notes to the Accounts' shall state whether the accounts have been prepared in accordance with applicable accounting standards (any material departures being disclosed and justified). These standards will be considered in detail in later chapters.

The concept of 'true and fair' is at the very heart of a company's accounts. It may seem odd, therefore, that the phrase is not defined. These three words were in fact used for the first time in *CA 1948*, although earlier Acts had used similar expressions (the first ever *Companies Act 1844* required companies to 'present a full and fair balance sheet', and the *1890 Act* required auditors to state whether the balance sheet was 'properly drawn up so as to exhibit a true and correct view').

'Truth', in the accounting context, does not equate with scientific truth. Costs and revenues for any accounting period, which is less than the full life of any particular venture, cannot be determined with precision. The word 'fair' can be thought of as embracing such words as 'clear', 'distinct', 'plain', 'impartial', 'just' and 'equitable'. The Financial Reporting Council issued a statement on 19 May 2008 (*FRC PN 222*) to the effect that, in the opinion of counsel, the true and fair requirement remains central to the preparation of financial statements in the UK, irrespective of whether they are prepared in accordance with international or UK accounting standards. The Chief Executive said, 'The FRC believes that this Opinion is an important confirmation that the "true and fair view" is a key contributor to the integrity of financial reporting in the UK'.

If accounts are produced which do not exhibit a true and fair view, the directors may be obliged to produce revised accounts which do show such a view – and this is so, even if the auditors have expressed a non-qualified audit opinion (see **2.17** *et seq* below). Both the Department for Business, Innovation and Skills (BIS) and the Financial Reporting Review Panel (FRRP) have procedures for receiving and investigating complaints regarding the annual accounts of companies in respect of apparent departures from the accounting requirements of the *Companies Acts* (including the requirement to give a true and fair view). The FRRP deals with public/large companies – the most likely companies to be affected – and BIS looks after all other companies.

Directors' report

2.16 For each financial year, the directors must, under *CA 2006, s 415*, append a directors' report to the company accounts. Amongst other matters, the report should contain a fair review of the activities of the company during the year and give details of directors and their shareholdings (even if these shareholdings are not beneficially held).

The report must be signed and attached to the accounts. As will be seen later, the auditors must review the directors' report and, if it is inconsistent with the accounts, must say so in their report.

The directors' report is sometimes a rather bland document to which little attention is paid. This can be a mistake. Many a Revenue officer has bolstered a technical argument (eg whether there has been a major change in the conduct of a business) by reference to comments made by directors in their report without full consideration of the consequences. Another area might be that of directors' shareholdings. This is the only place in the accounts where there might be an indication of the directors having acquired/disposed of shares. Moreover, it is not unknown for directors to be holding shares as nominees but yet be shown as beneficial owners of the shares according to the directors' report.

CA 2006, s 417 requires the directors' report to include a business review, which analyses the development and performance of the company, with a description of the principal risks. This applies to accounting periods starting on or after 1 October 2007, but does not apply to small companies.

2.17 *The Legal and Institutional Framework*

Auditors and the audit report

2.17 Companies must appoint auditors by virtue of *CA 2006, ss 485* and *489*. The auditors are usually appointed annually, although private companies may elect to dispense with the annual formality of reappointment. The auditors must themselves be drawn from a pool of suitably qualified and registered practitioners.

For each financial year, the auditors make a report to the members (ie shareholders). The report must state whether, in the auditors' opinion, the accounts have been prepared in accordance with *CA 2006* and, in particular, whether a true and fair view is given of:

– the state of affairs of the company at the financial year end; and

– the profit and loss of the company for the financial year.

As noted above, the auditors must report by exception if the directors' report is not consistent with the accounts.

The auditors are required by *CA 2006, s 498* to carry out investigations to check that proper accounting records have been maintained and that the accounts are in agreement with them. If this is not the case, they must say so in their report.

Although the auditors report to the members, they owe a duty of care to other users of the accounts and, in particular, to the tax authorities (although the strict legal extent of this remains to be clarified by the courts). Indeed, it was the Revenue who were most opposed to the concept of abolishing the audit requirement for the 'small' company. One consequence of the fact that the Revenue place some reliance on the audit process to 'police' the tax system is that non-limited companies (ie sole traders and partnerships) are more than twice (nearly three times) as likely to be selected for tax investigation than their incorporated counterparts.

The financial scandals of the late 1980s, early 1990s and early 2000s caused considerable public criticism of the accountancy profession and its perceived failure to detect problems within companies and to 'happily' issue 'clean' audit reports on accounts which, subsequently (and frequently only a short time after the signing of the audit report), are discovered to be hopelessly misleading. Part of the profession's defence has been that the public have misunderstood the relative roles of the company management and the auditors, and the nature of the audit itself. Perhaps to counter this, in May 1993, there was issued a new auditing standard *SAS 600*, which considerably amended the wording of audit reports. The revised auditing standard became effective for all accounting periods ending on or after 30 September 1993.

Several years ago, the wording in audit reports was amended to indicate that, in certain circumstances, the auditors had relied on directors' representations. It quickly became common practice for the audit report of most proprietorship companies to contain this wording. Nobody explained to the Revenue that this revised wording was not intended to imply anything sinister and, as a result, a number of inappropriate tax investigations were initiated. Revenue

The Legal and Institutional Framework **2.18**

officers *do* look at audit reports, so it is very important that tax practitioners (including Revenue officers) are fully conversant with the new formats and can understand the 'coded' messages contained therein.

The normal form of audit report will be the 'unqualified opinion' (or the 'clean' report). Exceptionally, the auditor may express a qualified opinion. Broadly, this will happen when:

- there is a limitation on the scope of the auditor's examination; or
- the auditors disagree with the treatment or disclosure of a matter in the financial statements.

The 'qualification' may be in the form of a disclaimer of opinion or, in extreme cases, an adverse opinion (ie in the auditor's opinion the accounts do not give a true and fair view). The relaxation of audit requirements for companies with small turnover is explained at **2.7** above.

Laying and delivering accounts

2.18 Under *CA 2006, s 437,* the directors should lay before the company, in general meeting, copies of the annual accounts and directors' and auditors' reports, although *CA 2006* permits the shareholders of a private company to elect to dispense with the annual formality of a general meeting at which the accounts need to be laid.

Under *CA 2006, ss 441, 451* and *452*, the directors must lodge similar documents with the Registrar of Companies.

The period allowed for the laying and delivering of accounts and reports is:

- for private companies, nine (previously 10) months after the relevant accounting period;
- for public companies, seven months after the relevant accounting period.

The Registrar of Companies can and does impose fines on directors for failure to meet these deadlines.

Small companies are provided with exemptions from the requirement to file accounts with the Registrar of Companies. Instead of 'full' accounts, small companies may file what are called 'abbreviated' (formerly known as 'modified') accounts. These give much less information to the outside world. It is understood that about 60 per cent of companies capable of making use of this exemption fail to do so, and file a full set of accounts instead. Medium-sized companies may lodge accounts with limited disclosures.

Listed (ie quoted) companies, whatever their size (although very unlikely to be anything other than large), are able, under *CA 2006, ss 426* and *427*, to send members a 'summary financial statement'.

HMRC does not recognise the distinction between large, medium and small companies, nor even between private and public companies. Although there are some distinctions in the *Taxes Acts* between listed (or quoted) companies

2.19 *The Legal and Institutional Framework*

and other companies, these are not relevant to the question of accounts and their delivery to the Revenue.

Under corporation tax self-assessment, companies are required to include with the return:

- accounts drawn up under UK company law;
- computations showing how the figures in the corporation tax return have been arrived at from the accounts; and
- other documents required under company law, eg directors' and auditor's reports.

HMRC send a notice to deliver a company tax return three to seven weeks after the end of the company's accounting period, and the return must usually be delivered within 12 months. A system of penalties exists to encourage compliance.

Senior Accounting Officers

2.19 Under *FA 2009, Sch 46*, large companies must appoint a Senior Accounting Officer (SAO) to be responsible for assuring HMRC that appropriate accounting arrangements are set up and maintained. According to Revenue Guidance, 'This measure addresses that potential "accountability gap" by making the SAO of a qualifying company responsible for ensuring that appropriate tax accounting arrangements are in place'.

LIMITED LIABILITY COMPANIES – THE INSTITUTIONS

The accountancy bodies

Accounts

2.20 In the 1960s, the UK accountancy bodies came together and set up the Accounting Standards Committee (ASC). They set about codifying accounting principles in specific areas. A series of proposed standards were published as Exposure Drafts (EDs), many of which, amended after consideration of representations made, were published as standards which were (and are) known as Statements of Standard Accounting Practice (SSAPs). These standards are intended to be applied to any accounts intended to exhibit a 'true and fair' view.

The Accounting Standards Board Ltd was designated as a standard-setting body from 20 August 1990 (*Accounting Standards (Prescribed Body) Regulations 1990 (SI 1990/1667)*, issued by the authority of *CA 1985, s 256*). That company immediately established a committee called the Accounting Standards Board (ASB) which began its task on 24 August 1990, effectively replacing the ASC.

The Legal and Institutional Framework **2.21**

The ASB is funded by the Government, the financial community and the accountancy profession. Board members are drawn from similar backgrounds. Its first action was to 'adopt' the extant SSAPs (then 22 in number) and institute a programme of additions and amendments. They issue exposure drafts known as Financial Reporting Exposure Drafts (FREDs), which lead ultimately to Financial Reporting Standards (FRSs). References, therefore, to applicable accounting standards in the *Companies Acts* relate to SSAPs and FRSs. From time to time, specific matters of accounting concern emerge which require a speedy authoritative statement. A sub-committee of the ASB, called the Urgent Issues Task Force (UITF), has been established to issue pronouncements on such issues. These are called Abstracts. The expectation is that accountants should apply the principles in the UITF Abstracts immediately. They are not strictly 'applicable accounting standards', but the likelihood is that a court would place considerable weight on such statements. Recently, a single comprehensive standard has been introduced for small companies (see Chapter 10).

Additionally, industrial groups have issued industry-specific Statements of Recommended Practice (SORPs). These are helpful guidelines, though with no statutory or other force.

In 2004, a new structure was put in place to regulate the accounting profession, and the Financial Reporting Council was created. This body comprises an executive and a number of operating bodies, ie the Accounting Standards Board, the Auditing Practices Board, the Professional Oversight Board, the Financial Reporting Review Panel, and the Accountancy and Actuarial Discipline Board.

Audit
In the 1980s, there came into being the Auditing Practices Committee, superseded in 1990 by the Auditing Practices Board (APB). As its name implies, its function was to standardise the process of auditing and audit reporting. Since 2002, the APB has been part of the Financial Reporting Council; its mandate is to establish high standards of auditing. This it has done through the issue of a series of standards. Since 2005, the APB has issued standards based on international auditing standards (ISAs), modified by the addition of certain UK-specific requirements. These standards are mandatory for statutory audits (ie the independent audit of a limited company's financial statements under the *Companies Acts*). Of most relevance is *ISA 700, The Independent Auditor's Report on General Purpose Financial Statements*.

The Stock Exchange

2.21 The Stock Exchange is a marketplace for trading in the securities of companies. Only the securities of public companies may be traded on the Exchange. Securities so traded are often described as 'quoted'.

There are presently two distinct markets: the more senior and important is the Official List, sometimes called the 'full market'. It is on this market that the shares of companies with household names trade. Technically, these shares

2.22 The Legal and Institutional Framework

are 'listed'. The junior market is the Alternative Investment Market (AIM). This only started in the summer of 1995, and includes smaller and younger companies.

The Stock Exchange monitors certain aspects of the performance of companies on these markets but, apart from a small number of minor disclosure requirements, no accounting rules additional to normal company law are imposed.

The rules which the Stock Exchange impose are codified in looseleaf publications bound in a yellow binder – the 'Yellow Book'.

HMRC do not consider the shares of companies on the AIM to be 'listed' or 'quoted', so such shares may qualify, for example, for Enterprise Investment Scheme (EIS) reinvestment relief, or for favourable business property relief in an inheritance tax context.

The City Code on Takeovers and Mergers

2.22 The 'City Code' exists to provide fair and equal treatment of shareholders in takeover situations. It applies *only* to public companies and is administered by the Panel on Takeovers and Mergers, which was established in 1968. Following the implementation of the EU Takeovers Directive in the UK, the City Code now has statutory effect.

Worthy bodies

2.23 In recent times, a number of worthy bodies have been appointed to issue reports and recommendations in relation to publicly quoted companies, the most notable being the Cadbury, Greenbury and Hempel Reports (named after their respective chairmen).

These bodies have issued suggested codes of practice (in such areas as the role of non-executive directors, the need for director remuneration committees, the disclosure of directors' options or pension benefits etc) which, whilst not enforced by statute, are widely recognised as being 'best practice'. The latest version of the Combined Code published by the Financial Reporting Council was issued in 2008.

THE ACCOUNTS OF NON-LIMITED COMPANIES

2.24 The vast majority of accounts prepared and submitted to HMRC are for sole traders and partnerships. It is somewhat surprising, therefore, that there are so few specific rules as to who can prepare accounts, how they are prepared, and what they should contain.

The following list identifies some of the main differences which exist in relation to accounts of sole traders and partnerships as compared to the accounts of limited companies:

The Legal and Institutional Framework **2.25**

- Persons preparing accounts do not need to have specific qualifications or be registered with a regulatory authority.
- There is no provision for audit.
- Until *FA 1998*, there was no requirement for accounts to exhibit a 'true and fair' view, nor to comply with particular accounting standards (see below).
- Apart from HMRC, there is no regulatory body, eg Registrar of Companies, with whom accounts are to be lodged, nor any regulatory body monitoring the quality of accounts preparation.
- Generally, HMRC require accounts to be prepared and submitted. 'Accounts' for this purpose include a balance sheet and profit and loss account.
- For some small businesses, ad hoc practices arise whereby balance sheets are dispensed with and a simple income/expenditure account is submitted.
- For very small businesses (turnover below £30,000), no proper accounts at all need to be submitted.

FA 2002, s 103(5) requires that taxable profits be calculated in accordance with generally accepted accounting practices. This was clarified in 2004 *(FA 2004, s 50)* as including international (ie EU–compliant, as set out in *Regulation (EC) 1606/2002*) as well as UK standards.

SUMMARY

2.25 This chapter contains some very important concepts. It may help to summarise the overall effect of the various provisions:

- The process of preparing and distributing the accounts of limited companies is highly regulated by an overlapping combination of *CA 2006* requirements and pronouncements of the various accounting and auditing regulatory bodies.
- Accounts must conform to one of several formats and generally comply with accounting standards.
- Companies may be classified in several different ways, but essentially the directors of all companies are responsible for preparing accounts which show a true and fair view, arranging for their audit and the distribution thereafter to shareholders, the Registrar of Companies etc.
- Accounts for this purpose include balance sheet, profit and loss, notes to accounts, directors' report and (in some cases) cash flow statements.
- Audit reports generally conform to one or another of the formats approved by the Auditing Practices Board. Audits may only be undertaken by suitably qualified individuals properly registered with an approved accountancy body.

2.25 *The Legal and Institutional Framework*

- Higher standards of record keeping for companies (compared to sole traders and partnerships) are required by company law and are expected by HMRC.

For unincorporated entities, however:

- Accounts preparation for sole traders and partnerships is neither regulated by law nor the accountancy bodies (although the accounting institutes have issued guidance on the preparation of such accounts); however, this has changed more recently (eg the *FA 1998* withdrawal of the 'cash' basis).

- No special qualifications for the preparation of such accounts are needed. Accounts need not show a true and fair view. No audit is required (generally).

- Such accounts normally comprise balance sheet and profit and loss account. In smaller cases, even less may be acceptable to HMRC.

Chapter 3

An Accounting Overview

3.1 Later chapters contain a detailed look at the fundamentals of how transactions are accounted for and presented in financial statements (or 'accounts' for short); in this chapter, the accounting for transactions is considered in basic overview.

3.2 At this stage, the focus is on UK GAAP; the next chapter introduces international accounting standards.

THE 'ENTITY' CONVENTION

3.3 The objective of preparing financial statements is to provide *useful* information to the reader of those financial statements. In order for the information provided to be 'useful', the accountancy profession has developed a number of 'conventions'.

A particularly relevant accounting convention to understand at this stage is the 'business entity convention'. This convention means that the financial statements of a business entity should show all the transactions, assets and liabilities of the business, and nothing else. This sounds sensible, but the importance of this convention can perhaps be explained by considering a business carried on as either a limited company or a sole trader.

3.4 Legally, a limited company is a separate legal entity; in other words, it is separate from its owners or 'shareholders', which means that it is able to own assets and incur liabilities in its own right. The shareholders do not own the assets or owe the liabilities directly; rather, they own a proportion or share of the company. Therefore, the balance sheet shows the assets and liabilities of the company. Any excess of assets over liabilities of the company ('net assets') is shown as being due to the owners of the company, ie the shareholders.

3.5 By contrast, a business carried on by a sole trader is not a separate legal entity; in other words, the business and the owner, or sole trader, are one and the same. Therefore, when the business incurs a liability, it is a

3.6 An Accounting Overview

liability of the sole trader and, when the business has an asset, it is owned by the sole trader. In principle, there is no reason why the sole trader should not prepare accounts showing all their assets, both personal and business, and all their liabilities, again both personal and business. However, the resulting information would not be as helpful as possible to the sole trader, who needs to understand how well the business is performing. Therefore, in order for the accounting information to be as useful as possible to the sole trader for managing the business, it needs to show the transactions, assets and liabilities of the business only, and to exclude all personal transactions, assets and liabilities not related to the business.

3.6 In summary, the business entity convention states that the accounts should show all the transactions, assets and liabilities of the business *as if the business were a separate legal entity from the owner(s)*, irrespective of the strict legal position of the business entity. This also means that the financial statements of all business entities have similarities, such as showing the business assets and liabilities of the business and showing any surplus of assets over liabilities as due to the owners of the business, although the terminology may differ (for example, 'shareholders' or 'proprietor').

3.7 The following analysis proceeds on the basis of a business carried on in limited company format.

THE BALANCE SHEET

3.8 The first key document in a set of 'accounts' is the balance sheet. Normally, it is in vertical format (see Chapter 2) and comprises a single page, or possibly two. It lists the assets and liabilities of the company by appropriate categories (see below).

3.9 For the sake of illustration, consider the balance sheet of ABC Ltd for the year ended 31 December 2009. Suppose its net assets at 31 December 2008 were £90,000, and at 31 December 2009 its net assets are £100,000.

In its most simplified version, the balance sheet will appear:

Example 3.1

	31/12/2009	31/12/2008
	£	£
Net Assets	100,000	90,000
Shareholders' Funds	100,000	90,000

This shows that the company's net assets, in other words the excess of its assets over its liabilities, 'belong' to the owners of the business, namely the shareholders for a limited company. The word 'belong' has been shown in quotation marks, because the shareholders do not own the net assets directly, nor are they directly responsible for the debts and liabilities, but, rather, they own a share of the separate legal entity that is the limited company. However, should the company be wound up, then any surplus assets after paying the company's liabilities would be liquidated and distributed to the company's shareholders.

3.10 It is important not to become bogged down by detail, and to see the balance sheet in this way first, before proceeding to the next level of refinement. Having mentally seen the balance sheet as in *Example 3.1*, it is possible to break down the figures and, in the second level of appreciation, the balance sheet might look like:

Example 3.2

	31/12/2009	31/12/2008
	£	£
Fixed Assets	100,000	105,000
Net Current Assets	50,000	35,000
Bank Loans	(50,000)	(50,000)
Net Assets	100,000	90,000
Share Capital	5,000	5,000
Reserves	95,000	85,000
	100,000	90,000

3.11 Already, useful analysis begins to be possible. The assets are broken down between fixed assets and net current assets. As will be seen later, the tax treatment of events affecting the two categories of assets is quite different. By splitting the assets in this way, it is possible to distinguish those assets which are expected to be used in the business over an extended period (ie the fixed ones) and those which 'turn over' more frequently (ie the current ones). A banker who is considering a loan to the company is likely to concentrate initially on the fixed assets, which are more suitable for having charges attached as security for the loan, whereas the current assets are less suitable for acting as security.

3.12 Current assets are those assets that are expected to be converted into cash within the next accounting period (generally one year), such as stocks

3.13 *An Accounting Overview*

and trade debtors (amounts due from customers for sales made on credit), plus bank and cash balances. Current liabilities are those liabilities that are expected to be paid within the next accounting period, such as trade creditors (amounts due to suppliers for purchases made on credit) and other liabilities, such as taxation payable, plus bank overdrafts and the proportion of bank loans repayable within the next year. The normal convention is to refer to 'net current assets' if current assets exceed current liabilities, and 'net current liabilities' if current liabilities exceed current assets. The net current assets are sometimes described as the 'working capital' of a business.

3.13 In the lower part of the balance sheet, the shareholders' funds have been split between the capital permanently tied up in the business – the share capital – and what are generally called 'Reserves', which usually includes accumulated profits not paid to the shareholders in the form of dividends. Reserves often also include items that have restricted uses, such as the share premium account (see **3.23**), or that cannot be distributed to shareholders until 'realised' via a transaction with a third party, such as a revaluation reserve (see **3.27**).

3.14 A major potential source of confusion arises here for the uninitiated. Accumulated profits not paid away in the form of dividends (or 'retained profits' for short) are generally called the balance on 'Profit and Loss' account. This must not be confused with the profit and loss account for the year, which will be seen (at **3.28** below) to be a document which records certain of the transactions of the year to determine the profit for that year, and which is attached to the balance sheet to form the 'accounts' for the year. When an accountant refers to the 'Profit and Loss' account, often it is only from the context that it can be deduced whether he is talking about the balance of retained profits (which appears on the balance sheet) or the document which records transactions for the year which is appended to the balance sheet. As an aid to the uninitiated, this book will use the following convention. When referring to accumulated profits shown on the balance sheet, the expression 'Profit and Loss' (with capitals) or 'retained earnings' will be used. When referring to the statement of annual transactions, the expression 'profit and loss' will be used.

3.15 All potential creditors are interested in the share capital, which is sometimes called the 'creditors' buffer'. It is the sum of money that the shareholders have contributed, and they can never get it back to the prejudice of the creditors. The retained earnings represent a pool of current and previous years' profit after tax. It is available to be paid away in the form of dividends. Two important points follow from this.

- First, because it represents profits already subject to (corporation) tax, if it is paid to shareholders as dividends or in connection with some other corporate transaction (eg a company buy-back of own shares), any tax in the shareholders' hands is mitigated by a tax credit which reflects the fact that it is paid out of a post-tax pool. So, getting these profits into shareholders' hands, by whatever mechanism, is generally tax efficient.

An Accounting Overview **3.20**

- Secondly, corporate law attempts to protect creditors' interests by making it difficult for the creditors' buffer to be reduced. The retained earnings are not part of the creditors' buffer. They can easily be paid out in the form of dividends. There are many corporate transactions where the law is very complex but there is an underlying theme. Whether the transaction is a merger, demerger, buy-out, buy-in, buy-back or whatever, providing the amount or value which exits a company under the arrangement does not exceed that which it could have paid out by dividend, then it is likely that corporate law will permit the transaction relatively easily.

3.16 A word of caution in connection with the word 'equity'. Strictly, the 'equity' or 'equity capital' means the money subscribed to a company on the issue of shares. In some circumstances, the word 'equity' is used to embrace the whole of the shareholders' funds (share capital plus reserves). One example of this is in considering 'gearing' ratios (see **3.37** below). The precise meaning in any particular usage can only be deduced from the context.

3.17 With only the analysis in *Example 3.2* to hand, quite complex questions can be considered and dealt with. Suppose that our colleague who had given us the set of accounts had said, '… in ABC Ltd, there are two equal shareholders. One is leaving and the object is for ABC Ltd to buy back his shares for £75,000. Can it be done, and is it tax efficient?'.

3.18 The answers immediately are 'Yes' and 'Yes'. If the shares are acquired for £75,000, this is less than the £90,000 which could have been paid out by dividend. Company law will permit the transaction. The payment can be treated in the same way as a dividend in the departing shareholder's hands, and his tax thereon mitigated by his tax credit.

3.19 The above analysis is simplistic and there are many 'ifs' and 'buts'. However, it does provide a starting point which comes from a very quick broad understanding of the outline balance sheet.

3.20 Moving on, the balance sheet can be developed to the next level of understanding:

3.21 *An Accounting Overview*

Example 3.3

				31/12/09			31/12/08
Fixed Assets	£	£	£	£	£	£	
Land/Buildings at Cost		50,000			50,000		
Plant/Machinery at Cost	100,000			100,000			
Less Depreciation	(50,000)	50,000		(45,000)	55,000		
			100,000			105,000	
Current Assets							
Stock		30,000			25,000		
Debtors		30,000			25,000		
Cash		30,000			20,000		
Current Liabilities							
Creditors	(25,000)			(20,000)			
Overdraft	(15,000)	(40,000)		(15,000)	(35,000)		
Net Current Assets			50,000			35,000	
Bank Loans			(50,000)			(50,000)	
NET ASSETS			100,000			90,000	
Shareholders' Funds							
Share Capital			5,000			5,000	
Reserves							
Share Premium			5,000			5,000	
Profit and Loss b/f		80,000			72,000		
Profit for Year		10,000			8,000		
Profit and Loss c/f			90,000			80,000	
			100,000			90,000	

Notation:

b/f = brought forward – the balance at the end of the previous year (and the balance at the start of the current year).

c/f = carried forward – the balance at the end of the current year (and the balance at the start of the next year).

3.21 By now, the balance sheet is beginning to look more formidable but, by retaining the overview which comes from seeing it through *Examples 3.1* and *3.2*, it is much easier to handle the increased detail of *Example 3.3*.

3.22 In the upper half of the balance sheet, it can be seen that, whilst land and buildings are not depreciated, plant/machinery is being depreciated. In later chapters, the correctness of this will be considered. Plant/machinery has an accounting written down value of £50,000. It is interesting to ask what the capital allowance 'pool' is and to contemplate the question of deferred tax (see Chapter 22). The upper half of the balance sheet now also shows the constituent elements of current assets and current liabilities. 'Current liabilities' include the capital element of long-term loans repayable within the next year. As explained in *Example 3.1*, the net assets at the balance sheet date 'belong' to the shareholders. The lower half of the balance sheet explains how these net assets have arisen.

3.23 The lower half of the balance sheet in *Example 3.3* shows the two main ways in which net assets (ie an excess of assets over liabilities) can arise in a business: through capital being introduced by the owners of the business, and via profitable trading with third parties. In a limited company, the share capital represents the *nominal value* of shares issued by the company to its shareholders. Whilst shares cannot be issued for less than their nominal value, they can be (and often are) issued for more than their nominal value, in which case the excess of the amount received by the company for the shares issued over and above the nominal value of the shares issued is recorded in the share premium account. Therefore, the total of the 'share capital' account and the 'share premium' account represents the total amount (either in cash or in assets) received by the company for the shares it has issued. As the share premium account arises at the point that the shares are issued by the company, it follows that the balance on this account is not affected by subsequent transactions in shares between shareholders, or by any increases or decreases in the value of shares after they have been issued. In other forms of business entity, such as sole traders or partnerships, there is no need for the capital introduced into the business to be split in this way; the description 'capital' generally is sufficient.

3.24 The lower half of the balance sheet also shows that this year's profit was £10,000, and last year's profit was £8,000. This is the profit after taxation and dividends to the shareholders for the year in question; in other words, the amount that *could* have been distributed to the shareholders each year, but which it has been decided (by the directors) should be retained within the company for investment in the business. This is not an irrevocable decision – as explained in **3.15** above, the balance remains available to be paid to shareholders as dividends in future years, if required. It also follows, from the fact that the profit after taxation and dividends is added to the balance on the Profit and Loss account brought forward from the previous year, that the balance on the Profit and Loss account (or 'retained earnings') within Shareholders' Funds represents the *cumulative* total of profits (less losses) earned after taxation less the *cumulative* amounts paid to shareholders as dividends, in both cases since the limited company was created. For partnerships and sole traders, the same logic applies, although payments to the owners of the business generally are referred to as 'drawings' rather than 'dividends'.

3.25 *An Accounting Overview*

3.25 Returning to the theme in **3.23** above, the two main ways in which the net assets of a business can change is, first, through capital being introduced into the business by the owners and, secondly, through trading with third parties. The increase in net assets between two balance sheets that was not provided by the shareholders is explained by the profit and loss account for the period between the two balance sheet dates.

Therefore, the profit and loss account can be viewed in two ways: as a record of transactions with third parties during a period of time; and as a reconciliation of how the net assets of the business have changed during the period. This is simply two different ways of viewing the same thing. However, understanding this point enables a distinction to be made between those transactions that are reflected in the profit and loss account and those that are merely movements between balance sheet categories.

An example may help: when a business purchases an item of stock from a third party, it has not earned a profit from the purchase, but has merely exchanged assets. It now has an item of stock, but its cash has reduced by an equal amount (or its liabilities have increased by an equal amount, if the purchase was on credit). Therefore, this transaction would not feature in the profit and loss account, but would be a balance sheet movement. When the business sells that item of stock to a third party (hopefully at a profit), the net assets of the business would change (increasing if the sale did generate a profit). This transaction would be reflected in the profit and loss account. The important distinction here is the *intention* to make a profit, rather than whether or not a profit was actually earned.

3.26 It also follows that a transaction that does not involve a third party, such as moving an item of stock from a warehouse to a retail outlet, would not be reflected in the profit and loss account. This may seem obvious for a single business, but the point will be more important when considering the accounts of groups of companies in Chapter 23.

3.27 The analysis above does contain some simplifications. For example, increases in net assets can arise through the periodic revaluation of assets. This will be discussed in more detail in Chapter 5. However, now we will look at the profit and loss account in more detail.

THE PROFIT AND LOSS ACCOUNT

3.28 This can be confusing, particularly in the limited company context. In a sole trader or partnership situation, the profit and loss account is relatively straightforward. Usually in vertical format, the sales revenue is compared to the direct cost (ie purchases) to arrive at a gross profit from which the various expenses are deducted to arrive at the net profit.

This is illustrated in *Example 3.4*, which reflects the same company and facts as in *Example 3.1*.

An Accounting Overview **3.30**

Example 3.4

		31/12/09		31/12/08
	£	£	£	£
Sales		1,000,000		900,000
Cost of Sales		(850,000)		(760,000)
Gross Profit		150,000		140,000
Rent/Rates	(10,000)		(9,000)	
Gas/Electric	(4,500)		(4,500)	
Travelling	(7,500)		(7,000)	
Wages	(100,000)		(96,000)	
Bank Interest	(1,000)		(1,000)	
Repairs	(4,000)		(3,000)	
Depreciation	(5,000)		(5,000)	
Audit	(3,000)		(2,500)	
		(135,000)		(128,000)
Net Profit		15,000		12,000

3.29 In the case of a sole trader or partnership situation, that would be the end of the matter. The profit would have been arrived at.

A limited company – as will be seen later – is more complicated. What is reproduced in *Example 3.4* is usually called the detailed profit and loss account, and generally does not form part of the statutory accounts which a company is obliged to prepare and lodge with the Registrar of Companies. Nevertheless, it is a document which HMRC needs to see.

3.30 A company is required to produce something called a 'statutory profit and loss account'. For ABC Ltd, this might look like:

Example 3.5

	31/12/09	31/12/08
	£	£
TURNOVER	1,000,000	900,000
Cost of Sales	(850,000)	(760,000)
Gross Profit	150,000	140,000

3.31 *An Accounting Overview*

	31/12/09	31/12/08
	£	£
Distribution Costs	(107,500)	(103,000)
Administrative Expenses	(26,500)	(24,000)
OPERATING PROFIT	16,000	13,000
Interest Payable and Similar Charges	(1,000)	(1,000)
PROFIT ON ORDINARY ACTIVITIES BEFORE TAXATION	15,000	12,000
Taxation	(3,000)	(2,500)
PROFIT FOR THE FINANCIAL YEAR	12,000	9,500
Dividends	(2,000)	(1,500)
RETAINED PROFIT FOR THE FINANCIAL YEAR	10,000	8,000

3.31 The important terms in this statutory profit and loss account are explained in later chapters. All that it is really necessary to understand at present is that, in many ways, the profit and loss account is subordinate or subsidiary to the balance sheet. The profit and loss account shows how the profit has been made, and reconciles the movement in net assets from one balance sheet to the next. Many tax practitioners and Revenue officers devote significant time and effort to the profit and loss account, no doubt seduced by the disarming fact that it is the natural place from which to pick up the 'profit per accounts' figure. However, there is much explanatory information in the balance sheet.

3.32 A word of caution is now necessary. In this simplistic model, the Profit and Loss account balance has been equated with the amount which a company can pay away in the form of dividends. In practice, this is often the case, but the question of the ability to pay dividends is in fact more complicated than this. Chapter 5 will develop these considerations further.

3.33 The analysis set out above is based on UK GAAP. Under international accounting standards, the profit and loss account is normally referred to as the 'income statement'. There are various other differences between a set of accounts prepared under UK GAAP and international accounting standards, including categorisation, terminology (as we saw in Chapter 2) and accounting treatments. A more detailed consideration of the major differences is set out in Chapters 2 and 4.

ACCOUNTING RATIOS AND JARGON

3.34 Before leaving this section on the taking of an overview, it is as well to consider some of the ratios and associated jargon that both preparers and readers of accounts often use. But first, a word of warning: contrary to the normal expectations of non-accountants, ratios do not have universally agreed definitions. There are many variations, and experienced financial analysts will not hesitate to amend standard definitions to meet their specific requirements more accurately. However, a selection of reasonably common ratios is shown below:

3.35 The first clutch of ratios is connected with profitability. The main ones are:

(a) Return on Capital employed = $\dfrac{\text{Profit before Interest and Tax}}{\text{Capital Employed}}$

where capital employed = Total assets less current liabilities or Shareholders' Funds plus long-term liabilities. (These are merely two different ways of expressing the same thing, as can be seen in *Example 3.3*.)

This ratio attempts to measure the overall profitability of a company or business. It compares the total return (or profit) before deducting any financing costs (interest on loans or returns to shareholders) and taxation. Financing costs can vary based on the split of total capital between equity (provided by the shareholders) and loans, and the taxation charge can vary based on the individual circumstances of the business. This ratio attempts to eliminate these sources of variation, to allow a more ready comparison to be made between different businesses.

(b) Profit Margin on Sales = $\dfrac{\text{Profit before Interest and Tax}}{\text{Sales}}$

This ratio is sometimes called the operating margin. It measures the average amount of profit made on each £100 of sales before deducting financing costs and taxation, again for the reasons set out in (a) above. As a general rule, any ratio that includes the word 'margin' in the title is expressing the return at a particular position in the profit and loss account as a percentage of the sales generated for the period.

(c) Gross Profit Margin or % = $\dfrac{\text{Gross Profit} \times 100}{\text{Sales}}$

This ratio focuses on the gross profit, which is the profit after deducting from turnover the 'direct' costs of making those sales. Therefore, it represents the profit earned before deducting the general overheads of the business.

These are the sorts of ratios used (particularly by Revenue officers) in deciding whether a business generates 'enough' profit. If the return on capital employed is low, the business may as well close down and put the capital realised on deposit. If the gross profit percentage is low compared to competitors, the Inspector may suspect that possibly not all profits are being declared.

3.36 *An Accounting Overview*

3.36 The next set of ratios considers 'liquidity' and working capital management. Liquidity considers the likelihood of a business being able to pay its liabilities as and when they fall due. Working capital management is a measure of how able a business is to convert its working capital into cash.

The alert reader may have noticed that, in *Example 3.3*, the current assets were listed in reverse order of liquidity, ie stock, debtors, cash. This is conventional if not entirely logical. In any event, the main ratios under this head are:

(a) $\quad$ Current Ratio $= \dfrac{\text{Current Assets}}{\text{Current Liabilities}}$

This ratio compares the current assets with the current liabilities, that is, the assets expected to be converted into cash within the next 12 months with the liabilities expected to be settled within the next 12 months. When expressed this way, it is reasonably easy to see that no account is taken of the conversion profiles (ie the timescale in which the assets are expected to be converted into cash and the liabilities are expected to be settled). Therefore, it is merely an *indicator* of solvency and, for this reason, the general 'rule of thumb' is that current assets should be twice the current liabilities (ie the ratio should be 2 or more) to be 'safe'. Similarly, a current ratio of less than 1 (where the current liabilities are more that the current assets) is generally considered to be a 'danger signal'. This is very much a generalisation, as some companies are able to operate successfully with current ratios of less than 1 more or less permanently. Examples include the major supermarket chains that make the majority of their sales for cash (or 'near cash', including credit card transactions), have extremely efficient supply chain management, and hold relatively low levels of stocks. They are also efficient in their treasury management operations, and invest a significant proportion of their cash flow in new stores and refurbishments.

(b) $\quad$ Quick Ratio $= \dfrac{\text{Current Assets} - \text{Stock}}{\text{Current Liabilities}}$

The Quick ratio (sometimes called the 'acid test ratio') is similar to the current ratio, except that it excludes stocks, which are the slowest of the current assets to be converted into cash. It is, therefore, a more rigorous measure of the company's ability to pay its debts as and when they fall due (but the caveats in (*a*) above, regarding no account being taken of the conversion profile, still apply) and it is not potentially impacted by, for example, excessive stock holdings, which the current ratio can be. The general 'rule of thumb' is that the quick ratio should be 1 or more to be 'safe'.

(c) $\quad$ Stock Turnover $= \dfrac{\text{Cost of Sales}}{\text{Stock}}$

Stock turnover compares cost of sales for the year with the value of stock held to support those sales. The calculation shows the average number of times each item of stock is sold in a year, a proxy measure of the efficiency of stock management. However, it should be noted that stock turnover averages vary enormously between industries. A similar measure is often seen, which merely inverts the ratio above and multiplies by 365 days, thereby giving the average number of days that each item of stock is held prior to sale.

(d)   Debtors Collection Period $= \dfrac{\text{Debtors}}{\text{Credit Sales per day}}$

The debtors collection period is the average number of days that a company's credit customers take to settle their invoices. This is a proxy measurement for the efficiency of credit management within a company and, again, industry averages vary enormously. Generally, the debtors collection period should be compared to the credit terms offered by the company to its customers, rather than being reviewed in isolation; the excess of the actual debtors collection period over the average credit terms offered being a more useful measure of the efficiency of credit management. Similar calculations can be made of the creditors payment period (the average number of days' credit taken by the company), and the difference between the two measures is often enlightening.

These ratios are of interest to lenders and financiers for reasons which are self-explanatory, particularly the last two. Slow-moving stock or extended credit periods are a sign that a business may be facing liquidity problems in the near future.

3.37   Next on the list come the so-called 'gearing' ratios. Conceptually, a business is financed by the proprietor's capital (shareholders' funds = share capital plus retained profits, in the case of a limited company) and borrowings. A business with a preponderance of borrowings is said to be highly geared. It is inherently risky, because borrowings have to be serviced, ie interest has to be paid. If times are hard, dividends can be cut or waived, but bank interest generally cannot. The various measures of gearing, expressed in limited company format, include:

(a)   Long Term Gearing $= \dfrac{\text{Long Term Debt}}{\text{Equity Shareholders' Funds}}$

(b)   Total Gearing $= \dfrac{\text{Total Debt}}{\text{Equity Shareholders' Funds}}$

(c)   Interest Cover $= \dfrac{\text{Profit before Interest and Tax}}{\text{Interest Payable}}$

Interest cover compares the pool of funds available to pay interest, namely profit after all costs but before interest and tax, with the interest payable. The greater the multiple, the 'safer' are the interest payments from the lender's perspective.

Clearly, financiers are interested in these ratios. There is a particular interest by HMRC in the area of international business. UK companies which have subsidiaries elsewhere in the world, or which themselves are subsidiaries of

3.38 *An Accounting Overview*

parent companies resident overseas, will have to address the question of 'thin capitalisation'. Most businesses financed at arm's length will have a mixture of both equity and loan. Within particular sectors and varying over time, there is a spectrum of likely gearing ratios. Where the funder is a connected party, such as a parent company, there is a tendency for the bulk of the funding to be on inter-company loan account. The subsidiary then has a small equity base and relatively large (inter-company) borrowings. In brief, it is very highly geared or, in tax jargon, 'thinly capitalised'.

Depending upon the tax jurisdiction and the provisions of the relevant Double Tax Treaty, HMRC can and do attack thinly capitalised companies and, if successful, treat part of the loans as 'quasi-equity'. What then appears to be inter-company interest is re-analysed by HMRC as inter-company dividend, and tax consequences then follow from this.

3.38 The final batch of ratios is those which might be called the investors' ratios, the principal amongst which are:

(a) Dividend Yield = $\dfrac{\text{Net Dividend per Share + Tax Credit}}{\text{Current Market Price of Share}}$

(b) Dividend Cover = $\dfrac{\text{Earnings per Share}}{\text{Net Dividend per Share}} = \dfrac{\text{Profit after Tax}}{\text{Total Net Dividend}}$

(c) Price/Earnings Ratio = $\dfrac{\text{Current Market Price per Share}}{\text{Earnings per Share}}$

(d) Net Assets per Share = $\dfrac{\text{Net Assets}}{\text{Number of Shares}}$

The most widely used of these ratios are the Price/Earnings ratio (usually called the PE) and the dividend yield. For quoted companies, these are reproduced daily in the *Financial Times*.

Both ratios are used *extensively* in discussing share valuations with the Shares Valuation Division (SVD) of HMRC.

In valuing controlling holdings of unquoted limited companies, it is virtually standard practice to identify a quoted counterpart or counterparts to 'guesstimate' an average typical PE for a 'similar' quoted company. If one discounts that by maybe a third or a quarter to reflect the lack of a market in the unquoted company sector and applies the discounted PE to the most recent profits after tax for the company to be valued, one arrives at a 'valuation'. As the reader may imagine, a great deal of further sophistication may be brought to bear on the matter, but in essence this is what happens.

In valuing minority holdings – say 25% or less – a similar procedure involving dividend yields is employed. However, unquoted companies frequently do not pay dividends, even if profitable, so this method of valuation can only proceed by speculating on what would be a reasonable dividend for the company to pay. This is loading speculation upon estimation upon 'guesstimation'. It represents one of the most imprecise areas within the tax system and is best suited to those with an artistic rather than scientific bent.

3.39 A final word of warning on ratios. Ratio analysis does not provide *answers* to questions such as 'How well has company X performed in the last year?'. Ratio analysis can be a useful way of analysing what has changed and by how much, but it cannot explain *why* the change has occurred or determine whether the performance has been *good or bad*. At best, ratio analysis provides sensible questions for further investigation, and the final judgement as to the quality of the performance rests with the analyst personally.

3.40 Armed now with an overview of how business activities are represented by figures on a page, with a feeling of how, in outline, to interpret these, with the jargon of analysis nestling under the wing, it is possible to move on to consider more specifically the ins and outs of financial statements. Before doing so, however, the next chapter introduces the key differences between UK GAAP and international accounting standards.

Chapter 4

Financial Statements – Which Version of Accounting Standards?

4.1 The Accounting Standards Board (ASB) issues Financial Reporting Standards (FRSs) in the United Kingdom. It has also adopted the Statements of Standard Accounting Practice (SSAPs) issued by its predecessor body, the Accounting Standards Committee.

4.2 Similarly, the International Accounting Standards Board (IASB) issues International Financial Reporting Standards (IFRSs), and it adopted the International Accounting Standards (IASs) issued by its predecessor body, the International Accounting Standards Committee.

4.3 Until 2004, UK companies followed UK Generally Accepted Accounting Practice (UK GAAP), as set out in the FRSs and SSAPs in issue at the relevant time. However, this changed following the European Commission's adoption of *Regulation (EC) 1606/2002* (the '*IAS Regulation*') in June 2002. European Commission 'Regulations' differ from 'Directives', in that they do not need to be passed into national law by each Member State's legislative process before becoming operative. The *IAS Regulation* required certain companies governed by the law of a Member State to prepare their *consolidated* financial statements in accordance with 'international accounting standards' for each financial year starting on or after 1 January 2005.

4.4 'International accounting standards' means IASs, IFRSs, and any related interpretations issued or adopted by the IASB and endorsed by the European Union. The key phrase here is 'endorsed by the EU'. This gives the potential for certain IFRSs and IASs not to be endorsed by the EU. This has only happened once, relating to certain aspects of the original *IAS 39* 'Financial Instruments'. *IAS 39* has since been amended by the IASB, and the EU has endorsed the amended version.

4.5 The companies covered by the *IAS Regulation*, and therefore *required* to prepare their *consolidated* financial statements in accordance with international accounting standards, are those with their securities admitted to a 'regulated market' in any Member State at the balance sheet date. Securities include both equity and debt instruments.

Financial Statements – Which Version of Accounting Standards? **4.9**

4.6 The *IAS Regulation* only applies to consolidated financial statements. Therefore, strictly, the individual company financial statements of the parent company and each of its subsidiary companies can continue to be prepared under UK GAAP (or other relevant GAAP for overseas companies). In practice, the parent company whose securities are admitted to a regulated market produces one document containing both the consolidated financial statements of the group and its own company financial statements, so it is often logistically easier to prepare both sets of financial statements under the same framework. However, the individual company financial statements of the subsidiary companies do not have to be prepared under international accounting standards. For example, in the 2009 Annual Report and Financial Statements of Tesco PLC, the group financial statements are prepared under international financial reporting standards, whereas the parent company's own financial statements are prepared under UK GAAP.

4.7 The *IAS Regulation* also gives the *option* for the consolidated and individual company financial statements of *unlisted* companies (ie those whose securities are not admitted to a regulated market) to be prepared under international accounting standards. Effectively, this is a one-off choice, since, once a company has elected to prepare financial statements under international accounting standards, they must continue to do so unless there is a material change of circumstances.

4.8 As a result of the *IAS Regulation*, there are now a number of possible permutations and combinations, and it is no longer possible to assume that the financial statements of UK companies have been prepared under UK GAAP:

- Listed companies are required to prepare their consolidated financial statements under international accounting standards.

- Listed companies often prepare their own company financial statements under international accounting standards, but do not always do so.

- The subsidiaries of listed companies may prepare their financial statements under either international accounting standards or UK GAAP.

- Unlisted companies may prepare their consolidated financial statements and their own company financial statements under either international accounting standards or UK GAAP, as may their subsidiary companies.

4.9 As the corporation tax liability of a company is based on its own company financial statements, rather than consolidated financial statements, the first question a tax practitioner needs to ask is, 'Which version of accounting standards has been used to prepare these financial statements?'. Even if one's clients are primarily unlisted companies, it is possible that some of them will have opted to use international accounting standards, rather than UK GAAP. Therefore, a tax practitioner needs to have a working knowledge of both UK GAAP and international accounting standards.

4.10 *Financial Statements – Which Version of Accounting Standards?*

4.10 There are many areas where international accounting standards and UK GAAP are practically identical, particularly at the basic accounting level. Even at the more advanced level, there are many overlaps and similarities. However, there are also numerous differences, particularly as one gets into the more advanced and technical areas of accounting and financial reporting. Furthermore, as the process of international harmonisation of national accounting standards continues, it would be reasonable to assume that some of the current differences between international accounting standards and UK GAAP will be reduced or eliminated over time, as UK standards are revised and reissued.

4.11 Bearing in mind that international standards are the product of consensus between a large number of countries, each with their own domestic sets of accounting standards, it is not surprising that there are differences in the terminology used between UK GAAP and IAS.

The following is a brief summary of the key differences:

UK GAAP	*International Standards*
Profit and Loss Account	Income Statement or Statement of Comprehensive Income
Turnover	Revenue
Stocks	Inventories
Debtors	Receivables
Creditors	Payables
Fixed Assets	Non-current assets
Creditors: amounts falling due within one year	Current liabilities
Creditors: amounts falling due after one year	Non-current liabilities
Profit and Loss (reserve)	Retained earnings.

4.12 As noted in the previous chapter, for tax purposes *ITTOIA 2005, s 25* and *CTA 2009, s 46* state that the profits of a trade must be calculated in accordance with generally accepted accounting practice, subject to any adjustment required or authorised by law in calculating profits for tax purposes. In 2004, clarification was made in terms of international accounting standards, and these are now as acceptable for tax purposes as UK GAAP.

4.13 The chapters of this book initially cover the basic accounting requirements in each area, but also summarise and explain the main differences between international accounting standards and UK GAAP in sufficient detail to give a reasonable working knowledge, albeit not to the level of detail required by an accounting and financial reporting expert.

Chapter 5

Back to Basics: Accounting Principles

5.1 It may appear odd that four chapters have already passed and yet the fundamentals of accounting are only now being mentioned for the first time. This mirrors the 'back to front' approach adopted over the years by the standard setting bodies and in the *Companies Acts*.

5.2 Prior to 1 August 1990, accounting standards were set by the Accounting Standards Committee (ASC). The standards set by this body are known as Statements of Standard Accounting Practice (SSAPs). Since 1 August 1990, the accounting standard setting role has been taken over by the Accounting Standards Board (ASB). The ASB adopted the standards originally set by the ASC but, when it issued new or replacement standards, they were known as Financial Reporting Standards (FRSs). As a result, there are both SSAPs and FRSs in issue.

5.3 The first attempt to articulate the fundamental principles was in 1971 on the issue of *SSAP 2: Disclosure of Accounting Policies* (*SSAP 1: Accounting for Associated Companies* was also issued in 1971). As will be seen shortly, *SSAP 2* was of a very generalised nature but at least it was a start. Over the years, many SSAPs and FRSs have been produced, but strangely there has been relatively little guidance concerning the distinction between 'capital' and 'revenue' expenditure (whatever those terms may mean), and relatively little in relation to timing issues for revenue and expense recognition. These are clearly fundamental issues for both accounting and tax purposes. In 1995, the ASB published, in a single package, its draft 'Statement of Principles'. This was intended to provide a conceptual framework for the future development of standards. It is still the subject of debate within the accountancy profession.

Meanwhile, *CA 1981* (later consolidated in *CA 1985* and continued in *CA 2006*) for the first time introduced a statutory framework (largely based on *SSAP 2*) and tightened up the disclosure requirements where departure from its provisions was made. *CA 1981* was the mechanism by which the European Community's Fourth Directive was introduced into UK law. This Directive required company accounts in Member States to be prepared in a standard format, and introduced the 'true and fair view' concept throughout Europe. (It had previously been a mainly UK concept.)

5.4 *Back to Basics: Accounting Principles*

The ASB in the UK issued its *Statement of Principles for Financial Reporting* in December 1999. The following year, *FRS 18*, entitled Accounting Policies, was issued to supersede *SSAP 2* and updates the discussion of the fundamental accounting concepts in *SSAP 2* to be consistent with the new *Statement of Principles*.

The International Accounting Standards Committee approved a *Framework for the Preparation and Presentation of Financial Statements* in 1989, which is the conceptual framework on which international accounting standards are based. It was adopted by the IASB in April 2001. The IASB's *Framework* draws on concepts and ideas developed in the US in relation to the theory behind financial reporting; and, in 2006, the IASB and the US FASB issued a discussion paper about 'converging' their two approaches, which has been the subject of much debate.

The following section describes the old *SSAP 2* and the legal requirements found in the companies legislation, which draw heavily on these ideas.

LEGAL REQUIREMENTS

5.4 In Section A of the Accounting Regulations (SI 2008/409 and SI 2008/410), five fundamental accounting principles are outlined. These are the broad assumptions which underlie the preparation of accounts. Their observance is presumed unless stated otherwise.

Fundamental accounting concepts

5.5

- **Going concern** Accounts are prepared on the assumption that the enterprise will continue for the foreseeable future. The term 'foreseeable future' is not defined precisely, although it is generally accepted that it should be for at least the following accounting period. To an extent, it depends on how far into the future it is reasonable to be able to expect the business to 'foresee' (ie forecast with a reasonable degree of accuracy), which in turn depends on the nature of the business being undertaken. A common misconception is that the 'going concern' concept implies that the current year's sales or profits will be maintained for the 'foreseeable future'. This is incorrect. The term 'going concern' means that the company is expected to continue in *operational existence*. This does not preclude losses or a significant curtailment in the scale of operations, such as asset sales or workforce redundancies – it merely means there will be no close-down.

- **Accruals** Revenues and costs are recognised when earned or incurred, not as money is received and paid. This enables revenues and costs to be 'matched' with each other. Therefore, profit is calculated after revenues have been offset by the costs and expenses incurred in generating that revenue.

- **Consistency**   This implies that like items will be dealt with consistently, both within an accounting period and from one year to another.
- **Prudence**   Revenues and profits will not be anticipated but only accounted for when ultimate realisation can be assessed with reasonable certainty. Conversely, provision is made for expenses or losses as soon as they are identified, even if precise quantification is difficult.

The foregoing are the four which essentially draw on the old *SSAP 2*. The fifth fundamental concept is colloquially known as the 'no offset' principle. What this means is that if, say, an enterprise buys a factory and takes a bank loan to fund it, the factory is included in the balance sheet as a separate item, and the loan, even though associated with the factory, is shown as a liability – current or long-term, as appropriate. There should be no netting off of the loan against the factory to disclose only the net 'investment' by the enterprise in the factory.

5.6   Any departure from the five accounting principles must be disclosed, justified and quantified.

ACCOUNTING BASES

5.7   These are the methods which have been developed over the years for expressing or applying the fundamental concepts to particular transactions.

HISTORICAL COST ACCOUNTING RULES

5.8   Section B of the Accounting Regulations (SI 2008/409 and SI 2008/410)deals with the 'normal' basis on which assets should be stated in accounts. This is called the historical cost basis and means, broadly, fixed assets are stated at cost and depreciated over their expected useful lives.

Current assets – mainly stocks, work in progress and debtors – are to be stated at cost or (if lower) net realisable value. Net realisable value, which is not defined in the legislation, means the anticipated future realisation less additional costs to be incurred in effecting that realisation.

There are specific rules for establishing how to measure the 'cost' of stocks and work in progress, and these are considered more fully in Chapter 13.

ALTERNATIVE ACCOUNTING RULES

5.9   Section C of the Accounting Regulations (SI 2008/409 and SI/2008/410) introduces the concept of 'alternative accounting rules'. In practice, this is not as alarming as it may sound.

In essence, it permits the use of 'current cost' accounting. This is something which was introduced in the 1970s at a time of high inflation.

5.10 *Back to Basics: Accounting Principles*

It represented an attempt to reflect the effect of inflation on a company's business. Current cost accounting had its own very detailed SSAP, but there was widespread dispute in the financial world as to the usefulness of the current cost concept and a lack of agreement as to the methods to be used in preparing current cost accounts. As inflation petered out, the SSAP was withdrawn and, with one or two rare exceptions, current cost accounts are not now seen.

5.10 However, one element of current cost accounting survives, and this is grafted on to the historical cost basis. This relates to the revaluation of fixed assets.

From time to time, companies may decide that the historical cost of its fixed assets – usually land and buildings, but possibly also plant/machinery – lags behind its current market value and, therefore, it would like to reflect that amount in its accounts. There are many commercial reasons for so doing. On the one hand, the asset base of a company is strengthened, and this may impress potential lenders. Gearing is improved, as assets (and hence shareholders' funds) increase whilst borrowings remain constant. On the other hand, return on capital falls. There are two reasons for this. First, profits themselves are likely to reduce (the only profit effect is in relation to depreciation; and, as shall be shown below, depreciation is calculated on the revalued amount, and is therefore likely to be higher than the depreciation calculated on the historic cost basis). Secondly, the capital employed (the denominator of the fraction) has increased.

It is important for the reader to appreciate what is happening here. It is not the revaluation itself that is causing a change in business performance. If a company has assets (usually land/buildings) which are worth more than the amount at which they are stated in the accounts, then that fact would need to be taken account of when judging the performance of the company. However, it is important to appreciate that a company is not *required* to incorporate the revaluation into its accounts.

An analyst aware of such facts would mentally adjust his thinking. A banker considering lending always wants an up-to-date value of the land/buildings so he can assess his security. The company which goes that one step further, and incorporates that valuation in its accounts, is merely reflecting that commercial reality so that all readers of the accounts are put in the same position, albeit only temporarily, as the valuation may not be updated each year.

It may appear strange that there is no legal requirement to revalue assets (upwards). So, two companies with identical profiles may produce different accounts – one revaluing, one not. Strange but true. The only time that companies are *obliged* to revalue is when there is a *permanent reduction* in the value of an asset. Prudence requires that this loss in value should be recognised. It is relatively rare to see land/buildings so written down, although adjustments do occur in relation to investment assets.

Revaluation reserve

5.11 It is necessary now to look at the mechanics for effecting a revaluation and the accounting for it.

Section C of the Accounting Regulations (SI 2008/409 and SI 2008/410) requires the establishment of a revaluation reserve. How this works may best be illustrated by the following example:

Example 5.1
Reproduced below is first the accounts of Company A which chooses not to revalue its assets. This is followed by the accounts of Company B which revalues its land/buildings and plant/machinery to £500,000 and £400,000 respectively at the end of Year 1. Neither company depreciates its land/buildings. Both companies depreciate the plant/machinery at the rate of 25% p.a. on the 'written down' value. In all other respects, Companies A and B are identical. Taxation is ignored. Note that this example has been deliberately simplified for ease of illustration – it is relatively rare for plant/machinery to be revalued, and buildings would normally be depreciated.

5.11 Back to Basics: Accounting Principles

Company A Balance Sheets

		Opening		Year 1		Year 2	
		£	£	£	£	£	£
Land/buildings			250,000		250,000		250,000
Plant/machinery	Cost	200,000		200,000		200,000	
	Depreciation	(100,000)		(125,000)		(143,750)	
	Net		100,000		75,000		56,250
Net current assets			100,000		200,000		380,000
Bank loan			(100,000)		(100,000)		(100,000)
Net Assets			350,000		425,000		586,250
Share Capital			100,000		100,000		100,000
Profit & Loss account			250,000		325,000		486,250
			350,000		425,000		586,250

Back to Basics: Accounting Principles 5.11

Company A profit & loss accounts

	Opening £	£	Year 1 £	£	Year 2 £	£
Turnover				1,000,000		1,200,000
Gross profit			200,000		300,000	
Expenses			(100,000)		(120,000)	
Depreciation			(25,000)		(18,750)	
Profit for the year				75,000		161,250

Company B Balance Sheets

		Opening £	£	Year 1 £	£	Year 2 £	£
Land/buildings			250,000		500,000		500,000
Plant/machinery	Cost	200,000		400,000		400,000	
	Depreciation	(100,000)		0		(100,000)	
	Net		100,000		400,000		300,000

5.11 Back to Basics: Accounting Principles

	Opening £	Year 1 £	Year 2 £
Net current assets	100,000	200,000	380,000
Bank loan	(100,000)	(100,000)	(100,000)
Net Assets	350,000	1,000,000	1,080,000
Share Capital	100,000	100,000	100,000
Profit & Loss account	250,000	325,000	405,000
Revaluation Reserve		575,000	575,000
	350,000	1,000,000	1,080,000

Company B profit & loss accounts

	Year 1 £	Year 2 £
Turnover	1,000,000	1,200,000
Gross profit	200,000	300,000
Expenses	(100,000)	(120,000)
Depreciation	(25,000)	(100,000)
Profit for the year	75,000	80,000

5.12 A large number of important conceptual points emerge from what is apparently a straightforward example.

At the end of Year 1, Company B revalues its plant and machinery to £400,000. At the start of that year (as shown in the opening balance sheet), the plant and machinery had a net book value of £100,000 (cost of £200,000 less accumulated depreciation of £100,000). This would seem to imply an uplift of £300,000 (valuation of £400,000 less £100,000 net book value). However, the revaluation at the end of Year 1 does not remove the requirement to charge depreciation for that year and to reflect that depreciation in the profit and loss account and the balance sheet. The profit and loss account needs to reflect the fact that the assets were used to generate that year's sales – hence, depreciation of £25,000 should be charged. The revaluation takes place at the end of Year 1 – *after* depreciation has been charged for the year.

The revaluation surplus may be analysed:

	£	
Revaluation land/buildings	250,000	
Revaluation plant/machinery	125,000	to original cost
	200,000	uplift from historical cost
	575,000	

The analysis of the revaluation surplus is interesting. As will be seen in Chapter 15, the method of accounting for the revaluation surplus of £325,000 on the plant and machinery accords with *FRS 15*. In **5.22** *et seq* below, reference is made to a statement issued by the accountancy bodies in relation to the determination of 'distributable profits'. To the extent of the write-back of depreciation in an asset revaluation (in *Example 5.1* above, £125,000 falls into this category), there are differences of opinion as to whether the £125,000 is distributable or not. If it is considered distributable, it may be preferable to transfer £125,000 from the revaluation reserve to the Profit and Loss account.

In Year 2, Company B charges depreciation of £100,000, considerably more than the depreciation on the historic cost basis would have been (£18,750, as shown for Company A). It is generally argued that this additional depreciation (£81,250) does not represent a realised loss, and an amount equal to that additional depreciation may be transferred from the revaluation reserve to the Profit and Loss account via a movement between the balance sheet reserves. (It will also feature in the disclosure of historical cost profits and losses required by *FRS 3*.) It is not permissible for this adjustment to be made through the profit and loss account statement.

It is interesting to compare and contrast some key features of Companies A and B at the end of Year 2.

5.13 Back to Basics: Accounting Principles

	Company A £		Company B £	
Profit for Year	161,250		80,000	
Return on Capital	$= \dfrac{161{,}250}{586{,}500}$	27%	$\dfrac{80{,}000}{1{,}080{,}000}$	7%
Gearing	$= \dfrac{100{,}000}{586{,}500}$	17%	$\dfrac{100{,}000}{1{,}080{,}000}$	9%

It is partly because of such 'anomalies' that *FRS 3* (see Chapter 7) requires the additional disclosure for those companies with revalued assets of what the profits would have been if the revaluation had not taken place.

5.13 This type of analysis is important for tax purposes, especially in the field of valuation. Most, but not all, valuations of companies proceed on an 'earnings basis'. That is, maintainable future earnings are estimated, and an appropriate multiple of these is selected to arrive at a value.

As can be seen above, Companies A and B have identical real trading performance, yet simply on the basis that one chooses to revalue, whilst the other does not, their apparent profits are very significantly different. Clearly, both companies are equally valuable, but the application of a profit multiple to each would produce vastly different results.

5.14 Another area of interest in the tax world relates to those circumstances in which tests are to be applied to determine, say, the 'closeness' of an individual's connections with a company.

Suppose an individual owns 10% of the equity of a company but additionally has provided £100,000 of loan capital. In a number of situations, the tax legislation concerns itself as to the degree of control such an individual may exert. He may exert significant control through his loan capital out of proportion to the fact that he only owns 10% of the equity. Therefore, there are tests (for example, in the Enterprise Investment Scheme (EIS) legislation) that require a notional liquidation to determine what proportion of the assets available would go to each shareholder.

In *Example 5.1* above, suppose a 10% shareholder of Company A was also the provider of the borrowings (instead of the bank) of £100,000. What he would be entitled to as a 'participator' on a notional liquidation at the end of Year 2 is:

	£	
Loan repayment	100,000	
10% shareholders funds	58,625	
	158,625	(158,625
=	23%	(586,250 + 100,000)

Back to Basics: Accounting Principles 5.16

In Company B, what he would be entitled to is:

	£	
Loan repayment	100,000	
10% shareholders funds	108,000	
	208,000	(208,000)
=	17%	(1,080,000 + 100,000)

The differences in the percentages can make the difference between falling foul, or otherwise, of 'anti-avoidance' legislation.

5.15 At this point, the important and fundamental concept of 'realised profits' is addressed. This is very important and must be borne in mind at all stages of a potential transaction – including the initial appraisal (see Chapter 3, especially the cautionary words in **3. 32** above).

5.16 *CA 2006, s 830* describes the circumstances in which companies can make distributions (in general parlance, 'dividends').

Distributions can only be made out of 'distributable profits'. For private companies, these comprise accumulated 'realised profits' (insofar as those realised profits have not already been distributed or 'used' for some other corporate transaction, eg a redemption of own shares) less accumulated 'realised losses'.

For public companies, *CA 2006, s 831* incorporates an additional restriction, namely that any net accumulated 'unrealised loss' must be retained and not distributed.

There is no definition of 'realised profits' or 'realised losses'.

The statutory rules limiting a company's ability to make distributions were introduced in 1980. At that time, it was provided that directors should research the history of their accumulated Profit and Loss balance (ie retained profit) to determine the extent to which it represented realised profit (which it probably did); but, providing the directors detected no specific information to the contrary, the company was entitled to assume that the balance of its profit and loss account at 22 December 1980 did constitute realised profit available for future distribution.

Because there is no statutory definition of what constitutes realised profits, the accountancy bodies have issued guidance. Essentially, this provides that if a FRS or an SSAP requires a profit (or loss) to be recognised in a profit and loss account, it should be treated as a realised profit (unless any particular FRS or SSAP states otherwise).

There is a particular problem where profits are 'realised' by virtue of transactions intra-group (see Chapter 23 for a fuller discussion of groups).

5.17 *Back to Basics: Accounting Principles*

5.17 The upshot of this is that, in examining the balance sheet of a company, care has to be taken to identify what reserves are capable of being distributed (ie paid away as dividends) and which are not so capable.

Reserves described as 'Profit and Loss account' are almost always distributable.

Reserves described as 'Share Premium', 'Capital Redemption Reserve Funds' or 'Revaluation Reserves' are not distributable.

The terms 'distributable' and 'non-distributable' rarely feature in the accounts themselves.

Further consideration to this aspect is contained in Chapter 23.

5.18 The ability (or inability) of a company to distribute its reserves is occasionally relevant for tax purposes.

ITA 2007, s 682 et seq concerns itself with the potential avoidance of tax by organising matters so that what would otherwise be liable to income tax is converted into a liability to capital gains tax. The basic supposition of the legislation is that a company which is in a position to pay a dividend organises its affairs so that an amount of money equivalent to the dividend finds its way into the shareholder's hands in apparently a capital form. If it can be demonstrated that no dividend could lawfully have been paid in the first place, then the provisions have no effect.

This point became relevant in *Shearer v Bercain Ltd* 53 TC 698. In that case, Company A acquired Company B. The latter paid a dividend (under group election) to the former. The Revenue alleged that A could, if it had wished, have paid that dividend out to its shareholders – and that various tax consequences followed from this. Company A successfully argued that it was prohibited by law from the onward payment of dividend. The courts agreed and the Revenue's claim was dismissed. (The company law on the distribution of pre-acquisition profits has now changed. The present law is discussed in Chapter 29)

Accounting policies

5.19 These are the specific accounting bases judged by the enterprise as most appropriate to employ in preparing its own accounts. The *Companies Acts* require the directors of a company to select suitable accounting policies and to apply them consistently.

5.20 For taxation purposes, the concepts do not normally cause offence. The 'accruals' concept is mirrored in the tax jargon by the expression 'earnings basis', which was given statutory effect by *FA 1998, s 46*.

5.21 For tax purposes, for periods of account ending on or after 1 August 2001, *FA 2002, s 64* and *Sch 22* apply, and provide a computational method to calculate the adjustment necessary for tax purposes. For periods of account ending after 1 January 2005, positive adjustments are charged as a receipt of the trade arising on the first day of the first period of account of the new accounting policy. Negative adjustments are allowed as a deduction in computing profits as an expense on the first day of the first period of account of the new accounting policy. There are special spreading rules for particular transitions, eg from a realisations basis to a mark to market basis (*ITTOIA 2005, ss 236–237*).

FINANCIAL REPORTING STANDARD 18 (FRS 18)

5.22 *FRS 18* 'Accounting Policies' was issued in December 2000 and essentially requires entities to adopt policies that are most appropriate to the entity and enable their financial statements to give a true and fair view.

The standard endorses the 'going concern' and 'accruals' concepts, but is different in some respects to *CA 2006*. In relation to going concern, even when a company is in financial difficulties, *FRS 18* will require the going concern basis to be used, unless the directors intend to liquidate the entity or cease trading, or have no realistic alternative but to do so. Disclosure is required of any material uncertainties or events or conditions that cast doubt on the entity's ability to continue as a going concern.

In relation to accruals, whereas the old *SSAP 2* had required matching of revenue and costs, *FRS 18* does not. The central concern with *FRS 18* is to reflect the effects in the period in which they occur. This means that costs incurred in the hope of future revenue can only be deferred if they meet the definition of 'asset'. Although *CA 2006* allows departures from accruals, *FRS 18* does not.

CA 2006 (and *SSAP 2*) policies of consistency and prudence under *FRS 18* have been subsumed within a statement of the objectives against which an entity should judge its accounting policy. These are specifically:

- relevance – ie useful for assessing the stewardship of management and for making economic decisions;
- reliability – ie presents faithfully the substance of transactions or events, is free from deliberate or systematic bias, is complete within the bounds of materiality and, where there is uncertainty, prudence has been exercised;
- comparability – achieved through a combination of consistency and disclosure; and
- understandability – 'capable of being understood by users having a reasonable knowledge of business and economic activities and accounting and having a willingness to study with reasonable diligence the information provided'.

FRS 18 takes a different approach to the question of uncertainty than did *SSAP 2*. In respect of prudence, for example, whereas *SSAP 2* required it to take priority over accruals, *FRS 18* says it is a response to uncertainty and, as such, must be balanced.

5.23 *Back to Basics: Accounting Principles*

5.23 *FRS 18* extends the disclosure requirements when there is a change in accounting policy. Details required include a statement of why the new accounting policy is considered to be more appropriate and, unless the effect is immaterial, a statement indicating the effect of the change in accounting policy on the results for the current and preceding accounting period.

DEVELOPMENTS IN FUNDAMENTAL ACCOUNTING CONCEPTS

5.24 The ASB's *Statement of Principles* is not entirely consistent with the legal requirements since, as noted earlier, it is based largely on *SSAP 2*. The ASB argues, however, that the inconsistencies do not go to the core of the principles and that the *Statement* has an important role to play in shaping future developments in the companies legislation. The *Statement* is also consistent with the IASB's *Framework*.

While the *Statement* maintains the accruals concept, it gives a slightly more restricted role to the notion of 'matching'. This means that some items may appear in the profit and loss account rather than the balance sheet under the *Statement*. Accounting standards issued after publication of the *Statement* are consistent with its approach, and the ASB has expressed confidence that these subtle changes are not a cause for concern in practice.

Chapter 3 of the *Statement* observes that information provided by financial statements should be relevant and reliable, comparable and understandable. The principle of materiality is preserved in the *Statement*, as is the principle of prudence.

Areas of inconsistency between the *Statement* and *CA 2006* include:

- Recognition – whereas *CA 2006* states that only profits realised at balance sheet date can be included in the profit and loss account, the *Statement* says that gains should be recognised if they can be measured with sufficient reliability and that sufficient evidence exists that they have actually arisen.

- Measurement – for some assets, *CA 2006* uses a different basis of measurement to that suggested in the *Statement*, particularly in relation to the use of current values.

In relation to the IASB *Framework*, materiality is treated differently, in that it is included as a 'quantitative' characteristic, whereas the *Statement* envisages it as relating to both size and nature of the item. The *Framework* describes going concern and accruals as underlying assumptions. The *Statement* does not describe them in this way, but adopts the same view as to their role and describes them in the same way.

The ongoing developments, particularly in relation to the convergence between UK and international standards and principles, are considered further in Chapter 32.

DIFFICULT ISSUES

Materiality

5.25 As a general rule, if the inclusion or exclusion of an item would affect the decisions of those who use financial statements, the item is material. In 1995, the ICAEW issued a paper 'Materiality in Financial Reporting' which was updated in 1996 and re-titled 'The Interpretation of Materiality in Financial Reporting' (*TECH 32/96*).

The following guidelines assist in determining whether something is material:

- The material fact may not be financial. That a company is, for example, breaking UN sanctions by trading with Iraq is a material fact, whatever the amounts involved.

- In monetary terms, materiality is a relative factor. £1,000 in the accounts of a multinational is immaterial. In the context of a corner shop, it may well be material.

- The degree of approximation or inherent uncertainty in the item under consideration affects the materiality. The share capital is capable of precise quantification. Virtually any departure from this would be material. The valuation of stocks and work in progress necessarily involves value judgements – precise quantification is not possible, and so greater latitude is possible.

- An amount may not be material in its own right, but may be associated with a critical point, ie its inclusion or exclusion may turn an overall profit into a loss, or vice versa. In that sense, the figure could be regarded as material.

The ICAEW issued a further technical release (*TECH 03/08*) in June 2008, which confirmed the continuing relevance of *TECH 32/96* and provides updated guidance by reference to recent developments in accounting standards and regulation.

In the tax context, the question of materiality also arises, although it is not mentioned anywhere in the *Taxes Acts*. In theory, HMRC would say that they are a pragmatic organisation. Perfection is not sought and they would only involve themselves in 'material' matters. In practice, the level of 'materiality' is determined by individual officers and, seemingly, has as much to do with their own immediate workload, their own seniority and their own predilections.

In general, though, it is fair to say that the scope which directors (and auditors) give themselves as regards materiality is much wider than that which most Revenue officers would permit. For example, in a sizeable private company, the fact that £50 per week petty cash is not fully vouched for might be regarded by the company and its auditors as not material. The Inspector might regard it as material in itself, and possibly as material in being indicative of a general attitude of the directors and the question of accounting for cash.

5.26 *Back to Basics: Accounting Principles*

In September 1997, a meeting between the Revenue and the Tax Faculty (of the ICAEW) produced an agreed minute, recorded in Tax 18/97, stating, 'The Revenue said that the usefulness generally of accounts was limited by the concept of materiality in their preparation'.

Some additional insight into the materiality factors for Revenue officers might be gleaned from their own attitude to adjustments to tax computations submitted to them. For larger concerns, where the integrity of the accounts are not generally questioned, Revenue officers restrict themselves to queries which might relate to technical adjustments, such as analysing repairs expenditure to identify possible capital expenditure. Their success is quantified and reported. Generally, no record is made unless the adjustment is at least £2,000 in terms of adjustment to profit.

In the investigation field, an examination of a current year's account can lead to adjustments to the taxable profits for that year, an extrapolation to earlier years and, in the more serious cases, to the imposing of interest and penalties. At present, the general rule seems to be that there is no extrapolation to earlier years unless the current year profit adjustment exceeds £1,000, and no imposition of interest and penalties unless the current year profit adjustment exceeds £2,000.

A further perspective is given in the Revenue press release of 18 May 1993 in which – in certain circumstances – tax computations rounded to the nearest £1,000 may be accepted. These self-imposed financial criteria give some indication of HMRC's ideas on materiality.

CAPITAL OR REVENUE

5.26 There is no formal accounting definition of the distinction between capital and revenue expenditure. Historically, it has been a kind of underlying fundamental accounting principle, but was not specifically dealt with in *SSAP 2* or *CA 2006*. More recent accounting developments are making the accounting difference of less significance, although for tax purposes the distinction is still important; however, in some areas such as the loan relationship rules (see Chapter 22), the capital/revenue divide is no longer relevant.

5.27 In the earliest days of accounting, an enterprise could tell 'how it was doing' by comparing its incomings and outgoings to arrive at a surplus (or deficit) of receipts over payments. Some small non profit-making organisations still do this but, for most trading activities, this was recognised as too crude.

For example, if during a particular year a building is acquired from which to trade, it is likely to last many years. It would not be a fair representation of the year's performance to charge the entire cost of that building against that year's income. This led to the evolution of the balance sheet, with expenditures such as property acquisitions being included there, rather than in the receipts and payments account (which then came to be called the profit and loss account).

Apart from the acquisition of long-term assets, such as a building, it was also recognised that other costs should be (more temporarily) included in the balance sheet rather than the profit and loss account. The cost of stock bought for resale but still unsold at year end should more fairly be matched against the sales income which normally arises in the following year. Therefore, such expenditure is included in the balance sheet but transferred back to profit and loss in the following accounting period.

So, the balance sheet evolved into a document in which two kinds of expenditures were reflected. These expenditures are said to produce 'assets'. Assets held for the long term are called 'Fixed'; assets held for the short term are called 'Current'.

The acquisition or enhancement or improvement of a fixed asset is called capital expenditure. Other expenditure, including the acquisition etc of a current asset, is called revenue expenditure.

5.28 The distinction between capital and revenue expenditure is crucial for tax purposes, not only because of the general requirement to determine taxable profits on the basis of commercial principles, but also because of the specific statutory prevention of tax deductibility of capital expenditure by *CTA 2009, s 53*.

Many tax cases have come before the courts (see Appendix A). No conclusive definition of capital expenditure has evolved, but the general characteristics of capital expenditure are that it tends to be exceptional (in the sense of not recurring, except at lengthy intervals), relatively large, and is incurred with a view to producing an enduring benefit. At this stage, the tax concept of capital and revenue expenditure is not essentially different from the accounting understanding which is expressed in **5.27** above (ie capital expenditure is that which is expended in acquiring etc a fixed asset), except in relation to the question of abortive expenditure. Expenditure which is intended to result in the acquisition of a fixed asset but which does not do so (eg professional costs in relation to the purchase of a property which ultimately does not proceed) is not included in the balance sheet, but is written off against the year's income. From the tax viewpoint, the courts have held that it is the purpose of the expenditure which is relevant. Thus, such expenditure is capital in nature, although not 'capitalised' in the balance sheet.

5.29 If accounting had developed down a capital/revenue path, it is possible that the courts (and HMRC) would have allowed the tax concept to evolve in a similar manner.

However, in the world of accounting, development has been focused more around the concept of an 'asset'. This, in turn, has emphasised the importance of the 'balance sheet' view.

The ASB's *Statement of Principles* makes no mention of capital or revenue. Rather, it takes as its starting point the balance sheet. The balance sheet should include 'assets' and 'liabilities'.

5.30 *Back to Basics: Accounting Principles*

'Assets' are defined as 'rights or other access to future economic benefits as a result of past transactions or events'.

'Liabilities' are defined as 'obligations to transfer economic benefits as a result of past transactions or events'.

This conceptual balance sheet approach to accounting remains the subject of debate (see Chapter 29 for a further discussion of this) within the accountancy profession.

5.30 In relation to capital/revenue problems, HMRC (and the courts) are much less inclined to give weight to modern accountancy input or to depart from (or develop) principles established by the courts at a time when only limited accountancy input was available. This is quite different from situations in relation to 'timing issues' (see below).

REVENUE (INCOME AND EXPENDITURE) – TIMING

5.31 Once the classification of an income or expense is accepted as not being 'capital' (ie it is of a revenue nature), it is necessary to determine into which accounting period it should fall.

In essence, this is an application of the accruals and prudence concepts. There is no essential difference between income and expense items.

Several accounting standards (eg *FRS 12* 'Provisions, contingent liabilities and assets') specifically address what are essentially timing issues. In general, HMRC accept the application of these standards for tax purposes.

There are two particular areas, however, where there remains room for debate – from both the tax and the accounting aspects.

When is a sale a sale?

5.32 There is no specific accounting standard on revenue recognition to answer this question. The *Statement of Principles* by implication addresses the issue, but only in a conceptualised way. Application Note G to *FRS 5* 'Reporting the Substance of Transactions' and *UITF Abstract 40* 'Revenue Recognition and Service Contracts' are concerned with revenue recognition, but do not set out to deal with the issue comprehensively.

Essentially, a sale is a sale when the buyer assumes from the seller the risks and rewards of the 'sold' asset, and the amount of revenue can be reliably measured.

5.33 There is an infinite variety of commercial transactions. Often, there is no uniquely 'correct' point in time at which to recognise the sale as having taken place.

For example, consider a house builder selling to the general public. The normal process is for a customer to decide to purchase, and then pay a deposit to secure a plot. (Sometimes, the 'deposit' is refundable if a completed sale does not result, but this is not universally the case.) The customer arranges a mortgage, and lawyers draw up a contract which is then exchanged, usually with the payment of a true (non-returnable) deposit. Sometime later – possibly four weeks – completion takes place. The balance of the purchase price is paid, and a conveyance to the customer takes place.

So, when did the sale take place? The placing of an initial 'deposit' by the customer will probably not be the appropriate point. The 'deposit' will be small, and in practice a significant number of such 'reservations' will not complete.

The exchange of contracts is a strong candidate. There is a legally enforceable contract, a significant deposit, and there will be few examples of cases where, following exchange, there will not be a completion.

An equally strong candidate would be the date of completion, as on that date legal ownership passes and the purchase price is fully satisfied.

In practice, completion date is the more common, but contract exchange date is certainly not unusual – it is not incorrect accounting and is acceptable to HMRC. Most (if not all?) accountants would regard the date of initial deposit as being far too imprudent.

When is an expense an expense?

5.34 Using accounting jargon, this question can be rephrased as 'when should a "provision" be made?'.

5.35 The word 'provision' is much used and misunderstood. A provision is an amount set aside in arriving at current profits to meet a future obligation arising out of past or present events. A provision is an expense deducted in arriving at profits. The future obligation may be contingent and/or uncertain in amount, but the important point is that the event giving rise to it has already happened.

A reserve, on the other hand, is not an expense. It is a sum set aside out of profits to meet future needs which may arise out of future events.

Accountants, Revenue officers and judges sometimes use the words 'provision' and 'reserve' as synonyms. It is important to appreciate the distinction.

5.36 In 1995, the ASB issued a discussion paper entitled 'Provisions'. There was concern that companies were trying to smooth out their trading results from year to year by making 'generalised' provisions. A particular abuse was identified in relation to acquisitions, when management of the acquiring company caused management of the target company to make large

5.37 *Back to Basics: Accounting Principles*

provisions for future expenditures at the date of acquisition – the consequence of which is to deflate pre-acquisition and inflate post-acquisition profits. That debate has resulted in the publication of *FRS 12* 'Provisions, Contingent Liabilities and Contingent Assets' (see Chapter 18).

5.37 The tax position in relation to provisions was clarified following the issue of *FRS 12*, at which time it was made clear that the accounting treatment of provisions would generally be followed for tax purposes, subject to the capital/revenue divide.

Chapter 6

Substance Over Form

6.1 Over the years, accountants have devoted much effort and ingenuity to devising schemes to keep certain items of finance off the balance sheet. These schemes relied on the transaction being accounted for in accordance with its strict legal form rather than by reflecting the true commercial substance.

Such off balance sheet finance items needed to be correctly accounted for before the accounts could give a true and fair view.

Attempts to tackle off balance sheet finance first began with Technical Release TR 603 published in December 1985, and have culminated in Financial Reporting Standard 5 which was issued in April 1994.

FINANCIAL REPORTING STANDARD 5 (FRS 5)

6.2 *FRS 5* is effective for all accounting periods ending on or after 22 September 1994, and applies to all transactions, regardless of when they were undertaken.

The stated objective of *FRS 5* is to ensure that the substance of an entity's transactions is reported in its financial statements. The commercial effect of the entity's transactions, and any resulting assets, liabilities, gains or losses, should be faithfully presented in its financial statements.

The approach taken by *FRS 5* is to adopt a new definition of assets and liabilities (this is consistent with the draft 'Statement of Principles'). The effect of applying these definitions is that transactions which were off balance sheet will be brought on balance sheet, subject to permitted exclusions.

FRS 5 mainly affects more complex transactions whose substance may not be readily apparent. Transactions requiring particularly careful analysis are those:

- which are linked with other transactions in such a way that the commercial effect can be understood only by considering the series of transactions as a whole;
- where legal title is separated from the risks and benefits of an asset (as in a finance lease); or
- where an option is included on terms that make its exercise highly likely.

6.3 *Substance Over Form*

Not only does *FRS 5* require items to be brought on balance sheet, but it also requires disclosure of a transaction sufficient to enable the user of the financial statements to understand its commercial effect.

Since accounting for the substance of transactions is at the core of *FRS 5*, it is not difficult to see that this leads to more scope for interpretation than if the accounting followed the strict legal form. It may well be that there is little consistency in how certain items are accounted for, and the Urgent Issues Task Force (UITF) may well be busy in this area.

Fundamental concepts

6.3 The fundamental concepts are defined as follows.

Assets

6.4 Assets are rights and other access to future economic benefits controlled by an entity as a result of past transactions or events.

Liabilities

6.5 Liabilities are obligations to transfer economic benefits as a result of past transactions or events.

Risk

6.6 Risk is uncertainty as to the amount of the benefit, including both potential for gain and exposure to loss.

Control in the context of an asset

6.7 Control, in this context, is the ability to obtain the future economic benefits relating to an asset and to restrict the access of others to those benefits.

Recognition

6.8 Recognition is the process of incorporating an item into the primary financial statements under the appropriate heading.

APPLICATION OF FRS 5

6.9 *FRS 5* is designed to ensure that the substance of transactions is accounted for. As has been mentioned, the fact that *FRS 5* is based on

Substance Over Form **6.10**

substance and not legal form allows for more liberal interpretations and the creation of grey areas.

FRS 5 includes seven Application Notes which give guidance on particular areas, and following these notes will usually be sufficient to ensure compliance with the standard. They also provide guidance on how *FRS 5* should be applied in other areas. The Application Notes are:

A.   Consignment stock;

B.   Sale and repurchase agreements;

C.   Factoring of debts;

D.   Securitised assets;

E.   Loan transfers;

F.   Private Finance Initiative and similar contracts (September 1998);

G.   Revenue recognition (November 2003).

METHODOLOGY

6.10   The approach of *FRS 5* is to analyse transactions according to the following methodology.

Identifying assets and liabilities
In determining this, one looks for new assets and liabilities, whether the entity has rights to the benefits by assessing the risks inherent in the benefits, and whether there is an obligation to transfer benefits.

Recognition of assets and liabilities
Where a transaction gives rise to an asset or a liability, that item should be recognised in the balance sheet if there is sufficient evidence of its existence and it can be measured from a monetary perspective with sufficient reliability.

Transactions in previously recognised assets
This part of *FRS 5* provides guidance on when assets and liabilities should be recognised in the financial statements and when assets and liabilities should cease to be recognised. There are three possibilities:

- Where a transaction in a previously recognised asset results in no significant change in an entity's rights or access to benefits relating to that asset, or exposure to risks inherent in those benefits, then the entire asset should be recognised in the balance sheet.

  An example where assets should get full, continued recognition in the balance sheet is a factored debt where the seller retains significant benefits and risks relating to the debt. The application of *FRS 5* to factored debts is covered in Application Note C.

6.11 *Substance Over Form*

- Where a transaction in a previously recognised asset transfers significant rights or other access to benefits relating to that asset, and all significant exposure to the risks inherent in those benefits, then the entire asset should cease to be recognised in the balance sheet.

    A simple example would be the sale of an item of plant or machinery for a non-returnable cash consideration.

- There are some special cases where the above treatments do not apply (see *FRS 5, paras 23* and *24*). In these cases, there will be a significant change in the reporting entity's rights to benefit and exposure to risk, but the above conditions are not met. These cases usually arise where a transaction has one or more of the following ingredients:

    – a transfer of only part of the item in question;

    – a transfer of all of the item but only for part of its life; and

    – a transfer of all of the item for all of its life, but where the entity retains some significant right to benefits or exposure to the risks inherent in those benefits. 'Significant' should be gauged in relation to the benefits and risks that are likely to occur in practice.

Transactions in previously recognised assets give rise to a grey area. Continued recognition or derecognition will be the clear treatment for most transactions but, as one gets into the special cases, the accounting treatment is not so clear-cut.

Where a special case arises, the description or the monetary amount relating to an asset should be changed, where necessary, and a liability recognised if an obligation to transfer benefits is assumed – put simply, show a new asset and/or a new liability in the balance sheet.

Linked presentation

6.11 FRS 5 goes on to discuss a 'linked presentation' for certain non-recourse finance agreements. The basic idea is that, where a transaction involving a previously recognised asset (which should continue to be recognised in the balance sheet – see above) is in substance a financing asset, but the financing entity 'ring-fences' the asset such that:

- the finance will only be repaid from the proceeds of the sale of the specific asset it finances, and

- the asset cannot be retained or re-acquired on repayment of the finance,

then the finance should be shown deducted from the gross amount of the asset on the face of the balance sheet, and not in a note – the linked presentation.

The linked presentation should only be used where six conditions are simultaneously satisfied (see *FRS 5, para 27*).

6.12 One aspect of the linked presentation worthy of note is how profit should be recognised. Profit should be recognised, on entering into the arrangement for which a linked presentation is used, only to the extent that non-returnable proceeds are in excess of the previous carrying value of the asset. Thereafter, any net profit or loss should be recognised when it arises and be included in the profit and loss account.

Offset of assets and liabilities

6.13 Assets and liabilities should not be offset. Aggregation of balances is permitted only where certain conditions are satisfied (see *FRS 5, para 29*).

This requirement mirrors the legal provisions concerning the offset of assets and liabilities in *SI 2008/409* and *SI 2008/410*.

Disclosure

6.14 Disclosure is key to *FRS 5*. The requirement is for the transaction to be disclosed in enough detail for the user of the financial statements to understand its commercial effect.

This disclosure is required, irrespective of whether assets or liabilities have been put on or taken off the balance sheet.

Where different types of asset or liability have been put on the balance sheet, the different nature of those assets should be explained.

PROFIT RECOGNITION

6.15 *FRS 5* could be considered as being just concerned with the balance sheet. This is not the case, although it seems to deliberately provide limited guidance on profit recognition.

Since the starting point in computing profits chargeable to corporation tax is the accounts profit, it is worth considering the effect of *FRS 5* on profit recognition. One type of transaction that *FRS 5* hopes to counter is that which is designed to accelerate profit. From a tax perspective, however, one might be more concerned with transactions to defer profits. Guidance on transactions designed to accelerate profits basically comes from *FRS 5*, Application Note B which considers sale and repurchase transactions. The Application Note indicates that, where no sale has taken place, no profit can be recognised.

Application Note G, issued in 2003 and taking effect for accounting periods ending on or after 23 December 2003, specifically deals with revenue recognition. This Application Note is designed to promote consistency in the face of divergent practices in this area.

DISTRIBUTABLE PROFITS

6.16 It will be recalled that a company can only pay a dividend out of 'distributable profits' (see Chapter 5). Distributable profits are not determined

6.17 *Substance Over Form*

by statute but by generally accepted accounting principles. Thus, if *FRS 5* requires that no realised profit should be recognised, distributable profits will be similarly affected.

FRS 5 applies to all transactions, regardless of when they are undertaken. If *FRS 5* requires the profit previously recognised on earlier transactions to be derecognised, then there will be a consequent effect on the accumulated Profit and Loss account. This will not affect dividends already paid, but will affect future dividends. To this limited extent, *FRS 5* can be regarded as retrospective.

INTERNATIONAL STANDARDS

6.17 There is no international standard dealing specifically with substance over form in the way that *FRS 5* does. For guidance on this thorny issue, one must look to the IASB's *Framework for Presentation of Financial Statements*. The *Framework* defines assets and liabilities in terms of 'economic benefits', and so substance in this context involves considering the commercial environment in which the entity is operating rather than the legal ownership or responsibilities.

TAXATION

6.18 *FRS 5* effectively promotes 'substance over form', with particular reference to off balance sheet transactions. There is no analogous taxation rule. Indeed, the Inland Revenue have said (Tax 18/97) that 'the resultant uncertainties in the application of *FRS 5* militates against its use as a core feature of the tax system'. However, 'substance over form' has echoes of *Furniss v Dawson* 55 TC 324 and there is scope for confusion. It is useful to understand the latest analysis on this subject.

Statutory construction v substance over form

6.19 There is no tax rule which permits tax to be levied on the basis of the substance of a transaction rather than on its legal form. This is the case, whether or not there is any underlying tax-avoidance motive.

There is only one principle. The relevant tax statute must be applied to the transaction as it is, not how the Inland Revenue (or anyone else) would like it to have been.

Where there is relevant and recent legislation (with its own anti-avoidance provisions), there may be a presumption that Parliament intended that legislation to be the determinant in establishing tax liability.

Otherwise – and in a restricted range of circumstances – it may be necessary to apply the rule of statutory construction first tentatively identified in *Ramsay (WT) Ltd v CIR* 54 TC 101 and subsequently developed in later judgments.

The 'Ramsay' principle

6.20 This can only apply where:

- there is a pre-ordained series of transactions (which are identified in advance and, once initiated, are highly likely to continue in sequence); and

- one of those transactions has been inserted for no commercial purpose, but solely to avoid tax (note that it is commercial *purpose* not commercial *effect* which is relevant).

If this is the case, then – subject to **6.21** below – the inserted step may be disregarded and liability determined by applying the statute to the other elements of the transaction.

Limitations on the principle

6.21 Recent cases have identified two further limitations of the '*Ramsay*' principle. First, there is the 'end result' test. At the end of the day, the series of transactions has a starting and an end point. The reinterpretation of the series of transactions must be consistent with those fixed points. For example, a sole trader may be selling his business.

He may firstly incorporate (under *TCGA 1992, s 162*) and allow the company to on-sell the business. The company should pay no capital gains tax on disposal (as a result of the uplift in base cost on transfer from sole trader). The Revenue cannot simply say that the incorporation was an artificially inserted step and treat the sale as having been made directly to the purchaser, because the true end result is that he ends up with shares in a company and the company ends up with the cash. Secondly, there is the limitation that the Revenue may not get the taxing result they want if that means altering the character of real transactions that have taken place. For example, an individual may be selling his company for £1 million. Before sale, he may pay a dividend of £500,000 and then sell his shares for £500,000. The only purpose of the dividend is to enable a lower total tax bill for the individual to be obtained. The 'end result' test does not help. In both cases, he ends up with £1 million before tax in his hands. However, the Revenue cannot simply say that what he did was equivalent to the disposal of shares for £1 million. The dividend was real. It created a different asset for sale. The purchaser acquired a company with a different balance sheet, with different potential for paying future dividends etc. The Revenue would not be able, therefore, to apply the '*Ramsay*' principle.

6.22 Within the past 15 years, the difficult issue of substance over form continued to be considered in the courts. The difficult case of *CIR v McGuckian* [1997] STC 908 was decided in favour of the Revenue, partly on the basis of conventional (*Furniss v Dawson*) analysis and partly by adopting a 'purposive' approach, ie by seeking to understand what kind of circumstances

6.22 Substance Over Form

the legislation was trying to get at, and deciding that, if the circumstances fit, the statute should bite. This is in fact getting a little closer to an *FRS 5* 'substance over form' argument.

In 2005, the House of Lords delivered its decision in *Barclays Mercantile Business Finance Ltd v Mawson* [2005] STC 1. The case involved a sale and leaseback arrangement between the Barclays group and the Irish Gas Board, and the claim for capital allowances. HMRC argued, essentially, that the expenditure was on 'financial engineering' and not on qualifying plant and machinery. The House of Lords, finding in favour of the taxpayer, noted that whether an expense is incurred is a legal question.

In 2008, the High Court delivered its decision in the *Astall* case [2008] EWHC 1471 (Ch), in which the taxpayer sought to deduct a loss arising from the transfer of discounted securities. The Special Commissioners had earlier found in favour of HMRC that the loss was not deductible, taking a purposive approach to interpreting the relevant legislation. Their decision was upheld by the High Court. The standing of the 'purposive' principle of interpretation is still, however, unclear. Further cases are needed to determine its scope and limitations.

Chapter 7

The Presentational Standards

7.1 In this section, a number of standards that relate to the presentation of facts and figures in the accounts will be considered. The innocuous description 'presentational' belies the significance of the subject matter of these standards for both accounting and tax purposes.

7.2 Chronologically, the earliest of these was *SSAP 3* 'Earnings Per Share'. As will be seen, this attempts to compute and present that part of a company's total profits applicable to a single shareholder (at its simplest, total profits divided by the number of shares). This was followed soon after by *SSAP 6* 'Extraordinary and Prior Year Items'. *SSAP 6* was generally regarded – as shall be seen later – as being susceptible to abuse and manipulation and, for this reason, was withdrawn and replaced with *FRS 3* 'Reporting Financial Performance'. *FRS 3* also had consequential effects for *SSAP 3*, which was subsequently replaced by *FRS 14* 'Earnings Per Share'. *FRS 14* has itself been superseded by *FRS 22* 'Earnings per share'. Meanwhile, *SSAP 25* 'Segmental Reporting' was introduced. This is a freestanding and relatively straightforward standard.

Further consideration of the standards will proceed on a logical rather than chronological basis, dealing first with segmental reporting, then with reporting financial performance, and finally with the computation and disclosure of earnings per share.

SEGMENTAL REPORTING

7.3 The *Companies Act 2006 (CA 2006)* requires all large companies to make limited additional disclosure – by way of Notes to the Accounts – where they carry on businesses of different classes, or serve different geographical markets. All that is required by statute is that the turnover and the profit or loss of each class, or the turnover relating to each separate market, be separately disclosed. Small and medium-sized companies need only disclose details for different geographical areas.

SSAP 25, introduced in June 1990, extends these limited disclosure requirements significantly in the case of certain companies.

7.4 *The Presentational Standards*

STATEMENT OF STANDARD ACCOUNTING PRACTICE 25 (SSAP 25)

Scope

7.4   *SSAP 25* applies only to public and certain highly specialised companies, and those companies which exceed the criteria for a medium-sized company by a factor of ten.

Indirectly, this provides an interesting perspective on the concept of 'true and fair'. If public and large/medium companies need to make the *SSAP 25* disclosures in order to give a 'true and fair' view, why should this not be the case for private and smaller companies? *SSAP 25* implies that 'true and fair' is not a 'black and white' concept but that there are various shades of grey. The disclosures required lead to an 'improved' true and fair view, but for private and smaller companies, that degree of improvement may not be material and therefore may be ignored. This is not entirely logical. In relative terms, segmental analysis may be just as significant for companies excluded by *SSAP 25*. The standard partly recognises this by encouraging those companies that are outside its scope to disclose the information anyway.

Reportable segments

7.5   The standard seeks to address the fact that many business entities carry on several classes of business or operate in several geographical areas. Each of these business classes or geographical areas may present different rates of profitability, different opportunities for growth, and different degrees of risk. The objective of the standard is to provide users with additional information to assist them in making judgements about the entity's performance and prospects.

7.6   *SSAP 25* envisages the breaking down of the activities of a company into reportable segments. Broadly, there are two criteria for identifying these segments. First, activities may be segmented by geographical area. Secondly, activities may be segmented by the class of business carried on.

There is clearly some subjectivity in identifying such segments. Any potential segment whose turnover represents less than 10% of the turnover of the entirety, or profit represents less than 10% of the total profits, or whose assets are less than 10% of the net assets of the entirety, is to be disregarded (as a separate segment).

The precise mechanism for determining the segmental boundaries is not important for present purposes. It is sufficient to note that those companies within the scope of *SSAP 25* are required to disclose, by means of a separate note to the accounts, certain additional information on a segment–by-segment basis.

Analysis by geographical segment is confusing. Company law identifies a geographical segment by destination (ie where the goods/services are supplied). *SSAP 25* primarily identifies a geographical segment by source

The Presentational Standards **7.9**

(where the goods/services are made), with separate additional disclosure if this is materially different from geographical segment by destination. Basically, such companies must disclose, for each segment:

- turnover (distinguishing between that generated with external customers, and that derived from other segments);
- results, before tax, minority interest and extraordinary items; and
- net assets.

7.7 *SSAP 25* recognises that publication of segmental information may, in certain circumstances, be prejudicial to the interests of the reporting entity. Therefore, *SSAP 25, para 43* allows information that the directors consider to be seriously prejudicial not to be disclosed, although the fact must be stated.

COMPARISON WITH INTERNATIONAL ACCOUNTING STANDARDS

7.8 The relevant international accounting standard is *IAS 14* 'Segment Reporting'. It applies to entities with publicly traded equity or debt securities (and entities in the process of issuing such securities) and, therefore, will not apply to all companies that are covered by *SSAP 25* (see **6.4** above).

In general, *IAS 14* is more prescriptive than *SSAP 25* and requires more extensive disclosures to be made. Whilst *IAS 14* requires segmental disclosures to be made for both business and geographical segments, it requires the primary segmentation to be determined, and greater disclosures to be made for the primary segmentation, including additions to fixed assets and depreciation, for example. The decision on which is the primary segmentation normally reflects the structure of the entity's internal financial reporting. Identification of individual segments should be based on components of the business that face similar risks and rates of return.

An important difference between *IAS 14* and *SSAP 25* is that *IAS 14* has no equivalent to the 'seriously prejudicial' exemption in *SSAP 25* (see **6.7** above).

TAXATION CONSIDERATIONS

7.9 There are several tax considerations to be borne in mind. Where companies carry on separate trades, the results of each trade need 'streaming' for many tax purposes (eg the carry-forward of losses). The segmental analysis adopted by the company may not correspond with the concept of separate trades. For example, a building company may have a domestic housing division and a commercial contracting division. It may report its results on a segmental basis, distinguishing the two activities, but is it carrying on one or two trades? If no segmental analysis had been adopted, there is little reason to suppose that HMRC would take the point and try to argue that two

7.10 *The Presentational Standards*

separate trades were being carried on. The mere fact of the segmental analysis appearing in the Notes to the Accounts may encourage a Revenue officer to run that argument.

7.10 If a tax problem of this type is faced, it is important to remember that the segmental profits reported in the accounts do not correspond with what would be regarded by HMRC as the fair measure of the profit of each trade.

In the first place, *SSAP 25* requires no adjustment for 'inter-segment' transactions. One segment may derive revenue from another at below cost, at cost, or subject to a mark-up. *SSAP 25* makes no recognition of this. For tax purposes, any inter-business trading should be accounted for at 'arm's length' pricing.

Equally, the allocation of common overheads (and the non-allocation of finance costs) by *SSAP 25* is by no means precise or accurate enough for tax purposes.

REPORTING FINANCIAL PERFORMANCE

7.11 Worldwide, there has been debate about the best way of reporting financial performance. By convention, and domestic corporate law, most countries have evolved a document called a 'profit and loss account' which purports to represent the principal measure of financial performance, but increasingly this has been seen to be insufficient. There are many profits and losses which are not reflected in the profit and loss account. A simple example would be revaluation surpluses, which are specifically forbidden under UK law from passing through profit and loss. Many of the emerging issues in accounting are likely to require recognition of gains and losses that may not fit comfortably into a traditional profit and loss account. Internationally, the general move is towards a single comprehensive statement of financial performance, in which all gains and losses are reported which could render the profit and loss account obsolete.

FINANCIAL REPORTING STANDARD 3 (FRS 3)

7.12 Conceptually, *FRS 3* 'Reporting Financial Performance' is one of the most important of the standards. It introduces a secondary measure of financial performance – the 'Statement of Total Recognised Gains and Losses'. This is held to be a primary accounting document of equal status to the profit and loss account. Some commentators suggest that this is the embryonic replacement of the profit and loss account. In practice, it has not been popular. Against the background of worldwide change, there are likely to be further developments.

FRS 3 also requires additional disclosures, and absorbs (and changes) the provisions of *SSAP 6*, principally in relation to the issue of 'extraordinary items'.

Disclosures – profit and loss account

7.13 A layered format is to be used in the profit and loss account itself, to highlight a number of important components of financial performance:

(i) results of continuing operations (including the results of acquisitions);

(ii) results of discontinued operations;

(iii) profits or losses on the sale or termination of an operation, costs of a fundamental reorganisation or restructuring, and profits or losses on the disposal of fixed assets; and

(iv) extraordinary items.

Examples of how such a profit and loss account might look are attached to *FRS 3*, and Example 2 from *FRS 3* is reproduced below:

7.13 The Presentational Standards

Example 7.1
Profit and Loss Account

	Continuing Operations 1993	Acquisitions 1993	Discontinued Operations 1993	Total 1993	Total 1992 as restated
	£ million	£ million	£ million	£ million	£ million
Turnover	550	50	175	775	690
Cost of Sales	(415)	(40)	(165)	(620)	(555)
Gross Profit	135	10	10	155	135
Net Operating Expenses	(85)	(4)	(25)	(114)	(83)
Less 1992 Provision			10	10	
Operating Profit	50	6	(5)	51	52
Profit on Sale of Properties	9			9	6
Provision for Loss on Operations to be Discontinued					(30)
Loss on Disposal of Discontinued Operations			(17)	(17)	
Less 1992 Provision			20	20	
Profit on Ordinary Activities Before Interest	59	6	(2)	63	28
Interest Payable				(18)	(15)
Profit on Ordinary Activities Before Taxation				45	13

76

The Presentational Standards 7.13

	Continuing Operations 1993 £ million	Acquisitions 1993 £ million	Discontinued Operations 1993 £ million	Total 1993 £ million	Total 1992 as restated £ million
Tax on Profit on Ordinary Activities				(14)	(4)
Profit on Ordinary Activities After Taxation				31	9
Minority Interests				(2)	(2)
[Profit Before Extraordinary Items]				29	7
[Extraordinary Items] (Included only to show positioning)				–	–
Profit For The Financial Year				29	7
Dividends				(8)	(1)
Retained Profit For The Financial Year				21	6
Earnings Per Share				**39p**	**10p**
Adjustments [to be itemised and an adequate description to be given]				Xp	Xp
Adjusted Earnings Per Share				Yp	Yp
[Reason for calculating the adjusted earnings per share to be given]					

A small additional amount of analysis is required to be disclosed by way of note to the accounts.

The significance of the 'earnings per share' calculation is explained below.

7.14 *The Presentational Standards*

7.14 The classification of activities in this way will highlight a number of tax problems:

- It may raise the question of how many trades the company is actually carrying on.

- Particularly in relation to 'close down' costs, problems may arise as to whether expenditures are being incurred post cessation of trade (generally not deductible) or, indeed, even if incurred before cessation, whether it can be said that the expenses are being incurred for the 'purpose of carrying on and earning profit'.

- For acquisitions, the main tax considerations relate to the values ascribed to the various assets acquired, coupled with the question of the deductibility of the 'costs' of acquisition.

- Even where there is no dispute as to what trade(s) is or are being carried on, 'changes' in what is being carried on can lead the Inspector to question whether there have been 'major changes in the nature or conduct of a trade', which can itself have tax consequences.

Disclosures – historical cost profits

7.15 *Example 5.1* illustrated the effect that a revaluation could have on the reported profits of an entity (via the depreciation charge). This can obviously be misleading. *FRS 3* requires, therefore, that a note to the accounts should effectively restate, in abbreviated form, the profit and loss account to show how it would have looked if no revaluation had taken place. An example of how this might appear (for the company in *Example 7.1* above) is shown below:

Example 7.2

Note of Historical Cost Profits and Losses

	1993 £ million	1992 as restated £ million
Reported Profit on Ordinary Activities Before Taxation	45	13
Realisation of Property Revaluation Gains of Previous Years	9	10
Difference Between Historical Cost Depreciation Charge and the Actual Depreciation Charge of the Year Calculated on the Revalued Amount	5	4
Historical Cost Profit on Ordinary Activities Before Taxation	59	27
Historical Cost Profit for the Year Retained After Taxation, Minority Interests, Extraordinary Items and Dividends	35	20

The Presentational Standards **7.16**

This looks deceptively simple, but is very difficult to understand.

7.16 This is how the actual accounts of such a company would look, and the intention of *FRS 3* is to provide more (and better) information to readers of accounts.

The 'profit on ordinary activities' – £45 million – can be easily seen as coming from the 'profit on ordinary activities' in *Example 7.1*.

The 'realisation of property revaluation gains *of previous years*' – £9 million – is not the 'profit on sale of properties' (which is for the current year - it is coincidental that this is also £9 million) taken from line 7 in *Example 7.1*.

How the figures are arrived at may be illustrated by the following assumed set of facts – but there are many (if not an infinite number of) possible configurations which could have boiled down to the same net position shown in the accounts.

Assume a property at original cost of £50 million has been depreciated at 2% p.a. on the straight line method.

This property is revalued at the end of Year 5 to £55 million. It continues to be depreciated at 2% p.a. straight line.

After 14 years, it is sold for £54 million.

	Historical Cost Basis £ million	*Revaluation Basis* £ million
Purchase Price	50	50
Depreciation for 5 Years at 2%	(5)	(5)
Revaluation	–	10
	45	55
Depreciation for further 9 years at 2%	(9)	(10)
Book Value before sale	36	45
Sale Proceeds	54	54
Profit on sale	£18	£9

In Years 5 to 14, there would have been a transfer cumulatively of £1 million from revaluation reserve, being the difference between depreciation on historic cost (£9 million) and on the revalued amount (£10 million), leaving a net £9 million revaluation reserve at the date of disposal, which represents the difference (£18 million – £9 million) on the profit computed on the historic cost and revalued amount bases.

7.17 *The Presentational Standards*

7.17 This may not be immediately clear, but for present purposes, the concern is to be able to compute the tax liability.

Subject to possible March 1982 valuations, and relief for indexation and sale expenses, the capital gains computation on the above transaction is:

	£ million
Sale Price	54
Cost	50
Gain For Tax Purposes	£4 million

So, the accounts 'proper' will show an accounting profit of £9 million – with a tax liability computed as though the profit were £4 million, and the note of historical cost profits and losses will show a profit of £18 million (£9 million already included in £45 million, an extra £9 million shown explicitly), again with a tax component based on a profit of £4 million. There is nothing wrong in this, because each of the figures is calculated on a different basis, but it may nonetheless be confusing.

Disclosures – recognised gains and losses

7.18 *FRS 3* requires the production of the statement of total recognised gains and losses. 'Recognised' does not mean 'realised' or 'distributable'. Some profits and losses do not pass through the profit and loss account but go direct to reserves (eg a revaluation surplus). The Statement of Total Recognised Gains and Losses (STRGL, pronounced 'struggle') is regarded as a primary accounting statement of 'equal' importance with the profit and loss account. Indeed, conceptually (and consistently with the ASB's *Statement of Principles'*) the STRGL may come to have more significance than the profit and loss account itself. The example below, based on the company in *Example 7.1*, illustrates how this statement might appear. Currency translation differences and prior year adjustments are specifically dealt with later in this book, and no attention need be paid to them at this stage.

Example 7.3

Statement of Total Recognised Gains and Losses

	1993	1992 as restated
	£ million	£ million
Profit for the Financial Year	29	7
Unrealised Surplus on Revaluation of Properties	4	6
Unrealised (Loss)/Gain on Trade Investment	(3)	7
	30	20

The Presentational Standards **7.19**

Currency Translation Differences on Foreign Currency Net Investments	(2)	5
Total Recognised Gains and Losses Relating to the Year	28	25
Prior Year Adjustment (as explained in note x)	(10)	
Total Gains and Losses Recognised Since Last Annual Report	18	

Disclosures – shareholders' funds and reserves

7.19 The paragraph above described the ways that *FRS 3* attempts to highlight to readers of accounts how the company has performed during the year. Of equal importance is the state of the company at the year end. This is effected by statements reconciling the movement in shareholders' funds, culminating with 'closing shareholders' funds' (which arithmetically equals 'share capital plus reserves') and a reconciliation of the closing balance on each individual reserve. The example below, again based on the company in *Example 7.1*, illustrates how this is achieved.

Example 7.4

Reconciliation of Movements in Shareholders' Funds

	1993	1992 as restated
	£ million	£ million
Profit for the Financial Year	29	7
Dividends	(8)	(1)
	21	6
Other Recognised Gains and Losses Relating to the Year (Net)	(1)	18
New Share Capital Subscribed	20	1
Goodwill Written Off	(25)	
Net Addition to Shareholders' Funds	15	25
Opening Shareholders' Funds (originally £375 million before deducting prior year adjustments of £10 million)	365	340
Closing Shareholders' Funds	380	365

7.20 The Presentational Standards

Reserves

	Share Premium Account	Revaluation Reserve	Profit & Loss Account	Total
	£ million	£ million	£ million	£ million
At Beginning of Year as Previously Stated	44	200	120	364
Prior Year Adjustment			(10)	(10)
At Beginning of Year as Restated	44	200	110	354
Premium on Issue of Shares (nominal value £7 million)	13			13
Goodwill Written Off			(25)	(25)
Transfer from Profit and Loss Account of the Year			21	21
Transfer of Realised Profits		(14)	14	0
Decrease in Value of Trade Investment		(3)		(3)
Currency Translation Differences on Foreign Currency Net Investments			(2)	(2)
Surplus on Property Revaluations		4		4
At End of Year	57	187	118	362

Note: Nominal share capital at end of year £18 million (1992 £11 million)

Disclosures – extraordinary and exceptional items

7.20 Exceptional items are those that derive *from* the ordinary activities of a company which, because of their size (either individually or in aggregate), need to be disclosed to give a true and fair view. Disclosure can be given by way of a note to the accounts or on the face of the profit and loss account (if that degree of prominence is necessary to give a true and fair view).

Extraordinary items are those that possess a high degree of abnormality, which arise from events or transactions *outside* the ordinary activities of the company, and are not expected to recur. The original *SSAP 6* definition did

The Presentational Standards **7.22**

not include the 'high degree of abnormality' test. In relation to the possibility of recurrence, the *SSAP 6* test was also somewhat weaker – an item could be extraordinary if it was expected not to recur frequently or regularly. The spirit of *FRS 3* is that there should be very few instances in which events or transactions are considered extraordinary.

As explained earlier, the essence of the changes is to prevent companies which have suffered losses from classifying them as extraordinary and somehow, therefore, making them less significant in evaluating the company's future prospects.

In theory, the classification of an item – usually an expense – as exceptional or extraordinary ought not to have a tax consequence. There may be, however, a temptation on the part of HMRC to regard such items (particularly those classified as extraordinary losses) as potentially excludable as trading profit deductions, on the basis of being outside the normal operations of the company. This is not the case. Each exceptional or extraordinary item must be considered on its own merits.

For example, a company may in a particular year suffer a one-off uninsured catastrophe, such as the burning down of its factory, with consequential loss of trading stock.

The loss on land/buildings and on stock would probably have been treated as extraordinary under *SSAP 6*, but will be exceptional under *FRS 3*. However, whilst no deduction would be had for the loss on land/buildings (capital), there should be a deduction for the loss of stock (revenue).

Disclosures – prior period adjustments

7.21 *FRS 3* also deals with what are defined as prior period adjustments.

There are two types of prior period adjustment:

- those arising from the correction of a fundamental error in earlier years' accounts; and
- those arising from a change in accounting policy.

7.22 When accounts are prepared, it is often necessary to make judgements – an example might be the extent to which bad debt provisions are needed. The provision made is no more than an estimate, albeit hopefully based on factual information and experience. With any estimate a degree of imprecision is inevitable, especially if the intention is to be reasonably (but not excessively) prudent. Therefore, it is likely that the provision will be higher or lower than ultimately required. That does not mean that the original accounts contained a fundamental error. The correction of the original bad debt provision in the later year is a normal current year accounting adjustment.

However, if it were discovered that, for the previous 10 years, a director of a company had been diverting, say, £10,000 p.a. of cash takings into his

7.22 The Presentational Standards

own back pocket, so that the accounts had shown a fundamentally incorrect position, then that circumstance would need rectification by means of a prior year adjustment. An example will best illustrate this.

Example 7.5

A company began trading on 1 April 1998. It has just prepared its draft accounts for the year to 31 March 2008, which in summary form are below:

		31/03/2008		31/03/2007
	£	£	£	£
Fixed Assets		100,000		80,000
Current Asset				
Stock:	170,000			
Debtors:	30,000			
Cash:	10,000			
Current Liabilities				
Creditors:	(30,000)			
Directors Loans:	(120,000)			
Net Current Assets		60,000		20,000
Net Assets		160,000		100,000
Share Capital		10,000		10,000
Profit and Loss b/f	90,000		70,000	
Profit For Year	60,000		20,000	
Profit and Loss c/f		150,000		90,000
		160,000		100,000
		31/03/2008		31/03/2007
		£		£
TURNOVER		1,000,000		850,000
Gross Profit		200,000		120,000
PROFIT BEFORE TAX		80,000		25,000
Taxation		(20,000)		(5,000)
RETAINED PROFIT FOR YEAR		60,000		20,000

The Presentational Standards **7.22**

Now suppose that it is discovered, before the 2008 accounts are finalised, that a director (who is also a controlling shareholder) has for each of the past 10 years under-declared turnover and profits by £10,000 p.a. This has been discovered by HMRC and a quick 'settlement' is agreed with them, the terms of which will be:

	£
Additional Profits Taxable 01/04/1998–31/03/2007	90,000
Additional Corporation Tax at 25%, say,	22,500
Interest and Penalties Thereon	22,500
Total Settlement	45,000
Additional Profits Taxable 01/04/2007–31/03/2008	10,000

(to be included on finalising the current accounts)

Reproduced below are the finalised accounts reflecting the above settlement:

		31/03/2008			31/03/2007
	£	£	£		£
Fixed Assets		100,000			80,000
Current Assets					
Stock:	170,000				
Debtors:	30,000				
Cash:	10,000				
Current Liabilities					
Creditors:	(77,500)				
Directors Loans:	(20,000)				
Net Current Assets		112,500	(x)		87,500 (i)
Net Assets		212,500			167,500
Share Capital		10,000			10,000
Profit and Loss b/f	90,000		70,000		
Prior Year Adjustment	67,500	(vi)	60,000	(ii)	
Profit and Loss as Restated b/f	157,500	(vii)	130,000		
Profit For Year	45,000		27,500		
Profit and Loss c/f		202,500			157,500 (v)
		212,500			167,500

7.23 *The Presentational Standards*

	31/03/98 £		31/03/97 £
TURNOVER	1,010,000	(viii)	860,000 (iii)
Gross Profit	210,000		130,000
PROFIT BEFORE TAX	67,500	(ix)	35,000
Taxation	(22,500)		(7,500) (iv)
PROFIT ON ORDINARY ACTIVITIES AFTER TAX	45,000		27,500

7.23 At first sight, this may appear very confusing. The following notes may assist.

In finalising the 2008 accounts, it is first necessary to restate the comparative 2007 figures:

(i) See attached explanation at (x) below.

(ii) There is a prior period adjustment in the 2007 accounts representing the errors of the eight preceding years.

The additional profits of these eight years were £80,000.

The extra tax on these profits was £20,000.

Therefore, the additional after tax retained profits are £60,000.

(iii) The extra £10,000 turnover for 2007 (which is Year 9 of the misappropriation) carries down the restated profit and loss account.

(iv) The additional £10,000 profit leads to additional tax of £2,500. The restated profit for the year is therefore £27,500.

(v) The restated retained profits b/f (£130,000), plus restated profit for the year (£27,500) gives restated profit c/f of £157,500.

The next step is to adjust the figures for 2008.

(vi) The prior year adjustment for this year reflects nine previous years of misappropriations. This is £90,000 of additional profits less £22,500 of tax, yielding a net £67,500 prior year adjustment.

(vii) The restated retained profit b/f is therefore £157,500 (£90,000 + £67,500). As a check, it can be seen that this is consistent with the closing restated retained profit of the 2007 period (as computed in (v) above).

The Presentational Standards **7.24**

(viii) The current year adjustment is to increase turnover (and profit) by £10,000, the consequential increase of £2,500 to the tax charge, leaving a net £7,500 increase in current year's profits (before exceptional items).

(ix) In 2008, there arises a payment of interest and penalties of £22,500 which, under *FRS 3*, is an exceptional item and therefore deducted in arriving at the profits for the year of £67,500 (£90,000 – £22,500).

Probably, the £22,500 would be broken down into constituent parts – interest on the one hand, penalties on the other – with the interest element included in the interest charge for the year, and the penalty part included in the administration costs or other non-specific overhead. If the amounts are material, these will be disclosed in the notes. (It is possible, though, that the interest charge is factored into the prior period adjustment.)

As the question of materiality is subjective, and the natural temptation of companies will be not to advertise the fact of their wrongdoing, it is possible that separate disclosure will not be made. Preparers of tax computations for companies recently subject to investigation should be aware that the interest and penalties – neither of which is tax deductible – may be incorporated in the accounts in a less than immediately obvious manner.

(x) The net current assets in the final accounts (£112,500) differ from the draft account (£60,000) by £52,500.

In the first place, the director has improperly withdrawn £100,000 of company funds over 10 years. He must be 'charged' with this. The amount owing to him by the company (apparently £120,000) needs reducing to £20,000.

On the other hand, the company has additional liabilities compared to the draft accounts of:

Extra tax for 2008	£2,500
Extra tax, interest and penalties for earlier years	£45,000
	£47,500

Therefore, an addition to creditors of £47,500 is required.

The total adjustment to net current assets is £52,500 (£100,000 – £47,500). Had the detailed figures for 2007 been available, the equivalent figures for 2007 (see (i) above) could have been derived.

7.24 It is worth commenting that the prior period adjustment (in this case, £67,500) would also appear in the Statement of Total Recognised Gains and Losses (see *Example 7.3* above).

7.25 The Presentational Standards

7.25 As mentioned above, prior period adjustments can also arise in relation to changes in accounting policy. For example, a house-building company may change its policy on income recognition. For nine years, it may consistently recognise a sale as taking place on exchange of contract, but in the tenth year it may change to the more prudent basis of recognising the sale as taking place on the date of completion. As in *Example 7.5* above, the balance sheet for Year 10 would incorporate an adjustment to reserves brought forward at the end of Year 9 to reflect the cumulative effects, up to and including Year 9, of the application of the new accounting policy to those past years. The comparative balance sheet for Year 9 would incorporate the cumulative effect for the eight previous years.

COMPARISON WITH INTERNATIONAL ACCOUNTING STANDARDS

7.26 The material covered by *FRS 3* is included in *IAS 1* 'Presentation of Financial Statements' (*IAS 1* also covers accounting policies and the format of financial statements) and *IAS 8* 'Accounting Policies, Changes in Accounting Estimates and Errors'. In summary, the requirements of *IAS 1* and *IAS 8* are generally less prescriptive, but broadly in line with *FRS 3*.

IAS 1 requires financial statements to include a Statement of Changes in Equity. The requirements are similar to the Statement of Total Recognised Gains and Losses required by *FRS 3*, except that *IAS 1* generally requires that gains and losses that were initially taken directly to reserves are 'recycled' through the Income Statement (the equivalent of the profit and loss account) on realisation. *IAS 1* is also specific in stating that 'extraordinary items' should not appear either on the face of the Income Statement or in the supporting notes. For practical purposes, this is no different from *FRS 3*.

TAXATION CONSIDERATIONS

7.27 Prior period adjustments resulting from a change in accounting policy are brought into the trading profits computation in the year of the change. Some may be spread over six years. This does not apply, however, to fundamental errors, which require restatement of prior period tax computations by way of an amendment to the corporation tax return.

EARNINGS PER SHARE

Financial Reporting Standard 22 (FRS 22)

7.28 *FRS 14* 'Earnings per Share' was issued in October 1998 and was effective for accounting periods ending on or after 23 December 1998. It only applies to entities whose shares are publicly traded. *FRS 14* was largely

The Presentational Standards **7.32**

based on its international equivalent, *IAS 33*, the main differences being of a detailed nature and the additional guidance provided by *FRS 14* compared to *IAS 33*. *FRS 22* replaced *FRS 14* effective for accounting periods beginning on or after 1 January 2005, the date that the IAS Regulation required publicly traded companies to prepare their consolidated financial statements in accordance with international accounting standards (see Chapter 2). It has the effect of implementing *IAS 33 (*revised in 2003) for entities that *choose* to disclose earnings per share but are not *required* to do so, so that all published earnings per share figures should be prepared on a consistent basis.

7.29 The PE ratio (see **2.20** above) is internationally one of the most widely used indicators of the value of a company and/or its ordinary shares.

The *Financial Times* publishes the share price of quoted companies and also quotes the PE. It derives this figure from the formula:

Share price = EPS × PE

ie PE = $\dfrac{\text{Share price}}{\text{EPS}}$

FRS 22 requires listed companies to compute and disclose their earnings per share in their accounts. That is the source from which the *Financial Times*, and others, can deduce the PE.

7.30 The basic idea is very simple. A company's earnings attributable to ordinary shareholders, ie profits after exceptional and extraordinary items (if any), tax, minority interests (for group accounts) and dividends in respect of non-equity shares (eg preference shares) are divided by the number of ordinary shares, to give the earnings (or profits) attributable to each individual ordinary share.

7.31 There are, however, difficulties when the number of ordinary shares in issue changes, or may change in the future (for example, because share options are in existence). In such cases, the weighted average number of ordinary shares needs to be used in the calculation of earnings per share.

The detail of the calculation is not important for the present purpose. All that is required to be understood is that computational adjustments are made to try to arrive at a fair measure of earnings truly attributable at the end of the year to the holder of a single ordinary share.

7.32 However, the question of share options is one with tax consequences, so it is relevant to understand what happens in this case and the terminology used. This can be illustrated best by example:

7.33 The Presentational Standards

Example 7.6

The profit and loss account reproduced below is for a company with 1,200,000 × £1 ordinary shares at the end of the year, having issued an additional 400,000 × £1 ordinary shares at full market value half way through the year. There are 100,000 × £1 preference shares paying a 10% (net) dividend each year. The directors have an unapproved share option scheme giving them the right to acquire (from the company) 250,000 × £1 ordinary shares at par at any time in the following seven years.

	£
TURNOVER	1,000,000
Gross Profit	600,000
PROFIT BEFORE TAX	300,000
Taxation	(80,000)
PROFIT FOR YEAR	220,000
Preference Dividends	(10,000)
Ordinary Dividends	(10,000)
RETAINED PROFITS	200,000
Earnings per share (basic)	21p
Earnings per share (fully diluted)	17.8p

7.33 The basic earnings per share is calculated thus:

Earnings (after tax, after preference dividend)	£210,000
Weighted average number of ordinary shares	
$\dfrac{800,000 + 1,200,000}{2}$	1,000,000
∴ Earnings per share (basic)	21p

7.34 *FRS 22* also requires the calculation of what is known as the fully diluted earnings per share. This is achieved by adjusting the denominator in the earnings per share calculation (shown above) to reflect the number of 'free' shares that would be issued if the options were exercised. Thus, in the example in **6.31** above, when the share options are exercised, the company receives £250,000 for the issue of 250,000 shares. If the fair value of those shares is, say, £4 per share, then had the shares been issued at full value, only 62,500 would have been issued. Effectively, 187,500 shares have been issued 'for free'.

Therefore, the revised earnings per share calculation would be:

Earnings	£210,000
Weighted average number of shares	
$\dfrac{987{,}500 + 1{,}387{,}500}{2}$	1,187,500
∴ Earnings per share (fully diluted)	17.68p

TAXATION CONSIDERATIONS

7.35 Earnings per share is basically a valuation tool and, given that it generally only applies to listed companies – where valuations for tax purposes proceed on the basis of quoted prices – it may appear not to have any direct tax relevance.

The two reasons for tax practitioners to be alert and aware of what is involved are, first, the effect that tax has (the Net/Nil basis, the deferred tax effect) on the calculation of a sensitive figure in the accounts; and, secondly, to be appreciative and understanding of the effects on the earnings per share of the structures to effect corporate transactions that have been designed essentially to achieve tax-driven goals.

Chapter 8

Post-Balance Sheet Events

8.1 There is a general principle that financial statements are prepared so as to reflect events occurring up to the balance sheet date, and based on conditions that existed at that date. Post-balance sheet events are those that occur after the balance sheet date, but may shed light on conditions existing as at that date. The question then arises whether the financial statements need to reflect these post-balance sheet events.

The ASB issued *FRS 21* in May 2004 as part of its project to converge UK GAAP with IAS. *FRS 21* supersedes *SSAP 17* and is consistent with the equivalent international standard (*IAS 10* 'Events After the Balance Sheet Date'), but tailored for UK entities. The standard aims to prescribe when an entity is required to adjust its financial statements to take into account events that occur after the balance sheet date, and also what disclosures need to be made in that regard. The *Companies Act 2006* (*CA 2006*) also requires disclosure in the directors' report of important events that affect the company or its subsidiaries and which occurred after the end of the year.

FINANCIAL REPORTING STATEMENT 21 (FRS 21)

8.2 Events after the balance sheet date are defined as those events, both favourable and unfavourable, that occur between the balance sheet date and the date on which the financial statements are authorised for issue. A distinction is made between two types of event: those that provide evidence of conditions existing at the balance sheet date (adjusting events), and those that are indicative of conditions that arose after the balance sheet date (non-adjusting events). Material adjusting events should be reflected via adjustments to the amount(s) recognised in the financial statements, whereas material non-adjusting events do not result in changes to the figures but, rather, are reflected by way of disclosure in the supporting notes. Immaterial events after the balance sheet date are not required to be reflected. The subjective issue of what is 'material' is discussed in Chapter 5.

8.3 *FRS 21, para 9* provides some examples of adjusting events:
- a court case may be resolved after the balance sheet date which confirms that the entity already had a present obligation at balance sheet date, and so should adjust a provision accordingly;

- a customer's bankruptcy subsequent to balance sheet date confirms that a loss already existed on trade receivables (unless the bankruptcy is because of events occurring after balance sheet date);
- the cost of assets purchased or the proceeds from the sale of assets before balance sheet date may only become calculable after that date; or
- there may be discovery of fraud or errors that show the financial statements were actually incorrect.

8.4 Non-adjusting events are only indicative, and so do not require changes in the amounts recognised. They may need to be disclosed, however, if they are material, such as destruction of a major production plant by fire, or abnormally large changes in asset prices or foreign exchange rates after the balance sheet date.

8.5 *FRS 21, para 21* provides that dividends to holders of equity instruments declared after balance sheet date should not be recognised as a liability at the balance sheet date. No obligation arises to pay dividends until they are authorised. In relation to dividends received, *FRS 21* requires that neither the investor nor the investee should adjust their accounts to reflect dividends declared after balance sheet date, which is a departure from common practice prior to *FRS 21*.

8.6 Calculation of current and deferred tax balances for financial reporting purposes requires reference to the tax rates and laws that have been 'substantially enacted' as at the balance sheet date (see Chapter 22). It may be, however, that announcements are made relating to changes in either the rates or computation of corporation tax; but, if they are not substantially enacted at the date of the balance sheet, they should not be recognised in the financial statements.

8.7 If there is a serious deterioration in operating results and financial position after the balance sheet date, then there may be a need to reconsider the appropriateness of the going concern assumption. If it is no longer appropriate, *FRS 21* requires a fundamental change in the basis of accounting, rather than an adjustment to the original basis.

8.8 In the case of non-adjusting events, *FRS 21* requires disclosure of the nature of the event and an estimate of its financial effect (or a statement that an estimate cannot be made, if that is the case).

INTERNATIONAL ACCOUNTING STANDARD 10 (IAS 10)

8.9 There are no appreciable differences between *FRS 21* and *IAS 10*.

8.10 *Post-Balance Sheet Events*

TAXATION

8.10 There are two areas in particular where tax problems arise in *FRS 21*-related circumstances.

Directors' emoluments and loan accounts

8.11 Directors' emoluments – especially bonuses – are often (and in most private companies, almost invariably) determined after the year end. The process is generally one of preparing draft accounts, seeing the results and then making a decision on the quantum of bonus. It is conventional to provide these bonuses in the year-end accounts by charging the bonus against profit, and crediting the director with what will be due (usually to his director's loan account). This accords with the accruals concept, and also because it is conventional (and universally applied) that this is an adjusting event, and not specifically because it gives additional evidence of conditions existing at the balance sheet date (although it is just about arguable that, at the balance sheet date, the principle of bonus payment had been determined and all that was awaited was a quantification).

Whether the company obtains a corporation tax deduction for that provision in these accounts is a question of timing (*CTA 2009, s 866*).

The main bone of contention with HMRC concerns the standing of the director's loan account and associated potential tax liabilities under *ICTA 1988, ss 160* and *419*. HMRC argue two points:

- At the time of crediting the director with his or her bonus, a PAYE obligation arises. He or she should therefore also be charged with the tax and national insurance (employees' contribution only). Effectively, only the net bonus should be credited.

- Although the credit is shown (via the adjusting post-balance sheet event mechanism) as having taken place at the year end, in fact it took place only when the amount was credited to him (generally within nine months of year end, to secure the corporation tax deduction). Thus the director's loan account needs rewriting on a chronological basis to determine the 'real' balances at various dates.

There is very little defence to these arguments (except to cite *Re Duomatic*, a non-tax case giving some support to the ability of a proprietor/director to award himself remuneration without the usual formalities). Failure to recognise and return these liabilities can (and sometimes does in practice) attract interest and penalties.

8.12 The example below illustrates the various differences which can arise in the balance on a director's loan account on three different bases:

Example 8.1 – Analysis of Director's Current Account

	Unacceptable for Accounting and Tax Purposes	Acceptable for Accounting but not for Tax Purposes	Acceptable for Tax Purposes
	£	£	£
Opening Balance	20,000	20,000	20,000
Drawings During Year	(12,000)	(12,000)	(12,000)
Gross Bonus Voted Six Months After Year End	7,000	7,000	–
PAYE on Year 1 Bonus	–	(2,500)	–
Balance at End of Year 1	15,000	12,500	8,000
Drawings During Year	(15,000)	(15,000)	(15,000)
Gross Bonus in Respect of Year 1	–	–	7,000
PAYE on Year 1 Bonus	(2,500)	–	(2,500)
Gross Bonus for Year 2 Voted Six Months After Year End	12,000	12,000	–
PAYE on Year 2 Bonus	–	(3,500)	–
Balance at End of Year 2	9,500	6,000	(2,500)
Drawings During Year	(20,000)	(20,000)	(20,000)
Gross Bonus in Respect of Year 2	–	–	12,000
PAYE on Year 2 Bonus	(3,500)	–	(3,500)
Gross Bonus for Year 3 Voted Six Months After Year End	22,000	22,000	–
PAYE on Year 3 Bonus	–	(6,000)	–
	8,000	2,000	(14,000)

8.13 *Post-Balance Sheet Events*

EXTENDED DEBATES

8.13 It is often many months after finalising accounts that submission is made to HMRC, who may raise queries, and the debate on these may span several years. The debate may be about stock valuation – inclusion of stocks at net realisable value, provisions for warranty claims, bad debt relief, long-term work in progress valuation or a host of other matters, all of which will themselves have reflected in them a post-balance sheet date consideration. However, if the year end is 31 March 2009 and the post-balance sheet period ended, say, on 30 September 2009, it may be 30 September 2010 when the subject is being discussed with HMRC. Much more information may be available at that later time, and it may be that, blessed with that hindsight, a different decision might have been made at 30 September 2009. That additional information may show new factors existing but unappreciated at 30 September 2009, or may show new developments since 30 September 2009. To what extent is this new information relevant to the debate about the tax liability for the year ended 31 March 2009?

There are two areas of relevance. First, the new information may provide comfort that the original assessment was made bona fide and on a reasonable basis. If a bad debt provision is made and, ultimately, the debtor becomes bankrupt with no possibility of a dividend to unsecured creditors, then a decision to provide for the bad debt taken well before bankruptcy is at least *prima facie* reasonable. On the other hand, if a company makes a bad debt provision against ten specific bad debts and, in the event, each and every one of them pays up, this just might jaundice the view that the company was less than reasonable in its initial assessment of recoverability. Secondly, although hindsight should not really play a part, it is simply flying in the face of human nature to disregard it. It is very normal for one side in a debate to claim the benefit of hindsight and the other to disavow it. The net effect is that, if the ultimate outcome is consistent with the earlier prediction, the argument is strongly bolstered. HMRC's Business Income Manual (BIM 31040) states, 'where facts are available they are preferable to speculative estimates. For tax purposes it is not acceptable to ignore facts if by doing so an unreal loss is provided for'.

Chapter 9

Related Parties

9.1 Tax legislation has long recognised the possibilities for 'manipulation' where transactions are not at arm's length. Almost every part of every tax statute has a mechanism for dealing with situations involving relatives, associates, participators and other connected persons. The mechanism is usually to replace the financial effect of the actual transaction with that which would have arisen had the parties been at arm's length.

Accounting and company law has been much less ambitious, restricting itself, in the main, to 'disclosure' rather than 'substitution'. In October 1995, *FRS 8* was published in order to extend the *CA 1985* requirement to disclose, and applies to accounting periods starting on or after 23 December 1995. The *Companies Act 2006* introduced new disclosure requirements in response to new EU requirements and draws on *IAS 24* (see below). In December 2008, the ASB issued an amendment to *FRS 8* to reflect the minimum disclosures necessary to comply with legal requirements on the definition of a related party and an exemption for wholly owned subsidiaries in *SI 2008/410*.

FINANCIAL REPORTING STANDARD 8 (FRS 8)

9.2 *FRS 8* is relatively straightforward, and the following discussion is based on the amended standard issued in 2008. The objective is to require disclosure of transactions with related parties, and the name of the party who ultimately controls the entity (whether or not there have been transactions with that party).

Related parties

9.3 Two parties are related where one controls the other, or both are controlled by the same source.

The concept is extended, however. Two parties are related where one has influence over the other which may inhibit the other from pursuing its own independent interest. Moreover, two parties entering into a transaction are related where both are subject to influence from the same source, such that one of the parties has subordinated its own interests.

9.4 *Related Parties*

9.4 The revised definition of related parties of an entity is as follows

'A party is related to an entity if:

(a) directly, or indirectly through one or more intermediaries, the party:

   (i) controls, is controlled by, or is under common control with, the entity (this includes parents, subsidiaries and fellow subsidiaries);

   (ii) has an interest in the entity that gives it significant influence over the entity; or

   (iii) has joint control over the entity;

(b) the party is an associate ... of the entity;

(c) the party is a joint venture in which the entity is a venturer ...

(d) the party is a member of the key management personnel of the entity or its parent;

(e) the party is a close member of the family of any individual referred to in (a) or (d);

(f) the party is an entity that is controlled, jointly controlled or significantly influenced by, or for which significant voting power in such entity resides with, directly or indirectly, any individual referred to in (d) or (e); or

(g) the party is a post-employment benefit plan for the benefit of employees of the entity, or of any entity that is a related party of the entity.'

Close family

9.5 This includes members of an individual's family, or members of his household, who may be expected to influence or be influenced by that individual.

Key management

9.6 Those persons having authority or responsibility for directing or controlling the activities of the entity, directly or indirectly, including any director.

Related party transactions

9.7 This includes the transfer of assets or liabilities or the performance of services by, to, or for a related party, irrespective of whether a price is charged.

The disclosures

9.8 *FRS 8* requires disclosure of information relating to control, and transactions and balances.

Control
The name of the immediate and ultimate controlling entity (whether or not there have been transactions with that entity) must be disclosed.

Transactions and balances
Details of material transactions (whether or not a price is charged) must be disclosed. The details include:

- the related parties' names;
- nature of relationship;
- description of transactions and amounts involved;
- any other elements necessary for a proper understanding of the financial statements; and
- details of amounts due to or from related parties, provisions for bad debts, and amounts written off in respect of debts to or from related parties.

Exemptions

9.9 There are several related party transactions which are not required to be disclosed by *FRS 8* on policy grounds or because disclosure is required elsewhere. These include:

- in consolidated accounts, any transactions that are eliminated on consolidation;
- transactions entered into between two or more members of a group, provided that any subsidiary undertaking which is a party to the transaction is wholly owned by a member of the group (replacing the previous exemption for 90% subsidiaries);
- transactions of pension contributions;
- transactions of employee emoluments;
- transactions with providers of finance (eg bankers) in the normal course of their business; and
- transactions with customers, suppliers etc who could be regarded as related because of the volume of business transacted.

9.10 *Related Parties*

INTERNATIONAL ACCOUNTING STANDARD 24 (IAS 24)

9.10 While the definition of related parties in *FRS 8* has now been brought into line with that in *IAS 24*, there are some residual differences between the two standards: *IAS 24* does not deal with the materiality of the disclosure (because *IAS 1* has already stated that IFRSs do not apply if items are not material); the actual disclosure requirements differ, in that *IAS 24* does not require the name of the related party, whereas *FRS 8* does; and, finally, the exemption applicable to the parent company in relation to transactions that are eliminated on consolidation is not present in *IAS 24*.

TAXATION

9.11 *FRS 8* is simply a matter of disclosure, and does not directly have a tax consequence. However, as tax law tackles in so many ways the potential loss of tax in transactions between 'connected' persons, *FRS 8* will bring to the attention of HMRC most of such transactions (at least in the corporate sector), whether or not there is any consequential tax adjustment. Practitioners in UK-linked traditional tax havens need to pay special attention to this. There are several points to note, as follows.

9.12 From time to time, the Inspector gets excited about 'disallowing' an expense incurred by company B (in an ABC group) on the grounds that the expense is incurred, at least in part, to secure a benefit for company C. These are generally not transactions with related parties (being transactions with the outside world) and *FRS 8* will not have application. Even if the transaction is between, say, B and C, providing they are wholly-owned subsidiaries, no disclosure will be required.

9.13 However, in a more indirect situation, where A, for example, exercises 'influence' over B (although not controlling it), then A might cause B to do something which B would not otherwise have done. This transaction may be disclosable under *FRS 8*. Can B be said in this situation to be incurring such an expense wholly and exclusively for its trade?

Chapter 10

Smaller Entities

10.1 Increasingly, there has been a move towards simplification for the smaller, entrepreneurial company. Company law was initially drafted in terms of rules which applied for all companies, with exemptions for the small (and sometimes the medium-sized) company. One important feature of the *Companies Act 2006* is that benefits are specifically provided for private companies, which will usually be small. These include:

- simpler model Articles of Association;
- removal of the requirement to have a company secretary;
- no need to have an annual general meeting, unless positively choosing to do so; and
- simpler rules on share capital, and decision making.

10.2 In relation to accounts, there is now a clear distinction between small and other sized companies. For large and medium-sized companies, accounts must conform to *SI 2008/410*, although medium-sized companies may lodge accounts with the Registrar which, to an extent, give only summarised information (*CA 2006, Part 7*).

Small companies must ensure that their accounts conform to *SI 2008/409*, and they may submit significantly less information to the Registrar of Companies – the so-called 'abbreviated accounts'.

10.3 As explained in **2.7** above, very small companies, with turnover not exceeding £6.5 million and a balance sheet total not exceeding £3.26 million, are not required to be audited (*CA 2006, s 477*).

10.4 There have also been developments in accounting standards, both UK and international.

FINANCIAL REPORTING STANDARD FOR SMALLER ENTITIES (FRSSE)

10.5 A small (as defined by company law) company may – but does not have to – decide to comply with one composite standard, that is the

10.6 *Smaller Entities*

FRSSE, rather than the many and varied standards (SSAPs, FRSs and UITF Abstracts) applicable to other companies. Broadly, all the SSAPs, FRSs and UITF Abstracts are simplified and reproduced in the FRSSE. The underlying principles are the same but the language is simpler, the calculations are not so complex, and there is a much reduced need for extensive disclosure. The FRSSE may be applied to all financial statements intended to give a true and fair view of the financial position and profit and loss. Because its use is linked to the *CA 2006* definition of 'small', FRSSE does not apply to large or medium-sized companies or groups or public companies. In 2004, the ASB issued a discussion paper suggesting incorporating the *Companies Acts* requirements, so as to provide a 'one stop shop' for small companies. The latest version of FRSSE became effective in April 2008 and incorporates relevant company law including *CA 2006* and relevant regulations. The revised FRSSE defines small companies as having a turnover of up to £6.5 million.

10.6 Reasonably sophisticated concepts are retained. There is still a (*FRS 5*-type) 'substance over form' provision. There remains the requirement to produce a Statement of Total Recognised Gains and Losses (per *FRS 3*), but not to produce a Cash Flow Statement (although optional production is encouraged).

10.7 There is, however, no automatic update of the FRSSE as the mainline standards are updated. The intention is to update the FRSSE periodically to bring it into line. There will, unfortunately, be periods in which the FRSSE will give a different accounting treatment to that of the ordinary standards.

THE IASB VIEW

10.8 The IASB have observed that over 95% of all companies around the world are SMEs. Full IFRS is designed to meet the needs of equity investors in companies in public capital markets. Users of SME financial statements are focused rather on short-term issues such as cash flows, liquidity and solvency. The stated objective of the IASB SME project, which commenced in 2003, is therefore to:

> 'develop an IFRS expressly designed to meet the financial reporting needs of entities that (a) do not have public accountability and (b) publish general purpose statements for external users. Examples of such external user include owners who are not involved in managing the business, existing and potential creditors, and credit rating agencies.'

In June 2004, the IASB issued a Discussion Paper entitled 'Preliminary Views on Accounting Standards for Small and Medium Sized Entities'. This document proposed a move away from a size test based on quantifiable measures such as turnover and number of employees. Instead, it proposed the adoption of qualitative tests, such as the extent to which the entity is publicly accountable. Most respondents to the discussion paper were of the view that IFRS is not suitable for small companies, and also that the qualitative approach to characterising eligible companies is more appropriate.

10.9 The IASB subsequently issued an exposure draft of the proposed *International Financial Reporting Standards for Small and Medium Sized Entities*, and then renamed it in May 2008 as *IFRS for Private Entities*. Following receipt of some 162 letters of comment, the IFRS for SMEs was published on 9 July 2009. The starting point for the SME standard is full IFRS, but then requirements are simplified in areas such as recognising and measuring assets, liabilities, income and expenses. Topics that are of no relevance to SMEs are removed, such as earnings per share, interim financial reporting, segment reporting, and special accounting rules for assets held for sale.

Chapter 11

Cash Flow Statements

11.1 A great many businesses fail because they run out of cash. There are many ways of presenting accounts that paint a picture which, to varying degrees, represent an accurate reflection of the state of affairs, but the bottom line is the extent to which a company can pay its debts as they fall due. If they cannot, disaster looms.

As the sophistication of accounting increased, there was the danger that this basic fact would be lost sight of and so, in 1975, there was issued *SSAP 10* 'Statement of Source and Application of Funds'. This required certain companies to append a supplementary statement to their accounts which attempted to identify where the 'funds' for the period had been generated, how they had been disbursed, and the resulting increase or decrease in working capital (ie stocks, debtors, cash and creditors).

One of the first tasks undertaken by the ASB was to review the operation of *SSAP 10*. (The ASC itself had been doing this and had issued Exposure Draft 54 with its proposals for change.) With effect from accounting periods ending on or after 23 March 1992, *SSAP 10* was withdrawn and replaced by *FRS 1* 'Cash Flow Statements'. As the name implies, the significance of 'cash' has been elevated to the prime position it deserves.

FRS 1 has been the subject of some criticism and, in December 1995, *FRED 10* was issued. This became the revised *FRS 1*, effective for accounting periods ending on or after 23 March 1997. It was subsequently amended by *FRS 9* 'Associates and Joint Ventures' regarding treatment of dividends received from associates and joint ventures for accounting periods ending on or after 23 June 1998.

Although there is no statutory requirement for companies to produce a cash flow statement, the *Statement of Principles* includes a cash flow statement as part of the set of primary financial statements.

FINANCIAL REPORTING STANDARD 1 (REVISED 1996) (FRS 1)

11.2 *FRS 1* applies to all entities whose accounts are intended to give a true and fair view (ie mainly limited companies) except:

- small companies (as defined in *CA 2006, s 382*, see Chapter 2);

- 90% owned subsidiaries (provided consolidated accounts and cash flow statements are prepared by the group and are publicly available); and
- certain specialised entities (eg building societies).

11.3 The format of the cash flow statement is specified by *FRS 1*. The cash inflows and outflows are to be classified under the following headings:

- operating activities;
- returns on investments and servicing of finance;
- taxation;
- capital expenditure and financial investment;
- acquisitions and disposals;
- equity dividends paid;
- management of liquid resources; and
- financing.

11.4 It is neither appropriate nor necessary to go into too much detail. The underlying principles can best be illustrated by the example (appended to the revised *FRS 1*) of a cash flow statement for a single company:

Example 11.1

XYZ LIMITED

Cash Flow Statement for the Year Ended 31 December 1996
Reconciliation of Operating Profit to Net Cash Inflow from Operating Activities

	£'000
Operating profit	6,022
Depreciation charges	899
Increase in stocks	(194)
Increase in debtors	(72)
Increase in creditors	234
Net Cash Inflow from Operating Activities	6,889
Cash Flow Statement	
Net Cash Inflow from Operating Activities	6,889
Returns on Investments and Servicing of Finance (Note 1)	2,999

11.4 Cash Flow Statements

	£'000
Taxation	(2,922)
Capital Expenditure	(1,525)
	5,441
Equity Dividends Paid	(2,417)
	3,024
Management of Liquid Resources (Note 1)	(450)
Financing (Note 1)	57
Increase in cash	2,631

Reconciliation of Net Cash Flow to Movement in Net Debt (Note 2)

Increase in Cash in the Period	2,631
Cash to Repurchase Debenture	149
Cash Used to Increase Liquid Resources	450
Change in Net Debt*	3,230
Net Debt at 1 January 1996	(2,903)
Net Funds at 31 December 1996	327

* In this example all changes in net debt are cash flows.

Notes to the Cash Flow Statement
Note 1. GROSS CASH FLOWS

	£'000	£'000
Returns on Investments and Servicing of Finance		
Interest received	3,011	
Interest paid	(12)	
		(2,999)
Capital Expenditure		
Payments to acquire intangible fixed assets	(71)	
Payments to acquire tangible fixed assets	(1,496)	
Receipts from sales of tangible fixed assets	42	
		(1,525)

	£'000	£'000
Management of Liquid Resources		
Purchase of treasury bills	(650)	
Sale of treasury bills	200	
		(450)
Financing		
Issue of ordinary share capital	211	
Repurchase of debenture loan	(149)	
Expenses paid in connection with share issues	(5)	
		(57)

Note 2. ANALYSIS OF CHANGES IN NET DEBT

	At 1 Jan 1996	Cash Flows	Other Changes	At 31 Dec 1996
	£'000	£'000	£'000	£'000
Cash in hand, at bank	42	847		889
Overdrafts	(1,784)	1,784		
Debt due within 1 year	(149)	149	(230)	(230)
Debt due after 1 year	(1,262)		230	(1,032)
Current asset investments	250	450		700
Total	(2,903)	3,230	–	327

Tax items in the cash flow

11.5 Only payments to and from the tax authorities in respect of a company's revenue and capital profits are included under the heading of taxation.

This means that tax on interest received or paid is included as part of the interest (ie interest receipts and payments are shown gross). Dividends are shown inclusive of any withholding tax, but not any other taxes such as underlying tax, that is not payable wholly on behalf of the recipient.

Moreover, VAT is not explicitly shown. VAT is basically excluded from the cash flow relating to the operating activities. If, however, irrecoverable VAT arises (the business is exempt or partly exempt for VAT purposes), that is not separately distinguished but added to the originating transaction value. Other forms of tax are also shown with the items to which they relate; for example, PAYE tax paid on behalf of employees is included under operating activities.

11.6 *Cash Flow Statements*

Capitalised interest

11.6 As can be seen in *Example 11.1* above, the notes to the cash flow are required to reconcile, amongst other things, the operating profit per the accounts with the net cash flow from operating activities.

FRS 1 requires interest paid to be included under returns on investments and servicing of finance, even where it has been capitalised in the accounts themselves. This can cause reconciliation problems.

Material non-cash transactions

11.7 If one business 'acquires' assets on finance leases whilst another buys for cash, they are substantially in the same economic position, but a strict application of *FRS 1* gives rise to a completely different cash flow statement for each enterprise.

FRS 1 requires that, where there are material transactions not resulting in movements of cash, these should be disclosed in the notes if knowledge of them is necessary for an understanding of the underlying transactions.

What this means is that the reader has to check with the notes to see if there are any transactions the substance of which is to generate a net cash flow not reflected in the cash flow statement itself. Whilst doing this, the reader should also check the notes for details of any restrictions preventing cash being remitted from one part of the business or group to another.

INTERNATIONAL ACCOUNTING STANDARDS

11.8 The international accounting standard on cash flow statements is *IAS 7* 'Cash Flow Statements'. The main difference between the two standards is the definition of 'cash'. *FRS 1* defines 'cash' much more strictly, as cash in hand plus deposits repayable on demand less overdrafts, whereas *IAS 7* defines 'cash' as above plus 'cash equivalents', which include short-term liquid investments that are convertible to known amounts of cash and subject to insignificant risk of changes in value. This can include short-term deposits of up to, say, three months' duration. Under *FRS 1*, movements in 'cash equivalents' are shown under the Management of Liquid Resources section.

FRS 1 allows an exemption for small entities from the requirement to produce cash flow statements, whereas *IAS 7* does not; it applies to all entities irrespective of size.

IAS 7 requires cash flows to be presented under only three headings: operating activities, investing activities, and financing activities (compared to the eight headings under *FRS 1*).

The components under the heading of 'operating activities' are those that determine the net profit or loss of the entity. To arrive at 'net cash from operating activities', payments of interest and income tax are taken into account, the cash flow being the balancing amount obtained from the opening and closing balances in the statement of financial position and the amount of the item reported in the income statement.

The heading of 'investing activities' captures cash flows related to the acquisition or disposal of any non-current assets and returns received in cash from investments including interest and dividends received.

The heading of 'financing activities' captures dealings with external providers of finance, such as equity and debenture holders.

In addition to the cash flow statement, *IAS 7* requires the disclosure of the components of cash and cash equivalents, reconciliation to the statement of financial position, the accounting policy used to determine what is included in cash and cash equivalents, as well as a commentary by management, and any other information likely to be relevant, such as the amount of any undrawn borrowing facilities.

TAXATION CONSEQUENCES

11.9 There are no specific or direct tax consequences arising from the cash flow statement itself, but there are several points to be borne in mind:

- The valuation of a company is generally determined by its ability to generate future profits, but this is modified to the extent that the business is able to generate cash. A cash generator is more valuable than a cash absorber. The cash flow statement can be used in debate with the Shares Valuation Office.

- In harsh recessionary times, companies sometimes cannot meet their corporation tax, PAYE and VAT liabilities on time. Instalment arrangements to pay arrears are sometimes possible. The production of a cash flow statement in support of a request can be useful.

- The underlying concept of the cash flow statement permeates much of the work involved in the world of tax investigation in terms of providing clues, particularly for small business taxpayers, about the real levels of profit.

PART II

BASIC ACCOUNTING ISSUES

Chapter 12

Revenue Recognition

12.1 It was not until the 1990s that pressure came to bear on the absence of UK guidance on revenue recognition. The ASB issued a Discussion Paper entitled *Revenue Recognition* in 2001. This was soon overtaken, however, by the move towards convergence with IAS. Rather than taking the revenue recognition project forward, the ASB instead contributed to the IASB project. The absence of guidance in the UK had led to inconsistent practices between, and even within, different industries. The view persisted that UK guidance was required, and so, in November 2003, the ASB issued limited guidance in the form of an Application Note to *FRS 5* 'Reporting the Substance of Transactions', which takes effect for accounting periods ending on or after 23 December 2003.

FRS 5: APPLICATION NOTE G

12.2 The Application Note does not attempt to deal with the subject in a comprehensive way; rather, it gives a brief overview of principles together with some specific guidance on five situations. It does not apply to transactions in financial instruments, insurance contracts or arrangements, as they are dealt with more specifically elsewhere in other accounting standards.

Under the heading of basic principles, the Application Note states that 'a seller recognises revenue under an exchange transaction with a customer, when, and to the extent that, it obtains the right to consideration in exchange for its performance'. This will usually entail recognition of a new asset, most likely a debtor.

In dealing with the situation where a seller receives payment in advance from customers, the Application Note recognises a liability equal to the amount received, which represents the obligations of the seller under the contract. As performance successively generates a right to consideration, the liability is reduced and that reduction is recognised as being revenue.

The Application Note further requires that revenue be measured at fair value of the right to consideration, which will usually be the price specified, net of any discounts, VAT and similar sales taxes. If the duration of the contract is such that the time value of money is material, the amount of revenue recognised should be the present value of expected cash inflows. Adjustment may be necessary to take into account the risk of default.

12.3   *Revenue Recognition*

Turnover is distinguished from exchange transactions, such as the sale of fixed assets, which are outside of operating profit and so not covered by the fair value requirement.

12.3   The five specific situations covered by the Application Note are:

Long-term contractual performance – additional guidance is provided here in relation to *SSAP 9* (see Chapter 14) in terms of the recognition of turnover derived from long-term contracts. Specifically, the Application Note shows how changes in a seller's assets or liabilities and related turnover should be recorded in relation to performance under incomplete long-term contracts.

Separation and linking of contractual arrangements, where a seller is required to provide a number of different goods or services to customers that may be unrelated but are sold as a package at a price below that which would be charged if each item were sold individually. The Application Note requires that a contractual arrangement should only be accounted for as two or more separate transactions when the commercial substance is that the individual components operate independently of one another. This separation is referred to as 'unbundling'. On the other hand, the commercial substance may require that two separate contracts be accounted for as a single transaction ('bundling').

Where a contractual arrangement consists of various components that operate independently, and a reliable fair value can be attributed to every component, the seller should recognise changes in assets or liabilities for each component as if it were an individual contractual arrangement. The Application Note offers a number of examples, including:

> 'A customer may purchase "off the shelf" packaged software from a seller, which also offers separately a support service that provides helpline assistance and advice about the package's operation. An analysis of the arrangement shows that the customer has no commercial obligation or requirement to purchase the support service; it is not needed for the software package to operate satisfactorily. The seller's performance is made up of two components and it should recognise turnover separately for each.'

The Application Note also deals with inception fees, which allow the customer to purchase goods or services over a period of time. If the fee and the charges represent the seller's return on the contract as a whole, the seller should report a liability for the fee to the extent to which it has not been included in turnover. If it can be shown that the seller has no further obligations to the customer in respect of the fee, the seller should record the fee as turnover on the date on which entitlement to it arises.

The Note also deals with the position of vouchers redeemable against future purchases from the seller. If the fair value of the voucher is significant in the context of the transaction, the transaction should be reported at the amount of consideration received less the fair value of the voucher, which represents a liability for future performance.

Bill and hold arrangements, where there is a transfer of title under a contractual arrangement but physical delivery takes place at a later date. The question then arises whether the seller should recognise turnover and a right to consideration, or continue to recognise the goods as stock. For the former to apply, the goods should be complete and ready for delivery, the seller should not have any significant performance obligations apart from safekeeping and delivery of goods, the goods should be separately identified from other stock, and the arrangement should be to the benefit of the customer and not the seller.

Sales with rights of return – rights of return may be explicit or implicit or arise under statute. The inclusion of such rights may affect the quantification of the seller's right to consideration. Changes in the seller's assets or liabilities should reflect the loss expected to arise from rights of return, and turnover should exclude the sales value of estimated returns.

Presentation of turnover as principal or agent – where the substance of a transaction is that the seller acts as principal, it should report turnover based on the gross amount receivable. Where the substance of a transaction is that the seller is acting as an agent, the commission should be reported as turnover, and sums receivable that are payable to the principal not included.

URGENT ISSUES TASK FORCE (UITF 40)

12.4 The ASB 2001 Discussion Paper on revenue recognition contained a chapter entitled 'Accounting for Incomplete Contractual Performance', in which it was stated that 'revenue should be recognised to the extent that the seller has performed and that performance has resulted in a benefit accruing to the customer'. Following the subsequent issue of Application Note G in 2003, there was some confusion about long-term contracts for services and the relationship between *FRS 5* and *SSAP 9*) and, in the interests of clarity, *UITF 40* was issued on 10 March 2005, effective for accounting periods ending on or after 22 June 2005.

Application Note G had stated that *SSAP 9* should be applied for long-term contracts such that turnover is ascertained according to stage of completion of the contract, the business and the industry in which the entity operates. The question that arose then was whether contracts for services should be similarly accounted for. *UITF 40* states that contracts that require services to be provided on an ongoing basis, ie repetitively, rather than the provision of a single service, do not fall to be accounted for as long-term contracts under *SSAP 9*. At para 16, *UITF 40* states

> 'The overriding consideration is whether the seller has performed, or partially performed, its contractual obligations. If it has performed some, but not all, of its contractual obligations, it is required to recognise revenue to the extent that it has obtained the right to consideration through its performance … Where the substance of a transaction is that the seller's contractual obligations are performed gradually over time, revenue is recognised as contract activity

12.5 *Revenue Recognition*

progresses ... Where the substance of the contract is that a right to consideration does not arise until the occurrence of a critical event, revenue is not recognised until that event occurs.'

Thus, contracts for services should not be treated as long-term contracts unless they involve the provision of a single service, or a number of services that constitute a single project.

INTERNATIONAL ACCOUNTING STANDARD 18 (IAS 18)

12.5 In general terms, *IAS 18* states that revenue should be recognised when it is probable that future economic benefits will flow to the entity and these benefits can be measured reliably. It applies to sale of goods, rendering of services and the use by others of entity assets yielding interest, royalties and dividends. The standard does not deal with leases, insurance contracts, financial instruments or other current assets, or agricultural assets and mineral ore extraction.

Revenue is income arising in the ordinary course of an entity's activities. The IASB's Framework defines income as 'increases in economic benefits in the form of inflows or enhancements of assets or decreases of liabilities that result in increases in equity'.

As with Application Note G, measurement is at fair value of the consideration received or receivable.

In relation to revenue from the provision of services, *IAS 18* requires it to be recognised by reference to the stage of completion of the transaction at the balance sheet date.

TAXATION CONSIDERATIONS

12.6 For tax purposes, income is generally earned when goods are provided or services completed, and the timing of invoicing and payments is not relevant. There is some case law dealing with income recognition for tax purposes. Revenue recognition was the subject of the dispute in *Symons v Weeks and ors* (1983) 56 TC 630 in the context of long-term contracts (see Chapter 14).

12.7 HMRC Help Sheet 238 outlines the income tax view of *UITF 40* for the year ended 5 April 2009 in a non-technical manner, and observes that it may require some businesses to change the way they deal with uncompleted work and recognise income. HMRC's Business Income Manual states at BIM 74201 that:

'FA98/S42 [now CTA 2009, s 46] and ITTOIA05/S25 require the profits of a trade, profession or vocation to be calculated according to GAAP subject only to the adjustments required or authorised by

Revenue Recognition **12.7**

law ... Therefore where there are changes in GAAP it follows that the computation of taxable profits must also change, subject to any overriding tax rule.'

FA 2006, Sch 15 allows the tax adjustment arising on the change in accounting policy made when first adopting *UITF 40* to be spread over a maximum of six years. The spreading rules will also apply on adoption of the similar rules in *IAS 18*, unless previously applied on prior adoption of *UITF 40*.

Chapter 13

Stocks and Work in Progress

13.1 The inclusion of stocks and/or work in progress is a virtually universal feature of financial accounts. For that reason, it is of utmost importance. The question, 'How much does this cost to make?', is one which non-accountants would expect accountants to be able to answer, yet it is also a question that many accountants dread, for the simple reason that there is never a uniquely correct answer.

As shall be seen, to answer the question requires, potentially, a significant number of subjective judgements to be made in order to ascertain an appropriate valuation of stocks and work in progress held at the year end. This creates room for differences of opinion, errors or fraud, leading to potential disputes. One of the results of this has been the proliferation of cases which have come to court over the years. There is no single other topic which has been the subject of so much tax litigation.

One reason for this is that year end stocks are 'self-balancing'. Stocks are not part of the double entry bookkeeping system. Any valuation of stocks at the end of the year appears in the accounts twice – in the balance sheet as current assets, and in the calculation of the cost of goods sold (opening stocks plus purchases less closing stocks) in the profit and loss account. Any overstatement of the value of year end stocks inflates the balance sheet and reduces the calculated value of cost of goods sold, thereby increasing the recorded profits for the year. This does not 'create' additional profits, because the closing stock for one year is the opening stock of the next year, but rather it has the effect of bringing forward into the current year profit that would otherwise not be recognised until next year. Given the subjective nature of stock valuation, this makes the manipulation of year end stocks a tempting target for the unscrupulous.

The reconciliation of year end stocks is also an area prone to difficulties and, therefore, errors. Inevitably, the physical stocks and the related documentation, such as purchase invoices, that trigger the accounting entries in the double entry bookkeeping system, arrive at different points in time. This makes matching the records of physical stocks with the accounting records (often known as 'cut-off') problematical.

SSAP 9 – introduced in 1975 and updated in 1988 – deals with the questions of stocks and work in progress. It is entitled 'Stocks and Long-Term Contracts'. Long-term contracts give rise to special considerations and are fully considered

Stocks and Work in Progress **13.4**

in Chapter 14. This chapter will deal only with stocks (defined to include work in progress other than that arising in long-term contracts).

In addition to *SSAP 9*, the provisions of the *Accounting Regulations* need to be borne in mind, and these are considered following the *SSAP 9* analysis.

STATEMENT OF STANDARD ACCOUNTING PRACTICE 9 (SSAP 9)

13.2 Essentially, *SSAP 9* is an application of the matching concept, tempered with a measure of prudence.

The costs of unsold or unconsumed stocks will have been incurred in the expectation of future revenue and profit. A 'carry forward' is needed so that these costs can be set against that future revenue ('matching'). However, if the circumstances are such that the future profit is unlikely to arise (eg due to obsolescence of the stock on hand), then the costs unlikely to be recovered should be charged against revenue in the year the likelihood of non-recovery becomes apparent ('prudence').

The terms will be defined below, but the above concepts lead to the proposition that stocks should be included in accounts at the lower of cost (matching) and net realisable value (prudence).

STOCKS

13.3   *SSAP 9* defines stocks as comprising:

- goods or other assets purchased for resale;
- consumable stores;
- raw materials and components purchased for incorporation into products for sale;
- products and services in intermediate stages of completion;
- long-term contract balances (dealt with separately in Chapter 14);
- finished goods.

Products and services in intermediate stages of completion are what might otherwise be termed 'work in progress'.

COSTS

13.4   These are explained to be the expenditures incurred in the 'normal course of business' in bringing the product or service to its present location and condition.

13.4 Stocks and Work in Progress

Costs would include the 'costs of purchase' (purchase price, import duties, transport, trade discounts, rebates and subsidies) and the 'costs of conversion'. 'Costs of conversion' include direct overheads (direct labour, direct expenses etc), production overheads, and other overheads (if any). SSAP 9 defines production overheads as overheads 'based on the normal level of activity'. The distinction between 'normal' (where costs incurred would be included in the calculation of stock valuation) and 'abnormal' (where costs would be charged directly to the profit and loss account) is an area of subjectivity which can be the source of disputes. For example, production time lost through a machinery breakdown may be considered to be 'abnormal'. However, it can equally well be argued that for machinery never to break down would also be abnormal, so that a 'normal' level of lost production time would be acceptable.

It may help to ponder at this stage what these terms mean and how the expenditures are classified.

All overheads should be classified according to function (production, marketing, selling, and administration). Generally, only the production overheads will be included in the stock valuation. An example will illustrate the position.

Example 13.1

A company is in its first year of trading. It manufactures widgets. During the year it has made and sold 80,000 widgets and, at the year end, it has 10,000 completed widgets in stock and 20,000 widgets that are precisely in a condition of 50% completion (and the assumption here is that 50% complete implies that 50% of the total eventual cost has been incurred).

An extract from the management accounts for the year is as below. Each overhead is analysed by function. Those relating to production are earmarked for inclusion in the stock valuation. The two final columns quantify the amount to be included in relation to the complete and incomplete widgets on hand at the year end.

Classification	Overheads	Total Costs	Completed Widgets on Hand	Incomplete Widgets on Hand
		£	£	£
Production	Factory Wages	100,000	10,000	10,000
Production	Factory Rent	10,000	1,000	1,000
Production	Electricity for Factory	10,000	1,000	1,000
Production	Machine Depreciation	20,000	2,000	2,000
Sales	Salesmen's Commissions	30,000	–	–

Stocks and Work in Progress **13.6**

Classification	Overheads	Total Costs	Completed Widgets on Hand	Incomplete Widgets on Hand
		£	£	£
Sales	Salesmen's Car Expenses	15,000	–	–
Office	Office Wages	25,000	–	–
Office	Office Rent	2,500	–	–
Office	Office Power	2,500	–	–
Office	Office Depreciation	1,000	–	–
General	Interest	10,000	–	–
General	Accountancy	5,000	–	–
	TOTAL OVERHEADS	£231,000	£14,000	£14,000

The amounts included in the two last columns above are determined by taking the fractional share of the overheads.

The total effective production for the year	=	80,000 + 10,000 + (50% × 20,000) 100,000
That represented by completed widgets on hand	=	10,000/100,000
	=	10%
That represented by incomplete widgets on hand	=	50% × 20,000/100,000
	=	10%

13.5 In the example above, therefore, closing stocks at the end of the first year would be:

Complete Widgets	14,000
Incomplete Widgets	14,000
	£28,000

13.6 Whilst all of the above seems fairly straightforward, again there are many 'grey' areas. The detailed allocation of costs to account categories inevitably differs between companies. For example, the production planner

13.7 *Stocks and Work in Progress*

may sit in the 'offices' and hence part of the office rent, power and depreciation may relate to this activity. A proportion of these costs could validly be included in the cost of production, as well as the direct costs of the production planner, but how much? Similarly, an employee may have a role that is partly related to production and partly related to non-production activities. How is the cost to be apportioned? Any basis of apportionment is necessarily arbitrary, and many businesses would consider any increase in the accuracy of cost allocation to be insufficiently material to warrant the time and effort involved.

In addition, there are circumstances in which expenses not normally identified as relating to production can be included in stocks. For example, a company may tender for what will be a very important contract. It may engage outside help specifically for the gaining of that contract. Some of its own staff may be permanently seconded to the task of securing that contract. If that contract is won, it might be reasonable to include those costs uniquely incurred in acquiring it (the contract) as part of the overall production costs and thence to be included in the stock valuation.

Another example might be in the area of interest. Most companies would regard interest payments as a general expense of running a company. But, if a company secures a particularly large contract, it may take out special banking facilities just for that contract. Interest arising would be uniquely identifiable with that contract, and might therefore be properly included as a production cost and thereby included in stock valuation (but see **13.13** below in relation to disclosure).

METHODS OF COSTING

13.7 In practice, it is often not possible to relate expenditure to specific units which are on hand at the end of the year. Approximations are therefore necessary, and problems arise in the two areas of relating costs to contracts, and calculating related costs.

Relating costs to contracts

13.8 Some contracts are treated as one-offs, and all costs relating to them are identified and accumulated. This is called 'job costing'.

Some contracts require numbers of identical units to be made. These are considered en bloc and costs are accumulated for the entirety, each individual unit taking its pro-rata share of costs. This is called 'batch costing'.

Some sophisticated businesses work out, from time to time, what the cost of producing items *should* be. This is called 'standard costing'.

There are other methods of greater or lesser degrees of sophistication. Management is charged with the task of selecting (and applying consistently) the method which is most satisfactory for that particular business. However, all methods of cost allocation involve subjective allocations of joint costs (where the underlying activities contribute to more than one contract), and the problems of arbitrary allocation are compounded when a production facility produces a number of different products.

Calculating related costs

13.9 Problems arise here when identical items have been made or purchased at different times. There are several candidates in the selection of the appropriate method:

- *First in, first out (FIFO)*. On this basis, it is assumed that those items in stock are the most recently bought or made.

- *Last in, first out (LIFO)*. On this basis, it is assumed that those items still in stock are those items which were made or bought at the earliest time.

- *Discounted selling price*. On this basis, the selling price is ascertained and the normal gross margin deducted to arrive at estimated cost.

- *Replacement cost*. On this basis, the replacement cost of the units on hand is used.

- *Base stock*. On this basis, it is assumed that there is a base level of stock (in number or quantity terms) which is always present and which is carried at an unchanging monetary amount from year to year.

SSAP 9 again provides that management should select the method most appropriate to the circumstances, but comments that LIFO and base stock are unlikely to be appropriate, that the discounted selling price method should be used with caution, and that the replacement cost basis should be used only as an approximation to 'net realisable value'. HMRC resist the use of the LIFO and base stock methods.

Essentially, therefore, the strongly preferred (and most frequently encountered) bases are the FIFO method and its variant, weighted average cost.

NET REALISABLE VALUE

13.10 As explained in **13.2** above, stocks should be included at the lower of cost or net realisable value. This evaluation usually needs to be made on an item-by-item basis.

'Net realisable value' is the estimated proceeds from the sale of the stocks less all future costs to completion and less all costs to be incurred in marketing, selling and distribution directly related to the items in question.

This is a different concept from 'market value'. The market value is simply the price that could be expected from a sale of the item in its condition at that time. The concept of market value does not figure in *SSAP 9*.

13.11 *Stocks and Work in Progress*

A simple example will illustrate how this works:

Example 13.2
A company sells high-fashion clothing and has 1,200 units of a particular line on hand at the end of the year. These units have cost £50 each. The company anticipates being able to sell 400 of the items in the short term at present prices (£100 per item). It then anticipates having to initiate a sale at which there will be incurred £10 per item of sales promotion, which will give rise to a sale of 400 items at £80 per unit. It then anticipates selling the remaining 400 through a dealer at £30 per unit. Its year-end stock valuation should be:

Number of Units	Cost to Date	Anticipated Sale Price	Promotion Costs	Net Realisable Value	Stock Valuation
	£	£	£	£	£
400	20,000	40,000	–	40,000	20,000
400	20,000	32,000	(4,000)	28,000	20,000
400	20,000	12,000	–	12,000	12,000
					£52,000

Whilst the analysis set out above may appear to be reasonably straightforward, given the facts presented, the estimation of future selling prices, volumes and selling costs is inevitably, in practice, subjective and prone to being influenced by optimism. In particular, the selling price achievable is often a function of the time available in which to attract a willing buyer.

DISCLOSURES

13.11   SSAP 9 provides that stocks should be stated at the lower of cost or net realisable value of the separate items of stock or groups of similar items. Stocks should be sub-classified in the balance sheet or notes to the categories specified in the *Accounting Regulations*.

Detailed provisions for the disclosure of long-term work in progress and payments on account thereof are provided. Chapter 14 effectively covers the *SSAP 9* provisions in this respect.

COMPANY LAW REQUIREMENTS

13.12   The legal requirements are set out in *SI 2008/410* for large companies and *SI 2008/409* for small and medium-sized companies (the '*Accounting Regulations*').

Stocks are to be stated at the lower of purchase price/production cost and net realisable value.

13.13 In determining production cost, there *must* be included the purchase price (plus expenses) of raw materials and consumables, plus other costs which are directly attributable to the production of the asset.

In addition, there *may* be included:

- a reasonable proportion of indirect overheads (but only insofar as they relate to the period of production); and
- interest on capital borrowed to finance the production of that asset (to the extent it accrues over the period of production).

If interest is included, then that fact should be disclosed and quantified in the notes to the accounts.

13.14 The method of determining the purchase price or production cost must be selected by the directors as that which is most appropriate to the circumstances of the company, but acceptable methods may be:

- FIFO;
- LIFO (unlikely to be appropriate under *SSAP 9*);
- weighted average price; or
- any other similar method.

13.15 If the replacement cost of stocks differs materially from the value as ascertained above, then this fact and a quantification of the difference should appear as a note to the accounts.

COMPARISON WITH INTERNATIONAL ACCOUNTING STANDARDS

13.16 The requirements of *IAS 2* 'Inventories' are similar to those of *SSAP 9* in most material respects, although more extensive disclosure may be given.

TAXATION CONSIDERATIONS

13.17 Following the enactment of *FA 1998, s 42*, HMRC now generally follows *SSAP 9* and *IAS 2* in relation to stock or inventory and work in progress. There are some exceptions, however: first, where the business is discontinued or stock is disposed of to connected persons, in which case market value must be used; and, secondly, in the case of appropriations of stock for private use. For the latter, the decision in *Sharkey v Wherner* (1955)

13.18 *Stocks and Work in Progress*

36 TC 275, which required the market value to be used for tax purposes, and not cost, has now been codified (*FA 2008, s 34, Sch 15*).

One recent controversy concerns the question of depreciation in stock. Following the decision of the Hong Kong court in the *Secan* case, HMRC published its view (in *Tax Bulletin 59*) on how depreciation in stock should be dealt with, specifically that full depreciation should be added back in the tax computation, irrespective of whether it was attributable to stock on hand at the end of the period. This view was successfully challenged in the joint appeal of *HMRC v William Grant & Sons Distillers Limited and Small (HM Inspector of Taxes) v Mars UK Limited* [2007] UKHL 15, and HMRC now accept that the depreciation attributable to closing stock will not be added back in the tax computation until such time as it is sold.

The valuation of work in progress is on the basis of the lower of cost and net realisable value. This applies to uncompleted service contracts, so that a profit or loss is not recognised for tax purposes until the contractual obligations have been fulfilled. In some circumstances, it may be appropriate to consider that professional work in progress should be treated as long-term contracts. In *Duple Motor Bodies v Ostime* (1961) 39 TC 537, the question of recognising overheads as part of work in progress was considered, but this decision pre-dates *SSAP 9* and the taxpayer's practice of only including direct costs in work in progress is no longer generally accepted accounting practice.

In the HMRC publication 'Working Together' issued in June 2003, a list of problems encountered by Revenue accountants includes: stock provisions not supported by the facts; long-term contracts not identified and properly accounted for; stock and work in progress valued on a basis related to an emergency sale rather than sale in the ordinary course of business; and work completed before the end of the year but invoiced afterwards not being correctly accounted for under *FRS 18*.

13.18 Certain trades have special considerations. The HMRC *Tax Bulletin* of August 1994 (at p 156) gives guidance in relation to motor dealers' stock valuation. Farming is even more specialised – see HMRC *Tax Bulletin* of May 1993.

Chapter 14

Long-term Contracts

14.1 A 'long-term contract' is one in which contract activity spans more than one accounting period. Technically, a company with a year end of 31 March which begins work on a contract on 1 January 2009 and completes it on 30 June 2009 has undertaken a long-term contract. However, *SSAP 9* provides that, despite this, in normal cases, only contracts exceeding one year should be accounted for as 'long-term' (unless a long-term contract of a duration of less than one year is so material to results that not to account for it as long-term would distort performance so that the accounts would not give a true and fair view). In practice, almost all contracts accounted for as 'long-term' have a duration of more than one year (often considerably longer).

14.2 The basic idea is that profits and losses on long-term contracts should be brought into account as the contract progresses rather than awaiting the final outcome, which may be many years down the line. Once again, the methods adopted apply a degree of 'matching' tempered with a dose of 'prudence'.

There are three concepts requiring understanding.

ATTRIBUTABLE PROFIT

14.3 This is that part of the total profit currently estimated to arise over the duration of the contract that fairly represents the profit attributable to that part of the work performed at the accounting date, calculated on a prudent basis. There can be no such attributable profit until the profitable outcome of the contract as a whole can be assessed with reasonable certainty. The point at which the final outcome of the contract can be assessed with reasonable certainty will depend on both the nature and terms of the contract, and the company's experience with such contracts. Until that point is reached, no profit should be reflected in the profit and loss account, although it may be appropriate to include an appropriate proportion of the contract's value as turnover (and an equal amount as costs) in order to reflect the level of activity during the year.

SSAP 9 does not prescribe the method to be used to calculate the profit attributable to the proportion of the contract completed as at the accounting date. The method needs to be appropriate to the specific terms of the contract

14.4 *Long-term Contracts*

in question, and it is the responsibility of the directors to determine the most appropriate method. However, *SSAP 9* specifically requires that any known inequalities of profitability in the various stages of a contract must be taken into account, as well as the estimated cost of any remedial work not recoverable under the terms of the contract.

There are a number of areas of inherent subjectivity here, including the determination of the point at which the final outcome of each contract can be foreseen with reasonable certainty and the estimation of future contract costs, including remedial work. Similar considerations apply to the estimation of foreseeable losses below.

FORESEEABLE LOSSES

14.4 These are the losses which are currently estimated to arise over the duration of the entire contract. This is required irrespective of:

(*a*) whether work has yet commenced on the contract;

(*b*) the proportion of work carried out at the accounting date; and

(*c*) the amount of profits expected to arise on other contracts.

PAYMENTS ON ACCOUNT

14.5 These are all amounts received and receivable at the accounting date in respect of contracts in progress.

14.6 A careful reading of the definitions of attributable profit and foreseeable losses will illustrate the asymmetry of the provisions.

Attributable profits include only a proportion of the overall anticipated contract profit (proportional to the work carried out), whereas foreseeable losses include the whole contract loss, even if work has not yet started.

Accounting for the attributable profit and foreseeable loss is straightforward, if taken slowly. Appendix 3 to *SSAP 9* explains the principles and gives a comprehensive example.

The basic idea is that, at the year end, the prospects of each contract are examined.

Whatever the outcome (profitable or otherwise), the contract is part complete so that a calculation is made of the effective turnover. It is as if a sale had been made (there is no actual sale as such, so this is a kind of substance over form adjustment). This turnover is treated as a sale, and the proceeds (which are assumed at this stage not to have been paid) are included in debtors (ie amounts owing to the company) under the title 'amounts recoverable on contracts'.

Then, an assessment is made of the costs relating to this turnover. This amount is charged against profits and not carried forward in the work in

Long-term Contracts **14.8**

progress valuation. The effect of this is to credit to profit any attributable profit (turnover less costs).

If there are foreseeable losses, these are charged against the profits for the year by being deducted from the value of closing work in progress.

14.7 There remains only the question of payments on account. If these relate to contracts which have been included in turnover on the basis above, any payments on account which are received effectively discharge the debtor which the company is carrying under the head 'amounts recoverable on contracts'. However, there may be contracts where a payment on account received exceeds the debtor being carried (ie in payment terms, the contract may be front loaded). In this case, the excess should be deducted from the residual balance sheet value of the contract work in progress. Any excess over that should be treated as a separate creditor balance.

14.8 In practice, non-accountants get most confused with the treatment of payments on account. The following example is designed to clarify this point:

Example 14.1
A company has just finished its first year in business. Apart from other transactions, it has entered into one long-term contract. It has expended £500,000 on the first phase and has just started, and spent £20,000, on the second phase. It expects to spend another £480,000. The sales value of the contract is £1,500,000 so it expects to make an overall profit of £500,000. It estimates that the profit attributable to the year's work on the first phase is £250,000 on an estimated effective turnover of £750,000 (there is no absolute reason for the linearity of these numbers; it is possible for profits to accrue disproportionately). It has no rights to any payment on account. Its accounts look like:

Profit and Loss Account

		£	
TURNOVER		5,000,000	(including £750,000 long-term contract)
Net Profit		1,000,000	(including £250,000 profit on long-term contract)
Balance Sheet			
Fixed Assets		100,000	
Current Assets			
Stock	100,000		(including £20,000 on phase 2)
Debtors	850,000		(including £750,000 in respect of 'amounts recoverable on contracts')

14.8 Long-term Contracts

	£
Cash:	100,000
Creditors:	(150,000)
Net Current Assets	900,000
Total Assets	1,000,000
Shareholders Funds	1,000,000

The £250,000 profit is included in net profit because £750,000 has been included in turnover, whilst £500,000 of contract work in progress has been written off against this (and not carried forward in the stock on the balance sheet).

Now consider two further scenarios: first, that the company receives a payment on account of £500,000; and, secondly, a payment on account of £1,000,000. In each case, these sums are received before the year end.

Payments on account do not impact on the profit and loss account.

The effect on the balance sheet in these scenarios is:

	Scenario 1		Scenario 2	
	£		£	
Fixed Assets		100,000		100,000
Current Assets				
Stock	100,000		80,000 (iii)	
Debtors	350,000 (i)		100,000 (ii)	
Cash	600,000		1,100,000	
Creditors	(150,000)		(380,000) (iv)	
Net Current Assets		900,000		900,000
Total Assets		1,000,000		1,000,000
Shareholders' Funds		1,000,000		1,000,000

(i) This is £850,000 less the payment on account of £500,000.

(ii) This is £850,000 less £750,000 of the payment on account. It is not possible to deduct any more because there is only £750,000 included under debtors in respect of amounts recoverable on (this) contract.

(iii) This is £100,000 less £20,000 of the payment on account. This occurs because stocks contain £20,000 of costs incurred on (phase 2 of) the contract.

(iv) This is £150,000 plus the balance of payment on account of £230,000 (£1,000,000 − £750,000 − £20,000).

COMPARISON WITH INTERNATIONAL ACCOUNTING STANDARDS

14.9 The equivalent international accounting standard is *IAS 11* 'Construction Contracts'. Despite the title of the standard apparently implying a narrower application than *SSAP 9*, the scope of the two standards is similar. The main differences between the two standards are that *IAS 11*, first of all, does not specifically require the calculation of attributable profit to take account of any known inequalities of profitability over the contract, and, secondly, does not require the distinction between amounts recoverable on contracts (shown under 'debtors' above) and work in progress (shown under 'stock' above) to be shown separately.

TAXATION

14.10 Foreseeable losses are accounted for under *SSAP 9*. In 1982, the accountancy bodies issued a paper, approved by counsel which, *inter alia*, confirmed that profits (and losses) included in long-term work in progress valuations represented realised profits (or losses) for *Companies Act* purposes. Providing the calculations have been effected properly and accurately, it is difficult to see any reason why the foreseeable losses, if any, should be disallowed for tax. Yet, for periods before 22 July 1999, Revenue *Statement of Practice* 3/90 required that profits and losses not be anticipated, based on accumulated case law. From that date, however, profits and losses recognised during the currency of long-term contracts are also recognised for tax purposes.

Chapter 15

Tangible Fixed Assets

15.1 Tangible fixed assets are assets that have physical substance and are held for use in the production or supply of goods or services, for rental to other entities or for administrative purposes. They are accounted for under *FRS 15*, which has effect for accounting periods ending on or after 23 March 2000. Investment properties are dealt with separately under *SSAP 19* although, during the period of construction, ie before they actually become investment properties, they are dealt with under *FRS 15*.

INITIAL MEASUREMENT

15.2 *CA 2006* specifies that, if historical cost accounting is used, the amount to be included for fixed assets is its purchase price (including incidental acquisition expenses but excluding trade discounts and rebates) or production cost. *FRS 15* expands on the *CA 2006* requirements in relation to the costs of production, other than finance costs. Only costs that are directly attributable to bringing the asset into working condition for its intended use are taken into account. Directly attributable costs are defined as:

(*a*) the labour costs of own employees (eg site workers, in-house architects and surveyors) arising directly from the construction or acquisition of the specific tangible fixed asset; and

(*b*) the incremental costs to the entity that would have been avoided only if the tangible fixed asset had not been constructed or acquired.

These include items such as purchase costs, stamp duties, site preparation and clearance, delivery and handling, installation costs and professional fees. In addition, the estimated cost of dismantling and removing the asset and restoring the site are capitalised, but only to the extent that such costs are also recognised as a provision under *FRS 12*. (The entity must have a legal or constructive obligation to dismantle and remove the asset and to restore the site – see Chapter 18) The recognition of an equal asset and liability avoids the estimated restoration costs being charged to the profit and loss account immediately; the charge to the profit and loss account arises over the period in which the asset is used, via depreciation of the capitalised estimated restoration costs.

If costs are directly attributed to a tangible fixed asset, they must be capitalised and cannot be written off in the current period, subject to a maximum, which is the recoverable amount as defined in *FRS 11* 'Impairment of Fixed Assets and Goodwill' (see below).

Some costs are identified as being not suitable for capitalisation, such as administration and general costs, site selection costs, abnormal costs such as correcting design errors, or industrial disputes.

START-UP COSTS

15.3 *FRS 15* identifies acceptable and unacceptable circumstances in relation to the question of whether costs associated with start-up, or commissioning, periods should be included. Acceptable circumstances arise in relation to the physical preparation of the asset for use, such that it is impossible to operate at normal levels because of the need, for example, to test equipment or run machinery in. A situation where an asset is capable of being used, but demand has not yet built up, would not be acceptable, and so costs incurred during such period will not form part of the tangible fixed asset.

In June 2004, *UITF Abstract 24* was published to deal with the question of start-up costs and requires that start-up costs should be treated consistently with similar costs incurred in relation to an entity's ongoing activities.

This raises the question of timing, ie at what point does capitalisation of costs cease? *FRS 15* states that it is when there are no further activities required that would make a material difference to the cost of the asset.

FINANCE COSTS

15.4 *CA 2006* allows for the inclusion of interest on capital borrowed to finance the production of the asset. *FRS 15* interprets 'interest' to include all finance costs as defined in *FRS 4*. Capitalisation of finance costs is not a requirement of *FRS 15*; companies can choose whether or not to capitalise such costs. If a policy of capitalisation of finance costs is chosen, it must be applied consistently rather than selectively. Where finance costs are capitalised, this should be done on a gross basis (ie before any tax relief). Capitalisation of finance costs should cease when the tangible fixed asset is ready for use. Disclosure of the accounting policy adopted, the aggregate amount of capitalised finance costs, and the amount capitalised during the accounting period need to be disclosed.

SUBSEQUENT EXPENDITURE

15.5 There are three circumstances where expenditure subsequent to initial acquisition of a tangible fixed asset should be capitalised:

15.6 *Tangible Fixed Assets*

- where it enhances the economic benefits of the tangible fixed asset in excess of the previously assessed standard of performance;
- where a component of the asset has been treated separately for depreciation purposes and that separate component is replaced or restored; and
- where there is a major inspection or overhaul that restores the economic benefits of the asset that have been consumed by the entity and already reflected in depreciation.

The last two circumstances relate to 'complex assets'. These are assets made up of components with significantly different estimated useful lives, each of which should be recorded and depreciated separately. Examples include a furnace that needs to be relined every five years, and an aircraft that requires a periodic major inspection and overhaul by law. When the subsequent expenditure is recognised, the costs and related depreciation of the component being replaced should be derecognised (ie removed from the fixed asset records). To the extent that the component being replaced has not been fully depreciated, this will result in a charge to the profit and loss account representing the remaining net book value being written off.

Subsequent expenditure that does not meet the criteria set out above, but maintains an asset's previously assessed standard of performance, should be charged to the profit and loss account as incurred. The depreciation of tangible fixed assets is dealt with in the next chapter.

ALTERNATIVE VALUATION BASES

15.6 The *Accounting Regulations* (as discussed in Chapter 5) allow for the use of alternative accounting rules, which gives companies the ability to revalue fixed assets selectively. One of the aims of *FRS 15* is to achieve a greater level of consistency in this regard, and it allows companies to choose to adopt a revaluation policy, in which case all revalued assets are required to be carried at their current value at balance sheet date. For properties, current value is the lower of the replacement cost and the recoverable amount, which itself is the higher of net realisable value and value in use. This is described as 'deprival value', ie the loss the entity would suffer if it were deprived of the asset. Where a revaluation policy is adopted, all assets in the same class must be revalued, preferably using a qualified valuer. The classes are those specified in the *Accounting Regulations*, the broadest categories being:

- land and buildings;
- plant and machinery; and
- fixtures, fittings, tools and equipment.

Frequency of revaluation is at the company's discretion, but cannot be less than five-year intervals.

For assets other than properties, ie those in the second and third categories above, the general rule is valuation at market value, where possible. If market values are not available, depreciated replacement cost may be used.

15.7 *CA 2006* allows an alternative valuation basis for tangible fixed assets; specifically, a fixed value may be used provided the assets are:

- not material to assessing the company's state of affairs;
- constantly replaced; and
- not subject to material variation in quantity, value or composition.

IMPAIRMENT

15.8 Both *CA 2006* and *FRS 11*, introduced in 1998, require companies to consider whether a fixed asset has been impaired, which essentially means that it has suffered a diminution of value. The objective of *FRS 11* is to ensure that:

- fixed assets and goodwill are recorded in the financial statements at no more than their recoverable amount;
- any resulting impairment loss is measured and recognised on a consistent basis; and
- sufficient information is disclosed in the financial statements to enable users to understand the impact of the impairment on the financial position and performance of the reporting entity.

15.9 Under *FRS 11*, the carrying amount of an asset is compared with its recoverable amount, and if the carrying amount is higher, the asset is written down. The recoverable amount is the higher of the net realisable value and the amount that could be expected to be obtained through using the asset (the value in use). The latter is calculated using the present value of cash flows that the asset is expected to generate. This is inevitably a rather subjective exercise, involving the estimation of future cash flows that the asset is expected to generate for the remainder of its estimated useful life, plus the selection of an appropriate discount rate for use in the present value calculations. Frequently, individual assets do not generate separately identifiable cash flows; cash flows tend to be generated by groups of assets. *FRS 11* permits the use of 'income generating units', being groups of assets that generate separately identifiable cash flows. This grouping of assets represents a further layer of subjectivity.

Impairment tests are only required where there is some indication that impairment has occurred. *FRS 11* gives a number of examples of indications of impairment (in para 10), including operating losses, obsolescence, adverse market changes, business reorganisations and the loss of key employees.

FRS 15 requires that tangible fixed assets, other than non-depreciable land, should be reviewed for impairment at the end of each reporting period when there is no depreciation charge on the grounds that it is immaterial, or the estimated useful economic life is more than 50 years.

15.10 *Tangible Fixed Assets*

Impairment losses should be recognised in the profit and loss account, unless the loss arises on a previously revalued asset, in which case it should be set against the revaluation reserve (and reflected in the statement of total recognised gains and losses – 'STRGL'), with any excess being charged to the profit and loss account. Where the impairment arises on an 'income generating unit' of assets, the impairment loss should be allocated to the individual assets comprising the income generating unit in the following order:

(1) goodwill;

(2) other intangible assets; and

(3) tangible assets (pro-rata or another more appropriate basis).

Any subsequent reversal of an impairment loss should be recognised in the profit and loss account to the extent that the original impairment loss was charged to the profit and loss account. Any excess is reflected in the revaluation reserve (and the STRGL).

GAINS AND LOSSES OTHER THAN THROUGH IMPAIRMENT

15.10 Essentially, these arise through either the revaluation of assets using the alternative accounting rules permitted by *CA 2006*, or on ultimate disposal of the asset.

CA 2006 requires a gain on revaluation, ie where the revalued amount is in excess of the net book value, to be included in the balance sheet in a revaluation reserve and reflected in the STRGL, unless the revaluation reflects the reversal of a previous revaluation loss that was charged to the profit and loss account, in which case the revaluation gain is credited to the profit and loss account up to the amount of the previously reflected loss, with any excess being reflected in the revaluation reserve. A revaluation loss is charged to the profit and loss account, again unless it is the reversal of a previous revaluation gain, in which case it is charged to the revaluation reserve up to the amount of the previously recorded gain and any excess is charged to the profit and loss account. *FRS 15* specifically requires that gains and losses on individual assets should be treated separately, rather than being aggregated and only the net gain or loss being accounted for.

Gains and losses on fixed asset disposals should be accounted for in accordance with *FRS 3* (see Chapter 7).

INVESTMENT PROPERTIES

15.11 Neither *FRS 11* nor *FRS 15* applies to investment properties, which are, instead, dealt with by *SSAP 19*, originally issued in 1981 and updated in 1992 and 1994. The basic requirement of *SSAP 19* is that investment properties are included in the balance sheet at their open market value. Changes in value are dealt with as movements in the revaluation reserve and reported in the STRGL.

An investment property is defined as an interest in land and/or buildings:

(*a*) in respect of which construction work and development have been completed; and

(*b*) which is held for its investment potential, any rental income being negotiated at arm's length.

The standard does not apply if the property is owned and occupied by the company for its own purposes.

Changes in the market value of investment properties should not be taken to the profit and loss account, but should be taken to the STRGL as a movement on an investment revaluation reserve.

INTERNATIONAL ACCOUNTING STANDARD 16 (IAS 16)

15.12 *IAS 16* 'Property Plant and Equipment' provides for revaluations at fair value – in practice, market value, as compared with the use of 'current value' under *FRS 15*. The fair value will take into account the fact that the asset might be used in a different way, ie it will take account of possible alternative uses. Value in use, under *FRS 15*, only takes account of the cash flows from continuing to use the asset in its current use. This can have a significant effect on the valuation of land and buildings in particular.

IAS 16 does not specify a maximum period between full valuation (*FRS 15* specifies five years). In addition, *IAS 16* does not require annual impairment reviews for assets that are either not depreciated, or depreciated over more than 50 years.

Chapter 16

Depreciation

16.1 As with stocks, depreciation is a virtually universal feature of financial accounts. It is also an area of accounting that is often misunderstood and many consider to be simple, which is not the case, as will be seen below. The tax consequences are much less than for stocks and work in progress although, as **16.19** below illustrates, these are not entirely negligible.

The requirement to provide depreciation, its method and disclosure are governed by *FRS 15* and the provisions of *SI 2008/409* and *SI 2008/410* (the '*Accounting Regulations*').

FINANCIAL REPORTING STANDARD 15 (FRS 15)

16.2 Depreciation is defined by *FRS 15* as 'the measure of the cost or revalued amount of the economic benefits of the tangible fixed asset that have been consumed during the period'. It further explains the notion of consumption as including 'the wearing out, using up or other reduction in the useful economic life of a tangible fixed asset whether arising from use, effluxion of time, or obsolescence through either changes in technology or demand for the goods and services produced by the asset'. Depreciation is often misunderstood to result in the fixed asset in question being reflected on the balance sheet at its current value as a 'used' asset – in other words, that depreciation reduces the original cost of an asset to its value as a 'used' asset. This is completely incorrect. The rationale for depreciation is that a business purchases an asset to use in its business, in order to generate income, over a number of accounting periods. Depreciation is merely the mechanism whereby the cost of the asset (or its revalued amount) is spread over the accounting periods that are expected to benefit from its use. This is an application of the 'matching' principle. Depreciation is entirely separate from market valuation.

The depreciable amount is the difference between either the cost or revalued amount and residual value, and it must be allocated to the profit and loss account in a systematic basis over the useful economic life of the asset concerned. The method used should be that which reflects as fairly as possible the pattern of consumption of the benefits. It is the responsibility of the

Depreciation **16.4**

directors to determine which depreciation method is most appropriate, and this should be done for each individual asset as it is brought into use. A number of 'tools' are available to calculate depreciation (discussed below), but it is the responsibility of the directors to choose which one best achieves the key objective for each individual asset, namely to best reflect the pattern of consumption expected from using that particular asset.

Even if the asset has increased in value over a period, there is still a need to charge depreciation to the profit and loss account, because some part of the economic benefits inherent in the asset has been consumed during the period. Valuation and depreciation should be viewed as two entirely separate issues.

Useful economic life and residual value take into account the following factors:

(*a*)   expected rate of use of the asset, by reference to expected capacity and physical output;

(*b*)   expected rate of physical deterioration through use or time passing, taking into account intended maintenance plan;

(*c*)   expected rate of economic or technological obsolescence; and

(*d*)   legal or other similar limits on use (for example, lease terms).

The estimation of both the useful economic life and the residual value are areas of subjectivity which will inevitably differ between companies and, possibly, also between similar assets used by a particular company. It is also apparent from the definition of useful economic life that this is not necessarily the same as the physical life of an asset.

Both the useful economic life and the residual value must be reviewed at the end of each reporting period and revised if necessary. In computing the residual value, no account is taken of any expected change in price levels.

METHODS OF COMPUTING DEPRECIATION

16.3   *FRS 15* leaves it to directors to select an appropriate method. The following are possible candidates: straight line method; reducing balance; and other methods.

Straight line method

16.4   This method requires the original cost, estimated useful life and estimated realisable value at the end of its life.

It is simple to operate, and revenues of successive accounting periods are charged with equal amounts of depreciation. But, if revenue is constant, the return on the asset (measured on net book value) will increase as the asset becomes older. Nevertheless, it is in common use.

16.5 Depreciation

Example 16.1

Original Cost of Asset	£8,400
Estimated Useful Life	4 Years
Estimated Scrap Value	£400
Annual Depreciation Charge	£(8,400 – 400)/4
	= £2,000

Where the pattern of consumption of an asset's economic benefits is uncertain, the straight line method of depreciation is normally used.

Reducing balance

16.5 In this method, the depreciation charge is calculated by applying a fixed percentage to the opening net book value of the asset (its cost or valuation less accumulated depreciation at the start of the accounting period).

For some assets (eg cars), this aligns the accounting treatment more closely to the taxation treatment. Moreover, this method results in higher depreciation in the earlier years (compared to the straight line method). This is said to be justified because the profit-earning capacity is greater and the costs of repair/maintenance less in these earlier periods. This method does, however, never quite succeed in writing down the cost of an asset to nil; and, for short-life assets in particular, very high depreciation rates are needed even to reach an approximation to this.

This, too, is a very commonly used method.

Example 16.2
The facts are the same as in *Example 16.1*. The two methods of computing depreciation can be compared.

	Straight Line	Reducing Balance
	£	£
Year 1	2,000	4,200
Year 2	2,000	2,100
Year 3	2,000	1,050
Year 4	2,000	525
TOTAL	8,000	7,875

(The reducing balance method has been computed at a depreciation rate of 50%.)

Other methods

16.6 There are occasions where the most appropriate method of depreciation is based on output or usage. This might be where the total output of an asset can be estimated with reasonable accuracy, and the use of the asset is expected to vary over time. A simple example may be a business that purchases a gravel pit, estimated to contain one million tonnes of gravel, for £1,000,000. It may be appropriate to depreciate the cost of the gravel pit at £1 per tonne of gravel extracted.

There are other alternatives, known variously as the 'sum of the digits', 'sinking fund', 'annuity' and 'replacement cost' methods. In practice, these are rarely seen and, therefore, are not considered further.

'COMPLEX ASSETS'

16.7 'Complex assets', referred to at **15.5** above, are assets made up of components with significantly different estimated useful lives, each of which should be recorded and depreciated separately. Examples include a furnace that needs to be relined every five years, and an aircraft that, by law, requires a periodic major inspection and overhaul. If a complex asset is acquired in a single transaction, it will be necessary to apportion the purchase price between the separate components in order to calculate the depreciation on each one. This apportionment inevitably involves a subjective exercise.

Land and buildings are treated as separate components, even when they are purchased in a single transaction. Freehold land has an unlimited life and therefore is not depreciated, whereas buildings do have a limited life and should be depreciated. Similarly, the building is likely to be made up of a number of components, such as the fabric, major components such as the central heating system, and general fittings.

REVALUATIONS

16.8 It is quite possible, and specifically permitted under the '*Accounting Regulations*', for fixed assets to be revalued. *FRS 15* states that the revalued amount and the remaining economic useful life should form the basis for the depreciation. *FRS 15* allows, subject to a requirement for consistency, either the opening or closing valuation balance to be used as the basis for depreciation. In practice, the determining factor tends to be the effective date of the revaluation. *FRS 15* specifically requires a depreciation charge to be made to operating profit, even if the asset has risen in value or has been revalued.

16.9 *FRS 15* requires the depreciation charge for each period to be recognised as an expense in the profit and loss account, unless it is permitted to be included in the carrying amount of another asset (such as a fixed asset

16.10 *Depreciation*

manufactured in-house or year end stocks). It does recognise that there may be situations where it is not appropriate to provide depreciation, in particular where the depreciation charge and the accumulated depreciation are immaterial, such that they would not reasonably influence the decisions of users of the financial statements.

PERMANENT DIMINUTION IN VALUE

16.10 If an event occurs which permanently diminishes the value of an asset (an uninsured accident, an unexpected obsolescence), and the then net book value is not expected to be recoverable in full, the net book value should be written down immediately to the recoverable amount. If it subsequently is perceived that the write-down was unnecessary, the write-down can be written back.

This could arise, for example, where expensive software expected to last five years was acquired. At the end of Year 2, new software comes on to the market, seemingly making all existing software obsolete. At that time, a company may write off the entire book value of the software. However, if, during Year 3, the industry comes to view the new software as flawed, with the result that the original software has, quite literally, a new lease of life, then at the end of Year 3 it may have the write-down of Year 2 written back. Of course, depreciation for Year 3 and later years will have to be provided on the restored book value.

Disposal of revalued property

16.11 The comprehensive example below shows how an asset may be acquired (and depreciated) in Year 1, revalued in Year 2, depreciated in Year 3, and sold at a profit in Year 4.

Example 16.3
In Year 1, a company buys a machine for £100,000. Its depreciation policy is 10% p.a. straight line, thus assuming an expected life of 10 years.

At the end of Year 2, this asset is revalued to £200,000.

In Year 3, it is depreciated (at 10% p.a. straight line. This presupposes that the machine will have an expected life of a further 10 years).

In Year 4, it is sold for £250,000.

The company makes annual trading profits of £100,000 before depreciation.

All other assets remain constant, other than an annual increase of £100,000 in the bank balance (derived from the trading profit).

Taxation is ignored.

Depreciation 16.12

	Year 1 £	Year 2 £	Year 3 £	Year 4 £
Freehold Land	100,000	100,000	100,000	100,000
Machine	90,000	200,000	180,000	–
Net Current Assets	–	100,000	200,000	550,000
	190,000	400,000	480,000	650,000
Share Capital	100,000	100,000	100,000	100,000
Profit and Loss	90,000	180,000	260,000	550,000
Revaluation Reserve	–	120,000	120,000	–
	190,000	400,000	480,000	650,000
TURNOVER	500,000	500,000	500,000	500,000
Profit Before Depreciation	100,000	100,000	100,000	100,000
Depreciation	(10,000)	(10,000)	(20,000)	–
Profit on Sale	–	–	–	70,000
Profit for Year	90,000	90,000	80,000	170,000

The Profit and Loss at the end of Year 4 is analysed:

Profit and Loss B/f	260,000
Trade Profit for Year	100,000
Profit on Sale of Machine (250,000 – 180,000)	70,000
Transfer from Revaluation Reserve	120,000
Profit and Loss C/f	550,000

An interesting feature of the above example is that, although a large profit has arisen on the machine over the Years 1–4 (cost £100,000, sold for £250,000), only £70,000 has passed through the profit and loss account. Had a revaluation not been made, the full profit over the period of ownership of the asset would have passed through profit and loss. This is one of the reasons that *FRS 3* requires the appending of a memorandum entitled 'Note of historical cost profits and losses'. Effectively, this is a rewriting of the profit and loss account to show what the profits would have been if there had not been a revaluation.

DISCLOSURES

16.12 The accounting policies with respect to depreciation must be disclosed under the *Accounting Regulations*. *FRS 15's* disclosure requirements are more extensive and cover:

16.13 *Depreciation*

- the depreciation methods used;
- the useful economic lives or depreciation rates used;
- total depreciation charge for the period;
- the material financial effect of a change in either the useful economic lives or residual values;
- the cost or revalued amount at the beginning of the period and at balance sheet date;
- the cumulative provision for depreciation or impairment at the beginning of the period and at balance sheet date;
- a reconciliation of the movements in the financial period, ie additions, disposals, transfers, depreciation, impairment losses, and reversals of past impairment losses;
- the net carrying amount at the beginning of the period and at balance sheet date; and
- any change in depreciation method used, together with the reason for the change.

STATEMENT OF STANDARD ACCOUNTING PRACTICE 19 (SSAP 19)

SSAP 19 specifically deals with the question of investment properties, as noted in the previous chapter.

16.13 The basic idea is that, when fixed assets are held as investments, rather than being used in the business operations, they are not 'consumed' in the process of earning revenue, and their current value is of more significance than any systematic provision for depreciation. This leads to the investment properties being included in accounts at market value. It is not necessary for formal valuations by qualified or independent valuers (except where a substantial proportion of the total assets of a major enterprise, such as a listed company, are represented by investment properties, in which case a formal valuation by an external valuer should be undertaken at least every five years), although the name and qualifications of the person effecting the valuation should be disclosed (as should the fact that he is an employee of the company, if that is the case).

16.14 *SSAP 19* was amended in July 1994 to change the requirements concerning the treatment of certain revaluation deficits that were inconsistent with the spirit of *FRS 3*.

Changes in the value of investment properties should not be taken to the profit and loss account, but should be shown as a movement on an investment revaluation reserve (and also reflected in the STRGL), unless the total of the investment revaluation reserve is insufficient to cover a deficit. In that case, if the deficit is considered permanent it should be charged to the profit and loss;

but, if non-permanent deficits arise, these should be charged to the investment revaluation reserve, even if this creates a negative balance on this reserve. (Prior to 1994, *SSAP 19* did not – although the *Companies Act* did – permit such a negative balance.)

There are several difficult areas relating to the application of *SSAP 19*.

Conflict with the Companies Act

16.15 The *Accounting Regulations* require that *all* fixed assets with finite lives should be depreciated. Under *SSAP 19*, investment properties are not depreciated.

Thus, in order to comply with *SSAP 19*, it is necessary to disclose the way(s) in which the *Companies Act* requirements have not been observed, the reason (usually a statement that it is in order to comply with *SSAP 19* and to give a 'true and fair view'), and the effect of non-observance.

Optional depreciation

16.16 *SSAP 19 requires* leased investment properties to be depreciated if their unexpired terms are less than 20 years. However, it *permits* leases of longer duration to be depreciated; but, if that option is exercised, it must be applied to all leases (ie all leases are depreciated, or only those with less than 20 years to run).

Confusion between leaseholds and investment properties

16.17 Leased properties are only investment properties if they are let to unrelated third parties. Otherwise, they are no different from other assets and, therefore, fall fairly and squarely within *FRS 15*.

Redesignation of property

16.18 Where the use of a property changes, so that, for example, an investment property loses its status, the balance on the investment revaluation reserve should be transferred to the revaluation reserve for non-investment properties. It is not as easy to spot such a change as might be thought. For example, a property-holding subsidiary may let a property at arm's length to a third party. The tenant may move out and the new tenant may be a company in the same group (as the then property company). It may even take over the existing lease. Not much has changed except that, because of the *SSAP 19* definition of investment properties (see **15.11** above), the property's status would have changed.

The opposite treatment applies, of course, when the status changes the other way round.

16.19 *Depreciation*

TAXATION

16.19 There is a tendency to think that depreciation is not a particularly relevant concept for tax purposes. The following points may go some way to demonstrate that this is not the case:

- Valuation of companies – on either asset or PE bases – is clearly dependent on the net book value of assets and the accounting profitability.

- The depreciation on assets held on finance lease is effectively allowed as a trading deduction (see Chapter 17 for further details).

- Deferred tax is a concept needing to be understood. In many cases, the deferred tax provision can be very quickly reconciled as being the difference between the book net written down value of the plant, machinery, fixtures and fittings and the tax written down value (ie the balance on the capital allowances 'pool'), multiplied by the company's rate of tax.

- Tax practitioners often get involved in 'transactions'. Apart from being able to understand from the accounts and accounting information what the likely tax outcome will be, an awareness of how the resulting accounts will look is important. Transactions often involve the disposal of assets (frequently the subject of previous revaluations). The aftermath of a transaction is often a revaluation of assets on 'fair value' lines.

- Capital gains roll-over potentials need to be watched, particularly where assets are reclassified from being investment to non-investment properties (and vice versa).

- Capital gains computations themselves need careful attention where the assets have been previously revalued, particularly where there have been intra-group transfers (whether or not there have been revaluations). It is essential to understand the accounting so that tax base values can be identified and reconciled with the accounting transaction. This is especially relevant under the *FA 1994* rules in relation to the elimination of capital loss relief deriving in whole or part from indexation allowance.

- Capitalisation of finance costs will not, in HMRC's opinion, convert 'income' into capital. A trading profits deduction will be available, but only to the extent that it is included in the depreciation charge. However, *FA 1996, Sch 9, para 14* specifically confirms, in the context of the loan relationship rules, that capitalised interest will be deductible as it is incurred. This relaxation only applies in relation to corporate debt, so would not apply, for example, when the borrower was not subject to UK corporation tax (eg an individual).

Chapter 17

Acquiring Assets on Finance

17.1 In the beginning, life was simple. If a trader who wanted to buy an asset did not have the money, he borrowed from a bank or other lender and made his purchase. The asset acquired was capitalised on the balance sheet and depreciated, the borrowing was a liability shown as such on the balance sheet, and repayments subsequently made reduced the liability in stages, with additional amounts representing a finance charge (or interest) being written off against profit and loss account. Depreciation was 'added back', capital allowances were available and the finance charge allowed as a Case I deduction.

17.2 Then there was hire purchase. In common parlance, one speaks of 'buying' assets on hire purchase. Strictly, though, a hire purchase contract involves the hiree in paying regular hire charges (rent) to the hirer for a period, at the end of which the hiree has the option to purchase the asset, usually at a nominal amount. Thus, during the course of the hire purchase period, the ownership of the asset does not strictly pass, although all the characteristics of ownership – risks and rewards – do transfer to the hiree. The tax statute recognises this and *CAA 2001, s 67* provides that, for tax purposes, the asset is treated as owned by the hiree. The tax consequences are then similar to **16.19** above.

17.3 Lease financing took off in the 1960s and 1970s largely as a means of off-balance sheet financing. If an asset is acquired on borrowed money, both the asset and borrowing appear on the balance sheet. The borrowing impacts on the company's gearing ratio. In an effort to 'disguise' their true outstanding liabilities, companies entered into various types of leases relating to the assets they needed in their businesses, many of which (in the same way as hire purchase contracts) transferred effective ownership of the asset to the lessee without transferring legal ownership. Until the introduction in 1984 of *SSAP 21*, the only impact of this type of transaction on the accounts was the annual rental paid which was charged to the profit and loss account. *SSAP 21* put an end to that by providing that, where assets are 'acquired' on hire purchase or (certain types of) lease terms, then the substance of the transaction is that effective ownership of the asset passes at the outset to the user of the asset, and that it should be so accounted. This represented the conventional way of accounting for hire purchase contracts but was a

17.4 *Acquiring Assets on Finance*

significant innovation for lease contracts. Therefore, all such assets should be capitalised and all such obligations under hire purchase or (certain types of) lease contracts shown as liabilities on a company's balance sheet. There is no doubt that this rationalisation has been very much for the good. Unfortunately, some of the computational work to give effect to the standard is a little complex, and it is unfortunate that, as shall be seen, the tax (and VAT, for that matter) treatment of assets on hire purchase and lease contracts remains different.

STATEMENT OF STANDARD ACCOUNTING PRACTICE 21 (SSAP 21)

17.4 *SSAP 21* applies to assets dealt with under hire purchase or lease contracts. It concerns itself with the accounting treatment in the accounts of both lessor and lessee. The former is more complex; fortunately, the latter is encountered much more frequently in practice.

17.5 Two basic situations are recognised. First, leases under which assets are supplied, so that effective ownership is *not* passed to the user, are called operating leases. An example may be a three-year lease of a new building. At the end of the three-year period, the tenant vacates the property, and full rights in the property revert to the landlord. The accounting treatment is very straightforward. The rentals payable are charged as expenses in the profit and loss account of the lessee, and brought into the lessor's profit and loss as amounts received or receivable.

17.6 Secondly, there is recognised the situation where the user becomes the effective owner of the assets. This is so under a hire purchase contract or under what is called a finance lease. A finance lease might arise where, say, an asset is leased for five years at a rental of £10,000 per annum, and may then continue under lease for another 15 years at £1 per annum (by which time the asset will be – or will already have been – scrapped). There is no realistic prospect of the lessee handing back the asset at the end of Year 5, even if he or she has no use for the asset. If the asset has value, he or she will pay the £1 p.a. and turn that value to account (by subleasing to a third party, for example).

Assets 'acquired' under hire purchase or finance leases are capitalised and depreciated. The obligations to pay are carried on the balance sheet as liabilities. Repayments are analysed between capital and finance charges (ie interest). The finance charge is written off to the profit and loss account. The computations can be complicated, and are best illustrated by examples, several of which appear at **17.15** *et seq* below.

17.7 Conceptually, the accounting treatment of hire purchase and finance lease contracts in the lessor's accounts are very similar, yet there are

Acquiring Assets on Finance **17.13**

some computational refinements which make the arithmetic potentially more difficult (see further **17.20** below).

Definitions

17.8 The following represent definitions of the main concepts introduced by *SSAP 21*.

Lease

17.9 A lease is a contract between a lessor and a lessee for the hire of a specific asset. The lessor retains ownership of the asset but conveys the right to the use of the asset to the lessee for an agreed period of time in return for the payment of specified rentals.

Finance lease

17.10 A finance lease is a lease that transfers substantially all the risks and rewards of ownership of an asset to the lessee. It should be presumed that such a transfer of risks and rewards occurs if, at the inception of a lease, the present value of the minimum lease payments, including any initial payment, amounts to substantially all (normally 90% or more) of the fair value of the leased asset. The present value should be calculated by using the interest rate implicit in the lease (as defined in **17.13** below). If the fair value of the asset is not determinable, an estimate thereof should be used.

Operating lease

17.11 An operating lease is any lease other than a finance lease.

Lease term

17.12 The lease term is the period for which the lessee has contracted to lease the asset and any further terms for which the lessee has the option to continue to lease the asset, with or without further payment, which option it is reasonably certain at the inception of the lease that the lessee will exercise.

Interest rate implicit in a lease

17.13 The interest rate implicit in a lease is the discount rate that, at the inception of the lease, when applied to the amounts which the lessor expects to receive and retain, produces an amount (the present value) equal to the fair value of the leased asset. The amounts which the lessor expects to receive and retain comprise (*a*) the minimum lease payments to the lessor, plus (*b*)

17.14 *Acquiring Assets on Finance*

any unguaranteed residual value, less (c) any part of (a) and (b) for which the lessor will be accountable to the lessee. If the interest rate implicit in the lease is not determinable, it should be estimated by reference to the rate which a lessee would be expected to pay on a similar lease.

Fair value

17.14 The fair value is the price at which an asset could be exchanged in an arm's-length transaction less, where applicable, any grants receivable towards the purchase or use of the asset.

OPERATION OF THE STANDARD – LESSEES

17.15 Lease rentals which become due on operating leases are charged to profit and loss under the 'matching' principle. For lease rentals due on hire purchase or finance lease, the best way of illustrating the operation of the standard is to consider the following simple example:

17.16

Example 17.1
A trader whose year end is 31 December wishes to acquire an asset on 1 January which 'costs' £10,000 (in the terms of the standard, this is its 'fair value').

The asset has an anticipated economic life of five years. He acquires the asset on a lease which provides for a down payment of £2,500, followed by annual payments of £2,500 for each of the next following four years.

The asset is capitalised on the balance sheet at its 'fair value', ie £10,000. Using the straight line method, depreciation of £2,000 p.a. will be charged to profit and loss over each of the following five years.

The question remains, though, as to how much will be included in the balance sheet and profit and loss account to reflect the obligations to the lessor under the lease, both as to capital and interest. The computation proceeds as follows:

Amount Effectively Loaned	= £7,500 (10,000 fair value – 2,500 down payment)
Amount to be Repaid	= £10,000 (4 × 2,500 excluding the down payment)
Finance Charge	= £2,500 (£10,000 repayable – £7,500 'loan')
Implicit Rate of Interest	= 12.6%

That the implicit rate of interest is 12.6% is demonstrated as follows:

Acquiring Assets on Finance **17.16**

Year	Average Amount Outstanding	Interest at 12.6%	Repayment on 1 January Following
	£	£	£
1	7,500	945	(2,500)
2	5,945	749	(2,500)
3	4,194	528	(2,500)
4	2,222	278	(2,500)
5	–	–	–
		2,500	10,000

The 12.6% is a figure which can be derived from actuarial tables; in practice, various approximation techniques are used – see **17.17** and **17.18** below.

The key to preparing a table such as the one set out above is the calculation of the average amount outstanding during each period. This depends on whether the payments due under the lease are made in advance or in arrears.

Effectively, the annual rental payment of £2,500 is being split into its capital (repayment of the 'loan') and interest elements in the table above. The interest element is charged to the profit and loss account, and the capital element reduces the capital sum due in the balance sheet.

The five-year extracts from balance sheets and profit and loss accounts may now be constructed:

Profit and Loss Account

Year	1	2	3	4	5	Total
Depreciation	2,000	2,000	2,000	2,000	2,000	10,000
Interest	945	749	528	278	–	2,500
	2,945	2,749	2,528	2,278	2,000	12,500

Balance Sheets

Year	1	2	3	4	5
Leased Assets Cost	10,000	10,000	10,000	10,000	10,000
Depreciation	(2,000)	(4,000)	(6,000)	(8,000)	(10,000)
Net Book Value	8,000	6,000	4,000	2,000	Nil
Creditors	8,445	6,694	4,722	2,500	Nil

In practice, the creditors figure would be analysed between amounts due within and without 12 months, and sub-analysed between capital and accrued interest. For example, the £8,445 figure at the end of Year 1 may be analysed:

17.17 *Acquiring Assets on Finance*

Capital	1,555
Accrued Interest	945
Due Within 12 Months	2,500
Due After More Than One Year	5,945
	£8,445 (= 7,500 capital + 945 accrued interest)

Conceptually, the example above is easy to understand. The finance charge of £2,500 was very readily identified. The only difficulty is the spreading of the £2,500 over the period in a mathematically accurate way. The above example uses precisely accurate actuarial tables. Computers – or even some calculators – can effect calculations like this quite readily. *SSAP 21* permits approximations to be used. The following examples show two of the different types of approximation met in practice.

17.17 The following method of allocating the finance charge is known as the 'sum of the digits' method.

This works by determining the number of payments to be made and calculating the sum of the total number of such payments. If, for example, there are 12 payments, the sum would be $1 + 2 + 3 \ldots + 12 = 78$. If there are n payments, the sum is given by the formula $n(n + 1)/2$.

The allocation of the finance charge is then weighted according to the number of payments not yet due.

This can be illustrated in relation to the facts in *Example 17.1*.

Example 17.2
The finance charge is £2,500.

This must be apportioned over the four payments paid on the anniversary of the down payment.

There are four payments. The sum of the digits is, therefore, 10, ie $(4 \times 5) \div 2$.

The allocation to the various years is:

Instalment	Number of Rentals Not Yet Due		
1	4	× 2,500 ÷ 10 =	1,000
2	3	× 2,500 ÷ 10 =	750
3	2	× 2,500 ÷ 10 =	500
4	1	× 2,500 ÷ 10 =	250
			2,500

17.18 An even greater simplification would be to allocate the finance charge on a straight line basis. On the facts of *Example 17.2*, this would lead to an allocation of £625, ie 2,500 ÷ 4, finance charge for each of the first four years.

17.19 A comparison of the three methods of allocation can be made thus:

Allocation of Finance Charge

Year	1	2	3	4	Total
Actuarial Basis	945	749	528	278	2,500
Sum of Digits	1,000	750	500	250	2,500
Straight Line	625	625	625	625	2,500

In general, the 'sum of the digits' basis is regarded as a sufficiently accurate approximation of the more precise actuarial basis. The straight line basis is not really acceptable, and should only be used when considering numbers that are relatively immaterial so that variations from the more precise basis would be too small to give any concern.

OPERATION OF THE STANDARD – LESSORS

17.20 For operating leases, the lease rentals due are taken to profit and loss as they arise. But, for hire purchase or finance leases, the computations are more difficult than that for lessees. This is because *SSAP 21* requires that the lessor should spread the finance charge in its profit and loss account in a way which fully reflects the lessor's cash investment in the asset at a particular time.

If a lessor buys an asset to lease, his cash investment is not only his immediate monetary outlay. He may receive 'credits' in the form of grants or accelerated tax allowances. He may also be making a profit on 'sale' of the asset itself, in addition to a financing profit.

17.21 A calculation is required which measures the effective capital outlay, after adjusting for all such items, and computing therefrom the implicit rate of interest. That rate is applied to the average capital invested in each accounting period to determine the amount of the finance charge to be taken to profit for that year.

The calculations can be horrendous. No useful purpose is presently served by taking this matter further.

17.22 In February 1997, an amendment was made to *SSAP 21* for lessors in receipt of tax-free grants. For accounting periods ending after 22 June

17.23 *Acquiring Assets on Finance*

1997, such grants should be treated as non-taxable income. Previously, *SSAP 21* permitted the grant to be 'grossed up' by the notional tax, thus enhancing profits before tax.

DISCLOSURES

17.23 Fairly extensive disclosure requirements were introduced by *SSAP 21*. Although the leased assets are capitalised, they are to be shown as a separate category to the straightforwardly owned assets. Alternatively, they may be integrated, but equivalent information on the leased assets must in this case be disclosed by note. The notes to the profit and loss account should analyse the depreciation charge between the owned assets and those on lease and hire purchase. Liabilities under finance lease and hire purchase contracts should be separately disclosed in creditors, and analysed as described in *Example 17.1* above.

PROBLEM AREAS

17.24 One of the main practical problems can be in distinguishing between operating and finance leases. Document titles can be misleading. Apparently contradictory titles such as 'Lease Purchase' appear.

Any arrangement giving the lessee the option to purchase from the lessor at the end of a period is a hire purchase agreement.

Any other arrangement needs careful scrutiny. The general temptation is for leasing companies and their clients to argue that the arrangements they have entered into represent operating and not finance leases (thereby allowing the asset and the related liability to be excluded from the balance sheet in order to reduce the impact on the company's gearing, as discussed in **17.3** above). Careful reading of the documentation and the small print of *SSAP 21* is needed before acquiescing to this view.

17.25 Leasing contracts can be complicated documents. It is not unusual for the terms to include a number of 'contingency' payment provisions, for example excess mileage charges in vehicle leases. The general rule is that only the minimum lease payments are taken into account in the calculations set out above. Any additional amounts due are accounted for when due (or when it is reasonable to assume that they will become due).

17.26 Accounting for leases continues to be the topic of debate and research. It is possible that future changes to accounting standards will result in the concept of operating leases being abolished, such that all leases (even short-term hire contracts) would result in property rights being reflected on the lessee's balance sheet.

Acquiring Assets on Finance **17.29**

17.27 It must not be overlooked that *FRS 5* (the 'substance over form' standard – see Chapter 6) may also apply to leases or other lease-related arrangements which do not fit squarely within *SSAP 21*. A particular example would be a sale and leaseback in which there are features providing that the leased asset is likely to be reacquired at the end of the lease period. *FRS 5* would require such a transaction – which takes the form of a lease – to be accounted for as merely a financing operation.

COMPARISON WITH INTERNATIONAL ACCOUNTING STANDARDS

17.28 *IAS 17* 'Leases' is similar to *SSAP 21* in many respects. However, there are two important differences.

First, *SSAP 21* places considerable emphasis on the so-called '90% test' (referred to in **17.10** above); *IAS 17* has no equivalent test. Instead, leases are classified as finance or operating, based on whether or not the terms of the lease transfer substantially all the risks and rewards of 'ownership' from the lessor to the lessee. The standard specifies a number of characteristics of finance leases, and an overall assessment needs to be made at the date of the lease's inception as to whether the terms of the lease, taken as a whole, indicate that the lease should be accounted for as a finance lease or an operating lease. This greater weight given to the other terms of the lease is likely to lead to some leases that have been classified as operating leases under *SSAP 21* being reclassified as finance leases under *IAS 17*.

Secondly, *IAS 17* requires a single lease of land and buildings to be split into two separate elements – one for the land and one for the buildings – and for each element to be separately classified as finance or operating. One of the characteristics of a finance lease given by the standard is that the lease term is for a major part of the economic life of the asset. This generally results in the land element of the lease being classified as an operating lease, whereas the buildings element is more frequently classified as a finance lease. The splitting of one lease into two elements, and accounting for each element differently, is a potential source of considerable confusion.

TAXATION

Hire purchase

17.29 The tax treatment is straightforward and non-contentious. *CAA 2001, s 67* provides that any agreement under which the hiree has an option to acquire the asset at the end of a period is a hire purchase contract, whether or not the option is exercised. Under *s 67*, for all tax purposes the asset is deemed to be owned by the hiree. If he or she does not exercise this option, the hiree has effectively 'disposed' of the asset.

17.30 *Acquiring Assets on Finance*

Operating leases

17.30 Again, the tax treatment is non-contentious. Payments becoming due under the lease, providing normal criteria are satisfied, qualify for tax deduction.

Finance leases

17.31 HMRC takes the view that the legal form of the transaction is that ownership remains with the lessor. Therefore, the correct tax treatment is to give a deduction for the rental payments made.

However, the view is that, on the accruals or matching concept, the rental payments should be spread over the period during which the trader will benefit from the use of the asset. This may extend well past the primary rental period and into the period during which only nominal amounts of rent are payable. For example, for an asset of value £10,000, a lease contract may provide for £4,000 p.a. to be paid for three years, and £1 p.a. thereafter for 20 years. If the life of the asset was 10 years, HMRC would want to spread the £12,000 on some basis or other over 10 years. In April 1991, the Revenue issued Statement of Practice SP3/91, in which they confirm that the spreading arrangements required under *SSAP 21* will be acceptable. In other words, the depreciation and interest charges which are charged to the profit and loss account annually under *SSAP 21* will be allowed as deductions. So, to the extent that subjectivity plays a part in estimating the useful life of an asset, and the particular depreciation policy (straight line, straight percentage etc) adopted, a trader can determine his own tax deduction.

The lessor is regarded as the owner of the leased asset for tax purposes and is entitled to capital allowances accordingly. See below, however, in relation to long funding leases.

The financing of cars

17.32 There are two simple rules to remember.

First, no VAT arises in the provision of hire purchase finance. So, if a car is 'bought' on hire purchase, the only VAT is the (irrecoverable unless no private use) VAT on the purchase price of the car. If a car is 'bought' on lease – whether operating or finance – VAT is chargeable on the rentals. Generally after 1 August 1995, a lessor will be able to recover the VAT on acquisition. However, he will charge VAT on lease rentals. Most registered traders will be able to claim 50% of this VAT back, whilst exempt (or partly exempt) traders will not be able (or only partly be able) to make a reclaim. The '50% rule' is rough and ready, but equitable if a trader changes his car about once every three years (when its depreciated value is about half the original cost). The lessor's ability to reclaim the VAT makes lease/buy decisions neutral from the VAT perspective for exempt traders.

Secondly, there are special rules for 'expensive' cars. Up until 5 April 2009 (31 March for companies), there were restrictions for cars costing more than £12,000. Under a hire purchase agreement, the capital cost of the car qualified for capital allowances up to a limit of £3,000 p.a. However, when the car was eventually sold, a balancing adjustment was made so that the total depreciation suffered over the period of ownership was allowed as a tax deduction. The finance charge for such 'expensive' cars may be (but is not usually) restricted. On the other hand, for leased assets, the whole of the lease charge is subject to restriction. The effective disallowance for leased 'expensive' cars is necessarily more than that for such assets 'bought' under hire purchase. *FA 2009* changed this position, and now there is a limitation based on the level of CO2 emissions.

Long funding leases

17.33 The concept of long funding leases was introduced in *FA 2006, Sch 8* and applies with effect from 1 April 2006. Where a lease is classified as a long funding lease, the lessor company is taxed on the finance element of the lease rentals as income. The lessee is then entitled to deduct the finance component of the rentals and is also entitled to capital allowances, but only if not claimed by the lessor. It is an optional regime, and both the lessee and lessor can decide not to apply it, thus remaining subject to the normal finance lease tax rules.

Chapter 18

Provisions and Contingencies

18.1 Accounting for provisions and contingencies is covered by *FRS 12* 'Provisions, Contingent Liabilities and Contingent Assets', which was introduced in 1998. It was developed in parallel with the equivalent international accounting standard, *IAS 37*.

18.2 The driving force behind the approach to provisioning was the desire to curb the perceived abuse known as 'big bath' provisions. This occurred when, for example, Company A took over Company B, and at the point of takeover, large provisions were made for 'reorganisations'. This had the effect of increasing the apparent goodwill on purchase (written off direct to reserves – a practice now not possible under *FRS 10*) and inflating post-acquisition profits, as later costs could be charged to the provision (often without adequate disclosure, so that trading results appeared to be dramatically improved under the new management).

18.3 The overall impact of the standard was to restrict the circumstances in which provisions were permitted, compared to previous practice, and to increase disclosures. The former impact was considered to be contentious, as it appeared that the prudence concept was being down-graded, and the standard was the subject of significant opposition.

18.4 It was also recognised that the concept of a provision overlapped to some extent with the concept of a contingency and, unless these two were brought together under a single head, there might be room for companies to be influenced as to whether an item was a provision or contingency, depending upon the alternative accounting treatments.

FINANCIAL REPORTING STANDARD 12 (FRS 12)

Provisions

18.5 Provisions can be distinguished from other liabilities (such as trade creditors and accruals) because there is uncertainty as to the timing or amount of future expenditure required in settlement.

18.6 The key definitions in *FRS 12* are summarised below.

Provisions

A provision should be recognised when:

(1) an entity has a present obligation (legal or constructive) as a result of a past event;

(2) it is probable that a transfer of economic benefits will be required to settle the obligation; and

(3) a reliable estimate can be made of the amount of the obligation.

Unless these conditions are met, no provision should be made.

Present obligation

A present obligation is one that exists at the balance sheet date and the entity has no realistic alternative to settling that obligation.

Legal obligation

An obligation that derives from a contract or legislation.

Constructive obligation

An obligation that derives from past practice or published policies, such that a valid expectation is created on the part of third parties that the entity will discharge certain responsibilities.

Past event

The event giving rise to the obligation occurred prior to the balance sheet date.

Probable transfer of economic benefits

A transfer of economic benefits is considered to be probable if it is more likely than not (ie a probability of more than 50%).

Reliable estimate

FRS 12 acknowledges that the use of estimates is an essential part of the preparation of financial statements and that this is particularly so for provisions that are, by their nature, more uncertain than other balance sheet items. However, the standard explicitly states that a sufficiently reliable estimate should be capable of being made, except in extremely rare cases.

The standard anticipates that estimates will be calculated using a weighted average of the range of possible outcomes and their likely financial impact.

18.7 *Provisions and Contingencies*

18.7 When the standard refers to a provision being recognised, it means that the liability should be reflected in the balance sheet. This is only permitted when all the conditions in 18.6 above are satisfied at the balance sheet date.

Essentially, what this means is that a company cannot just look forward and see that it will incur an expense next year, and therefore provide for it this year. It should only provide this year if it is already legally or constructively committed to it.

18.8 Three particular situations are identified:

- No provisions should be made for future operating losses. This includes situations where loss-making operations are planned to be closed – the future operating losses are reflected in the profit and loss account as and when incurred. It was not uncommon for provisions to be made for future operating losses, particularly following a corporate takeover or change in management, prior to *FRS 12*.

- However, a net loss on an onerous contract (one which will inevitably result in a loss and for which the company would be liable to pay compensation if the contract was unfulfilled) should be provided for. To be classed as an onerous contract, the unavoidable costs (being the lower of the cost of exiting the contract and the cost of fulfilling the contract) must exceed the economic benefits expected to be received under the contract. Examples include unavoidable payments under a lease that is no longer being used in the business, such as vacant leasehold premises, contracts to sell products at a loss, or contracts to purchase products in excessive quantities or at prices that will result in a loss being made on use or sale. Provision should only be made for the *least net* cost option.

- Provisions for restructuring of the entity's operations should only be made when the organisation is demonstrably committed to the reorganisation and cannot realistically withdraw. As a minimum, this requires a detailed plan to have been approved by the directors and for the implementation of the plan to have been started or announced to those affected by it prior to the balance sheet date. (If these conditions are not met until after the balance sheet date, then no provision should be made but, instead, disclosure should be made by way of a post-balance sheet event note to the financial statements.) Provision should only be made for direct expenditure necessarily arising from the reorganisation and not associated with the continuing activities of the entity. Therefore, provision must not be made for costs such as retraining or relocating continuing staff – these costs will be reflected in the profit and loss account when incurred, as part of the profit or loss on continuing activities.

18.9 The requirements of *FRS 12* mean that the common previous practice of building up provisions for future expenditure, such as repairs and maintenance expenditure, over a number of years is no longer permitted on the grounds that there is no present obligation at the balance sheet date. However,

Provisions and Contingencies **18.16**

provision can still be made for warranties and sales returns, as the obligating event is considered to be the sale of the products in question.

18.10 In summary, *FRS 12* restricts the circumstances in which provisions are permitted to be made compared to previous practice.

18.11 *FRS 12* requires extensive disclosure relating to provisions, including, for each class of provision, a reconciliation of the movements between the balance sheet dates, and narrative disclosure of the nature of the obligation and an indication of the uncertainties about the amount and timing. Provisions need to be reviewed at each balance sheet date and adjusted to reflect the current best estimate. The standard also requires that a provision is only used for expenditure for which the provision was originally created. Whilst this may seem obvious, it was not always the case in the past!

18.12 There will be occasions when making the disclosures required by the standard could be seriously prejudicial to the interests of the entity, for example when the entity is in dispute with another party and legal action is pending. In such 'extremely rare' cases, only the general nature of the dispute needs to be given, together with the reasons why.

18.13 The Appendices to *FRS 12* give extensive guidance on the application of the standard, including a decision tree to assist in distinguishing between provisions and contingent liabilities, and numerous examples of situations where provisions may be required and illustrative disclosure notes.

Contingent liabilities

18.14 The basic idea is that, when conditions exist at year end such that the outcome of a situation will only be confirmed by future uncertain events that are not wholly within the entity's control, then this is termed a contingent liability. Essentially, this only applies to one-off situations, not to the normal uncertainties inherent in accounting estimates (such as economic lives of fixed assets, net realisable amount of stocks etc), for example, a pending court case against the company.

18.15 The term 'contingent liability' also applies where a provision has not been made because it is not probable that a transfer of economic benefits will be required (ie a probability of less than 50%), or the amount is not capable of accurate quantification (in extremely rare circumstances). In other words, contingent liabilities are 'provisions' that failed one or more of the conditions in **18.6** above.

18.16 Contingent liabilities should not be recognised in the balance sheet, but disclosure needs to be made. If the possibility of loss is remote, no provision or disclosure is needed.

18.17 *Provisions and Contingencies*

Contingent assets

18.17 Contingent assets are defined as possible assets that arise from past events and whose existence will be confirmed only by the occurrence of future uncertain events not wholly within the entity's control.

Contingent assets should not be recognised in the balance sheet. Disclosure by way of a note is required where an inflow of economic benefits is probable (ie a probability of more than 50%). The prudence concept drives the lack of symmetry with the treatment of provisions and contingent losses.

INTERNATIONAL ACCOUNTING STANDARDS

18.18 The international standard dealing with provision is *IAS 37* 'Provisions, Contingent Liabilities and Contingent Assets'. There are no appreciable differences between this and *FRS 12*.

TAXATION CONSIDERATIONS

18.19 Prior to 1998, accounts which contain provisions for contingent losses were almost invariably the subject of discussion with the Revenue who rarely permitted, at least in the first instance, a deduction for corporation tax purposes of the amount provided.

18.20 The Revenue's authority for its view was based on the case of *Spencer (James) & Co v IRC* CS 1950, 32 TC 111. In this case, a company claimed that, as soon as an accident was suffered by an employee, a liability to pay compensation arose, even though liability might not have then been admitted. An estimate of such liabilities was included in its accounts as a deduction from profits. The Court of Session (the case went no further) held the deduction was appropriate to the year in which the principle of liability was established or admitted. Thus, the taxpayer company lost its case.

The first comment to make is that the appeal was heard well before the publication of *SSAP 18*, and no expert accountancy evidence was given. The Lord President was clearly feeling his way when he said: 'I use the vague word "established" advisedly for we are now in the region of proper commercial and accountancy practice rather than of systematic jurisprudence'. With hindsight, it is a great pity that he was not aided in this respect. In later cases (*Southern Railway of Peru Ltd v Owen (Inspector of Taxes)* HL 1956, [1957] AC 334 and *CIR v Titaghur Jute Factory Ltd* CS 1978, 53 TC 675), House of Lords dicta have indicated that *Spencer* should *not* be regarded as laying down any general principle or rule of law.

The issue of *FRS 12* in 1998 changed this view, by providing a complete code of when provisions must be made and when not, as well as rules for quantification of provisions. HMRC's Business Income Manual (BIM 46535) observes that:

'FRS 12 does not change our view of tax law, but it clearly has changed GAAP. In particular, many provisions, which formerly accorded with GAAP, will no longer do so. It follows that those provisions, even if they were formerly allowable for tax purposes, will no longer be.'

For tax purposes, the deductibility of provisions is subject to the capital/revenue distinction, as well as adjustment for disallowable expenditure.

Chapter 19

Pensions

19.1 This is a very important and controversial area of accounting. Employers' responsibilities for pension fund deficits and what they can do (legally and illegally) with surpluses is topical and contentious. Liabilities can pass from one employer to another (in takeover situations) by agreement or by operation of law. This aspect of the legal system (both national and EC) is in a state of development and the position is not always clear. In any takeover where there is in existence a defined benefit scheme (as defined below), potential pension fund liabilities are a major point of concern.

SSAP 24 was introduced in 1988. As companies adopted its provisions, the Revenue became worried that the tax law and practice in relation to the deductibility of pension contributions by employers might be disturbed. Changes were incorporated in *FA 1993* to negate this possibility. In November 2000, *FRS 17* replaced *SSAP 24*.

19.2 The adoption of *FRS 17* reflects an important shift in view on how pensions should be accounted for. The old view is that pension costs should be matched against the period of employee service to give an even charge. One consequence of this, however, is that it leads to a misleading view of a company's financial position. More recent thinking, for both the ASB and IASB, is that the focus should shift to ensuring that the company's financial position is less misleading, although it is recognised that this could lead to some variation over time in the pension costs taken to the profit and loss account.

19.3 Defined contribution schemes, where a percentage of salary is contributed, giving certainty as to costs but considerable uncertainty as to future benefits, created few difficulties for accounting. It is defined benefit schemes, where the cost to the employer is uncertain, that are more problematic and require actuarial assessment of cost.

STATEMENT OF STANDARD ACCOUNTING PRACTICE 24 (SSAP 24)

19.4 *SSAP 24* was essentially an application of the matching concept under the old view of accounting for pensions. The accounting objective was that the employer should recognise the expected cost of providing pensions on a systematic and rational basis over the period during which he derived benefit from the employees' services. It applied where there were both contractual and non-contractual (ie ex gratia) arrangements. Pensions included other post-retirement benefits, but not social security or redundancy payments.

FINANCIAL REPORTING STATEMENT 17 (FRS 17)

19.5 The objective of *FRS 17* is to ensure that the financial statements reflect the assets and liabilities related to an employer's retirement benefit obligations and their funding at fair value, and that the operating costs of provision of retirement benefits are recognised in the period in which the benefits are earned by the employees. This gives rise to two issues: the way that scheme assets and liabilities are calculated; and the way that pension costs are calculated.

19.6 Valuation of assets and liabilities under *FRS 17* is different from that under *SSAP 24*. Essentially, assets are valued at fair value (compared to actuarial valuation), and liabilities are discounted using the current rate of return on AA rated corporate bonds (compared to expected rate of return on scheme assets). A pension scheme surplus or deficit is recognised in full in the company's balance sheet. The movement in the scheme surplus or deficit is analysed into:

- current service cost – recognised in the profit and loss account within operating profit;
- interest cost and expected return on assets – recognised as a net financial item in the profit and loss account; and
- actuarial gains and losses – recognised in the STRGL.

Actuarial gains or losses arise as a result of either changes in the present value of the defined benefit obligation, or changes in the market value of the pension plan assets.

19.7 The introduction of *FRS 17* was controversial and, in August 2006, the FRRP published the findings of a review into disclosures of defined benefit pension schemes. The levels of compliance with *FRS 17* (or *IAS 19* – see below) were high, in particular in relation to *FRS 17*.

INTERNATIONAL ACCOUNTING STANDARD 19 (IAS 19)

19.8 Following amendment in 1998, *IAS 19* now uses an asset or liability approach that requires the pension fund to be valued regularly. The one area where there is a difference between *FRS 17* and *IAS 19* is actuarial gains. Under *IAS 19*, actuarial gains can be dealt with in two ways:

19.9 *Pensions*

- *The 10% corridor approach* – if the actuarial gains or losses are more than 10% of the present value of the defined benefit obligations or more than 10% of the market value of the plan assets, then the excess gains or losses are taken into the income statement spread over the average remaining lives of current employees. If they are less than 10%, they can be recognised in the income statement.

- *The 'equity recognition' approach* – under this approach, it is acceptable to recognise the actuarial gain or loss immediately in the profit or loss. The downside of this approach is that it may create volatility in the statement of financial performance.

It is the ability to spread forward the actuarial gains or losses in excess of the 10% corridor that is the key difference between the standards.

TAXATION

19.9　It is easy to overlook the taxation consequences arising in relation to the accounting for pension liabilities. Matters to be borne in mind include:

- Deductions for trading profit purposes for approved pension schemes are given on a payments basis and not an accruals basis (*FA 2004, s 196*). Considerable timing differences (and hence deferred tax) can arise due to the differing tax and accounting bases.

- Provision is made for the deduction to be spread over a number of periods in certain circumstances. Spreading of deductions may be required under *FA 2004, s 197* where there is an increase over 210% in the level of employer contribution from one period to the next.

- Particular problems can arise with ex gratia payments on termination of employment. These are covered in the Revenue Statement of Practice *SP 13/91*.

- The proper provision for pension scheme liabilities (or even assets) is essential for valuation purposes.

- In passing, it is worth alluding to the VAT status of pension schemes. Particularly in the smaller company scheme, the person running the company and the main trustee of the pension scheme might be one and the same individual. The pension scheme may own (possibly on a sale and lease-back arrangement) the property from which the company trades. It is important to ensure that, if it can, the pension scheme registers for VAT and that all pension scheme costs (including audit etc) are invoiced in the name of, and paid by, the pension scheme, and not the name of the company.

Chapter 20

Employee Share Ownership Plans

20.1 This is a big topic, with both accounting and taxation aspects which are controversial. Many companies set up share schemes through vehicles known as Employee Share Ownership Plans (ESOPs). Typically, these are ways of rewarding employees in the form of shares in their employer company, often with tax benefits attached to them. That company sets up a trust (the ESOP), and transfers cash to the trustees, who then acquire shares in the employer company. In due course, those shares are distributed to employees.

Share-based payments are problematic from an accounting viewpoint. The question arises, in the case of employees, whether they are given in their capacity as shareholders, or as employees. If the former, then arguably no charge should be made to the profit and loss account or income statement. If the latter, then the cost should be recognised as a reward for employment, along with other forms of employee remuneration. This latter view has prevailed in both UK and international accounting standards. But, having decided to recognise a charge on share-based payments, a number of consequential issues arise, such as how should they be valued, when, and over what period of time?

UK GAAP

20.2 When *FRS 5* was published, observers wondered whether the assets held by the trustees, pending distribution to employees, should be regarded as 'assets' of the sponsoring company. On the face of it, that might appear to conflict with the company law requirement that a company cannot hold shares in itself.

20.3 It was to deal with this company law problem that *UITF Abstract 13* was published. Its principal thrust was to explain that, although it may be contrary to company law for a company to own shares in itself, it was not illegal for a company to show as an asset in its own balance sheet the 'asset' – represented perhaps by shares in itself held by ESOP trustees – being the future benefit the company enjoys from the workforce motivated to earn the right to have the shares appropriated to them. *UITF Abstract 17*, entitled 'Employee Share Schemes', was issued in October 2000 and subsequently

20.4 Employee Share Ownership Plans

revised in 2003, and was concerned with the measurement and timing of the charge to be recognised by companies in the profit and loss account.

20.4 *FRS 20* was issued in April 2004 and supersedes *UITF Abstracts 13* and *17*. It is mandatory for accounting periods beginning on or after 1 January 2005 for listed entities, and 1 January 2006 for unlisted entities (other than those applying FRSSE – see Chapter 10). The standard specifies the accounting treatment for share-based payments, which includes all types of executive and employee share option and purchase plans, as well as transactions with suppliers of goods and services by way of share-based payments.

20.5 *FRS 20* recognises three types of share-based payment, and sets out measurement principles for each. These are:

- equity-settled share-based payment transactions, where the entity receives goods or services in return for 'equity instruments';
- cash-settled share-based payment transactions, where the liability to a supplier of goods or services is based on the prices of the entity's 'equity instruments'; and
- transactions for which, in return for goods or services, the choice is given as to settlement by cash or by issue of 'equity instruments'.

For equity-settled transactions, fair value is used as the measurement principle, and the timing is related to the date the entity obtains the goods or the services are rendered. In the case of employee services, however, the fair value as at the grant date is used. The rationale for using the grant date is that it is at that time that the value of the shares most closely aligns with the services for which they are a reward. If there is not a market price, then an appropriate valuation technique can be used. In estimating the fair value, vesting conditions (see below) are not to be taken into account.

20.6 *FRS 20* requires that, where share options are granted to employees, the value of the options is to be treated as an expense over the period in which services are received from employees in exchange for the options. Sometimes, conditions are put on the exercise of the options, referred to as 'vesting conditions'. If there are no vesting conditions, the expense is recognised immediately. If there are such conditions – for example, employees may be required to continue working for the entity for a specified period of time or meet certain performance targets – then the expense is spread, usually over the period until such time as the options are exercised. There is also a possibility that the options may be cancelled, either by the employer or by the employee.

If the vesting conditions are not met, the cost in the profit and loss account is reversed, ie the options are treated as not having been granted in the first instance. Where the options are cancelled by the employer, all unamortised costs are immediately recognised.

INTERNATIONAL STANDARDS

20.7 The international standard dealing with employee benefits, *IAS 19*, only covered disclosure requirement for share-based payments. It did not deal with questions of measurement of payments and timing of recognition. In February 2004, the IASB issued *IFRS 2* 'Share-based Payment'. *FRS 20* and *IFRS 2* adopt the same approach to share-based payments.

TAXATION CONSIDERATIONS

20.8 For tax purposes, the accounting treatment of employee share schemes is irrelevant. Earlier confusion about the treatment of employee share schemes was dealt with by legislation, specifically *FA 2003, Sch 23*, which provides a specific tax deduction for providing employees with shares which satisfy certain qualifying conditions.

The deduction is the same, whatever method is used to fund the employee share schemes; it does not make any difference whether a trust is used in conjunction with a scheme, whether new shares are issued, or whether existing shares are purchased in the market.

The statutory deduction, therefore, overrides the accounting treatment. For periods starting on or after 1 January 2003, this is the exclusive statutory provision for tax deductions relating to share-based payments to employees.

Chapter 21

Government Grants

21.1 Government grants may take a variety of forms, to cover specific items of expenditure or to fund the acquisition of certain property, plant or equipment. They may be in monetary form, or non-monetary form. Accounting for Government grants is reasonably straightforward, since it is usually clear what the purpose of the grant is and any conditions that may attach to it.

UK GAAP

21.2 In April 1974, the ASC published *SSAP 4 'The Accounting Treatment of Government Grants'*. This was subsequently revised in July 1990, when its scope was widened to embrace the accounting treatment of all forms of government (local, national and international) assistance, including grants, equity finance, subsidised loans and advisory assistance.

Concepts

21.3 The principles underlying *SSAP 4* represent an application of the accruals concept, tempered with a measure of prudence. The main thrust of the standard is the 'matching' of the grant or other assistance with the expenditure to which it relates, with some circumstances (such as the possible repayment of grants) being accounted for on a prudent basis, ie refrain from anticipating revenue and profits before they can be recognised.

Revenue-based grants

21.4 Where a grant is received as a contribution to a specific revenue expenditure, it should be taken to the profit and loss account. If the expenditure spans more than one accounting period, then an appropriate part of the grant should be carried on the balance sheet as deferred income, and released to profit and loss as the expenditure to which it relates is incurred.

Where expenditure has been incurred and a grant is expected but not yet received, then, providing that the ultimate receipt is reasonably certain, the amount of grant receivable should be taken to the profit and loss account and treated as a current asset in the balance sheet.

There can be circumstances in which the grant is made available for the purpose of achieving a particular objective, such as the creation of a specified number of jobs, and the precise expenditure to which it relates is not uniquely defined. *SSAP 4* requires that an assessment of the expenditure incurred on achieving the objective be made and the grant matched with that.

Capital-based grants

21.5 Capital-based grants are to be taken to the balance sheet and amortised over the expected useful life of the asset attracting the grant. *SSAP 4* recognises two ways of achieving this objective:

- the grant is treated in the balance sheet as a separate asset (deferred income) and credited to profit and loss on a basis consistent with the asset depreciation policy; or

- the grant is deducted from the purchase/production price of the relevant asset and depreciation is based on the net amount.

Although these two alternatives are recognised, it is further commented that the latter treatment probably offends against the *CA 1985* fundamental accounting concept of 'no off-set' (see **5.5** above). In practice, therefore, it is rare to see anything other than the first of these alternatives adopted.

Repayments

21.6 Some forms of assistance are potentially repayable. If this is the case, then so long as the possibility of repayment exists, a note to the accounts should explain and quantify this contingent liability (contingent liabilities are covered in Chapter 18).

When the repayment of a grant becomes probable, prudence dictates that it should be provided for immediately. Where only part of the grant has thus far been credited to profit and loss – and there is, in consequence, a balance remaining on the balance sheet under the heading 'deferred income', then the amount probably repayable is first used to reduce the deferred income account and only the balance charged against the current year profit and loss account.

INTERNATIONAL STANDARDS

21.7 *IAS 20* 'Accounting for Government Grants and Disclosure of Government Assistance' deals with the recognition, measurement and disclosure of Government grants and other forms of Government assistance, and adopts the same approach as *SSAP 4*.

Following concerns about the standard's consistency with both the IFRS *Framework* and US GAAP, the IASB decided to amend *IAS 20* in February 2004, to bring it into line with *IAS 41* 'Agriculture'. Following discussion of

21.8 *Government Grants*

specific issues arising from this in July of that year, in February 2006 it was decided to defer further work on *IAS 20* pending progress on other related projects. In December 2007, the IASB further discussed accounting for Government grants in the context of the Emissions Trading Scheme project, but decided to limit the latter's scope rather than attempt to deal with all Government grants. The project on *IAS 20* remains inactive at the time of writing.

TAXATION CONSIDERATIONS

21.8 The UK tax law follows the accounting treatment where the grant is treated as income rather than capital. In the case of capital grants, the tax treatment of grants and other assistance is determined by other factors than the way in which they are accounted for. The legislation making the grants available is frequently associated with rules which determine their tax status, and if not, there remains some room for debate as to the precise tax treatment which is appropriate (cf *Seaham Harbour Dock Co v Crook (Inspector of Taxes)* HL 1931, (1931) 41 L1 LRep 95).

Probably the greatest difficulty to the tax practitioner is actually understanding, from the accounts, precisely what is going on. There now follows a series of examples to illustrate the principles discussed in the paragraphs above.

Revenue grant relating to current year

21.9

Example 21.1
A company incurs £10,000 expenditure in the year in respect of a marketing exercise, for which a grant of £5,000 was received. There is no balance sheet consequence. The profit and loss account in summary form for the year would appear:

Profit and Loss Account

	£
TURNOVER	500,000
Gross Profit	200,000
Distribution Costs	(50,000)
Administrative Expenses (including 10,000 marketing costs)	(60,000)
Other Operating Income (being the grant)	5,000
Net Profit	95,000

Government Grants **21.10**

If the £5,000 had been received by the year end, it would have been included in the bank balance. If it had not yet been received, it would be included in the balance sheet under the heading of debtors.

Revenue grant relating to expenditure over several years

21.10

Example 21.2
The same company in fact undertakes a bigger marketing project, costing £50,000, for which it will receive a grant of £25,000 in total. At the year end, only £20,000 had been incurred and nothing had actually yet been received. The accounts would look like:

		£
TURNOVER		500,000
Gross Profit		200,000
Distribution Costs		(50,000)
Administrative Expenses (including 20,000 marketing costs)		(70,000)
Other Operating Income (being the grant)		10,000
Net Profit		90,000
	£	£
Fixed Assets		1,000,000
Current Assets (including grants receivable 10,000)	300,000	
Current Liabilities	(200,000)	
Net Current Assets		100,000
Total Assets		1,100,000
Share Capital		100,000
Profit and Loss		1,000,000
		1,100,000

The example appears straightforward. As only £20,000 has been incurred and that will attract a grant of £10,000 ultimately, the net expense of £10,000 is debited to the profit and loss account. That part of the grant receivable referable to the expenditure incurred is included on the balance sheet as a debtor.

21.11 *Government Grants*

Capital-based grant

21.11

Example 21.3
A company buys a machine for £100,000 which it depreciates at 25% p.a. (on original cost), thereby writing the asset off over four years. It receives a grant of £40,000 in respect of the purchase. The accounts reflecting this are:

	£
TURNOVER	1,000,000
Gross Profit	200,000
Depreciation	(25,000)
Grant Receivable	10,000
Net Profit	185,000
	£
Fixed Assets (including machine at depreciated cost 75,000)	500,000
Net Current Assets	100,000
Accruals and Deferred Income (being unamortised balance of the grant)	(30,000)
Total Assets	570,000
Share Capital	100,000
Profit and Loss	470,000
	570,000

Capital-based grant – grant repayable

21.12

Example 21.4
The same facts as *Example 21.3* exist, but at the beginning of Year 2, it is discovered that a term of the grant assistance has been breached and, after discussion, £35,000 is paid back by the company. The accounts at the end of Year 2 would look like:

	£
TURNOVER	1,200,000
Gross Profit	250,000
Depreciation	(25,000)
Grant Repayable	(5,000)
Net Profit	220,000

	£
Fixed Assets (including machine at depreciated cost 50,000)	475,000
Net Current Assets	315,000
Accruals and Deferred Income	Nil
Total Assets	790,000
Share Capital	100,000
Profit and Loss	690,000
	790,000

The £35,000 repayable first reduces the anticipated future credits to the profit and loss account (the £30,000 deferred income), with the balance of £5,000 being charged to the profit and loss account. The net charge to profit and loss has been a credit of £5,000 (+ £10,000 − £5,000) which correctly corresponds to the ultimate net grant received (£40,000 − £35,000).

FRS 3 specifically requires that, if the amounts are material, they should be disclosed as exceptional.

Chapter 22

Accounting for Tax

22.1 The relationship between accounting profit and tax profit is complicated, and this is reflected in the debates about how best to represent a company's tax liabilities in its financial statements. Accounting for VAT is straightforward, as shown below. Accounting for tax on profits, corporation tax in the UK, or income tax under international accounting standards, is more difficult because of the different way in which the two systems, accounting and tax, calculate annual profit. This difference creates a need to segregate a company's tax liability in the financial statements into two components: current tax and deferred tax. In this chapter, accounting for VAT is discussed briefly before moving on to the more difficult issue of accounting for corporate income tax.

ACCOUNTING FOR VAT

Statement of Standard Accounting Practice 5 (SSAP 5)

22.2 In essence, the position with regard to accounting for VAT is very simple.

Turnover should be reported net of recoverable VAT. Irrecoverable input VAT should be attributed to the relevant expenditure and included as part of its cost. Amounts owing to or from HMRC should be included in the balance sheet under the heading of creditors ('other creditors including taxation and social security') or debtors, as appropriate.

22.3 The only real problems arise in relation to those companies which are partially exempt for VAT purposes.

Where an expense can be uniquely attributed to a supply, then the character of the expense (and its related VAT) is determined by the nature of the supply. Some input VAT is not directly attributable, and an apportionment of non-attributable VAT needs to be made to standard (or zero) rated supplies, on the one hand, and exempt supplies on the other. That part attributed to exempt supplies will be irrecoverable.

22.4 The attribution described above is in relation not only to revenue or expense items, but also to capital items. For example, an insurance broker may have a computer system which services both his normal commission-based work (basically exempt) and also his advisory work, for which he renders a charge (basically standard-rated). It is necessary in this case to agree an apportionment with HMRC, and only a proportion of the input tax on acquisition is reclaimable. The non-reclaimable VAT should be treated as an additional part of the cost price of (in this case) the computer, and depreciated in the normal way.

ACCOUNTING FOR CORPORATE INCOME TAX

22.5 There are two UK standards that deal with accounting for income tax: *FRS 16*, which considers current tax, that is the tax attributable to the current year's profit; and *FRS 19*, which deals with deferred tax.

Accounting for Current Tax: FRS 16

22.6 *FRS 16* came into effect in 1999 and superseded *SSAP 8*, which had been in operation since 1974.

The preamble states that '[t]he objective of this FRS is to ensure that reporting entities recognise current taxes in a consistent and transparent manner'. Current tax is defined as being 'the amount of tax estimated to be payable or recoverable in respect of the taxable profit or loss for a period, along with adjustments to estimates in respect of previous periods'.

One issue that arises in accounting for current tax is how to deal with income that carries tax credits, for example dividends received, on which withholding tax has been paid and which are paid out of profits which have borne their own corporate income tax. There was a time when it was thought appropriate to include all tax credits when reporting such income, but the current *FRS 16* requires that only taxes which are directly borne by the recipient, ie withholding tax, should be shown; thus, dividends, interest and other receipts should be shown gross of any withholding tax, but not any underlying tax.

Another issue that arises is what rate of tax to use to calculate the tax on the accounting profit for the year: the rate applicable for that year, or the rate applicable when the event gives rise to a tax effect? The previous standard, *SSAP 8*, used the latest known rate. *FRS 16*, however, requires that the tax should be calculated using 'tax rates and laws that have been enacted or substantially enacted' as at the date of the balance sheet.

The standard requires separate disclosure of the current tax expenses (or income) of UK tax and foreign tax, both distinguishing between the tax estimated for the current period and any tax that relates to prior periods. The following is an example of the profit and loss account disclosure taken from *FRS 16*:

22.7 Accounting for Tax

FRS 16: Illustration of Profit and Loss account disclosure

	£000	£000
UK Corporation tax		
Current tax on income for the period	a	
Adjustments in respect of prior periods	b	
	c	
Double tax relief	(d)	
		e
Foreign Tax		
Current tax on income for the period	f	
Adjustments in respect of prior periods	g	
		h
Tax on profits on ordinary activities		i

Accounting for Deferred Tax: Financial Reporting Standard 19

22.7 *SSAP 15* dealt with 'Accounting for Deferred Tax', but was superseded in December 2000 by *FRS 19*. A full understanding of deferred tax requires an understanding of both accounting and tax principles. Many tax advisers are intimidated by the jargon and the facility which accountants and auditors seem to possess to think through conceptual accounting adjustments so quickly. In essence, though, accounting for deferred tax is straightforward. It is not difficult to acquire a sufficient understanding to be able to talk to accountants and auditors on an equal footing.

22.8 Before getting into the detail, it may help to consider three very simple examples so that the basic idea can be grasped.

Example 22.1
A company makes accounting profits of £100,000. During the year it buys a machine for £100,000 which it depreciates by £10,000 in its accounts. It pays corporation tax at a hypothetical rate of 20%. It will qualify for capital allowances at 25% p.a. on a reducing balance basis. It does not anticipate the need to acquire new machines in the foreseeable future.

The profit and loss account for the company may be prepared on two bases, A and B, as below:

Accounting for Tax **22.9**

	Basis A	Basis B
	£	£
TURNOVER	1,000,000	1,000,000
Cost of Sales	(800,000)	(800,000)
Gross Profit	200,000	200,000
Overheads	(100,000)	(100,000)
PROFIT BEFORE TAX	100,000	100,000
Taxation	17,000 (i)	(20,000) (ii)
PROFIT FOR YEAR	83,000	80,000
(i) Accounting Profits	100,000	
Depreciation	10,000	
	110,000	
Capital Allowances	(25,000)	
	85,000	
Taxation (20%)	17,000	
(ii) Accounting Profits		100,000
Taxation (20%)		20,000

Basis A accounts for the actual tax arising in the year. Basis B acknowledges that, at the end of the day, the new machine costing £100,000 will be written down over time by £100,000, albeit at different rates for accounting and tax purposes. Over the life of the machine, accounting profits will suffer by the charging of depreciation of £100,000, and there will be £100,000 of tax allowances. The difference between the accounts and tax write-down is, therefore, only a timing difference and not an absolute difference. It is not prudent to take this timing difference to profit (as it will reverse in later periods), so the tax charge for the year will be increased by £3,000 (£20,000 – £17,000), that tax being described as deferred tax.

22.9

Example 22.2
A company in its first trading period makes an accounting loss of £100,000, and there are no adjustments to its accounting profits, so its taxable loss is also £100,000. It confidently expects to make accounting profits in future years.

The profit and loss account for the company may be prepared on two bases, A and B, as below:

22.10 Accounting for Tax

	Basis A	Basis B
	£	£
TURNOVER	1,000,000	1,000,000
Cost of Sales	(950,000)	(950,000)
Gross Profit	50,000	50,000
Overheads	(150,000)	(150,000)
LOSS BEFORE TAX	(100,000)	(100,000)
Taxation	Nil	20,000
LOSS FOR YEAR	(100,000)	(80,000)

In Basis A, the actual tax on the results of the year is charged to profit and loss. In Basis B, it is recognised that the losses of £100,000 will reduce future tax liabilities by £20,000 (20% × 100,000), and so this (deferred) asset is identified and reflected in the accounts.

22.10

Example 22.3
The facts are the same as *Example 22.1*, except that the accounting profits for the year (after the machine has been depreciated by £10,000) are only £5,000.

There are at least three possible ways in which the profit and loss account may be prepared, A, B and C, as below:

	Basis A	Basis B	Basis C
	£	£	£
TURNOVER	1,000,000	1,000,000	1,000,000
Cost of Sales	(800,000)	(800,000)	(800,000)
Gross Profit	200,000	200,000	200,000
Overheads	(195,000)	(195,000)	(195,000)
PROFIT BEFORE TAX	5,000	5,000	5,000
Taxation	Nil(i)	2,000(ii)	(1,000)(iii)
PROFIT FOR YEAR	5,000	7,000	4,000
(i) Accounting Profits	5,000		
Depreciation	10,000		
	15,000		

Accounting for Tax **22.11**

	Basis A	Basis B	Basis C
	£	£	£
Capital Allowances	(25,000)		
Taxable Loss	(10,000)		
Taxation (20%)	Nil		
(ii) Tax Loss as above		(10,000)	
Future Tax Relief (10,000 × 20%)		2,000	
(iii) Tax on Accounting Profits (5,000 × 20%)			1,000

Basis A accounts for the actual tax arising in the year. Basis B goes further, in identifying that this year's tax loss of £10,000 will ultimately yield a tax saving of £2,000, and takes credit for this. Basis C merely charges tax on the accounting profits of the year.

22.11 *FRS 19* is all about determining which is the correct accounting treatment in the circumstances outlined above. It requires that companies use a 'full provision' basis, which is different to the 'partial provision basis' previously required by *SSAP 15*. The full provision method requires the tax effect of gains and losses to be fully accounted for. Under the previous partial provision method, only tax liabilities that were expected to arise were accounted for, which then required the judgement of management to assess this likelihood, which went against the thinking of international standards.

In *Example 22.1*, *FRS 19* provides that the correct accounting treatment should be Basis B. It would contradict the 'matching concept' to do anything else.

However, in *Example 22.2*, the taking of a credit in the current year for future tax relief is felt to be too imprudent, because the future tax relief is dependant upon (uncertain) taxable profits arising in future years.. Hence, the correct basis for accounting in that case is Basis A.

Where, however, there is a deferred tax charge for the year, to that extent (and to that extent only) any future tax benefits (of losses, for example) may be set against any future tax contained in the deferred tax charge. Thus, in *Example 22.3*, the correct basis is C: Basis A fails to take account of the timing difference (see *Example 22.1*), and Basis B is too imprudent in taking full credit for future tax relief; Basis C achieves the acceptable compromise.

In fact, the tax charge in *Example 22.3* can be re-analysed in a way that illustrates even more clearly what is happening:

22.12 *Accounting for Tax*

Deferred tax charge for timing difference between depreciation and capital allowances (25,000 − 10,000) × 20%	(3,000)
Deferred tax credit for future value of tax losses 10,000 × 20%	2,000
Net charge to profit and loss	(1,000)

Timing differences

22.12 *FRS 19* is all about timing differences. Timing differences are described as 'differences between an entity's taxable profits and its results as stated in the financial statements that arise from the inclusion of gains and losses in tax assessments in periods different from those in which they are recognised in financial statements'. That is, they arise from the inclusion of incomes/expenditures in tax computations in periods different from those in which they are included in accounts.

Examples include:

- depreciation charges (contrasted with capital allowances);

- pension contributions and other post-retirement benefits (accruals for accounts, payment for tax);

- interest or development costs capitalised in the accounts, but treated as revenue expenses and allowed as incurred for tax purposes;

- unrelieved tax losses (accruals for accounts, set against future profits for tax); and

- assets revalued in the financial statements, but the revaluation gain only becomes taxable if and when the asset is sold.

Timing differences originate in one accounting period and are capable of reversing in a later period or periods. *FRS 19* does *not* deal with permanent differences between accounts and tax computations, defined as being 'differences between an entity's taxable profits and its results as stated in the financial statements that arise because certain types of income and expenditure are non-taxable or disallowable, or because certain tax charges or allowances have no corresponding amount in the financial statements'. Examples include disallowances for entertaining, or other statutorily prohibited deductions.

Deferred tax is simply the tax attributable to such timing differences.

Quantification – the liability method

22.13 There are several possible candidates for the recognised method of computing the deferred tax, but that adopted by *FRS 19* is called the 'liability method'. This is in line with worldwide trends, but goes against the US deferral method.

In the *FRS 19* regime, the deferred tax provision is calculated at the rate of tax which is estimated to apply when the timing difference reverses. It is generally not known what the future rate will be, so the current rate is used in setting up a provision, but this should be reviewed in later years, as rates change.

For example, in Year 1, a timing difference of £1,000 saves a company £200 tax. A deferred tax charge of £200 is made. In Year 2, it becomes clear that the company is now making large profits and its anticipated future tax rate will be 30%. If the £1,000 timing difference still exists at the end of the year, in theory an additional deferred tax charge of £100 (£300 – £200) should be established.

To provide or not to provide

22.14 In the UK, it was long-standing practice not to provide fully for deferred tax. The rationale for this was that, in management's view, the entire liability would not be paid in the future, as a result of timing differences, because there will be future investments that result in further deferral. So, traditionally, the deferred tax liability would be reduced to take into account the impact of anticipated future investments. However, *FRS 19* now requires full provision, even though the effect may be to build up large liabilities over time, particularly for companies with continuous capital expenditure qualifying for capital allowances.

With the advent of fair value accounting, another issue that arises is whether deferred tax should be recognised when fair value adjustments are made. *FRS 19* requires that, when an asset is continuously revalued to fair value, deferred tax should be recognised in the profit and loss account. These are usually financial investments and current assets that are 'marked to market'.

Revaluations: non-monetary assets

22.15 Non-monetary asset revaluation is an area of some confusion. Generally, revaluations produce surpluses, and this analysis will proceed on that footing.

Where an asset is revalued, the question arises as to whether the tax which would (or would possibly) arise on its disposal at that value should be accounted for. *FRS 19* requires that deferred tax should be recognised if the company has entered into a binding agreement to sell the revalued asset. If it is more likely than not that a rollover claim will be made on disposal, so that no liability would arise, then no provision is necessary. If a liability would arise on sale, but there are no plans to realise the asset so that, in the foreseeable future, no liability will crystallise, no provision need be made.

Deferred assets

22.16 Deferred tax assets as well as liabilities may exist. However, on grounds of prudence, such assets should only be accounted for to the extent that they are recoverable. Deferred tax should only be recognised if it is likely that the company will make sufficient suitable taxable profit to cover the reversal of any underlying timing differences. In making the decision whether

22.17 *Accounting for Tax*

there will be suitable taxable profit, all available evidence must be considered, and account can be taken of tax planning opportunities (*FRS 19*, para 25).

A potential deferred asset arises in respect of trading losses carried forward to future periods. This may be set off against a deferred tax liability, but, to the extent that it exceeds any such liability, it may only be recognised as an asset in its own right subject to strict criteria.

Discounting

22.17 *FRS 19* allows companies to discount their deferred tax assets and liabilities, based on the number of years between the balance sheet date and the time at which the underlying timing difference is expected to reverse. Discounting is permitted, but not required, under *FRS 19* where deferred tax liabilities will not be settled for some time.

Disclosures

22.18 Deferred tax should be recognised in the profit and loss account for the period, unless it is attributable to a gain or loss that has been recognised in the statement of total recognised gains and losses, in which case that is the place for recognising the deferred tax involved. All deferred tax in the profit and loss account should be included under the heading 'tax on profit or loss on ordinary activities'.

Net deferred tax liabilities should be classified as provisions for liabilities and charges in the balance sheet, with net deferred tax assets being classified as debtors, under a separate heading if material.

The notes to the accounts should show:

- changes in deferred tax balances (before discounting) arising from:
    - the origination and reversal of timing differences;
    - changes in tax rates and laws; and
    - adjustments to the estimated recoverable amount of deferred tax assets arising in previous periods; and
- where applicable, changes in the amounts of discount deducted.

The notes to the financial accounts are also required to highlight any circumstances that affect the current and total tax charges or credits for the current period and those of future periods.

INTERNATIONAL ACCOUNTING STANDARDS

22.19 International accounting standards do not specifically deal with VAT and similar indirect taxes. *IAS 18*, para 8 explains why it is not necessary to have an explicit standard on this:

'Revenue includes only the gross inflows of economic benefits received and receivable by the entity on its own account. Amounts collected on behalf of third parties such as sales taxes, goods and services taxes and value added taxes are not economic benefits which flow to the entity and do not result in increases in equity. Therefore, they are excluded from revenue.'

IAS 12 Income Taxes

22.20 *IAS 12* requires that current tax for the current and prior periods should be recognised as a liability to the extent that it has not yet been settled, and as an asset to the extent that the amounts already paid exceed the amount due. The benefit of a tax loss which can be carried back to recover current tax of a prior period should be recognised as an asset. Current tax assets and liabilities should be measured at the amount expected to be paid to (or recovered from) taxation authorities, using the rates and laws that have been enacted or substantively enacted by the balance sheet date.

For deferred tax, *IAS 12* requires the use of the liability method, which is consistent with *FRS 19* in the UK, but uses the concept of 'temporary' differences rather than 'timing' differences. Paragraph 5 of *IAS 12* says that temporary differences are 'differences between the carrying amount of an asset or liability in the statement of financial position and its tax base'. The idea of temporary differences is broader than, but includes, timing differences. The conceptual difference here is that the 'temporary difference' approach effectively provides for the tax that would be payable if the company were to sell its assets at the balance sheet date for their carrying values, whereas the 'timing difference' approach focuses only on the future reversal of timing differences.

There are also significant practical differences in the way that *FRS 19* and *IAS 12* deal with deferred taxation. In particular, provisions are required under *IAS 12* in the following circumstances:

- on revaluation of a non-monetary asset, regardless of whether or not it is intended to be sold or whether rollover relief would be claimed;
- on the sale of assets even where the gain has been rolled over into other assets;
- on the unremitted earnings of subsidiaries, associates and joint ventures; and
- on the adjustment to fair value of non-monetary assets on the acquisition of a business.

IAS 12 also does not permit discounting of deferred tax liabilities.

TAXATION CONSIDERATIONS

22.21 The tax practitioner needs to be particularly familiar with *FRS 19* or *IAS 12* for two principal reasons:

22.21 *Accounting for Tax*

- First, there may well be a need to liaise with auditors in computing deferred tax provisions for accounts and auditing purposes. The tax practitioner needs, therefore, to understand what he or she is doing and why.

- Secondly, and perhaps more importantly, in relation to company valuation matters.

Company valuations are frequently required for tax purposes. These may be on an 'asset basis', 'PE basis', 'dividend yield basis' or, indeed, a combination of all three.

In relation to the assets basis, it is clearly necessary to understand what the assets are. Has deferred tax been provided (or merely noted in the accounts)? If it is provided, should the fact that it may not crystallise for several years result in its value being discounted for valuation purposes? Deferred assets (eg future tax relief on current losses) may not be carried in the accounts as an asset, but often, when companies are sold, a certain additional amount may be paid if the company comes with tax losses. The position was even more interesting when 31 March 1982 valuations were being effected. In those days, first-year allowances for plant and machinery were 100%, and several different types of stock relief had been in place. Potential deferred tax balances at that time were quite large.

The position is similar when valuing on a PE basis, although the relevant deferred tax is that for the year, and not the cumulative balance on the balance sheet.

Whilst Revenue officers frequently do not understand (nor do they really need to) deferred tax adjustments, the same is not true of the Shares Valuation Division. It is quite possible to spend considerable time in correspondence with them on the extent to which, in any particular case, the deferred tax should be allowed to influence a value.

PART III

ADVANCED ACCOUNTING ISSUES

Chapter 23

Groups

23.1 This chapter considers in detail the question of 'groups' and related matters. The diversity and complexity of modern business life leads to interrelated economic activity being carried on through more than one company.

In the most straightforward situation, Company A trades with Company B. There is no other relationship between A and B, nor between their shareholders. There are no special further considerations.

If the same individuals own the shares in both A and B, there are few special accounting considerations, and the two companies would not be regarded for company law or accounting purposes as being part of a 'group' or as being 'associated' companies. HMRC would not recognise the two companies as forming a 'group' for corporation tax purposes but would regard them as being 'associated'. For VAT purposes, HMRC would recognise the companies as being part of the same 'group'.

If A and B had different shareholders but A had, say, a 20% holding in B, then company law and accounting principles would recognise A and B as 'associated' companies, but not normally as constituting a 'group'. HMRC would concur that there was no 'group', but would recognise that the companies were 'associated'.

If A held 51% of the equity of B, then company law and accounting principles would recognise a 'group' situation. HMRC would agree for VAT, but would accept the relationship as creating a 'group' for some, but not all, corporation tax purposes.

If A held 100% of the equity of B, then all parties would agree that a group relationship had been established between A and B.

The conclusion from these introductory thoughts on the concept of 'groups' and 'associated' companies is that company law and accounting principles go hand in hand, but that HMRC has such different ideas of the meaning of the phrases 'group' and 'associated' company for VAT and corporation tax purposes that it would have been better if they had found different words to describe the envisaged relationships.

23.2 *Groups*

CORPORATE LAW

23.2 The directors of companies have particular obligations under the *Companies Act 2006* ('*CA 2006*') to prepare, lay, and deliver accounts, as has been fully explained in Chapter 2.

Under *CA 1985, s 227*, if, at the end of a financial year, a company is a 'parent company', the directors must prepare 'group' accounts. 'Group' accounts must be 'consolidated' accounts and include a group balance sheet and a group profit and loss account. Very broadly, 'consolidated' accounts are produced by amalgamating the assets and liabilities, revenues and expenditures of the individual companies, and presenting an overall position. Numerous examples are given, in **23.15** *et seq* below, of the adjustments that are typically required if the overall position shown is to be meaningful. The formats must follow the *Accounting Regulations*, and the group accounts must show a true and fair view. In brief, most of the requirements relating to individual companies are carried over and apply to the group accounts themselves.

Parent companies

23.3 The language of *CA 2006* refers to parent undertakings (or parent companies) and their mirror image – subsidiary undertakings (or subsidiary companies).

In fact, the concept of parent was introduced in *CA 1989*. The original (and earlier) terminology was that of 'holding' company. Group accounts were required for holding companies and their subsidiaries.

Before *CA 1989*, the establishment of a group relationship was relatively straightforward. If Company A owned 51% or more of the equity of Company B, then a holding/subsidiary relationship existed. This simplistic approach led to companies effecting transactions through other entities which effectively they controlled (and whose liabilities they often underwrote) but which technically were not (applying the 51% test) subsidiaries and, therefore, were not required to be consolidated. In those circumstances, readers of accounts could not obtain a full view. The jargon expression for this is 'off balance sheet financing'. This is a very topical issue and it is worthwhile pondering at this stage a very simple example.

Example 23.1
A company, A Ltd, has a balance sheet as shown in the first column below. As can be seen, its 'gearing' (see **3.37** above) is 100%. Gearing is a measure of risk. If a company is highly geared, it is highly borrowed and is very susceptible to increases in interest rates or downturns in trade. Most of the companies failing in the recessions of the early 1990s and late 2000s were highly geared.

A enters into a transaction where it borrows £1,000 and buys new fixed assets for £1,000. The degree of risk inherent in this transaction is very high.

The effect on the balance sheet is shown in the second column below. The increased risk is reflected in the gearing – now 200%.

A new company, B, is formed. A takes 50% of the shares for £1, and some other entity (probably a finance house) takes the other 50% (for £1). B then borrows £1,000 and acquires the new fixed asset for £1,000. Arrangements are then entered into between A and B so that A enjoys the full pleasure (and pain) associated with the new asset and its borrowings. Effectively, A 'owns' the asset and the borrowing but, applying a crude 51% criterion for defining holding/subsidiary relationship, no group accounts would be prepared to reflect this. So, A would have entered into an inherently risky transaction, effectively increasing its gearing to 200%, yet its accounts – as shown in the third column – would not reflect this. Because A and B do not constitute a group, no group accounts would be required, so the reader of the accounts would be misled about the financial position of A and related entities.

	Original Balance Sheet £	Acquisition through A £	Acquisition through B £
Fixed Assets	1,000	2,000	1,000
Investment in B Ltd	–	–	1
Net Current Assets	1,000	1,000	999
Borrowings	(1,000)	(2,000)	(1,000)
Net Assets	1,000	1,000	1,000
Share Capital	100	100	100
Profit and Loss	900	900	900
	1,000	1,000	1,000
Gearing	1,000 / 1,000 = 100%	2,000 / 1,000 = 200%	1,000 / 1,000 = 100%

23.4 So, in an attempt to frustrate this kind of device, *CA 1989* introduced changes. For group accounting purposes a new concept – the parent/subsidiary relationship – was created. In particular, these changes are such as to cause Company A, in the example above, to prepare group accounts which would reflect the underlying substance of the financing transaction. The definition of the parent/subsidiary relationship – in *CA 1985, s 258* – is summarised below.

A parent/subsidiary relationship exists:

- where the parent holds or controls a majority (51%) of the *voting* rights (formerly, a majority of the equity capital was needed);

23.5 *Groups*

- where the parent is a shareholder and can appoint a majority of the board of directors of the subsidiary;
- where the parent has a dominant influence (ie it can instruct the directors of the subsidiary to act as it wishes);
- (broadly) where the parent holds 20% or more of the shares in the subsidiary and either it actually exercises a dominant influence or the parent and subsidiary are actually managed on a unified basis.

The parent/subsidiary definition is based on the concept of 'control'. Control of a company's operations is exercised by that company's directors and, therefore, if a shareholder can determine who is appointed to the Board, they effectively have control of the company. Appointment of directors is normally exercised by the ordinary shareholders via a majority resolution at the company's AGM, which is why the emphasis is on votes, rather than simply the number of shares. However, the definition above also acknowledges that there are other methods of controlling the appointment (or actions) of directors (such as via shareholder agreements).

The concept of control is also reflected in the consolidated group accounts. The directors of the parent company, through their control over the appointment and instruction of the directors of the subsidiary companies, have effective control over the operations of all the subsidiaries. The shareholders of the parent company will wish to assess the performance of the directors by considering the results generated from all the operations under their management control, and hence the consolidated group accounts need to reflect all the revenues and costs (and, therefore, profits) and all the assets and liabilities of all of the companies in the group.

23.5 The other major change in the definition of parent/subsidiary concerns holdings in excess of 20%.

A good example of the working of the new definition is in relation to joint ventures. A number of these proceed on a precise 50:50 footing, with perhaps one of the joint venturers actually running the operation as part and parcel of its own operations. Many of the 'Pubcos' (ie companies established to run public houses) have entered into such joint ventures with breweries. Under the old rules, neither 'Pubco' nor 'Brewco' would be regarded as the parent of 'Jointco'. Under the new provisions, 'Pubco' would be regarded as a parent (and, therefore, 'Jointco' would be consolidated into 'Pubco's' group accounts) – because the public houses are managed on a unified basis with 'Pubco's' other outlets – but 'Brewco' would not be regarded as a parent (and, therefore, 'Jointco' would not be consolidated into 'Brewco's' group accounts).

23.6 As explained in **23.2** above, parent companies must prepare group accounts in the form of consolidated accounts. *CA 1985, Sch 4A* gives some guidance on the meanings of these terms, but these are considerably amplified in *FRS 2*, which is the accounting standard for the preparation of group accounts. This is dealt with in detail in **23.10** below.

23.7 *CA 1985, s 231* together with *Sch 5* provide that the group accounts must disclose details of companies which are consolidated (names and relevant shareholdings) and give brief details of other related undertakings – companies which are not subsidiaries but where there is some lesser relationship (eg a 10% shareholding).

There are, in theory, circumstances in which subsidiary companies may be excluded from the consolidation process (*CA 1985, s 229*). It is very rare for these to apply.

23.8 There are, however, a number of exceptions which do frequently apply. These include:

- only the ultimate parent company need prepare group accounts (*CA 1985, s 228*);
- the parent company may omit its own profit and loss account from its own annual accounts if it prepares group accounts (providing the quantum of its own profit and loss is disclosed in the group accounts) (*CA 1985, s 230*);
- a parent company need not prepare group accounts if the group is small or medium-sized and is not an ineligible group (*CA 1985, s 248*).

Basically, an ineligible group is one in which any of its members are public companies, a bank, or an authorised person under the *Financial Services Act 1986*.

A group is small or medium-sized in any financial year if it falls within the financial parameters below, for that year and the preceding one (if there is a preceding one). The following figures are contained in *CA 2006, s 383 for 'small' groups and s 466 for 'medium' groups..*

Small or medium-sized group

23.9 A small or medium-sized group must satisfy at least two of the following criteria:

Small group

Aggregate Turnover	Not more than £5.6 million net (or £6.72 million gross)
Aggregate Balance Sheet Total	Not more than £2.8 million net (or £3.36 million gross)
Aggregate Number of Employees	Not more than 50

Medium-sized group

Aggregate Turnover	Not more than £22.8 million net (or £27.36 million gross)
Aggregate Balance Sheet Total	Not more than £11.4 million net (or £13.68 million gross)
Aggregate Number of Employees	Not more than 250

23.10 *Groups*

The gross and net figures are before and after the making of consolidation adjustments described more fully below.

ACCOUNTING PRINCIPLES

Financial Reporting Standard 2 (FRS 2)

23.10 The original accounting standard dealing with the preparation of group accounts was *SSAP 14*. This was updated (largely to reflect the *CA 1989* changes) and replaced by *FRS 2*, effective for accounting periods ending on or after 23 December 1992.

FRS 2 substantially incorporates the provisions of *CA 2006* in relation to the definitions of the parent/subsidiary relationship, and the circumstances in which consolidated accounts must be prepared, and the practicalities of the consolidation process, are more fully covered. These are perhaps best illustrated by a series of examples. However, before proceeding with the examples, it is worth summarising the objectives which are to be achieved by the consolidated group accounts.

Objectives and preparation of consolidated accounts

23.11 The primary purpose of preparing accounts is to enable the owners of the business (the shareholders) to assess the performance (or stewardship) of those managing the company on their behalf (the directors). In the context of a group of companies, as discussed in **23.4** above, this means that the consolidated group accounts need to show all the trading results, assets and liabilities of all the companies in the group to reflect the operations under the control of the parent company directors. In order to achieve this objective, consolidated accounts need to be prepared *as if the group were a single entity*, despite the fact that, legally, each company in the group is a separate entity. In other words, the consolidated accounts need to reflect all transactions with third parties outside the group.

23.12 This is the same basis on which the accounts of a single business are prepared. Imagine a simple business – a shop. The business is organised as two operations: the stores department and the retail space. In order to control the two operations, each maintains separate accounting records. Whenever an item of stock is moved from the stores to the retail space, appropriate entries would be made in the accounting records, but the published accounts for the overall business would not reflect a purchase or sale, or amounts due between the stores and the retail space, or a 'profit', because all that has happened is that an item of stock has moved location – there has been no transaction with parties outside the business. The same principles apply to the preparation of consolidated accounts for a group of companies. Transactions between the individual companies making up the group need to be 'eliminated', so that the resulting consolidated group accounts reflect only transactions with third parties. These 'eliminations' (often referred to as consolidation adjustments) are *not* reflected in the accounting records or published financial statements of the subsidiary companies; for each subsidiary, these are valid transactions with third (albeit connected) parties. Instead, the consolidation adjustments are made centrally, solely for the purpose of preparing consolidated group accounts. The adjustments are undertaken outside the double entry accounting records, although they must 'balance' (ie the debits must equal the credits) or the consolidated accounts will not balance.

23.13 The process for preparing consolidated accounts can best be visualised as a large spreadsheet, with the columns representing each of the companies in the group. The rows show all the information in the profit and loss account, balance sheet and the supporting notes of the financial statements of each company. The preparation of consolidated accounts starts with what is often referred to as an 'aggregation'. This is merely adding across all the columns to give total (or aggregated) figures for each item. Balancing consolidation adjustments are then made to the aggregation in order to eliminate transactions between the companies in the group in order to derive the consolidated accounts, reflecting transactions between the companies in the group and third parties outside the group.

23.14 Having discussed the objectives and process of preparing consolidated accounts, it is now appropriate to proceed with a number of illustrative examples.

Basic consolidation

23.15 Company A forms a 100% subsidiary, Company B, by subscribing £10,000 for 10,000 £1 ordinary shares. Both trade for a number of years. There are no inter-company transactions or dividends. Taxation is ignored. Their separate balance sheets and profit and loss accounts are shown below, as are the consolidated counterparts.

Example 23.2

	Company A	Company B	Group
	£	£	£
Fixed Assets	100,000	50,000	150,000
Investment in B	10,000	–	–
Net Current Assets	50,000	30,000	80,000
Bank Loans	(50,000)	(10,000)	(60,000)
	110,000	70,000	170,000

23.16 *Groups*

	Company A	Company B	Group
	£	£	£
Share Capital	20,000	10,000	20,000
Profit and Loss	90,000	60,000	150,000
	110,000	70,000	170,000

	Company A	Company B	Group
	£	£	£
Sales	1,000,000	700,000	1,700,000
Cost of Sales	(850,000)	(600,000)	(1,450,000)
Gross Profit	150,000	100,000	250,000
Expenses	(135,000)	(90,000)	(225,000)
Net Profit	15,000	10,000	25,000

As can be seen, the consolidation process is straightforward. In its simplest form, when there are no transactions between the group companies, this merely amounts to the arithmetic cross-addition of the separate components of each group company's individual accounts, with one exception – the original investment by A in B is a transaction between group companies and, therefore, it needs to be eliminated if the consolidated accounts are to reflect only transactions with third parties.

23.16 What has to be imagined is that A carried on B's activities itself. In that circumstance, there is no 'investment' by A in the share capital of B, and no B to issue shares. Imagine that B's activities are merely a division of A, and that the division has its own bank account. All that would have happened is that A would have moved funds from one bank account to another. The overall bank balances of A would not have changed – one account would have increased by £10,000 and the other reduced by the same amount. So, A's investment and B's issue of shares 'disappear', or 'cancel', on consolidation. This may seem stunningly obvious but, as some of the examples below will illustrate, some of the effects on consolidation are anything but so easy to comprehend, and it is important to fully understand the basic principles before progressing to the next level. It is also obvious that, if B's share capital (and that of any other subsidiaries in a more complex group) is eliminated on consolidation, the share capital shown in the consolidated accounts will *always* be the share capital of the parent company only.

23.17 It must be remembered, though, that A and B remain separate legal entities. If the directors are considering the payment of a dividend, it is Company A's Profit and Loss to which reference must be made – not the group's Profit and Loss. (If there are small retained profits in the parent company but large group retained profits, then subsidiary companies can declare dividends to reduce their retained profits and increase that of the parent. There are some tax planning opportunities in this – see the comments after *Example 23.5* below.) Equally, if B owes money to a third party, recourse cannot be had by that third party to the separate entity, A.

Consolidation adjustments – inter-company trading – unrealised profits

23.18

Example 23.3
The same facts apply as in *Example 23.2*, except that B sells part of its output to A.

During the year, its sales turnover with A is £100,000 in goods which cost it £80,000, thereby making a profit of £20,000. At the year end, A has managed to sell precisely one-half of those goods on to third parties for £55,000.

The separate and consolidated accounts reflecting these facts are:

	Company A £	Company B £	Group £
Fixed Assets	100,000	50,000	150,000
Investment in B	10,000	–	–
Net Current Assets	50,000	30,000	70,000
Bank Loans	(50,000)	(10,000)	(60,000)
	110,000	70,000	160,000
Share Capital	20,000	10,000	20,000
Profit and Loss	90,000	60,000	140,000
	110,000	70,000	160,000

	Company A £	Company B £	Group £
Sales	1,000,000	700,000	1,600,000
Cost of Sales	(850,000)	(600,000)	(1,360,000)
Gross Profit	150,000	100,000	240,000
Expenses	(135,000)	(90,000)	(225,000)
Net Profit	15,000	10,000	15,000

23.19 *Groups*

This is an important example with significant tax consequences. It is worthwhile ensuring that it is fully understood.

When completing the consolidation, recognition needs to be taken of the fact that, at the year end, A is holding stock of £50,000 (one-half of that acquired from B). This stock originally cost B £40,000 (1/2 × £80,000) on which it made a profit of £10,000 (1/2 × £20,000) on selling to A. B's accounts correctly show the sales turnover of £100,000 and profit of £20,000 on the inter-company sale. A's accounts correctly show the purchase for £100,000 and reflect the profit on the part sale of that stock by year end. It is necessary to eliminate the inter-company turnover (from the group point of view, it is just like moving stock round from one department to another) and to eliminate the profit on that part of the inter-company sales which, at year end, has not been crystallised by an onward sale to the outside third parties.

Therefore, on consolidation, the sales revenue of B needs reducing by £100,000 and, likewise, the cost of sales expense of A needs reducing by the same amount. Additionally, A is holding stock at a cost to it of £50,000 which has only cost the group £40,000. It is necessary, therefore, to eliminate the £10,000 profit recorded by A that has not yet been crystallised. The consolidation adjustment is to reduce the group stocks (and hence group profit) by £10,000. This is manifested by reducing stocks (included in the net current assets) in the balance sheet by £10,000, with a corresponding £10,000 increase in the group cost of sales.

From the tax point of view, the position is curious. All other things being equal, A will pay tax on profits of £15,000, and B will pay tax on profits of £10,000, whereas the group profit is only £15,000.

The missing £10,000 is the unrealised profit on the inter-company sales. *There is no tax relief for this.* In a group situation, any internally generated profits which have not come to fruition by onward sale out of the group by year end will generate an unnecessary tax liability for the period. It is possible to avoid this either by ensuring that the timing of such inter-company transfers are such that, at year end, there is no unrealised profit, or by arranging group affairs so that inter-company transfers are on a 'consignment' or 'sale or return' basis, so that Company B in our example would only count the transfer as a 'sale' at the point in time that A makes the onward sale.

Consolidation adjustments – inter-company loans

23.19

Example 23.4
The same facts apply as in *Example 23.2*, except that, over the year, A has lent £20,000 to B on a no-interest basis.

The separate and consolidated accounts are:

	Company A	Company B	Group
	£	£	£
Fixed Assets	100,000	50,000	150,000
Investment in B	10,000	–	–
Loan to B	20,000	–	–
Loan from A	–	(20,000)	–
Net Current Assets	30,000	50,000	80,000
Bank Loans	(50,000)	(10,000)	(60,000)
	110,000	70,000	170,000

	Company A	Company B	Group
	£	£	£
Share Capital	20,000	10,000	20,000
Profit and loss	90,000	60,000	150,000
	110,000	70,000	170,000
Sales	1,000,000	700,000	1,700,000
Cost of Sales	(850,000)	(600,000)	(1,450,000)
Gross Profit	150,000	100,000	250,000
Expenses	(135,000)	(90,000)	(225,000)
Net profit	15,000	10,000	25,000

This is a much simpler example, with no tax consequences. The inter-company loans merely 'net off' in the consolidation process. There is no effect on group profit.

Consolidation adjustments – inter-company dividends

23.20

Example 23.5
The same facts apply as in *Example 23.2*, except that Company B pays a dividend of £12,000. Assume the payment has been made under a 'group' election for tax purposes. The separate and consolidated accounts reflecting this are:

23.20 Groups

	Company A £	Company B £	Group £
Fixed Assets	100,000	50,000	150,000
Investment in B	10,000	–	–
Net Current Assets	62,000	18,000	80,000
Bank Loans	(50,000)	(10,000)	(60,000)
	122,000	58,000	170,000
Share Capital	20,000	10,000	20,000
Profit and Loss	102,000	48,000	150,000
	122,000	58,000	170,000

	Company A £	Company B £	Group £
Sales	1,000,000	700,000	1,700,000
Cost of Sales	(850,000)	(600,000)	(1,450,000)
Gross Profit	150,000	100,000	250,000
Expenses	(135,000)	(90,000)	(225,000)
Net Profit	15,000	10,000	25,000
Other Income	12,000	–	–
Dividends	–	(12,000)	–
Net Profit	27,000	(2,000)	25,000

This example brings out several interesting features.

As with inter-company loans, the inter-company dividends 'cancel'. The eventual group balance sheet and profit and loss account are identical in *Examples 23.4* and *23.5*. However, inter-company dividends do have consequences for the group as a whole.

As was explained in **3.15** above, many corporate transactions rely on the availability of retained profits. The inter-company dividend has transferred retained profits from B to A. If A (for example) had been contemplating a purchase of own shares for £95,000, it would have found it very difficult in the circumstances of *Example 23.4*, but relatively easy in the circumstances of *Example 23.5*.

Taxation, specifically ACT, was ignored in the example (or effectively ignored by assuming that advantage was taken of a 'group' election not to account for ACT). If there is in existence a group election, it is still possible for a subsidiary company to account for ACT on dividends paid to its parent.

Groups **23.21**

If a parent company is contemplating a dividend to its shareholders, say three months after its year end, it will be approximately 18 months (nine months after the end of the following accounting period) before it can recover that ACT. If, shortly before the year end, the subsidiary had paid a dividend to the parent and accounted for the ACT, it (the subsidiary) would have been able to recover the ACT roughly nine months later, and the parent would be able to frank the outgoing dividend with the tax credit on the dividend from the subsidiary. The payment, therefore, of an inter-company dividend prior to year end reduces by six months the period which the group is deprived of the ACT. All this changed from April 1999 when ACT was abolished.

The example also illustrates that dividends are paid out of retained profits, not merely out of current profits. B's current profits are £10,000, but a dividend of £12,000 can be paid because there are sufficient accumulated retained profits. The likelihood would be that, if B elected to pay ACT on a dividend of £12,000, the ACT recovery would be partly against the tax on the year's profits (of £10,000) and partly by carry back against earlier years' corporation tax.

Consolidation adjustments – accounting policies

23.21

Example 23.6
The same facts apply as in *Example 23.2*, except in relation to the accounting policy in relation to sales recognition.

A recognises a sale as having taken place whenever a contract is exchanged. B recognises a sale as having taken place only at the point at which a contract is completed (detailed consideration of accounting policies in relation to recognising 'revenue' is in Chapter 12). At the year end, B has one sales contract which cost B £80,000, but which it is contracted to sell for £100,000. Completion takes place satisfactorily shortly after year end.

The separate and consolidated accounts reflecting this are:

	Company A £	Company B £	Group £
Fixed Assets	100,000	50,000	150,000
Investment in B	10,000	–	–
Net Current Assets	50,000	30,000	100,000
Bank Loans	(50,000)	(10,000)	(60,000)
	110,000	70,000	190,000
Share Capital	20,000	10,000	20,000
Profit and Loss	90,000	60,000	170,000
	110,000	70,000	190,000

23.22 Groups

	Company A	Company B	Group
	£	£	£
Sales	1,000,000	700,000	1,800,000
Cost of Sales	(850,000)	(600,000)	(1,530,000)
Gross Profit	150,000	100,000	270,000
Expenses	(135,000)	(90,000)	(225,000)
Net Profit	15,000	10,000	45,000

In preparing consolidated accounts, it is important for a consistent set of accounting policies to be applied. If individual companies adopt different accounting policies, it is necessary to make adjustments when completing the consolidation.

The example above applies the policy adopted by A in the consolidated accounts, causing an adjustment to B's figures to reflect the extra sales revenue and profit in counting the transaction contracted for but not complete at year end as though it were a sale.

It may appear strange that a company has such latitude in selecting an accounting policy in relation to sales (or anything else for that matter) which can have a significant effect on accounting profit (and hence tax liability). *This is by no means an uncommon situation. Example 23.6* above could well represent the accounts of a group of house builders. The familiar cycle of house purchase – exchange of contracts (plus deposit) followed by a delay of (say) four weeks, climaxed by 'completion' – does not really permit an unambiguous answer to the question, 'when has the sale taken place?'. In practice, either date of contract or date of completion is acceptable (in both tax and accounting terms), although the favoured (and more prudent) basis is to use date of completion.

The main accounting requirements are that accounting policies should be disclosed and applied consistently from year to year (see Chapter 5).

Minority interests

23.22

Example 23.7
The same facts apply as in *Example 23.2*, except, at the time of A's subscription for 10,000 × £1 ordinary shares in B, there was also an outsider who subscribed for 2,500 × £1 ordinary shares in B (thus making B an 80% subsidiary of A ((10,000/12,500) × 100)).

The separate and consolidated accounts reflecting this are:

Groups 23.22

	Company A	Company B	Group
	£	£	£
Fixed Assets	100,000	50,000	150,000
Investment in B	10,000	–	–
Net Current Assets	50,000	32,500	82,500
Bank Loans	(50,000)	(10,000)	(60,000)
	110,000	72,500	172,500
Share Capital	20,000	12,500	20,000
Profit and Loss	90,000	60,000	138,000
Minority Interest	–	–	14,500
	110,000	72,500	172,500
	Company A	Company B	Group
	£	£	£
Sales	1,000,000	700,000	1,700,000
Cost of Sales	(850,000)	(600,000)	(1,450,000)
Gross Profit	150,000	100,000	250,000
Expenses	(135,000)	(90,000)	(225,000)
Minority Interest	–	–	(2,000)
Net Profit	15,000	10,000	23,000

The consolidation process proceeds by initially treating B as though it were a 100% subsidiary (ie the whole of B's assets, liabilities, revenues etc are cross-added or aggregated for inclusion in the group accounts), reflecting the fact that the directors of A effectively *control* B. It is then necessary to reflect the fact that A only *owns* 80% of B, the remaining 20% being owned by the 'outsider'. That part (20%) of B's profits, assets and liabilities which are 'owned' by outsiders (the so-called 'minority interest') are separately identified on both the balance sheet and the profit and loss account.

The consolidated balance sheet shows that the 'minority interest' are entitled to £2,500 of B's share capital plus 20% of B's retained profits (ie 20% × £60,000 = £12,000). Therefore, in total, the minority interest is entitled to £14,500 (£2,500 + £12,000) of the group's assets. Equally, it is entitled to 20% of the current year's profits for B, which amounts to £2,000 (20% × £10,000).

There is no particular taxation consequence on the minority interest question, except perhaps as a reminder of the appropriate percentage holding by outsiders. This helps in determining whether the percentage shareholding tests are satisfied for the various tax tests in establishing group status.

23.23 Groups

Where an Inspector is investigating or challenging the pricing of any inter-company trading between A and B, it is sometimes useful to highlight the outside interest in B. Any artificial pricing of transactions would have third party consequences in addition to tax ramifications and, therefore, (arguably) are less likely to have occurred.

Acquisitions

23.23

Example 23.8
The same facts apply as in *Example 23.2*, except that B may have traded for one year before A acquired its shareholding. At the end of B's first year of trading, A acquired the entire share capital from the then owner for £20,000. B's own accounts for the first year of trading (and, therefore, as at the date of acquisition by A) were:

	£
Fixed Assets	15,000
Net Current Assets	5,000
Bank Loans	(5,000)
	15,000
Share Capital	10,000
Profit and Loss	5,000
	15,000
Sales	150,000
Cost of Sales	(120,000)
Gross Profit	30,000
Expenses	(25,000)
Net Profit	5,000

Several years later, the separate and consolidated accounts for A and B are:

Groups 23.23

	Company A £	Company B £	Group £
Fixed Assets	100,000	50,000	150,000
Investment in B	20,000	–	–
Goodwill on Consolidation	–	–	5,000
Net Current Assets	40,000	30,000	70,000
Bank Loans	(50,000)	(10,000)	(60,000)
	110,000	70,000	165,000
Share Capital	20,000	10,000	20,000
Profit and Loss	90,000	60,000	145,000
	110,000	70,000	165,000

	Company A £	Company B £	Group £
Sales	1,000,000	700,000	1,700,000
Cost of Sales	(850,000)	(600,000)	(1,450,000)
Gross Profit	150,000	100,000	250,000
Expenses	(135,000)	(90,000)	(225,000)
Net Profit	15,000	10,000	25,000

This is an important example, which occurs frequently in situations abundant with tax planning opportunities.

The figures have been contrived to make them as similar to the actual facts of *Example 23.2* consistent with bringing out the salient points. The only difference between the individual company balance sheets in *Examples 23.2* and *23.8* is that, in the latter, the acquisition cost of shares in B is £20,000 (not £10,000). This additional expenditure is assumed to have reduced A's bank balance by £10,000, so net current assets are stated at £10,000 less than in *Example 23.2*. The other balance sheet totals are identical in both *Examples 23.2* and *23.8*.

Although the individual accounts are very similar, the consolidated accounts are quite different.

The consolidated accounts have to reflect the fact that, when the shares in B were purchased for £20,000, the net assets were only £15,000 (represented by share capital of £10,000 and retained profits of £5,000). A has therefore paid £5,000 more than the (book) value of the net assets of B as at the date of acquisition. This additional expenditure is normally called 'goodwill', hence the entry on the group balance sheet 'Goodwill on Consolidation'.

The remaining £15,000 of the purchase price paid represents the book value of B's net assets at the date of acquisition, and is eliminated against B's share

23.24 Groups

capital (£10,000, as in the previous examples) and the retained profits of B (the remaining £5,000) *as at the date of acquisition*. The group retained profits of £145,000 comprise all of A's retained profits (£90,000) and all of B's retained profits which have been earned since A acquired B (£60,000 – £5,000 = £55,000).

Quoted companies are often more interested in shareholder perception than in tax mitigation. Their objective is to show that an acquisition is successful and good profits accrue post acquisition. At the time of a share purchase, the target company is encouraged to be extremely prudent in preparing pre-acquisition accounts (stock write-downs, bad debt provisions etc). This has the effect of depressing pre-acquisition profits and inflating post-acquisition profits. It can either create or augment a loss problem under *ICTA 1988, s 768*.

Unquoted companies are generally more interested in protecting the tax position, and their wish is to avoid an *ICTA 1988, s 768* problem. If the target company is in a loss position, it may be best to err on the side of optimism in preparing pre-acquisition accounts (in addition to disclaiming capital allowances) to make the pre-acquisition target company's losses as small as possible. There may even be mileage in ensuring the target company makes pre-acquisition profits (such matters as small companies corporation tax rates are in point). Of course, group relief considerations need also to be borne in mind.

Accounting for acquisitions is both difficult and contentious, and is considered in more detail in Chapter 29, which discusses the concepts of 'fair value' accounting (intended to frustrate the manipulation of pre-acquisition asset values), treatment of acquired 'goodwill', and the use (and abuse) of an alternative method of accounting for acquisitions (the so-called 'merger accounting' method).

Disposals

23.24

Example 23.9
The same facts apply as in *Example 23.8*, except at the end of the period A sells its holding in B for £100,000 (all received in cash at year end). Taxation is ignored.

The individual and consolidated accounts reflecting this are:

	Company A	Company B	Group
	£	£	£
Fixed Assets	100,000	50,000	100,000
Investment in B	–	–	–
Net Current Assets	140,000	30,000	140,000
Bank Loans	(50,000)	(10,000)	(50,000)
	190,000	70,000	190,000

	Company A	Company B	Group
	£	£	£
Share Capital	20,000	10,000	20,000
Profit and Loss	170,000	60,000	170,000
	190,000	70,000	190,000
Sales	1,000,000	700,000	1,700,000
Cost of Sales	(850,000)	(600,000)	(1,450,000)
Gross Profit	150,000	100,000	250,000
Profit on Sale of B	80,000	–	25,000
Expenses	(135,000)	(90,000)	(225,000)
Net Profit	95,000	10,000	50,000

As far as A is concerned, it has disposed of an asset for £100,000 which cost £20,000, and therefore has made a profit of £80,000. As far as the group is concerned, it has disposed of net assets of £70,000 (the net assets of Company B) and the original premium on acquiring those assets – ie Goodwill on Consolidation – amounting to £5,000; therefore, from the group point of view, a profit of £25,000 (£100,000 – £70,000 – £5,000) arises.

For a tax practitioner, the group profit on disposal of a subsidiary is a very confusing figure. The best advice is to ignore it. In a real example, the facts are likely to be much more complicated – the original goodwill on consolidation is likely to have been amortised or written off one way or another in earlier years, and there are likely to have been inter-company dividends and even a pre-disposal dividend strip. The tax consequences on the profit/loss on disposal are determined from the individual company accounts.

An important tax point is to consider the effective date of disposal. From the accounting point of view, it is the date on which control passes – usually completion. For capital gains purposes, it is the date of contract and, for group relief purposes, the effects of *ICTA 1988, ss 409* and *410* need watching.

Financial Reporting Standard 9 (FRS 9)

23.25 A company may have a subsidiary and, as has been seen above, there are rules providing for the preparation of consolidated accounts. At the other extreme, a company may make a simple investment in another company. There are no special rules for the accounting of a simple investment. However, there are intermediate investments in companies or other entities which fall

23.26 *Groups*

short of creating parent/subsidiary relationships but in which the investor is something more than a passive financial investor. It has long been recognised that such investments need an appropriate intermediate accounting treatment. Indeed, this was the subject of the very first accounting standard (*SSAP 1*). For accounting periods ending on or after 23 June 1998, *SSAP 1* was replaced by the more comprehensive *FRS 9*.

23.26 *FRS 9* first recognises something called an 'associate'. This is an entity – usually a company – in which the investor company holds a long-term 'participating' shareholding (a holding of 20% or more is presumed enough to qualify) and over which the investor exercises significant influence in how the business is run, what investments it may make, and in relation to dividend policy.

Equity accounting

23.27 This is the name given to the method of accounting in a group's consolidated accounts for associates, as illustrated in the following example.

Example 23.10
In addition to the two companies, A and B, from *Example 23.2*, a third company, C, is formed during the year. A subscribes £10,000 for the issue of 10,000 × £1 ordinary shares in C, which represents 25% of the ordinary voting equity. The separate and consolidated accounts are as follows:

	Company A £	Company B £	Company C £	Group £
Fixed Assets	100,000	50,000	120,000	150,000
Investment in B	10,000	–	–	–
Investment in C	10,000	–	–	17,500
Net Current Assets	40,000	30,000	50,000	70,000
Bank Loans	(50,000)	(10,000)	(100,000)	(60,000)
	110,000	70,000	70,000	177,500
Share Capital	20,000	10,000	40,000	20,000
Profit and Loss	90,000	60,000	30,000	157,500
	110,000	70,000	70,000	177,500

	Company A	Company B	Company C	Group
	£	£	£	£
Sales	1,000,000	700,000	800,000	1,700,000
Cost of Sales	(850,000)	(600,000)	(600,000)	(1,450,000)
Gross Profit	150,000	100,000	200,000	250,000
Expenses	(135,000)	(90,000)	(170,000)	(225,000)
Net Profit	15,000	10,000	30,000	25,000
Share of Profit in C	–	–	–	7,500
Net Profit	15,000	10,000	30,000	32,500

For an associated company, therefore, there is no cross-adding of assets, liabilities, revenues and expenditures. This is because C is not controlled by A's directors. The investment in the associate is shown on the group balance sheet at cost, plus the group share of post-acquisition retained profits. A note to the accounts should analyse this figure to show the group's share of the associate's net assets. The group's profit and loss account for the year includes the group's share of the current year's profits of the associate.

Gross equity method

23.28 *FRS 9* then goes on to identify a higher-level involvement which it describes as a joint venture. A joint venture is an arrangement with characteristics between those of a subsidiary and an associate. This arises where two or more parties come together to exercise control over a venture where there is a contractual relationship giving the participants rights – possibly of veto – over strategic policy decisions, and providing a framework for settling disputes or even termination of the venture.

In *Example 23.10* above, Company A had 25% of the equity in Company C. If another unconnected company had 75%, then C would probably be no more than an associate of A. But if A was one of four investors in C, each holding 25%, it is likely that there would be a shareholders' agreement between the four shareholders which would deal with issues of veto, resolution of disputes, arrangements for termination etc. In that circumstance, C would probably represent a joint venture interest by A.

23.29 *FRS 9* requires slightly more information on joint venture companies to be disclosed on the face of the accounts than it does for 'mere' associates. It designates the prescribed method of accounting as the 'gross equity' method.

In the profit and loss account, using the equity method of accounting, only the group's share of the associate's profits is shown. Using the gross equity

23.30 *Groups*

method, the group's share of the joint venturer's turnover is also shown. In the balance sheet, using the equity method, a single entry comprising the net investment in the associate is shown; whereas, using the gross equity method, it is necessary to include a breakdown of the group's share of the gross assets and gross liabilities of the joint venture company.

23.30 The balance sheet and statutory profit and loss account of the ABC Group, in *Example 23.10*, can now be presented in the two different scenarios for Company C:

	C is an Associate Company £	C is a Joint Venture Company £
Fixed Assets	150,000	150,000
Investments in Associates	17,500	–
Investments in Joint Ventures		
Share of Gross Assets	–	42,500
Share of Gross Liabilities	–	(25,000)
Net Current Assets	70,000	70,000
Bank Loans	(60,000)	(60,000)
	177,500	177,500
Gross Turnover including share of Joint Ventures	1,700,000	1,900,000
Less share of Joint Ventures	–	(200,000)
	1,700,000	1,700,000
Cost of Sales	(1,450,000)	(1,450,000)
Gross Profit	250,000	250,000
Expenses	(225,000)	(225,000)
Group Operating Profit	25,000	25,000
Share of Operating Profit:		
in Joint Ventures	–	7,500
in Associates	7,500	–
Retained Profit for Group and its Share of Associates and Joint Ventures	32,500	32,500

23.31 Finally, *FRS 9* identifies an 'arrangement' which does not give rise to either an associate or joint venture relationship because there is no trading entity. An example might be where a land owner permits a building company to build a house on his land under an agreement to share in the eventual sale proceeds. The only trader is the house builder. There is no separate entity in which the two parties have an interest which is carrying on any trade. In these circumstances, each member of the arrangement merely incorporates into his own accounts those assets or liabilities (or shares in those assets or liabilities) that are his.

23.32 In addition to the accounting for associates and joint ventures in the accounts, disclosures by way of note need to be made. *FRS 9* sets out the detailed disclosures, which become increasingly wide once certain thresholds are breached. These initially come into play where the aggregate of all interests in joint ventures and associates exceeds 15% of the investor group's main financial parameters (assets, liabilities, turnover, average profit), and become even more extensive if any single joint venture or associate exceeds 25% of the investor group's financial parameters.

COMPARISON WITH INTERNATIONAL ACCOUNTING STANDARDS

23.33 *IAS 27* 'Consolidated and Separate Financial Statements' is broadly similar to *FRS 2* 'Accounting for Subsidiary Undertakings'. There are some detailed differences in the definition of a subsidiary and in the exemptions from the need to prepare consolidated group accounts, but these differences would only apply in exceptional circumstances. The mechanics of consolidation are the same under UK and international standards.

23.34 The requirements of *IAS 28* 'Investments in Associates' are reasonably similar to *FRS 9* 'Associates and Joint Ventures'. The main difference relates to loss-making associates, where *IAS 28* only requires the recognition of losses until the point where the investor's interest is reduced to nil, unless the investor has legal or constructive obligations to make payments on behalf of the associate, whereas *FRS 9* requires losses to continue to be recognised. *FRS 9* also requires additional disclosures for material associates.

23.35 The requirements of *FRS 9* on accounting for joint ventures are generally more prescriptive than its international counterpart, *IAS 31*. Whereas *FRS 9* only allows equity accounting (as set out at **23.28** to **23.32** above), *IAS 31* allows proportionate consolidation as an alternative. (Under proportionate consolidation, the appropriate proportion [based on the investor's percentage holding in the joint venture] of each line item in the joint venture's accounts is consolidated.) In addition, the difference referred to in **23.34** above also applies to joint ventures. There are also differences of presentation and disclosure between the two standards, particularly when the thresholds referred to in **23.32** above are exceeded.

TAXATION

Corporation tax

23.36 Until the late 1990s, group accounts were not directly relevant for corporation tax purposes. However, *Finance (No 2) Act 1997, s 47* defines a finance lease (for the purpose of certain capital allowance calculations) as including any arrangements which would fall, under normal accountancy practice, to be treated as a finance lease in any consolidated group accounts of which the company is a member. This followed on the heels of similar provisions in *FA 1997, s 82* in relation to finance lessors. Increasingly, therefore, group accounts can be seen to be very significant for corporation tax purposes.

23.37 There is no direct tax concept of the joint venture. Joint ventures conducted through special purpose companies may qualify as consortia; where there is no such company, the joint venture may amount to no more than a partnership between the joint venturers.

23.38 The concept of a 'group' for the purposes of corporation tax and company law (hereafter taken to include the very similar accountancy principles) is similar.

Both proceed on the basis of a parent company with equity stakes in one or more subsidiaries. Both recognise that the key concept is 'control'. However, tax and company law address the question differently.

Tax law recognises precise numerical hurdles to satisfy before acquiring group status: the 75%/90% tests for group and consortium relief (*ICTA 1988, s 402*) and the 75% test for capital gains exemption on inter-company transfers (*TCGA 1992, s 171*). But this raises the question, '75% of what?'. Definitional provisions then deal with this point. The definitions have evolved slightly differently for each tax purpose over time. Sometimes, regard has to be had for holdings of 'ordinary share capital' (as specifically defined), sometimes it is necessary to take into account potential future additions of shares (via options), and sometimes regard has to be had to notional distributions of income (or assets on liquidation) to determine whether the investor satisfies the relevant percentage hurdle. This has the benefit of objectivity and certainty, but leaves open the possibility of contrivances whereby what does not genuinely constitute a group is so regarded because it falls within the precise tax parameters.

Company law has developed differently and tackled the 'control' point more subjectively. Whereas a 51% holding of voting power is conclusive, lesser holdings which leave the investor company with a 'dominant influence' are deemed to create the parent/subsidiary relationship. This is more subjective and less precise than the tax regime. The potential abuse is that directors and 'weak' auditors will 'stretch' the interpretation of 'dominant influence' to suit their purposes.

This means that there will be many situations where company and tax law reach different conclusions as to whether a group has been created – and not just because of a basic difference in rules (eg 51% test for company law, 75% for group relief) – but because of other, more subtle differences.

23.39 The concept of 'associated company' is completely different in company and tax law. It is unfortunate that the same terms are used. (To be precise, company law uses the term 'related company' which is defined slightly differently from 'associated company' in *SSAP 1*, but the terminology 'associated company' is much the more common.)

For tax purposes, the expression 'associated company' connotes the common control of two companies (*ICTA 1988, s 416*). Control (51%) can be expressed either through a holding of shares by one company in another – direct or indirect – or by a commonality (51%) of shareholders without any holding of shares – direct or indirect – by either company in the other.

23.40 To complete the confusion, the VAT concept of group is different again, being closer to the corporation tax concept of associate. Fortunately, the VAT regime does not contemplate any relationship for which the term 'associate' should apply.

VATA 1983, s 43 provides that companies within a group may elect one member to be the 'representative member' for the group, and account for the whole of the group's VAT to HMRC. Inter-group transfers are outside the VAT net, but all companies within the group are jointly and severally liable for the group VAT debt.

For VAT purposes, two companies form a group where one controls the other, or both are controlled by another person (including a partnership).

Control is succinctly defined by stating that one company controls another where *CA 2006* would constitute the investor company as the 'holding company' of the investee company or where an individual is taken to control a company where, if he had been a company, *CA 2006* would have regarded him as the 'holding company' of the investee company.

The attentive reader will recall mention of the 'holding' company concept in **23.3** above. As explained there, the holding company definition is retained for some – but not group accounting – purposes. One of these is that of the definition of a group for VAT purposes.

23.41 The upshot of all this is that group accounts must be prepared in accordance with company law and accounting requirements. HMRC may deny that a group relationship has been created at all for corporation tax purposes (less than 51%), or accept that a group exists for some, but not all, tax purposes (51%–75%), or accept that a group exists for most tax purposes (more than 75%). Meanwhile, HMRC may accept the existence of a group for VAT (providing 51% satisfied) but, rather quirkily, would accept as a group those companies which are under common control but with

23.42 *Groups*

no cross-shareholding. Company law and accounting requirements would not recognise any relationship in this latter situation. HMRC would regard such a relationship as leading to the companies under common control being associated for corporation tax, a concept unknown for VAT. A company lawyer or accountant would be completely baffled.

23.42 There is no better conclusion to this section than to quote Singleton J in the case of *Briggenshaw v Crabb* 30 TC 331, where he said '… if you go on spending your time on Finance Acts and the like, it will drive you silly'.

Chapter 24

Foreign Currency Translation

24.1 This is a uniquely difficult subject. Whilst relatively few accounts include exchange differences, when this problem arises it tends to involve large numbers, so it is important to get it right. The current tax rules essentially follow the accounting rules, but did not always do so.

From the accounting point of view, the rules are contained in *SSAP 20*, although this is superseded by *FRS 23* for listed companies from 2005. *SSAP 20* was introduced in 1983, some eight years after *ED 16*, six years after *ED 21* and three years after *ED 27*, all of which sought to address the problem. The time lag is indicative of the difficulties in securing some kind of agreement on how the matter should be tackled. The price of that consensus is a degree of vagueness in the terminology, and a number of different options available to companies. Some commentators have identified up to 3,000 different accounting alternatives inherent in the standard! A complete exposition of these will be beyond the scope of this book.

FRS 23 was issued in December 2004 and has the effect of implementing *IAS 21* 'The Effects of Changes in Foreign Exchange Rates'. It supersedes *SSAP 20* for all listed entities for accounting periods on or after 1 January 2005. Other entities are permitted to apply *FRS 20*, so long as they also apply certain other FRSs. In 2005, amendment was made to *FRS 23* (*IAS 21*) in relation to net investments in a foreign operation. Companies not using *FRS 23* (*IAS 21*) will continue to use *SSAP 20*.

STATEMENT OF STANDARD ACCOUNTING PRACTICE 20 (SSAP 20)

24.2 *SSAP 20* envisages essentially two types of situation in which the translation of foreign currency has an accounting relevance. First, for individual companies, transactions (buying/selling goods, buying/selling fixed assets, acquiring/disposing of investments) may occur which are denominated in foreign currency. Over time, the rates of exchange vary, and exchange differences on translation arise. *SSAP 20* deals with the accounting treatment of these. It is essentially these types of exchange differences which impact on tax computations. Secondly, groups may operate with foreign subsidiaries who keep their accounting records in foreign currency. In preparing the

24.3 *Foreign Currency Translation*

group consolidated accounts, the results of the foreign subsidiary need to be translated into sterling, and exchange differences can arise here. *SSAP 20* also deals with the accounting effect of this translation. These exchange differences arise only in the consolidated accounts, and are therefore of limited relevance for tax purposes.

INDIVIDUAL COMPANIES

24.3 There are several specific situations to consider. The general theme, though, is that exchange differences, whether gains or losses, whether accrued or realised, should be taken to profit and loss.

Buying and selling assets

24.4 A company may buy or sell an asset at a price denominated in foreign currency. *SSAP 20* provides that, normally, the best way of accounting for that transaction is to translate the price into sterling at the rate applying when the transaction is entered into. Exceptionally, if the transaction is covered by a related or matching forward contract, the rate of exchange in the contract may be used. Alternatively, *SSAP 20* permits the use of the average rate of exchange for the year (not defined, incidentally) – at least during periods of non-volatility in exchange rates – rather than the precise rate applying at the date of the transaction.

But to keep matters simple, in many real-life situations, acquisitions and disposals are generally translated at the rates applicable at the date of contract. *Examples 24.1* and *24.2* illustrate how this works in practice.

Year end adjustments

24.5 Once non-monetary assets (plant, machinery, investments – including equity investments) have been translated into sterling, no further retranslations should be effected, and therefore no exchange differences arise, except in the circumstance described in **24.9** below.

24.6 However, monetary assets in existence at the end of an accounting period (debtors, creditors, cash/bank balances) should be translated into sterling at the rate applicable at the year end. It is likely that this will give rise to an exchange gain or loss.

The situation could arise that a company makes a sale in a foreign currency. It is due to receive a fixed amount of foreign cash. As described in **24.4** above, it translates this into sterling at the sale date and carries the debtor in its books. At the year end, the customer may not have paid. He still owes the same fixed amount of foreign currency, but its sterling equivalent may have changed from that relevant at the date of the sale itself. This represents an accrued exchange gain or loss. *SSAP 20* provides that this accrued gain or loss should be taken to the profit and loss account. This is quite unusual, in that the prudence principle generally militates against the taking of anticipated profit into the results of the year. Notwithstanding this, the basic proposition is that both accrued gains and losses on monetary assets should go to profit and loss. *Examples 24.3, 24.4* and *24.5* illustrate the point.

Realisation of monetary assets and liabilities

24.7 At some stage, the monetary asset, eg the debtor described in **24.6** above, will be converted into cash, ie the debtor pays. At that point, the foreign currency with which he pays is, generally, converted to sterling, and an actual exchange gain or loss is made, compared to the sterling equivalent at which the debt is carried in the books (which, if everything takes place within a single accounting period, will be the amount at the date of the transaction; or, if an accounting date occurs between the date of transaction and payment, it will be the amount computed at the year end). *SSAP 20* provides that this exchange gain or loss, not surprisingly, should also be taken to the profit and loss account. *Example 24.3* illustrates the point.

Long-term monetary items

24.8 *SSAP 20* gives special consideration to long-term monetary assets – generally being loans received or given. It is considered that, despite their long-term nature, there should be a retranslation of these into sterling at each successive year end, and that the accrued exchange gain or loss thereby arising should be taken to profit and loss. This is quite unusual. Generally, prudence would militate against the taking into profit of an accrued gain which might not be realised for many years down the line. *SSAP 20* specifically discusses this point but decides that symmetry of treatment (of gains and losses) is the correct method, except where there are doubts about the convertibility or marketability of the currency in question. In other words, whilst it may be satisfactory to accrue a gain on a US dollar loan, it may not be on a Russian rouble one. *Examples 24.4* and *24.5* are in point.

Matched long-term borrowings

24.9 An exception to the general rule is envisaged in situations where, for example, a company raises a foreign loan in order to finance the acquisition of a foreign equity investment. The exchange risk on the loan is effectively hedged against the inherent exchange differences on the underlying net assets of the foreign company. But, as **24.5** above[explains, the equity investment would not be retranslated at each successive accounting date, whereas, under **24.8** above, the 'associated' loan would.

Subject to conditions, *SSAP 20* allows the equity investment to be retranslated into sterling at successive year ends, but the exchange difference should be

24.10 *Foreign Currency Translation*

taken directly to reserves, and not pass through the profit and loss account. The exchange differences on the loan, to the extent of the transfer to reserves on the equity investment, may also be taken direct to reserves, with any surplus or deficit going through the profit and loss account. What this simply means is that exchange movements on long-term loans may be 'franked' against the movement on the associated equity investment. Where the loan and the cost of the foreign equity investment are equal, the exchange gain and loss will cancel. There will only be a surplus (or deficit) where the value of the equity investment has permanently reduced (eg by poor trading) below the amount of the associated loan, where the loan has been partially repaid, or where the hedging is in a different currency from the investment. *Example 24.6* shows how this works.

The *UITF 19* recently issued clarifies that, in the circumstances where exchange gains or losses are taken straight to reserves and reported in the Statement of Total Recognised Gains and Losses (STRGL), any attributable tax charges and credits should be accounted for in the same way.

GROUP CONSOLIDATED ACCOUNTS

24.10 *SSAP 20* recognises that groups may incorporate foreign subsidiaries which account in the local (ie foreign) currency. In the UK parent company's own accounts, any exchange differences (on the equity investment or on transactions with its own subsidiary) will be dealt with as in **24.3** *et seq* above. Different questions are posed, though, in relation to the group consolidated accounts.

24.11 There are some circumstances in which, although a foreign subsidiary has been incorporated, its activities are really no more than an extension of the UK parent. For example, this might be the case where a UK company sets up a foreign subsidiary solely to act as a selling agency, receiving stocks from the investing company and remitting the proceeds back to the parent.

SSAP 20 provides that, in circumstances like this, the accounts for the subsidiary should be translated using the 'individual company rules' (technically called the 'temporal method' – ie those described in **24.3** *et seq* above). Exchange differences are then, apart from the exception relating to matched long-term borrowings (see **24.9** above), taken through profit and loss. But, for all other situations, a different method is prescribed, which is known as the 'closing rate/net investment' method.

Closing rate/net investment method

24.12 Under this method, the amounts in the balance sheet are translated into sterling at the rate prevailing at the year end. Generally, the profit and loss account is also translated at the year end rate. (*SSAP 20* permits the profit and

Foreign Currency Translation **24.15**

loss account to be translated at the 'average rate' for the year. 'Average rate' is not defined, and its use generates yet another potential exchange difference – that between the translation of the profit and loss account at average rate and at year end rate. This is an unnecessary source of confusion for the reader and, for present purposes, will be disregarded.)

What this boils down to is, in fact, quite simple if represented diagrammatically, as below:

	$	£ Equivalent 01/01/09	£ Equivalent 31/12/09	Exchange Difference
Net Assets at 01/01/09	1,000,000	700,000	750,000	50,000
Profit for Year	500,000		375,000	
Net Assets at 31/12/09	1,500,000		1,125,000	50,000

The profit for the year is translated at the closing rate. This is simply a translation, and does not generate an exchange difference. Translating the year end net assets effectively means translating the opening net assets (year end = opening + profit for year; profit for year has already been translated). Therefore, the only exchange difference arises from the retranslation of the opening net assets at the year end. (NB There is a slight complication if capital injections or withdrawals have been made during the year, but this is not considered here.)

24.13 *SSAP 20* provides that such exchange differences should be taken direct to reserves. *Example 24.6* illustrates how this is done.

Quasi-equity

24.14 It is recognised in *SSAP 20* that parent companies may finance foreign subsidiaries by loan rather than share capital (in tax terminology, such foreign subsidiaries may be 'thinly capitalised', although the accounting and tax criteria do not precisely coincide). Such long-term loans should be treated as effective equity. Any such loans are treated as though they were equity, and any exchange differences thereon are taken directly to reserves. This is only for the treatment of exchange differences, though. The loans are not share capital and should not be shown as such (even less so since *FRS 4* – see Chapter 22).

Matching

24.15 An adjustment similar to that in **24.9** above is also recognised for consolidated accounts purposes. This arises where, within a group, foreign

24.16 *Foreign Currency Translation*

borrowings have been used to finance the acquisition of a foreign equity investment. The accounting for this can be very tricky – especially where the borrowing is not in the same currency as the foreign investment itself! It is an aspect of the subject beyond the realm of this book.

FRS 23 AND IAS 21

24.16 *FRS 23* and *IAS 21* introduce some concepts and definitions that are not used by *SSAP 20*, in particular, functional and presentational currency. Functional currency refers to the currency used in the primary economic environment that the entity operates in. Presentational currency refers to the currency in which the entity's financial statements are presented, which may or may not be the same as the functional currency. So, a company must identify its functional currency and translate its foreign transactions and operations into that functional currency. It may also then have to translate the results into a presentational currency.

In a company's own accounts, individual transactions in a foreign currency are recorded on initial recognition, at the spot rate (not the forward rate) between the functional and foreign currency at the date of the transaction.

At the balance sheet date, foreign currency and monetary items are translated using the closing rate. Non-monetary items that are measured using historical cost are translated at the exchange rate at the date of the transaction. Those that are measured at fair value in the accounts are translated using the exchange rate at the date on which the fair value was determined.

Exchange differences on the settlement of monetary items, or on translation of monetary items, are recognised in the profit and loss, except for items that form part of the net investment in a foreign operation. Some gains and losses are recognised in the STRGL, in which case the foreign exchange differences are also recognised there.

FRS 23 and *IAS 21* are consistent (except that *IAS 21* does not recognise the distinction between profit and loss account and STRGL).

COMPARISON WITH INTERNATIONAL ACCOUNTING STANDARDS

24.17 *FRS 23* embodies *IAS 21* 'The Effects of Changes in Foreign Exchange Rates' for listed companies with effect from periods beginning on or after 1 January 2005.

24.18 For companies continuing to follow *SSAP 20*, the main differences compared to *IAS 21* are as follows:

- *SSAP 20* allows transactions to be translated at matching forward contract rates, whereas *IAS 21* requires the spot rate to be used.

- *SSAP 20* allows the translation of a foreign entity's profit and loss account, for the purposes of inclusion in the consolidated accounts, using either the closing rate or the average rate. Use of the closing rate for translating the profit and loss account is not permitted by *IAS 21*.

TAXATION

24.19 The following represents a *brief* résumé of what is a most complex question. In any real situation, there can (unfortunately) be no substitute for the hard graft of coming to terms with the legislation and, where necessary, the case law.

The current system

24.20 In 2002, the intermediate system (see **24.21** below) was abolished for companies and foreign exchange gains and losses were assimilated into the loan relationship rules (see Chapter 27). In most cases now, there is no need for special computations for tax purposes.

In general, exchange gains or losses on shares held by a company will be brought into account in the capital gains computation, with a few exceptions. Where shares are dealt with under the special 'shares as debt' loan relationship rules, the resulting credits or debits are computed using fair value accounting, which will include exchange differences for shares denominated in a foreign currency. Exchange gains and losses can arise on shares which are held as trading stock, in which case they will form part of the company's trading profits and not be brought within the loan relationship regime.

The disregard regulations under the loan relationship rules allow companies to continue to use matching, and therefore the treatment in SSAP 20 will apply. There are complex anti-avoidance provisions relating to foreign exchange matching.

The intermediate system

24.21 This was introduced by *FA 1993, Pt II* and came into force on 23 March 1995. The legislation is over 50 pages long, supplemented by a number of 'Regulations' contained in statutory instruments (see **24.1** above). Assurances were given during the debate on the primary legislation concerning matters that would be included in the Regulations (giving scope for *Pepper v Hart & Others* [1992] STC 898, HL type future debates). There were also transitional provisions for some assets or transactions which have not yet matured and which have been dealt with initially under the old regime. These rules were specifically designed to align the tax and accounting treatment.

It is important to appreciate that the rules applied to most companies, but did not apply to sole traders or partnerships.

24.22 *Foreign Currency Translation*

There has been, since the 1990s, a certain paranoia within HMRC to prevent any avoidance or unfair or improper tax advantage, and this accounts for the length and complexity of the legislation. It must also be said that, at the very top end of international conglomerates, there are transactions which are terrifically complicated and it must be very difficult to conceive of simple tax rules to accommodate these. It may have been possible to introduce a simplified scheme for the 'smaller company', but this approach is not adopted in the legislation.

THE OLD SYSTEM

24.22 This system continues for all non-companies. There is no specific existing separate statute law on the taxation of exchange differences. *ITTOIA 2005, s 25* requires a business to compute its profit in accordance with GAAP, and so it follows that exchange rates used in the business accounts are also acceptable for computing trade profits, so long as it accords with GAAP. According to BIM39507, traders may use London closing rates when translating foreign currency amounts into sterling in their accounts. Equally, they may use other exchange rates, such as an exchange rate quoted by their bank, or the monthly average rates published by HMRC for VAT purposes. Exchange differences are dealt with by consideration of the underlying transactions from which they derive.

The first problem arises in relation to whether the transaction on which the exchange difference arises is on capital or income account. Purchases of stock and provision of working capital are clearly on income account. Purchase of a machine and associated borrowing is clearly on capital account. But what if the machine is bought out of overdraft? Is an exchange difference on a foreign currency overdraft on capital or income account?

The capital/income distinction may lead to exchange differences being dealt with under capital gains rules or under income tax rules.

Under capital gains rules, there is no 'accrual' of gains or losses. Under income tax rules, accruals are taken into account.

Under capital gains rules, liabilities are not chargeable assets. Therefore, exchange differences on liabilities (such as loans) do not give rise to taxable gains or losses. In the tax jargon, they are 'nothings'.

Matching and hedging problems abound. If a business has monetary assets and monetary liabilities of the same amount in the same currency, any exchange differences that arise will be cancelled out, ie they are 'matched'. Where assets and liabilities are matched in a particular currency, and so no exchange differences are recorded in the profit and loss account, the tax computation follows this, regardless of whether the assets or liabilities are capital or revenue in nature.

If a business holds an investment in a foreign entity, such as shares, and hedges the investment by borrowing, *SSAP 20* allows the investment to be treated as a monetary asset which means that gains or losses are taken to reserves. BIM39522 specifies that the exchange differences taken to reserves, along with the corresponding gains or losses, should not be regarded as taxable or allowable.

Exchange gains or losses on a currency contract are treated as trading transactions for tax purposes, unless the contract hedges a capital asset or liability, in which case they are treated as being capital.

24.23 The remainder of this section is designed to pick out from the legislation those parts which are needed to understand the day-to-day transactions most likely to be met in practice.

Basic proposition

24.24 The starting point is that the legislation attempts to follow accounting practice. Thus, the *SSAP 20* rules for individual unlisted companies not choosing to use *FRS 23* and *IAS 21* are directly relevant.

Exchange gains and losses on monetary assets and liabilities are essentially calculated in accordance with **24.3** to **24.8** above. Non-monetary assets (eg equity investments) continue to be dealt with under existing capital gains rules (except to the extent of a 'matching election' – see **24.25** below).

It is then necessary to identify whether these derive on trading account (no distinction between capital or income) or non-trading (eg pure investment).

Trading exchange gains and losses realised (or accrued) are treated as taxable trading receipts or deductible trading expenses, as they are reflected in the accounts.

Non-trading exchange gains and losses realised (or accrued) are treated differently. As a result of amendments made by the loan relationship legislation in the *Finance Act 1996*, they are now effectively amalgamated with and treated like losses or gains arising on corporate debt. All such exchange gains are accumulated to an amount (as the legislation calls it) 'A'. All exchange losses are accumulated to an amount 'B'. If A exceeds B, the excess will be charged to tax as a non-trading loan relationship. If B exceeds A, relief will be given, effectively as though the excess were a management expense of an investment company (ie the usual management expense set-offs, surrender under group relief rules etc).

Matching

24.25 Where an equity investment is matched by foreign company borrowing as a hedging mechanism, there are two possible treatments. One is for the investment to be dealt with under the capital gains rules as it is a non-monetary amount, whilst the loan is a monetary liability taxed as a non-trading loan relationship. The alternative calculation of exchange gains or

24.26 *Foreign Currency Translation*

losses which might, by election, apply is to effectively match the exchange gains and losses on the loan and investment to give no net liability.

Deferral of unrealised gains

24.26 In some ways, this is a generous provision. *SSAP 20* provides that exchange gains or losses on long-term borrowings should be charged to the profit and loss account each year. The basic proposition of the loan relationship rules is that these accrued differences will be taxed, or be tax deductible, as they arise in a manner depending on whether they relate to trading or non-trading matters.

The rules also introduce the possibility of companies being able to defer in part the tax liability following from an accrued gain on a long-term monetary asset or liability into the following accounting period.

Broadly, the relief applies on a claim. The corporation tax profit for the company is computed, ignoring group relief or any *FA 1993, s 139* relief. Amount A, being 10% of this corporation tax profit, is calculated. Amount B (the difference between the total of unrealised losses and gains on similar assets) and Amount C (the difference between the total amount of exchange gains in respect of certain assets/liabilities and the total exchange losses on similar assets/liabilities) are calculated.

Then, there is computed (B – A), and (C – A). The lower of these two amounts is then available for relief.

The relief comprises the deferral of liability until the next accounting period. However similar calculations in the next period may lead to further deferral, and so on.

EXAMPLES

24.27 It is quite possible, and not entirely surprising, that a good many readers may by this stage be dizzy. A number of simple worked examples now follow, which show how to account for (and comment on the tax treatment of) exchange differences in a number of different circumstances.

24.28 The case of the purchase of raw materials from a French supplier, the price denominated in sterling.

Example 24.1
Company A has a year end of 31 December.

On 1 June 2009 it purchases raw materials from France for a contracted amount of £20,000. The exchange rate is then £1 = 1.15 Euros. It takes two months' credit and then pays the £20,000. The exchange rate then is £1 = 1.10 Euros.

Exchange rate considerations are a red herring. The transaction was effected in sterling. There is no accounting exchange difference and, therefore, no tax consequence in either the old or new system.

24.29 The case of the purchase of raw materials from a US supplier, the price denominated in US dollars. Consideration paid before accounting year end.

Example 24.2
Company B has a year end of 31 December.

On 1 June 2009 it purchases raw materials for $100,000. The then exchange rate is £1 = $1.50. It takes two months' credit and pays on 1 August 2009 at a time when the exchange rate is £1 = $1.55.

The transaction is initially recorded at the rate of exchange applying at the date of purchase (1 June 2009). The goods are treated as having cost £66.667 $\left(\frac{100,000}{1.5}\right)$.

When payment is made, an amount of £64,516 is paid over £66.667 $\left(\frac{100,000}{1.5}\right)$.

An exchange gain of £2,151 (66,667 − 64,516) arises.

In accounting terms, the exchange gain is taken to profit in the year ended 31 December 2009.

Under the old taxation rules, the gain is taxable as a trading receipt, because it arises in regard to a revenue (ie not capital) matter (purchase of stock).

Under the new taxation rules, the gain is also taxable as a trading receipt, because it arises on trading (ie not investment) account.

24.30 The case of the purchase of raw materials from a US supplier, the price denominated in US dollars. Consideration paid after the year end.

Example 24.3
Company C effects the same transaction as Company B in *Example 24.2* above, except that it delays payment until 1 February 2010, at which time the exchange rate is £1 = $1.45. The exchange rate at 31 December 2009 is £1 = $1.48.

In accounting terms at 31 December 2009, there is an accrued exchange loss of £901 $\left(\frac{100,000}{1.5} - \frac{100,000}{1.48}\right)$. This is charged to profit and loss for the year ended 31 December 2009. In the following year, there is a further exchange loss of £1,398 $\left(\frac{100,000}{1.48} - \frac{100,000}{1.45}\right)$. This is charged to profit and loss for the year ended 31 December 2010.

24.31 Foreign Currency Translation

Under the old taxation rules, both the exchange loss of £901 and that of £1,398 would be allowable trading deductions in the years ended 31 December 2009 and 31 December 2010 respectively. This is so, even though the £901 is not realised but only accrued at 31 December 2009. For the measurement of trading profits, an accruals method is appropriate.

Under the new taxation rules, both the losses of £901 and £1,398 are allowable deductions in the years ended 31 December 2009 and 31 December 2010 respectively.

24.31 The case of taking out a loan denominated in US dollars.

Example 24.4
Company D has a year end of 31 December.

On 1 July 2009 it takes out a five-year loan of $200,000 from an American bank. The then rate of exchange was £1 = $1.55. At 31 December 2009, the rate of exchange was £1 = $1.50.

In accounting terms, at the taking of the loan, its sterling equivalent was £129,032 $- \left(\frac{200,000}{1.55}\right)$. At the year end, the sterling equivalent is £133,333 $- \left(\frac{200,000}{1.5}\right)$. In other words, the liability in sterling terms has increased by £4,301. An accrued exchange loss of £4,301 arises. For accounts purposes, this is charged to profit and loss for the year ended 31 December 2009.

Under the old tax rules, because the loan is capital (ie long-term) in nature, it is not a trading deduction. It is not a chargeable asset (because it is a liability!) for capital gains purposes. The exchange loss is, therefore, ignored for tax purposes.

Under the new rules, presuming the money is used for the purpose of the company's trade, then even though only an accrued loss, it is allowable as a trading deduction for the year ending 31 December 2009.

24.32 The case of an equity investment in an Australian company in Australian dollars, financed by a loan denominated in Australian dollars.

Example 24.5
Company E acquires a 10% equity stake in an Australian company costing A$300,000 on 1 July 2009 when the exchange rate is £1 = A$2.15. It regards this as a fixed asset and so accounts for it as such. At the same time, as a hedge against the exchange risk, the company borrows A$300,000. At the year end (31 December 2009), the exchange rate is £1 = A$2.3.

Foreign Currency Translation **24.33**

In accounting terms, the equity investment is matched with the related borrowing. There is an exchange loss on the investment of £9,100 $\left(\frac{300,000}{2.15} - \frac{300,000}{2.3}\right)$ which is matched with the exchange gain of £9,100 on the A$ loan. There is no net exchange loss or gain taken to profit/loss or to reserves.

This investment and loan fall to be dealt with under the capital gains rules. No gain or loss arises in the year because no gain or loss is realised. If, in the following year, the investment is sold and the loan repaid, then an exchange gain or loss is effectively incorporated in the capital gain computation on disposal of the investment; but, as the loan is not an asset, it is completely ignored for tax purposes.

In the new set of tax rules, there will seemingly be two possible tax treatments. The first is that the investment – not being a monetary asset – will continue to be dealt with under capital gains legislation. The borrowing is a monetary liability. At each year end, it should be translated to sterling. Not being on trading account, any exchange profit is taxable as a non-trading loan relationship, and any exchange loss is relieved as though it were a management expense. On the figures above, the £9,100 will be taxed for the year ending 31 December 2009. The alternative treatment will be to elect to effectively match the exchange gains and losses on the investment and loan to give no net liability. Once made, the election stays in effect until the asset is disposed of or matching ceases.

24.33 The case of a company preparing group accounts with an American subsidiary in which it has owned 100% of the equity since its inception.

Example 24.6

Company F is a UK company which has owned 100% of the issued share capital of an American company, G Inc, since inception (at which date the exchange rate was £1 = $1.60).

The exchange rate at 1 January 2009 was £1 = $1.50, and at 31 December 2009 it was £1 = $1.60.

Summary individual and group balance sheets and profit and loss accounts for the year ending 31 December 2009 are reproduced below:

24.33 *Foreign Currency Translation*

	F Ltd	G Inc	G Inc	Group
	£	$	£	
Net Assets	1,000,000	480,000	300,000	1,200,000
	1,000,000	480,000	300,000	1,200,000
Share Capital	100,000	160,000	100,000	100,000
Reserves	900,000	320,000	200,000	1,100,000
	1,000,000	480,000	300,000	1,200,000
TURNOVER	10,000,000	6,400,000	4,000,000	14,000,000
Net Profit After Tax	250,000	160,000	100,000	350,000

In accounting terms, there are no exchange differences in translating the profit and loss account – there is simply a translation using the closing (at 31 December 2009) exchange rate.

The analysis of group reserves can be deduced as follows: an exchange difference arises from the retranslation of G Inc's net assets at 31 December 2009 (compared to 1 January 2009) rates (see **24.12** above). For G Inc, it can be seen:

Net Assets at 31 December 2009	$480,000
Profit for Year	$160,000
Net Assets at 1 January 2009	$320,000
Sterling Equivalent 1 January 2009 (£1 = $1.50)	£213,333
Sterling Equivalent 31 December 2009 (£1 = $1.60)	£200,000
Exchange Loss	£13,333
Hence, group reserves can be analysed:	
Reserves 1 January 2009	£763,333
Exchange Loss	£(13,333)
Profit for Year	£350,000
Reserves 31 December 2009	£1,100,000

Fortunately, none of this impacts on either F Ltd or G Inc's tax liabilities under either the old or new tax rules, as these differences arise solely in the consolidated accounts.

Chapter 25

Goodwill and Intangible Assets

25.1 This is yet another major area of contention within the accountancy profession. *SSAP 22* was issued in 1984 (updated in 1989) and, as will be seen, strongly encouraged the immediate write-off of goodwill, although permitting capitalisation followed by annual amortisation. Within seven months of the update, a new exposure draft (*ED 47*) was published, taking precisely the opposite view. That was severely criticised and was not proceeded with. In December 1993, the ASB published a discussion paper on the question of accounting for goodwill. Amendments to this paper were proposed in 1995, following which heated public meetings were held. *FRED 12* on goodwill and intangibles was issued on 27 June 1996. In December 1997, *FRS 10* – dealing with goodwill and intangible assets – was published.

FINANCIAL REPORTING STANDARD 10 (FRS 10)

25.2 Goodwill itself is not an 'asset'. Intangible assets (licences, quotas, copyrights, franchises, trademarks, etc) form a spectrum, which at one end makes them difficult to distinguish from goodwill, whilst at the other they more closely resemble separate assets. Because of this similarity and overlap, the *FRS 10* rules for identification, amortisation and impairment of goodwill and other intangibles are similar.

Initial recognition

25.3 Purchased goodwill and intangible assets should be capitalised as assets (at fair value – see **25.11** below). Internally generated goodwill should not be capitalised. However, internally developed intangible assets may be capitalised, but only where they have a readily ascertainable market value. A 'readily ascertainable market value' is defined in *FRS 10* as a value that is established by reference to a market where:

- the asset belongs to a homogeneous population of assets that are equivalent in all material respects, and
- an active market, evidenced by frequent transactions, exists for that population of assets.

25.4 *Goodwill and Intangible Assets*

This is a restrictive definition and, therefore, in general, the costs of developing internally generated intangible assets will be written off to the profit and loss account as incurred.

Amortisation

25.4 Broadly, capitalised goodwill and intangible assets should be amortised (ie depreciated) over the period of their expected use. This requires an assessment of their useful lives, an exercise that inevitably requires subjective judgements to be made. There is a (rebuttable) presumption that the useful life should not exceed 20 years. The useful life can only be taken to be more than 20 years where the asset is capable of continued measurement (so that annual impairment tests can be made If the life is considered indefinite, so that no amortisation takes place, this technically breaches the *Companies Act 2006*. A note to the accounts would have to explain that departure from the detailed provision of the *Companies Act* was needed to provide a 'true and fair view'. Note that 'indefinite' is not the same as 'infinite'; it merely means that the estimated useful life is sufficiently long that it cannot be measured with any degree of precision. In the context of the wording of *FRS 10*, this would need to be considerably longer than 20 years.

Impairment reviews

25.5 An impairment review (see Chapter 15 is needed to ensure the goodwill or intangible asset has not fallen below its recoverable amount (the higher of net realisable value and value in use). Where the goodwill or intangible asset is amortised over a period not exceeding 20 years, the impairment review need only be done at the end of the first period following acquisition, or if events or changes in circumstances occur that indicate the carrying amount may not be recoverable. If amortised over a period of longer than 20 years (or not amortised at all), impairment reviews should be effected every year.

Revaluation

25.6 Goodwill should not be revalued, but intangible assets having a readily ascertainable market value may be revalued. If a revaluation is effected, then all intangibles of the same class should be included in the revaluation process. This requirement prevents selective revaluations covering only those intangibles that have increased in value. Further revaluations should occur often enough to ensure the carrying value does not materially differ from the market value.

Negative goodwill

25.7 Negative goodwill is to be shown on the face of the balance sheet, separately disclosed below the 'Goodwill' heading. It should pass through the profit and loss on a systematic basis. Insofar as the negative goodwill does not exceed the fair value of any non-monetary assets, it should pass through profit and loss as those non-monetary assets are depreciated or sold. Any excess of negative goodwill over the fair value of any non-monetary assets should be written back to profit and loss over the period expected to benefit from that negative goodwill.

Transitional rules

25.8 If application of *FRS 10* requires a change of accounting policy, then it should be accounted for as such, ie there should be a prior year adjustment (see Chapter 7). For many companies, *FRS 10* does require such a change. This is because goodwill on acquisition was allowed, under *SSAP 22*, to be written off immediately to reserves. Most acquiring companies did this, as there would not be any subsequent amortisation change to profit and loss. However, the ASB recognised that this may not be practicable. Therefore, reinstatement is not required of:

- goodwill on acquisitions pre-23 December 1989 where the information cannot be obtained without unreasonable expense or delay; or
- all goodwill eliminated before the issue of *FRS 7*; or
- all goodwill previously eliminated.

FINANCIAL REPORTING STANDARD 7 (FRS 7)

25.9 This deals with the thorny topic of 'fair value' determination where the acquisition method of accounting is applied.

The reason for the concern has been the lack of uniformity adopted in takeover situations and the perceived adoption of 'creative accounting' by many acquiring companies.

In simple terms, when an acquiring company purchases a target company, it estimates the fair value of the underlying assets it acquires and compares this with the consideration given to determine the goodwill (positive or negative) arising on the acquisition. That goodwill is then dealt with under *FRS 10*, as described above. Profits and losses after acquisition are included in the group profit and loss account.

Two particular areas of abuse have been prevalent.

First, acquiring companies were anticipating certain post-acquisition costs (such as the cost of a restructuring) and treating this as a liability on acquisition. Whilst this would increase the amount of goodwill, it inflates the post-acquisition profits of the target and hence the group because, when the restructuring costs are incurred, they were charged against the provision set up immediately following the acquisition, rather than against the post-acquisition profit and loss account.

25.10 *Goodwill and Intangible Assets*

Secondly, there was a certain vagueness about how the fair values themselves should be determined. For example, should a long-term debt not carrying interest be incorporated at its nominal or present value (applying discounted cash flow techniques)?

It is to counter these and other potential problems that *FRS 7* was introduced. The stated objective of the standard is to ensure that, when a business entity is acquired by another, all the assets and liabilities that existed in the acquired entity at the date of acquisition are recorded at fair values, reflecting their condition at that date. All changes to the acquired assets and liabilities, and the resulting gains and losses, that arise after control of the acquired entity has passed to the acquirer are reported as part of the post-acquisition performance of the acquiring group.

Assets and liabilities

25.10 *FRS 7* provides that only those assets and liabilities which the acquired entity has at the date of takeover should be taken into account. In other words, changes which may arise resulting from the acquirer's intentions should be disregarded. For example, provisions for future reorganisation costs are ignored unless already internally planned by the target company, as are the costs of integrating the acquired business into the group. Similarly, it is not permitted to make provision for future operating losses. These costs are to be charged to the post-acquisition profit and loss account.

The assets and liabilities to be taken into account may not all be reflected in the balance sheet. Pension scheme surpluses, or the deferred tax asset represented by future tax relief on past profits, may not be accounted for in the accounts of the target company. If, for example, the purchase price reflects an element relating to the benefit of tax losses, this would appear as goodwill unless the value of the assets is brought into the fair value calculation.

VALUATION BASIS

25.11 *FRS 7* defines 'fair value' as 'the amount at which an asset or liability could be exchanged in an arm's-length transaction between informed and willing parties other than in a forced or liquidation sale'. The application of this definition to specific classes of assets is as follows:

- **Tangible fixed assets**: market value, if assets similar in type and condition are traded on an open market; or, if such a market does not exist, depreciated replacement cost. The fair value should not exceed the 'recoverable amount' of the asset. The 'recoverable amount' is defined as the greater of net realisable value and value in use.
- **Stocks and work in progress**: lower of replacement cost and net realisable value.
- **Quoted investments and traded commodity stocks**: market prices.

- **Monetary assets and liabilities**: the amount expected to be received or paid, discounted, if material, to present value.

Whilst the term 'fair value' implies a reasonable degree of objectivity, it is apparent that the definitions set out above leave significant scope for subjectivity in the estimation of fair values. For the unscrupulous, this also gives scope for deliberate manipulation.

COST OF ACQUISITION

25.12 Where there are contingent future payments (eg on an 'earnout'), the best estimate of such future payment should be made and subsequently adjusted in later accounting periods.

The cost of acquisition is the amount of cash paid plus the fair value of any other consideration given.

Acquisition expenses are to be included as costs of acquisition. Only the incremental costs (such as fees paid to merchant banks, lawyers, accountants etc) are included in this head. Costs which would otherwise have been incurred (eg costs of maintaining an acquisitions department, or other management remuneration) should be written off to the profit and loss account. (This should discourage HMRC from trying to disallow such costs on capital/revenue grounds, although the 'wholly and exclusively' test needs watching, as does the tax status – trading, investment, hybrid – of the acquiring company.) Any costs associated with the issue of shares and other capital instruments are not included here, but are dealt with under *FRS 4* (see Chapter 27).

BUSINESS BOUGHT FOR RESALE

25.13 Special rules apply where businesses are bought for resale in the short term.

DETERMINATION OF FAIR VALUE

25.14 The following example – based on the example originally incorporated in Appendix 3 to *SSAP 22* – shows how a fair value might be determined in practice.

25.14 *Goodwill and Intangible Assets*

Example 25.1
Calculation of fair value

Acquisition – XYZ Ltd Date – 19/02/89

Consideration – 100,000 £1 ordinary shares were issued to acquire the following assets. The fair value of the consideration, using the mid-market price on 18/02/89 of £3.06, was £306,000, giving rise to goodwill of £100,000.

	Book Value	Revaluation	Provisions	Accounting Policy Alignment	Other Major Items	Fair Value to the Group
	£'000	£'000	£'000	£'000	£'000	£'000
Fixed Assets						
Intangible	–	–	–	–	80(f)	80
Tangible	160	20(a)	–	–	–	180
Investments	20	5(b)	–	–	–	25
Current Assets						
Stock	40	–	(9)(c)	(2)(e)	–	29
Debtors	35	–	(8)(d)	–	–	27
Investments	10	–	–	–	–	10
Cash at Bank	12	–	–	–	–	12
Total Assets	277	25	(17)	(2)	80	363
Liabilities						
Provisions						
Pensions	30	–	–	–	–	30
Taxation	45	–	–	–	10(g)	55
Other	10	–		–	–	10
Creditors						
Debenture	2	–	–	–	–	2
Bank Loans	15	–	–	–	–	15
Trade Creditors	30	–	–	–	–	30
Other Creditors	10	–	–	–	–	10
Accruals	5	–	–	–	–	5
Total Liabilities	147	–	–	–	10	157
Net Assets	130	25	(17)	(2)	70	206

	Adjustments	Explanations
(i)	**Revaluations**	
	Note a	Increases in value of freehold properties since last revaluation in 1981.
	Note b	Increase in value of shares in investment since purchase in 1983.
(ii)	**Provisions**	
	Note c	Write-down following reassessment of realisable value of stock which is more than one year old.
	Note d	Provision for doubtful debts following reassessment of realisable value.
(iii)	**Accounting Policy Alignments**	
	Note e	Change of stock valuation from weighted average cost to FIFO which is used by the group.
(iv)	**Other Major Items**	
	Note f	Recognition of intangibles – relating to publishing titles and brands acquired.
	Note g	Adjustment of deferred tax arising from the incorporation of fair values.

Accounting treatment

Acquisition – positive goodwill and intangibles

25.15 Once the amount of goodwill or intangible cost is established, a policy decision is needed as to the period over which the expenditure is to be amortised (usually). Although 20 years is not a 'default' period, it is likely that many companies will choose to write off over that period, particularly as it is difficult to determine the economic useful life of goodwill with any degree of objectivity.

Acquisition – negative goodwill

25.16 This will not be that unusual an occurrence. Failing subsidiaries may be disposed of by large groups, perhaps to a management buy-out team, at a discount to net assets. Provided the fair value of the net assets is more than the consideration, there will be negative goodwill. *FRS 10* provides that negative goodwill should be shown on the face of the balance sheet under the head 'Goodwill' and amortised. This is best illustrated by an example.

25.16 *Goodwill and Intangible Assets*

Example 25.2

Company A purchases Company B for £200,000. Fair values attributed to the assets show the following.

	£'000	£'000
Land and Buildings	200	
Plant and Machinery	100	
Non-monetary Assets		300
Net Working Capital	300	
Monetary Assets		300
Total Assets		600
Consideration Given		(200)
Negative Goodwill		400

NOTE: Net working capital is assumed to be represented by monetary assets for the purposes of this illustration.

Land and buildings are depreciated straight line at 2% p.a. Plant and machinery is depreciated straight line at 10% p.a. The residual goodwill is to be taken to profit and loss over 20 years.

Calculation

1. Negative Goodwill — 400
   Non-monetary Assets — 300
   Surplus — 100
   Total — 400

2. Depreciation on Non-monetary Assets: Land and Buildings — 4
   Plant/Machinery — 10
   Total — 14

3. Surplus negative goodwill (of 100) is credited to profit and loss over 20 years. Therefore, annual credit 5.

4. Therefore, at the end of Year 1, the amount of negative goodwill can be analysed:

	£'000
Negative Goodwill at Start	400
Transfer to Profit and Loss (14 + 5)	(19)
Negative Goodwill Carry Forward	£381

Goodwill and Intangible Assets **25.18**

It can be seen that the negative goodwill comprises two elements. In the first instance, the negative goodwill is, as far as possible, identified with non-monetary assets acquired (ie those which are generally depreciated). To the extent that these are depreciated, negative goodwill is released to profit and loss. Any excess negative goodwill is credited to profit and loss over its estimated useful life.

Realised profits – distributable profits

25.17 *SSAP 22* paid particular attention to this matter. As many companies did not restate earlier years using the *FRS 10* exemption (see **25.8** above), this is still relevant.

Dividends can only be paid out of distributable profits. Dividends are paid by individual companies – not groups. Therefore, the question of realised or distributable profits is one which is most directly relevant to individual companies.

When goodwill on acquisition was immediately written off to reserves (as was permitted under *SSAP 22*), it was not because it had fallen to negligible value overnight. It was not a realised loss. Therefore, the immediate write-off did not reduce realised or distributable profits, even though it may have had that appearance, especially if written off against Profit and Loss account balance. As the years go by, the value of the goodwill is consumed (if it had been capitalised, it would have been amortised). Each year, the equivalent of an amortisation charge has the effect of redesignating that part of the unrealised loss on the goodwill write-off into a realised one, and thus to that extent reducing realised and distributable profits.

25.18 This can be illustrated by an example:

Example 25.3

Company A bought the assets of Company B at 31 December 1993 for £1 million. The fair value of the assets was £500,000. The goodwill of £500,000 was written off to reserves. The goodwill is expected to have a life of 10 years. The balance sheet at 31 December 1998 of Company A is below. What is the maximum dividend Company A could pay?

	£'000
Net Assets	500
	500
Share Capital	100
Retained Profits	400
	500

25.19 *Goodwill and Intangible Assets*

On the face of it, a dividend of up to £400,000 could be paid. However, the £500,000 goodwill purchase has been written off to Profit and Loss. It is not entirely a realised loss. Had it accounted for the acquisition on the alternative *SSAP 22* basis or under the now mandatory basis of *FRS 10*, the £500,000 would have been capitalised and only £250,000 (5/10 × £500,000) would have been amortised. Therefore, the maximum dividend is:

	£'000
Retained Profits Per Accounts	400
Plus Non-realised Loss on Goodwill	250
	650

25.19 Extensive disclosures are required by *FRS 10*. The financial statements should describe the method used to value intangibles. Full information on positive and negative goodwill and each class of intangible asset should be separately disclosed. Reconciliations of movements dealing with acquisitions and disposals are also required.

COMPARISON WITH INTERNATIONAL ACCOUNTING STANDARDS

25.20 The international standard dealing with intangible assets (*IAS 38*) differs in a number of respects from UK GAAP. One important distinction relates to the coverage of the standard. While *FRS 10* only recognises intangibles that can be sold separately from the business, *IAS 38* actually *requires* recognition of non-separable assets where they arise from contractual or other legal rights. This means that, in a business combination, for example, more intangibles will be recognised under IFRS (*IFRS 3*) than under UK GAAP.

Another distinction relates to the amortisation of goodwill. Whereas *FRS 10* requires the amortisation of purchased goodwill with a finite useful life, *IAS 38* does not allow amortisation and *requires* annual impairment testing. In the case of goodwill also, *FRS 10* contains the rebuttable presumption of a 20-year life, whereas *IAS 38* contains no such presumption.

Under *IAS 36*, once an impairment loss has been recognised in relation to goodwill, it cannot subsequently be written back. This is based on the presumption that any increase in value following impairment is a result of internally generated goodwill, which cannot be recognised under *IAS 38*.

In the case of negative goodwill arising on a business combination, *FRS 7* requires recognition as a separate item within goodwill, and allows for its attribution to the profit and loss over time. *IFRS 3* requires immediate recognition as a gain in the profit and loss.

TAXATION

25.21 There are several relevant points arising.

The substitution of fair value in determining the quantum of goodwill purchased applies whenever a business (and associated assets) is acquired.

The contract may provide for land/buildings to be bought for £1 million, stock and work in progress for £1 million, and no consideration for all or any other assets. However, to account for the transaction properly, all assets must have attributed to them a fair value and, arithmetically, a balancing figure – being goodwill – may emerge. This will encourage HMRC to consider challenging the amounts attributed to assets in the contracts. In particular, *CAA 1990, s 150* is in point.

More common is to see goodwill emerge on consolidation. In itself, this gives no tax problem: when the shares in a company change hands, the vendor suffers a capital gain or loss, and the purchaser obtains a capital gains base cost on the shares bought and sold. The value of underlying assets is irrelevant.

THE INTANGIBLES REGIME

25.22 In 2002, a radical change was made to the tax treatment of intangible assets, including goodwill. A completely independent regime was created to deal with such assets, with the aim of aligning the tax treatment with the accounting treatment. The regime has effect from 1 April 2002 and is relevant for companies only. The broad outline is that a company's debits and credits in respect of intellectual property and other intangible assets, including goodwill, are only recognised for tax purposes when they are recorded in the profit or loss. The following is an outline of the relevant provisions of *CTA 2009, Part 8* (drawing heavily on the accompanying Explanatory Notes).

Definitions are provided of the terms 'intangible asset' and also 'intangible fixed asset', the latter including an important general extension to the original rules (contained in *FA 2002, Sch 29*), such that, if an asset is an intangible fixed asset, then so is any option, or other right to acquire or dispose of that asset. Goodwill is specifically brought within the intangibles regime by *CTA 2009, s 715*. In identifying the relevant accounting amounts from which the related tax amounts are derived, the term 'GAAP Compliant Accounts' is used; arguably, a more neutral term than 'correct accounts' in the old legislation.

'Credits' arise on receipts recognised when they accrue, for example royalties, but amounts received on realisation of the intangible fixed asset are dealt with separately. Credits include an upward revaluation of the intangible financial asset and certain releases of negative goodwill (see above). They will also arise on reversal of previously allowed accounting losses.

Debits arise in relation to expenditure, and *CTA 2009, s 727* puts beyond doubt that these rules do not apply to expenditure on tangible assets, even though they may appear to come within the definition. An example provided

25.23 *Goodwill and Intangible Assets*

in the Explanatory Notes is that of expenditure on cars used by company staff promoting the company's brand name.

Deductions are available for expenditure that is not capitalised but written off during the period in which it was incurred, such as expenditure in respect of maintaining an asset, or expenditure on an acquisition that proves abortive.

25.23 Deductions for amounts written off for intangible fixed assets that have been capitalised are provided by *CTA 2009, s 729*. Importantly, companies are given the option to take relief at a fixed rate (4% per annum) by *CTA 2009, s 730*. This means that the tax deduction for the cost of acquiring very durable assets, which are either not amortised in the accounts or are amortised over a very long period of time, is available or accelerated.

Realisation of intangible fixed assets (including goodwill) is dealt with separately by *CTA 2009, Part 8, Chapter 4*. Realisation is defined in *CTA 2009, s 734* by reference to GAAP. Rules are provided for quantifying the credits and debits for intangible fixed assets previously written down for tax purposes, and those not (for example, where they are sold soon after acquisition). In the case of partial realisation, *CTA 2009, s 737* determines the appropriate portion of the tax written-down value or cost of the asset to be written off.

CTA 2009, Part 8, s 740 provides for abortive realisation expenditure to be a debit, that is, expenditure in relation to a transaction that would have been a realisation if it had been carried through to completion, which would not otherwise be allowable.

CTA 2009, Chapter 6 deals with how credits and debits are given effect for tax purposes and, consistent with the loan relationship rules (see Chapter 27), distinguish between intangible fixed assets that are used for trading purposes and those that are not. In both cases, all the credits and debits are brought into account as revenue items for tax purposes, although different rules apply depending on the nature of the business activity, eg trading, property etc.

The charge to corporation tax on non-trading gains on intangible fixed assets is provided in *CTA 2009, s 751*.

In taking intangibles out of the capital gains tax regime, the need arose to consider the possibility of a sale followed by reinvestment in another intangible fixed asset. Rollover relief is provided in these circumstances (in *CTA 2009, Part 8, Chapter 7*) which creates a departure from the accountancy treatment.

Certain assets are excluded from the intangibles regime, most importantly those that are held for a non-commercial purpose. Because the intangibles regime is autonomous, such provision is necessary because it does not contain rules that apply elsewhere, such as the prohibition on expenses not wholly and exclusively for the purposes of a trade. Also excluded are assets on which capital allowances claims have previously been made, rights over intangible assets, and financial assets.

Goodwill and Intangible Assets **25.23**

In relation to computer software, where it is acquired together with hardware, it is treated as not being within the intangibles regime (consistent with the UK GAAP accounting treatment, but not IFRS). Software acquired other than together with hardware is within the regime, although companies may elect to exclude it, for example where the capital allowances treatment would be more generous.

Chapter 26

Research and Development Expenditure

26.1 The accounting for research and development expenditure is relatively straightforward. Part of the reason for this is that the strong thrust both of the accounting standard and the *CA 2006* is to require all research expenditure, and to encourage all development expenditure, to be written off against profits in the year in which it is incurred.

STATEMENT OF STANDARD ACCOUNTING PRACTICE 13 (SSAP 13)

26.2 *SSAP 13* was introduced in 1977 and revised in 1989. Research and development expenditure is distinguished from non-research-based activity by the presence or absence of an appreciable element of innovation. The SSAP itself gives examples of types of activity falling within or outside the ambit of 'research and development'. In practice, whilst it may be difficult to define, it is relatively easy to recognise.

DEFINITIONS

26.3 *SSAP 13* breaks down research and development expenditure into: pure (or basic) research; applied research; and development.

Pure (or basic) research

26.4 This comprises experimental or theoretical work undertaken primarily to acquire new scientific or technical knowledge for its own sake, rather than directed towards any specific aim or application.

Applied research

26.5 This comprises original or critical investigation undertaken in order to gain new scientific or technical knowledge, and directed towards a specific practical aim or objective.

Development

26.6 This comprises the use of scientific or technical knowledge in order to produce new or substantially improved materials, devices, products or services, to install new processes or systems prior to the commencement of commercial production or commercial applications, or to improve substantially those already produced or installed.

ACCOUNTING TREATMENT

26.7 Subject to the comments in the next paragraph, all expenditure on both pure and applied research should be written off in the year incurred through the profit and loss account.

All fixed assets (buildings, machines etc) bought or constructed to provide facilities for research and development should be capitalised and depreciated (under *FRS 15* principles).

All development expenditure should be written off in the year it is incurred through profit and loss account except in circumstances detailed below, when it *may* be deferred to later periods. The use of the word 'may', rather than 'must', was deliberate. It was not the intention of the standard to compel directors to capitalise development expenditure, presumably on the grounds that any new development has an element of speculation, in that there is no certainty of success, but to give them the option of so doing if they decided it was appropriate in the circumstances. However, the standard goes on to state that, if an accounting policy of deferral of development expenditure is adopted, it should be applied to all developmental projects that meet the criteria below.

The criteria are:

- there is a clearly defined project;
- the related expenditure is separately identifiable;
- the outcome has been assessed with reasonable certainty, both as to technical feasibility and the ultimate commercial viability;
- future sales revenues should exceed the development costs incurred, and to be incurred, and all related production and sales costs; and
- adequate resources exist, or are reasonably expected to be available, to enable the project to be completed and to provide any consequential increases in working capital.

The determination of whether a specific developmental project has met these criteria is a subjective exercise involving numerous assessments as to uncertain future events.

26.8 Where such development expenditure is so deferred (ie carried as an asset in the balance sheet and not charged to revenue through the profit

26.9 *Research and Development Expenditure*

and loss account), it should be amortised (ie depreciated). The period of amortisation begins with the beginning of commercial production. Each year, a part of the cost is transferred to profit and loss, to match up with revenues produced, to give a fair measure of profit. The amortisation method selected should reflect the anticipated sale or use of the output from the development project or the period during which benefits are expected to be derived, as appropriate. Amortisation does not need to be on a straight line basis.

26.9   SSAP 13 requires an annual review of the deferred development costs, to determine whether the conditions (as specified in **26.7** above) still hold.

DISCLOSURES

26.10   A company's accounting policy in relation to research and development should be disclosed, along with the total amount of research and development charged against profit and loss, analysed between the current year's expenditure and amounts amortised from deferred expenditure, and the movements on deferred development expenditure during the year (incorporating opening and closing balances). *SSAP 13* requires the disclosure of research and development charged to profit and loss, and its analysis, only for public limited companies, their subsidiaries, certain financial institutions, and companies which exceed by a factor of ten the criteria for defining a medium-sized company under *CA 1985* (as amended).

COMPANIES ACT REQUIREMENTS

26.11   *SI 2008/409* and *SI 2008/410* (the '*Accounting Regulations*') specifically prohibit the costs of research from being capitalised on a balance sheet.

Both formats 1 and 2 make provision for the inclusion of 'Development Costs' in the balance sheet, but the *Accounting Regulations* require that development costs should only be capitalised in 'special circumstances'. The special circumstances are not defined, but any company so capitalising this type of expenditure is required in its accounts to state its reasons, and to state the period over which the expenditure is to be written off.

Under the *Accounting Regulations*, the directors' report should give an indication of the company's activities in the field of research and development.

Under *CA 2006, s 844*, capitalised development costs are to be regarded as a realised loss for the purposes of determining the distributable profits of a company, *unless* there are special circumstances (not defined) justifying the directors in deciding that such expenditure will not be regarded as a realised loss. If the directors believe this to be the case, they should say so and justify it in a note to the accounts.

What all this means is that a company has to be very sure that it will recover these capitalised costs, and directors are put on notice that this is the case. The pressure is directed at encouraging immediate write-off (which is what many companies do).

COMPARISON WITH INTERNATIONAL ACCOUNTING STANDARDS

26.12 The international accounting standard dealing with research and development expenditure is *IAS 38* 'Intangible Assets', which was issued in March 2004. As the title of the standard suggests, it deals with a wider range of intangible assets. As far as research and development expenditure is concerned, the two standards are broadly similar. The main difference is that *SSAP 13* permits a choice as to whether or not to capitalise development costs when the criteria specified in **26.7** above are satisfied, whereas *IAS 38* requires capitalisation if the criteria are satisfied. However, the subjectivity of the criteria is such that it would be relatively easy to avoid capitalisation by failing to provide adequate evidence, if required.

IAS 38 also specifically does not allow development costs incurred before the criteria are satisfied (and therefore written off to the profit and loss account) to be retrospectively reinstated on the balance sheet after the criteria are met. *SSAP 13* does not address this issue.

TAXATION

26.13 The tax rules follow accounting in terms of the way research and development is defined, so the question of whether expenditure qualifies as research and development in the first instance is dealt with as an accounting issue. Note, however, that HMRC suggest that guidelines provided by the Department of Business, Innovation and Skills (formerly Department of Trade and Industry) will take priority over the accounting standards in this regard. Once identified as qualifying expenditure, the tax rules vary depending on whether the expenditure is of a capital or revenue nature (irrespective of whether it is capitalised in the accounts).

Capital expenditure on research and development qualifies for 100% capital allowances, ie it is written off in full for tax purposes. Revenue expenditure may be eligible for an enhanced deduction for tax purposes when incurred, depending on the size of the company. For SMEs, 175% of eligible expenditure can be deducted, and for large companies 135%. These rates of deduction were increased in *FA 2008* from the previous rates of 150% and 120% respectively. For this purpose, an SME (from 1 August 2008) is one with less than 500 employees and either an annual turnover not exceeding €100 million or a balance sheet total not exceeding €86 million.

Chapter 27

Financial Instruments

27.1 It is a widely held misconception that the various rules and regulations relating to financial instruments are only really applicable to financial institutions and large, complex businesses with sophisticated treasury functions. Unfortunately, this is not the case. The increasing use of a wide variety of financial instruments has led to the creation of a range of controversial financial reporting standards, which have a potential impact on a wide range of businesses. One of the most problematic aspects of financial instruments is their recognition, measurement and dealing with rapidly changing values. Common financial instruments include:

- cash;
- trade and loan debts;
- debt and equity investments;
- derivatives; and
- convertible debt instruments.

Here, the debt/equity divide is important for a number of reasons, including the effect it may have on a company's gearing ratios and, therefore, perceived creditworthiness. A financial instrument creates a financial asset for one party and a financial liability for the other party. Financial assets can be distinguished from tangible assets, such as buildings, and also from intangible assets such as patents. In considering whether a financial asset, liability or equity instrument exists, the legal status is key: there must be a contractual right enforceable by law. Derivatives are a particularly complex form of financial instrument and they have particularly volatile values, since their existence is premised on settlement of an agreement at some future date, and values are linked to changes in other items, such as interest rates or commodity prices.

The ASB first aired its view on this complex subject in a discussion paper in 1991, and followed this up in December 1992 with *FRED 3*. Most of the *FRED 3* proposals were subsequently adopted in *FRS 4*. In September 1998, *FRS 4* was replaced by *FRS 13* for banks and financial institutions; and, in December 2004, it was replaced by *FRS 25* for all entities in relation to disclosure and presentation. *FRS 26* was also issued in December 2004, and implements the measurement and hedging requirements of international standards (see below). In the UK, *FRS 26* is subject to the *Companies Act*

2006, and so UK entities using it will not be able to take full advantage of the fair value option in *FRS 26*.

FINANCIAL REPORTING STANDARD 25 (FRS 25)

27.2 *FRS 25* is concerned with the presentation of financial instruments in the financial statements, and applies to all entities for accounting periods beginning on or after 1 January 2005. Central to the presentation requirements is the classification of financial instruments as debt or equity, with consequences for the treatment of interest expense and dividend payments. The standard looks to the substance of the contractual arrangements rather than their legal form. Preference shares have long been problematic in this regard, since they have characteristics of both equity and debt.

FRS 25 requires that classification be made at the point of initial recognition of a financial instrument, and that classification cannot subsequently be changed. A financial liability is defined as:

(a) A contractual obligation:

  (i) to deliver cash or another financial asset to another entity (eg a payable);

  (ii) to exchange financial assets or financial liabilities with another entity under conditions that are potentially unfavourable to the entity ...

(b) A contract that will or may be settled in the entity's own equity instruments and is:

  (i) a non-derivative contract for which the entity is or may be obliged to deliver a variable number of its own equity instruments (eg an instrument redeemable in its own shares to the value of the carrying amount of the instrument); or

  (ii) a derivative contract over own equity that will or may be settled other than by the exchange of a fixed amount of cash (or another financial asset) for a fixed number of the entity's own equity instruments ...

An equity instrument is any contract that carries a residual interest in the assets of an entity after its liabilities have been deducted. A distinguishing feature is an *obligation* to deliver cash or another financial asset to the holder, which is not present in the case of equity instruments where the right to receive dividends is at the issuer's discretion. Financial liabilities, therefore, include bonds and bank loans, as well as mandatory redeemable preference shares and 'puttable' instruments, where the holder has the right to put the instrument back to the issuer for cash or another financial asset. In 2008, the ASB issued an amendment to *FRS 25* in relation to puttable instruments that impose a delivery obligation only on liquidation. Prior to the amendment, such instruments would have been treated as a financial liability, but following

27.3 *Financial Instruments*

the amendment (which was made as a result of a similar amendment to the relevant international standard) they are classified as equity.

The question of whether there is an obligation to deliver cash or another financial asset can be obscured where it is not explicit, but rather is an indirect term or condition of the instrument. *FRS 25 para 20* ensures that, where an entity can avoid the transfer of cash or another financial asset by settling with an agreed *non*-financial obligation, then it will nonetheless be treated as a financial liability.

27.3 Another difficult area is where there is a contingent settlement provision such that the obligation to deliver cash or another financial instrument only arises in the event of some future, uncertain event beyond the issuer's and/or holder's control. This could include, for example, changes in the law such as taxation changes, or changes in key performance indicators. In these cases, the issuer does not have an *unconditional* right to avoid the obligation to deliver cash or another financial asset, and so the instrument will be taken to be a financial liability, unless the contingent settlement provision is not genuine or if the settlement can only be required in the case of the issuer's liquidation.

Compound instruments must be separated into their liability and equity components. The fair value of the liability component is first calculated to establish the initial carrying amount, and then deducted from the fair value of the whole instrument; the residual amount therefore represents the equity component. If a compound instrument contains an embedded derivative, then the value of the embedded derivative must be allocated to the liability component. Compound instruments can be extremely complex, and further consideration of them is beyond the scope of this book.

Having classified the financial instrument as either equity or financial liability, the treatment of interest, dividends, gains and losses is as follows:

- interest, dividends, losses and gains relating to a financial liability (or component of a compound instrument) are recognised as income or expense in the profit and loss; and

- distributions to equity holders are debited directly to equity, as are transaction costs of equity transactions.

The disclosure requirements in *FRS 25* have been superseded by *FRS 29*, although many entities using UK GAAP are exempt from using *FRS 29*.

FINANCIAL REPORTING STANDARD 4 (FRS 4)

27.4 The requirements of *FRS 4* relating to measurement of debt apply to companies that are not applying *FRS 26* (see below), and also to shares that are presented as liabilities in accordance with *FRS 25*.

FRS 4 applies to all capital instruments, with the exception of warrants issued to employees under employee share schemes, leases accounted for under *SSAP 21*, and equity shares issued as part of a merger.

Immediately after issue, capital instruments are accounted for at the net proceeds of the issue, which are defined as 'the fair value of the consideration received on the issue of the instrument after deduction of the issue costs'. In later accounting periods, the carrying amount of the debt is increased by the finance charge for the period and reduced by any actual amounts paid.

Finance costs are allocated to the profit and loss account over the term of the debt by applying a constant rate to the carrying cost, and are included under the heading of 'interest payable'. Finance costs are defined as 'the difference between the net proceeds of an instrument and the total amount of the payments (or other transfers of economic benefits) that the issuer may be required to make in respect of the instrument' (*FRS 4*, para 8).

FRS 4 originally included, in Application Notes, examples of its application to 15 types of capital instruments. These were withdrawn on the issue of *FRS 25*, although, in some cases, the accounting treatment remained the same.

FINANCIAL REPORTING STANDARD 13 (FRS 13)

27.5 *FRS 13* 'Derivatives and Other Financial Instruments: Disclosures' was issued in September 1998. It does not apply to entities that have adopted *FRS 26* (see below), but applies to all other entities that have one or more of their capital instruments listed or publicly traded on a stock exchange and all banks and similar institutions.

Derivatives are defined as 'financial instruments that derive their value from the price or rate of some underlying item'. They include such instruments as interest rate swaps, which derive their value from an interest rate, and forward contracts that derive their value from foreign exchange rates.

All entities are required to provide narrative disclosures of the entity's risk profile and risk management policies, in the operating and financial review (or similar), so long as they are brought within the scope of audit. Numerical disclosures are also required in relation to their interest rate profile. In addition, a maturity analysis is required for all financial liabilities.

Companies are required to disclose aggregate fair values and carrying amounts for each category of financial asset and liability. For normal corporates (basically, not banks or financial institutions), instruments held or issued for trading must be disclosed separately from those used for risk management (hedging) purposes.

FRS 13 does not impose any additional disclosure requirements beyond *FRS 18* in relation to accounting policies.

FINANCIAL REPORTING STANDARD 26 (FRS 26)

27.6 *FRS 26* 'Financial Instruments: Recognition and Measurement' is concerned with the recognition and measurement of financial liabilities. It may

27.7 *Financial Instruments*

only be adopted as part of a suite of standards consisting of *FRS 23* (exchange rates), *FRS 24* (hyperinflationary economies), *FRS 26*, and *FRS 29* (financial instruments: disclosures).

FRS 26 was issued in December 2004 and applies to accounting periods commencing on or after 1 January 2005 for listed entities following UK GAAP, and 1 January 2006 for unlisted entities whose financial statements are prepared in accordance with the fair value accounting rules set out in the *Companies Act 2006*.

According to the ASB summary, *FRS 26* requires:

- '• all derivatives and all financial assets and financial liabilities that are held for trading to be recognised and measured at fair value. All changes in those fair values to be recognised immediately in the profit and loss account (P&L);
- • all loans and receivables held as assets and all financial assets that are being held to maturity to be initially recognised at fair value but subsequently measured at cost-based amounts;
- • all other financial assets ('available-for-sale financial assets') to be recognised and measured at fair value with gains and losses recognised immediately in the statement of recognised gains and losses (STRGL); and
- • all other financial liabilities to be recognised at fair value but subsequently measured at cost-based amount.'

An entity can choose to use fair value measurement for a financial asset or liability that would otherwise be measured at a cost based amount. This choice must be made on initial recognition and if chosen, all changes in fair value should be recognised in the profit and loss immediately.

FINANCIAL REPORTING STANDARD 29 (FRS 29)

27.7 *FRS 29* only applies to entities applying *FRS 26* and, for those that use it, it replaces *FRS 25* (above). According to the ASB summary, disclosures required are:

- '• information on the significance of financial instruments for an entity's financial position and performance;
- • information about exposure to risks arising from financial instruments. These include, where relevant, certain minimum qualitative disclosures about credit, liquidity and market risks together with descriptions of management's objectives, policies and processes for managing those risks. Quantitative disclosures are also required to provide information about the extent to which the entity is exposed to risk, based on information provided internally to the entity's key management;
- • the entity's objectives, policies and processes for managing

Financial Instruments **27.11**

capital. This would include quantitative data about what the entity regards as capital, and whether the entity has complied with any capital requirements and if it has not complied, the consequences of such non-compliance.'

INTERNATIONAL STANDARDS

27.8 There are no appreciable differences (within the scope of this book) between the international accounting standards and UK GAAP in this area for the following standards:

- *FRS 25* equates to *IAS 32*;
- *FRS 26* equates to *IAS 39*; and
- *FRS 29* equates to *IFRS 7*.

TAXATION CONSIDERATIONS

27.9 In the budget of November 1993, it was announced that the Revenue was instituting a comprehensive review of the tax treatment of interest (and similar) payments between companies (but not individuals). This subsequently resulted in new legislation which is considered at **27.14** below.

27.10 The question of tax deductibility of incidental costs of raising loan finance is dealt with in *ITTOIA 2005, s 58*. This is retained for non-companies, but such costs incurred by companies are now dealt with as described in **27.14** below.

Although *ITTOIA 2005, s 58* grants relief, it is not completely unambiguous as to which year or accounting period relief should be forthcoming. *FRS 4* has highlighted this vagueness. Until now, the presumption has been that relief is available when the incidental costs are incurred; but, as *FRS 4* obliges the spreading of those costs over the period of the relevant instrument, there could be an argument for spreading the relief over those years (it is, after all, not *that* different from *Gallagher v Jones; Threlfall v Jonesa* [1993] STC 537, CA – see Appendix A).

Indirect issues

27.11 The tax statutes are littered, in an ad hoc way, with attempts to differentiate equity which is not really equity, or loans that are not really loan capital. Examples of these are:

- The treatment of interest on certain loans as though it were equivalent to the payment of dividends contained in *ICTA 1988, s 209*.
- The treatment of 'loan creditors' as 'participators' for close company purposes under *ICTA 1988, s 417*.

251

27.12 *Financial Instruments*

- Thin capitalisation issues involving subsidiary/parent companies in different tax jurisdictions.
- Control tests, for example, in determining associated company status under *ICTA 1988, s 416* (the greater part of the assets in a winding-up test).
- The concept of 'equity holder' for group relief purposes (*ICTA 1988, s 413, Sch 18*).
- The definition of 'ordinary share capital' in *ICTA 1988, s 832(1)* – used for many tax purposes – does not sit easily within any distinction recognised by the *Companies Acts* or by *FRS 4*.

Whilst many anomalies remain, recent changes have resulted in greater harmonisation of accounting and tax principles.

RECENT TAX DEVELOPMENTS

27.12 As already indicated, the tax rules relating to financial instruments have historically been a 'hotchpotch' of separate provisions, with seemingly little connection to the treatment of the relevant costs in the accounts.

The rules were particularly difficult to understand when dealing with hedging contracts, with many costs associated with such contracts being non-deductible, whilst some gains were taxable when the contracts unwound.

The uninitiated – and perhaps, sometimes, the initiated as well – were often struggling to grasp the different tax treatments of a number of defined debt instruments, such as deep discount securities, deep gain securities, qualifying convertible securities, and so on.

The 1990s, however, saw a three-pronged attack to bring the tax treatment of financial instruments more into line with the figures shown in the accounts, for companies only. This radical shake-up comprised:

- the foreign exchange legislation (*Finance Act 1993*);
- the financial instruments legislation (*Finance Act 1994*) for derivatives; and
- the corporate debt legislation (*Finance Act 1996*) for loan relationships.

The rules relating to each area, although apparently a simplification, are long, complex and often a very tough read.

The foreign exchange rules have already been discussed in Chapter 24. The other two areas will be outlined here.

27.13 Partnerships and sole traders are not included in the new regime and, for them, the old rules are still in force.

The old rules operate on the principle that the constituent parts of related transactions should all be looked at separately and the tax rules applied accordingly. What this means is that tax mismatches can occur where, for example, capital losses arising on one element of the transaction cannot be set off against income tax profits on another element.

SP14/91 eased this problem to some extent by allowing a form of matching for tax purposes when the financial instrument is economically matched to another transaction.

Irrespective of matching, HMRC are also prepared to treat the costs of an interest hedge as a trading deduction, so long as the hedge is with respect to borrowings to finance a trade. However, tax mismatch problems remain for non-trading businesses and traders who are trying to hedge borrowing drawn for capital reasons.

Since first being introduced, the regime has been amended on numerous occasions and finally rewritten as part of the Tax Law Rewrite process into *CTA 2009, Part 5* (Loan Relationships), *Part 6* (Relationships Treated as Loan Relationships) and *Part 7* (Derivative Contracts).

Loan relationships

27.14 The explanatory notes to *CTA 2009* observes that the phrase 'loan relationship' is used for familiarity, even though the legislation covers more transactions than those originally conceived of as 'loan relationships' (Explanatory Notes, p 161, para 1038).

Profits and deficits on loan relationships are calculated using 'credits' and 'debits', distinguishing between trading and non-trading loan relationships. The general rule is stated in *CTA 2009, s 295(1)* that 'all profits arising to a company from its loan relationships are chargeable to tax as income'. A loan relationship is where a company stands in the position of a creditor or debtor as respects any money debt, and the debt arises from a transaction for the lending of money (*CTA 2009, s 302(1)*). A money debt is one that falls to be settled by payment of money, by transfer of a right to settlement under a debt that is itself a money debt, or by the issue of any share in any company (*CTA 2009, s 303(1)*).

Where a company is a party to a loan relationship for the purposes of a trade, the credits in respect of that relationship for the period are treated as receipts of the trade and, therefore, form part of the trade profits computation for the period (*CTA 2009, s 297(2)*). Conversely, debits are treated as deductible expenses in calculating trade profits (*CTA 2009, s 297(3)*). It is made clear (*CTA 2009, s 297(4)*) that this overrides the prohibitions against deductibility of capital expenditure (*CTA 2009, s 53*), expenses not wholly and exclusively for the purposes of trade, and unconnected losses (*CTA 2009, s 54*).

Non-trading profits and deficits are dealt with by *CTA 2009, Part 5, Chapter 16*. Non-trading credits and debits are essentially those that are not 'trading' credits and debits. Where the former exceed the latter, non-trading profits arise; where the latter exceed the former, a non-trading deficit arises (*CTA 2009, s 301(4)–(7)*).

27.15 *Financial Instruments*

The rules also deal with 'related transactions', that is, where there is any disposal or acquisition, in whole or in part, of rights or liabilities under a loan relationship *(CTA 2009, s 304(1))*.

CTA 2009, Part 5, Chapter 3 also deals with the general loan relationship rules; in particular, it provides for the application of GAAP where the accounts do not comply with GAAP.

27.15 'The general rule is that the amounts to be brought into account by a company as credits and debits for any period ... are those that are recognised in determining the company's profit or loss for the period in accordance with generally accepted accounting practice' *(CTA 2009, s 307(2))*.

CTA 2009, s 307(3) states that:

'The credits and debits to be brought into account in respect of a company's loan relationships are the amounts that, when taken together, fairly represent for the accounting period in question:

(a) All profits and losses of the company that arise to it from loan relationships and related transactions ...;

(b) All interest under these relationships; and

(c) All expenses incurred by the company under or for the purposes of those relationships or transactions.'

Expenses are further described *(CTA 2009, s 307(4))* as those incurred directly:

'(a) in bringing any of the loan relationships into existence;

(b) in entering into or giving effect to any of the related transactions;

(c) in making payments under any of those relationships or as a result of those transactions; or

(d) in taking steps to ensure the receipt of payments under any of those relationships or in accordance with any of those transactions.'

Prior period adjustments for accounting purposes are brought to account for tax purposes in the profit and loss for the period to which the re-statement relates *(CTA 2009, s 308(2))*.

CTA 2009, s 313(1) specifically refers to the use of amortised cost basis accounting or fair value accounting.

Where the accounting rules allow credits or debits in respect of loan relationships to be brought into account in determining the value of a fixed capital asset or project, the tax rules override this and required treatment under the loan relationship rules; that is, in this situation, the normal accounting rules are not followed *(CTA 2009, s 320)*.

Where credits and debits on loan relationships are taken directly to reserves, they are treated for corporation tax purposes as if they had been taken to the profit and loss *(CTA 2009, s 321)*.

Non-lending relationships

27.16 *CTA 2009, Part 6* brings within the loan relationship rules those money debts which do not fall within the definition of 'loan relationships' in *CTA 2009, s 302*, because they do not arise from a transaction for the lending of money. These may or may not involve discounts and are referred to as non-lending relationships (based on *FA 1996, s 100*). *CTA 2009, s 483* brings exchange gains or losses on currency holdings and liabilities into the loan relationship regime by treating them as money debts. This part does not apply to amounts dealt with under the derivatives regime (see below), or intangible assets regime (see Chapter 25).

CTA 2009, Part 6, Chapter 6 deals with alternative finance arrangements, ie those that comply with Shari'a law, as falling within the loan relationship regime.

Derivative contracts

27.17 The regime is the result of a lengthy process, and it needed three consultative documents to reach the final version:

- 'Tax Treatment of Swap Fees', issued 14 March 1989;
- 'Financial Instruments: The tax treatment of financial instruments for managing interest rate risk', issued 29 August 1991; and
- 'Financial Instruments: Draft clauses on the tax treatment of financial instruments for managing interest rate and currency risk', issued 20 August 1993.

There were also a Statement of Practice, SP14/91 concerning financial futures and options, and an Extra-Statutory Concession, ESC C17 concerning interest rate and currency swaps.

Unfortunately, the resultant legislation which aims to bring the tax treatment of costs into line with the accounting treatment is lengthy, complicated and detailed, incorporating the usual battery of transitional and anti-avoidance provisions. The current rules are now contained in *CTA 2009, Part 7*, an outline of which follows.

Derivative contracts are defined in *CTA 2009 s 576*. As explained in the Explanatory Notes (p 218, paras 1511–14), there are three conditions:

1. It is a relevant contract, as defined in *CTA 2009, s 577*, essentially that it derives its value from underlying subject matter that is subject to changes in market prices or other factors.
2. It meets the 'accounting conditions' in *CTA 2009, s 579*, ie the contract either is treated by the relevant standard as a derivative or as a financial asset or liability, or has underlying subject matter within certain categories.
3. Some other provision of the Act does not prevent it from being a derivative (this excludes underlying land and shares).

27.18 *Financial Instruments*

CTA 2009, s 589 excludes some contracts from being derivatives because of their underlying subject matter such as intangible fixed assets.

In most cases, the company's accounting treatment of its derivatives is followed in identifying and quantifying the credits and debits that make up the profits and losses on derivative contracts for tax purposes (Explanatory Notes, p 215, para 1490).

If the contract is held for the purposes of trade, then receipts and expenses go into trading profits. If not, they go into non-trading loan relationships. In a number of cases, particularly where the underlying subject matter of the derivative is land or shares, the profits fall within the capital gains rules as chargeable gains. So, generally, profits on derivative contracts are treated as chargeable to corporation tax as income, even if treated as capital under GAAP, but some are chargeable as capital gains.

SUMMARY

27.18 This chapter has presented only a very brief overview of both the accounting and tax rules relating to financial instruments. It has been a fast-changing area of law and regulation in recent years; one of the first in which there has been deliberate alignment, albeit incomplete, between the accounting and tax treatment so that the tax now follows the accounts. The added complication of debates in the international arena has also made this a particularly controversial area.

Chapter 28

Corporate Transactions – The Theory

28.1 This chapter pulls together several features which have appeared in various earlier parts of the book. The purpose is to present in unified form those aspects of accounting practice and company law which most frequently occur in the world of corporate transactions (buy-outs, buy-ins, reorganisations etc). To some extent, the concepts will be developed further. For completeness, some comments are added on related matters which, although not directly relating to accounting or taxation, appear so frequently that the practitioner needs a working familiarity. In the following chapter, a number of worked examples illustrate in practical terms how these principles are applied.

THE PRICE OF LIMITED LIABILITY

28.2 Most companies are incorporated under the *Companies Acts* and have 'limited liability'. A private limited company has the word 'Limited' (or 'Ltd') at the end if its name; a public company has the words 'Public Limited Company' (or 'plc') appended to its name.

What this means is that the shareholders put up a certain amount of capital – the share capital – and the company can then trade. That share capital is at risk if things go wrong, but the shareholders' risk is *limited* to the amount they put up in the form of share capital. This is a very valuable protection for the investor. The proprietor of a business carried on in unlimited form (eg sole trader or partnership) is completely at risk for the whole of any trading losses suffered, right up to the point of personal bankruptcy.

The shareholder in a limited liability company is, therefore, in a privileged position, but there is a price to pay. First, the company is subjected to a strict regime of publicity. As has been seen, companies must produce very detailed accounts with formidable disclosure provisions. These accounts must be filed with the Registrar of Companies within time limits. The accounts are open to inspection by the public at large. Secondly, there are strict rules as to what funds shareholders may withdraw from companies. Creditors need to know that the comfort they derive from the fact that shareholders have put up risk capital will not be undermined by the shareholders withdrawing this cash when things start to go wrong. It is the protection of creditors' interests which drives many of the following considerations.

28.3 Corporate Transactions – The Theory

RESERVES

28.3 *Example 3.2* (at **3.10** above) illustrated a very simple balance sheet, in which it was shown that the net assets of a company are equal to the (issued) share capital plus the reserves. The balance sheet formats permitted by *SI 2008/409* and *SI 2008/410* (the '*Accounting Regulations*') expand a little on this. For example (see *Schedule 1* to the *Accounting Regulations*), part K of the balance sheet of *Format 1* appears as follows:

'Capital and Reserves

I   Called-up share capital

II   Share premium account

III   Revaluation reserve

IV   Other reserves

    1   Capital redemption reserve

    2   Reserve for own shares

    3   Reserves provided for by the articles of association

    4   Other reserves

V   Profit and loss account'

Each of these is worthy of comment in its own right.

Called-up share capital

28.4 A company's Memorandum of Association used to specify the maximum capital which any particular company may issue. For example, it may provide that a company's capital is £10,000, represented by 10,000 × £1 ordinary shares. By resolution, a company may amend this (although it may need to amend its own Articles to permit it to do so). One of the changes made in the *Companies Act 2006* was to remove this requirement, and a company is no longer required to specify its authorised capital. It must, however, have a fixed nominal value for shares and, for a public company, this must be denominated in either sterling or euros (*CA 2006, s 765*).

28.5 It is important to distinguish between the capital which a company is capable of issuing, and that which has been issued. The same company may have the legal capacity to issue 10,000 × £1 shares but, at a point in time, it may have issued only, say, 5,000 × £1. It is only the issued share capital which is at risk. If this company were to fail, the £5,000 (if the shares were issued at £1 per share) put up by the shareholders could well be lost, but unhappy creditors would not be able to ask shareholders to stump up another £5,000.

28.6 Shareholders may be willing to give additional comfort to potential creditors. Suppose that, for the company above, shareholders only have £5,000 in cash but are willing to risk a potential loss of £10,000. In this circumstance, it is possible to issue 10,000 × £1 shares, each share being part paid to the tune of 50 pence. At that point in time, the shareholders would only have paid 10,000 × 50 pence, ie £5,000, but if things go wrong the company could demand that the other 50 pence per share be paid in. The language of the *Companies Acts* is to describe the 10,000 shares as having been allotted, but that only 50 pence (per share) has been called (note 12 to the balance sheet formats). The called-up share capital is, therefore, the nominal amount of share capital which has already been paid for by shareholders. (Another way of giving creditors comfort is to allot additional shares paid for, not in cash but by a redesignation from distributable reserves, ie a bonus issue – see **28.9** and **28.11** below.)

28.7 Except in very controlled situations, the allotted share capital cannot be paid back to shareholders (nor can uncalled capital in respect of shares already allotted be extinguished). The controlled situations are designed to ensure that creditors' interests are not prejudiced, and include: the repayment of redeemable share capital (ie share capital which, on issue, is stated to be redeemable – and only then if conditions are met); repayment of capital under court supervision (*CA 2006, s 645*); the purchase by a company of its own shares (*CA 2006, Part 18, Chapter 4*); and the distribution, in a winding-up by a liquidator, of surplus funds to shareholders once all other creditors have been paid in full.

Share premium account

28.8 Although a company may have its capital denominated at a certain amount, eg £10,000, being 10,000 × £1 ordinary shares, it is not obliged to issue those shares at a price of £1.

For example, Mr A starts a company and injects £5,000 in return for 5,000 × £1 ordinary shares. The company may prosper and, after a year or two, he finds it agreeable to invite Mr B to join in. As the company is successful, the shares may be worth more than £1. He could sell some of his shares to Mr B for, say, £2. That would give him a capital gain. Alternatively, he could cause the company to issue 5,000 × £1 ordinary shares, *but at a price of £10,000*. Mr B is paying £2 per share. This is not a disposal by the company (hence, no capital gains tax). The company is issuing £5,000 (in nominal value) of shares, but is receiving £10,000. The additional called-up share capital (see **28.6** above) is £5,000. The surplus £5,000 is called 'share premium'.

28.9 Where a company issues shares (for cash or otherwise) at a premium, it is required by *CA 2006, s 610* to create a share premium account. In accounting terms, it is very similar to called-up share capital (hence its proximity in the balance sheet formats under the *Accounting Regulations*). Permitted uses of the share premium are very limited.

Under *CA 2006, s 610*, the issue expenses involved, when new shares or debentures are issued, may be written off against this account. Companies are no longer able to write off the preliminary expenses of setting up the company.

28.10 *Corporate Transactions – The Theory*

It is possible to apply to the courts to utilise the share premium (*CA 2006, s 645* – and the definition in *CA 2006, s 610(1)* in other ways. This is often done in relation to large corporate takeovers. Company X issues shares to Company Y shareholders in return for Company Y shareholders transferring their (Company Y) shares to Company X. Company X issues its shares at a premium. The goodwill arising (fair value accounting – acquisition accounting – see **28.27** below) may, with court sanction, be written off against share premium account.

Under *CA 1985, ss 611–613*, share premiums may not need to be created in certain circumstances (see **28.34** below). The company can use the share premium account to pay up new shares to be allotted to members as fully paid bonus shares.

28.10 It is absolutely forbidden for shares to be issued at a discount (although it is possible to create a class of shares with a nominal value less than other shares, which in other respects rank *pari passu* with those other shares).

Revaluation reserve

28.11 When assets are revalued, a revaluation reserve must be created (*SI 2008/410, Sch 1, Pt 2, section C, para 35*). How this works was described in Chapter 5.

On a revaluation, there is a potential conflict between *para 35* and *FRS 15* in relation to the previous depreciation (see **5.12** above).

The revaluation reserve is a statutory reserve which can only be used for the purposes for which the statute provides. One such purpose is the payment of bonus shares.

Redenomination reserve

28.12 A company is generally free to issue shares in any currency it wishes and may use a mixture of denominations. *CA 2006, s 622* introduces a new procedure to allow a company limited by shares to redenominate its share capital more easily (whereas previously it had to cancel existing shares, requiring court approval, then issue new ones). A redenomination of a company's share capital does not affect members' rights, in particular their dividend entitlements. If a company reduces its capital as a result of a redenomination, it must transfer an amount equal to the value of the reduction to a non-distributable reserve, known as the redenomination reserve (*CA 2006, s 628*). This reserve may be used to pay up shares to be allotted to existing members as fully paid bonus shares.

Capital redemption reserve

28.13 As will be seen in **28.39** below, in certain circumstances, a company may purchase its own shares. These shares are then treated as cancelled.

Generally, this cancellation is effected by transferring the reduction in issued share capital to a special non-distributable reserve called the capital redemption reserve (*CA 2006, s 733*). The capital redemption reserve is virtually untouchable, except under court approval.

Reserve for own shares

28.14 This is rarely seen and, unlike share premium, revaluation and capital redemption reserves, is not created by virtue of the *Companies Acts*.

If, say, a financier injects *redeemable* share capital into a company, it will only be possible to redeem those shares in the circumstances described in **28.39** below. A term of his putting up the redeemable capital might be that the company should 'save up' to ultimately pay him out, and there may be required an annual transfer from potential distributable profits (usually Profit and Loss account) to a 'non-distributable' reserve (ie reserve for own shares) which will ultimately be used to create the capital redemption reserve on redemption. The reserve for own shares is described as 'non-distributable', not on the basis of company law – such reserves are technically distributable (and they need to be, as it is only out of distributable profits that share redemptions can generally be made) – but on the basis that the company has agreed with the financier, by contract, not to distribute it (for the time being).

Reserves provided for in own Articles

28.15 This is very unusual, but for whatever reason a company may require the creation of a reserve which may have specified uses (and non-uses). A company can always, of course, change its Articles (although normally this requires a 75% majority vote of shareholders).

Other reserves

28.16 As a matter of policy, a company may provide other reserves. In themselves, these have no legal significance. An example might be a plant replacement reserve. An asset may cost £1,000, with a life of five years, at the end of which a replacement may cost £2,000. Only £1,000 of depreciation may be written off over the five years. The company may wish to provide for the whole £2,000 of anticipated replacement cost. Therefore, over the five years, it may build up a further reserve of £1,000 to reflect this, ie it holds back £1,000 from being available for distribution because it has a future anticipated commitment.

28.17 There is no statutory reason why there cannot be a negative balance on the other reserves. This is occasionally seen in those cases where purchased goodwill was written off on acquisition, creating an immediate negative reserve. Nowadays, this method of accounting would not be acceptable according to *FRS 10* (see Chapter 25).

28.18 *Corporate Transactions – The Theory*

Profit and loss

28.18 In simple terms, this represents the cumulative total of previous years' after-tax profits, insofar as not distributed in the form of dividends.

As a starting point, it is a good assumption that it is capable of distribution in the form of dividends or of being utilised for similar purposes (such as the funding of share redemptions or the issue of bonus shares), but there are a number of refinements to this which are considered in **28.19** to **28.26** below.

If a company suffers cumulative losses, then it will have a negative balance on its Profit and Loss account. Public (but not private) company directors have an obligation (*CA 2006, s 656*) to call an extraordinary general meeting of shareholders whenever the net assets fall to half or less of the called-up share capital.

DISTRIBUTABLE PROFITS

28.19 Before the *Companies Act 1980*, there were very few statutory rules regarding the level of distributions a company could make. The prime authority was common law, which imposed some restrictions (for example, by prohibiting returns of capital). The common law provisions still exist, although the comprehensive statutory code introduced in 1980, and now found at *CA 2006, ss 830–831*, is generally used as the source for identifying what distributions are possible.

28.20 As explained in Chapter 6, under the *Companies Acts*, distributions can only be made out of net realised profits not otherwise utilised (for public companies, net unrealised losses must also be taken into account). Generally, reference should be had to the last published accounts to determine this (*CA 2006, s 836*).

28.21 There is no definition of 'realised profit' (or 'realised loss'). The ICAEW's publication Tech 03/09 attempt to give guidance. Generally, those items taken into account in determining the true and fair measure of profit do represent realised profits or losses (eg the foreseeable profit on a long-term contract is believed to be 'realised' for the purpose of *CA 2006, s 830*). Regard must also be had to the (as yet, not fully developed) concept of the 'cash' test (see Chapter 5).

28.22 Where a company capitalises development costs, there is an onus on the directors to establish that such costs do not represent realised losses (*CA 2006, s 269* – see **26.11** above).

28.23 There are particular problems in relation to revalued assets. As explained in Chapters 5 and 16, the effective write-back of depreciation when an asset is revalued above its book value is not normally accounted for.

The whole of the revaluation surplus – revalued amount less book value – is taken to the non-distributable revaluation reserve. However, the status of the depreciation effectively written back is unclear. It *may* be distributable. Any proposed distribution (or similar transaction) proposing to treat such write-back as distributable should not be made without obtaining legal opinion.

Equally, where an asset is revalued upwards, the additional depreciation (depreciation on revalued asset less depreciation on basis of no revaluation) may not – and probably is not – a realised loss (certainly the revaluation itself did not produce a realised profit – so why should the additional depreciation create a realised loss?).

Finally, when a revalued property is sold, the previous unrealised revaluation surplus becomes realised (assuming a sale at a price above the book value of the revalued asset). This revaluation surplus which becomes realised does not pass through profit and loss, but is transferred directly from the revaluation reserve to Profit and Loss (*Example 16.3* at **16.11** above illustrates this).

28.24 Distributions in kind (not previously mentioned in this book) are specifically dealt with under *CA 2006, ss 845–846*. A typical situation might be where a company holds the whole of the issued share capital of a subsidiary at cost (of say £100). These shares may now be worth £1 million, and the company may wish to distribute those shares (say, as part of a demerger arrangement). There may be insufficient realised profits (ie distributable profits) to make the distribution. The shares may be revalued to £1 million (creating an undistributable revaluation surplus of £999,900) and then, for the purpose of the distribution *in specie* of those shares, *s 846* permits the unrealised revaluation surplus to be regarded as realised.

Although, in strictness, the revaluation should be effected and reflected in the accounts which are used – under *CA 2006, s 836* – to determine the level of distributable profits, in practice the formal revaluation often does not take place. (This is risky and not recommended.)

28.25 Particular problems arise in relation to goodwill (both positive and negative). This is fully explained in Chapter 25.

29.26 Finally, following any combination of business entities, there is the question of the extent to which the combined amount of distributable profits may be amalgamated for potential onward distribution. This is a complex problem associated with two different methods of accounting – the so called 'acquisition' and 'merger' accounting concepts. These are wide issues in themselves, to which separate consideration will be given.

ACQUISITION ACCOUNTING

28.27 When Company A acquires (for the sake of illustration) the entire share capital of Company B (thereby forming a group with A as parent), this

28.28 *Corporate Transactions – The Theory*

is normally accounted for using the 'acquisition' accounting method. An example of this is shown at **23.23** above.

One of the features of acquisition accounting is that, in the group accounts, the 'fair value' of the consideration given is apportioned over the various underlying assets of the target company. This is done so as to identify the goodwill – positive or negative – implied in the deal (*Example 25.1* at **25.24** above demonstrates how this is done). It is unusual for the subsidiary company to revalue its own assets (if it does, this is called 'push down' accounting), but the group accounts are consolidated on the basis of the revalued figures, and the goodwill on consolidation is dealt with in line with *FRS 10*. The quantification and accounting for purchased goodwill, in particular where acquisition accounting is used, are contentious issues, now addressed by *FRS 7* (see **25.9** above).

28.28 If the consideration paid for the acquisition of shares in Company B comprises (in whole or part) the issue of new shares in Company A, then, if the 'fair value' of the shares issued is determined to be greater than their nominal value, the excess should be credited to the share premium account (see **28.8** above).

28.29 It is important to acknowledge, though, that groups as such do not make distributions. Individual companies make distributions. In the example above, after the acquisition, Company B may pay a dividend but it will go to Company A. Company A may pay a dividend – and that will go to its shareholders. The group, as such, is not a legal entity. The group's accounts reflect dividends and distributions by individual companies, but the group cannot in its own right pay dividends. Therefore, group accounts are irrelevant for the purpose of determining distributable profits.

MERGER ACCOUNTING

28.30 Even experienced accountants become confused on this topic and fail to retain the distinction between individual companies and groups. It is essential to the understanding of this difficult concept that the analysis considers each separately.

Individual companies

28.31 There are some situations whereby Company A comes to own Company B that are not really 'takeovers' in the generally accepted sense. It may be that there is a simple internal group reorganisation involving no ultimate change in ownership. Or, it may be the coming together of two companies, not involving the passing of cash but being a pooling of interests. In that sense, in general terms, the underlying reality is of a merger rather than a takeover.

28.32 There are no accounting standards or guidelines which distinguish – at the individual company level – between acquisitions which are 'takeover' in type, and those which are 'internal reorganisation' or 'merger' in type. The accounting standards and guidelines cover only the group accounts treatment of these situations. However, company law – at *CA 2006, ss 612 et seq* – does address these differences and their ramifications in relation to the individual company accounts.

28.33 When Company A issues new shares to acquire existing shares in Company B, *CA 2006, s 610* requires the value of the new Company A shares to be determined for the purpose of establishing a share premium account (see **28.8** above).

28.34 However, under *CA 2006, s 612*, a company (such as Company A in **28.24** above) is permitted (it is not completely clear whether the section is compulsory) not to create a share premium in certain circumstances. So, if Company A issues 100 × £1 shares, even though 'worth' £1 million, the acquisition in A's accounts is recorded as one which takes place at £100 (ie the cost of the investment is shown at £100 in A's accounts and no share premium is created).

Broadly, *s 612* relief applies to a transaction in which Company A obtains at least a 90% holding in the equity shares of Company B. Similar provisions in *s 611* apply to group reorganisations. Both *ss 612* and *611* apply to any shares issued by A in such circumstances – even if the bulk of the consideration is in the form of cash. (This is illustrated in *Example 28.1* below as 'Option 1'.)

Just to confuse matters, some companies which use *section 612* do record in their own balance sheet the fair value of the cost of the investment, but instead of creating a share premium account they create a non-statutory merger reserve. (This is illustrated in *Example 28.1* below as 'Option 2'.)

So, the balance sheet of Company A issuing 100 × £1 shares on the acquisition of the shares in Company B, worth £1 million, could appear in any of the three possible variations:

Example 28.1

	Without s 612 Relief	With s 612 Relief Option 1	With s 612 Relief Option 2
	£	£	£
Cost of Investment	1,000,000	100	1,000,000
Other Assets, say	1,000,000	1,000,000	1,000,000
Total Assets	2,000,000	1,000,100	2,000,000

28.35 *Corporate Transactions – The Theory*

	Without s 612 Relief	With s 612 Relief Option 1	With s 612 Relief Option 2
	£	£	£
Share Capital	500,100	500,100	500,100
Share Premium	999,900	–	–
Merger Reserve	–	–	999,900
Profit and Loss	500,000	500,000	500,000
	2,000,000	1,000,100	2,000,000

GROUP ACCOUNTS

28.35 *SI 2008/409* and *SI 2008/410* (the '*Accounting Regulations*') deal with the form and content of group accounts. *Paragraph 7 of Schedule 6* onwards deals with 'acquisition and merger accounting'.

The basic proposition is that acquisition accounting should be used unless certain conditions are satisfied, in which case, merger accounting *may* be used.

The conditions for the adoption of merger accounting include that the acquiring company must be obtaining at least a 90% holding in the target company, and that at least 90% of the fair value of the consideration must be represented by the nominal value of shares issued by the acquiring company. Subject to that, the adoption (of merger accounting) must conform with 'generally accepted accounting principles or practice'.

Thus, effectively, the relevant SSAP or FRS provides the circumstance and methodology.

Accounting principles

28.36 SSAP 23 contained much of the original thinking on the subject, but it was not universally accepted and has now been effectively superseded by *FRS 6*, which was amended in 2009 to take into account the *CA 2006* provisions.

28.37 FRS 6 attempts to move away from denying mergers by reference to arithmetic criteria, but maintains that a conceptual consideration of the underlying transaction be made. It provides that merger accounting should be used whenever it is not prohibited by the *Accounting Regulations*, and all the following criteria are satisfied:

1. No party to the combination is portrayed as either acquirer or acquired, either by its own board or management or by that of another party to the combination.
2. All parties to the combination, as represented by the boards of directors or their appointees, participate in establishing the management structure for the combined entity and in selecting the management personnel, and

such decisions are made on the basis of a consensus between the parties to the combination rather than purely by exercise of voting rights.

3. The relative sizes of the combining entities are not so disparate that one party effectively dominates the combined entity merely by virtue of its relative size. Such domination by the larger party would be contrary to the concept of a merger as a substantially equal partnership between the combining parties.

4. No more than an immaterial proportion of the fair value of the consideration received, under the terms of the combination or related arrangements, by shareholders of any party to the combination in exchange for equity shares, is represented by non-equity consideration (or equity shares carrying substantially reduced voting or distribution rights). Where one of the combining entities has, within the period of two years prior to the combination acquired equity shares in another of the combining entities, the consideration for this acquisition should be taken into account in determining whether this criterion has been met.

5. No equity shareholders of any of the combining entities retain any material interest in the future performance of part only of the combined entity.

28.38 The mechanics of merger accounting are straightforward. There are no fair value adjustments. The (trading) results of the combining entities are brought into the financial statements of the year in which the combination occurs (for acquisition, the results are only combined from the date of acquisition). The difference between the nominal value of the shares issued (plus other consideration) and the nominal value of the shares received in exchange (plus existing share premium, if any) should be shown as an adjustment on consolidated reserves. This adjustment should not be described as goodwill. The costs of effecting the merger should be written off through group profit and loss. *Example 29.13* at **29.36** illustrates how this all applies.

PURCHASE OF OWN SHARES

28.39 A corporate transaction – with particular tax consequences – frequently encountered in practice is the purchase by a company of its own shares. It is useful to understand the company law and accounting aspects.

28.40 Under *CA 2006, Part 18, Chapter 4*, a company may purchase its own shares, subject to conditions. Prior authorisation in the Articles is no longer required (*CA 2006, s 690*). The shares may originally have been issued as 'redeemable shares', ie there was some target date on which it was always intended that the shares would be redeemed, or they may have been issued in the normal course of events (ie not specifically as redeemable shares). If the Articles do not permit a self-purchase, the Articles can be changed with shareholder (usually 75%) consent.

28.41 Except for redeemable shares, various shareholder approvals are required to effect purchases of own shares. These depend upon whether the

28.42 *Corporate Transactions – The Theory*

shares are being acquired on a stock exchange, or are being bought as part of an 'off market' deal (as will always be the case for non-quoted companies). *CA 2006, s 694* enables a company to enter into a contract for an off market purchase of its own shares, conditional on the contract being approved by shareholders, which saves time in this process.

28.42 The basic proposition which applies to all companies is that shares may only be purchased 'out of distributable profits' (*CA 2006, s 687*). Put bluntly, if a company proposes to acquire a proportion of its own shares at a price of £150,000, then there must be at least £150,000 of distributable profits available (ie usually, there must be a balance of at least £150,000 on the Profit and Loss account). The logic for this is clear: if a company may legally pay a dividend (of, say, £150,000) to its shareholders (thereby reducing creditors' comfort), it should also be able to pay £150,000 to them by way of buying in their shares. To prevent the £150,000 of distributable profits being effectively used twice, the accounting for the buy-back has the effect of reducing the level of subsequent distributable profits. *Example 29.9* at **29.24** below illustrates how this happens.

28.43 A relaxation to the above is provided where the share purchase is effected wholly or partly via the issue of new shares. *Example 29.10* at **29.27** below illustrates this.

28.44 Once own shares are redeemed or purchased by a company, they are 'cancelled' under *CA 2006, s 688*. A capital redemption reserve may need to be created (see **28.13** above) under *CA 2006, s 733*.

28.45 A further relaxation applies only to private companies. Under *CA 2006, s 709*, private – but not public – companies may, to a limited extent, purchase their own shares out of capital (and not out of distributable profits). This does potentially prejudice the position of creditors, so the formalities are somewhat extensive. These include the passing of a special resolution of shareholders (75% majority), the making by the directors of a statutory declaration of the company's expected solvency in the following 12 months, the obtaining of an auditor's comfort letter, and advertisement in the *London Gazette*. Shareholders and creditors are given statutory rights of objection.

28.46 Provided these obstacles are overcome, a private company may reduce its capital in this way. To account for the transaction, the so-called 'permissible capital payment' must be computed. This is equal to the price of the shares to be redeemed, less any available distributable profits, less the proceeds of any fresh share issue made for the purpose of the redemption. In other words, as far as is possible, the redemption is to be made out of distributable profits (and new share issues). Only the excess can be considered for the reduction in capital.

28.47 If the permissible capital payment plus the proceeds of issue of new shares is less than the nominal value of the shares to be redeemed, the amount of the difference should be taken to capital redemption reserve. If more, then any excess may be deducted from any existing balance on capital redemption reserve, share premium, fully paid issued share capital or revaluation reserve. *Examples 29.11* and *29.12* at **29.30** and **29.33** below illustrate this.

DEMERGERS

28.48 A demerger is the name given to the arrangement whereby a single company carrying on two or more activities, directly or through subsidiaries, reorganises so that each activity is carried on by a separate free-standing company.

There is no special corporate regime. A demerger is in effect no more than a distribution *in specie*.

Example 28.2

Oldco holds the shares in two trading companies, X Ltd and Y Ltd. It is desired to 'break' the group, so that X and Y are separate free-standing companies.

A simple technique to achieve this would be:

- Reorganise the share capital of Oldco into A shares and B shares.
- The A shares carry all the rights (to dividends, distributions in the course of winding up etc) deriving from X Ltd.
- The B shares carry similar rights to Y Ltd.
- A dividend *in specie* on the A shares (comprising the shares in X Ltd) is declared.
- A dividend *in specie* on the B shares (comprising the shares in Y Ltd) is declared.
- Oldco is left as a shell company, and A and B are now separate free-standing companies.

In practice, demergers tend to be more complex – largely for tax reasons. *Examples 29.14* and *29.15* at **29.39** and **29.42** below illustrate this.

FINANCIAL ASSISTANCE

28.49 'Financial assistance' is a buzz phrase which crops up in many corporate transactions. It is essential that everyone involved in such deals is aware of its broad terms.

28.49 *Corporate Transactions – The Theory*

Under *CA 2006, s 678*, a public company may not give financial assistance in connection with the purchase of its own shares. Thus, it may not, for example, give charges over its assets for the purpose of raising finance which will then be used to buy its shares. This is a very common situation in management buyouts (eg where the management form Newco; a bank lends Newco cash secured on Target's assets; and Newco uses the cash to purchase Target's shares).

Public companies may never give financial assistance. As recommended by the Company Law Review (Final Report, para 10.6), the prohibition on private companies giving financial assistance for a purchase of own shares has been abolished and, as a consequence, the relaxation for private companies (sometimes referred to as the 'whitewash' procedure) is no longer required. The provisions in *CA 1985, ss 155–158* have, therefore, been repealed and are not carried forward in *CA 2006*.

Chapter 29

Corporate Transactions – The Practice

29.1 In the last chapter, all the relevant accounting practice and corporate law was pulled together to give a comprehensive theoretical background to the way in which corporate transactions are – or should be – accounted for.

This chapter considers a number of examples to illustrate how these principles are applied. A brief commentary, including tax points, follows each case.

REORGANISATION

29.2 The first two examples consider how to account for the situation where two companies under common control, but not being part of a group, are brought together in a group structure.

Example 29.1
Companies A and B are under common ownership. Summarised balance sheets at 31 December 2008 are:

	A	B
	£	£
Net Assets	500,000	300,000
Share Capital	10,000	1,000
Profit and Loss	490,000	299,000
	500,000	300,000

To create a group structure on 1 January 2009, A issues 1,000 new shares (in A) to the shareholders in B, in return for the transfer to A by them (the shareholders in B) of their shares in B. Thereby, a group with A as parent and B as subsidiary is formed. The opening individual and group balance sheets are:

29.3 Corporate Transactions – The Practice

	A	B	Group
	£	£	£
Net Assets	501,000	300,000	800,000
Share Capital	11,000	1,000	11,000
Profit and Loss	490,000	299,000	789,000
	501,000	300,000	800,000

29.3 The issue of shares by A need not give rise to a share premium account by virtue of *CA 2006, s 612*. The group accounts qualify under *FRS 6* for merger accounting, so fair value accounting is not necessary.

From the tax point of view, the transaction is straightforward. A clearance under *ICTA 1988, s 707* and one under *TCGA 1992, s 138* would normally be applied for. No *ad valorem* stamp duty should arise by virtue of *FA 1986, s 77*.

One interesting tax side issue is that, although there is no fair value accounting, the capital gains base cost of the B shares now held by A will be the fair value of those shares at the date of transfer. Any such transfer effected shortly before the onward sale of the B shares (by A) would probably risk the retrospective withdrawal of the *TCGA 1992, s 138* clearance, unless the sale possibility had been mentioned. In that case, though, clearance would probably not be given.

29.4 A slight variation in the way of achieving the same object as in *Example 29.1* is shown below.

Example 29.2
The same two companies as in *Example 29.1* wish to form a group. A new company is formed, Newco, which has only 2 × £1 shares in issue. That company might then issue 10,000 new shares (in Newco) to the shareholders in company A, and 1,000 new shares (in Newco) to the shareholders in company B in return for the A and B shareholders transferring their shares to Newco. The individual and group balance sheets would be:

	Newco	A	B	Group
	£	£	£	£
Net Assets	11,002	500,000	300,000	800,002
Share Capital	11,002	10,000	1000	11,002
Profit and Loss	Nil	490,000	299,000	789,000
	11,002	500,000	300,000	800,002

Corporate Transactions – The Practice 29.6

29.5 The accounting and tax analysis of the above configuration is almost identical to that in **29.3** above.

ACQUISITION OF ASSETS

29.6 The next example illustrates how a company should account for the acquisition of a business where the purchase is of assets (and not of the shares of a trading company).

Example 29.3

A company's year end is 31 December 2008. On 1 January 2008, it purchases for £500,000 a business formerly carried on by two individuals in partnership as a going concern. By agreement with the two individuals, the £500,000 is allocated between the assets in a particular way, and the legal documentation reflects this. The acquiring company believes that the allocation could not really be said to represent a 'fair' apportionment over the 'true' value of the assets. The relevant numbers are:

	Contract Documentation	Fair Value
	£	£
Property	250,000	150,000
Plant	200,000	100,000
Stock	50,000	75,000
Goodwill	–	175,000
	500,000	500,000

The draft balance sheet for the year ending 31 December 2008 is shown below, accounting for the acquisition using the contract documentation allocation. Alongside is shown the final balance sheet prepared under *FRS 7* and *FRS 10*.

	Draft	Final
	£	£
Property	750,000	650,000
Plant	300,000	200,000
Goodwill	–	140,000
Net Current Assets	150,000	150,000
	1,200,000	1,140,000
Share Capital	200,000	200,000
Profit and Loss	1,000,000	940,000
	1,200,000	1,140,000

29.7 *Corporate Transactions – The Practice*

29.7 Even though this is a purchase of assets, *FRS 10* requires 'fair' values to be substituted. Goodwill of £175,000 therefore arises, and this has to be amortised over a period (in this case, over five years by equal annual write-offs through the profit and loss account). By attributing an extra £25,000 to purchased stock, then – assuming it is all sold by year end – the annual profits will be reduced by the additional stock cost of £25,000.

29.8 Although this accounting is what should happen, there are many practical instances in which the contract allocation is assumed to represent 'fair value'. To do anything else is to invite a three-way discussion (or argument) between buyer, seller and HMRC. If buyer and seller agree on the fair allocation, then, unless the values they attach to the various assets are outrageous, it can be difficult for the Revenue officer to substitute an alternative allocation and attempt to impose liability on that basis.

INCORPORATION OF A SOLE TRADER BUSINESS

29.9 The next example considers the incorporation of a sole trader business.

Example 29.4
At 31 December 2008, the balance sheet of a sole trader business is as below. All assets are stated at their fair value, except for goodwill which is reckoned to be worth £100,000. The proprietor of the business does not wish to tie up all his capital account in the form of shares. He therefore transfers the whole of the business and its assets to a new company, Newco, in return for the issue of 1,000 new Newco shares plus £50,000. The £50,000 is left on loan account with the company. (Newco was formed a few weeks before the transaction. There are 2 × £1 ordinary shares in issue.) The opening company balance sheet is shown next to that of the closing sole trader.

	Sole Trader	Ltd Company
	£	£
Net Assets	300,000	300,002
Goodwill	–	100,000
Director's Loan Account	–	(50,000)
	300,000	350,002
Proprietor's Capital Account	300,000	–
Share Capital	–	1,002
Share Premium	–	349,000
	300,000	350,002

29.10 In an unincorporated business, the proprietor's capital account (= capital introduced + accumulated profits − cumulative drawings) takes the place of shareholders' funds (= share capital + accumulated profits − cumulative dividends).

The fair value of the net assets transferred is £400,000 (£300,000 + £100,000), and the consideration is £50,000 left on loan account, together with the issue of 1,000 × £1 shares. A share premium of £349,000 therefore arises. An accounting policy will be needed to amortise the goodwill (*FRS 10*).

From the capital gains point of view, a partial rollover under *TCGA 1992, s 162* is available (only partial, because the consideration is partly in the form of loan account). One way of avoiding the restriction of rollover is to draw £50,000 in cash out of the sole trader shortly before the incorporation, then incorporate wholly in return for shares, and finally reintroduce £50,000 on loan account into the company shortly after. Such a manoeuvre should be undertaken so as not to constitute a preordained sequence of events.

ACQUISITION OF A SUBSIDIARY

For cash

29.11 There now follows the first of a series of examples in which Company A acquires Company B.

Example 29.5
At 31 December 2008, Company A purchases the whole share capital of Company B for £1,000,000. The fair value of B's assets is £800,000.

The purchase price is paid in cash and is funded by the issue of an additional 100,000 × £1 ordinary shares at £5 per share (taken up by the existing shareholders of A) and the obtaining of bank borrowings of £500,000.

Total costs of the exercise are estimated at £10,000 relating to the issue of new shares, £10,000 bank arrangement fee and £20,000 professional fees in relation to the due diligence and negotiation of the acquisition (stamp duty is ignored).

The individual and group balance sheets immediately after acquisition are:

	A £	B £	Group £
Investment in B	1,030,000	–	–
Goodwill	–	–	230,000
Other Net Assets	500,000	700,000	1,300,000
Total Net Assets	1,530,000	700,000	1,530,000

29.12 Corporate Transactions – The Practice

	A £	B £	Group £
Share Capital	200,000	100,000	200,000
Share Premium	390,000	–	390,000
Profit and Loss	940,000	600,000	940,000
	1,530,000	700,000	1,530,000

29.12 Some explanation of the above may assist.

In A's accounts, the purchase price plus associated costs of B's shares is £1,040,000 (£1,000,000 + £10,000 + £10,000 + £20,000). But a share premium of £400,000 has been created on the share issue undertaken to fund the acquisition. That part of the costs relating to the raising of the shares (£10,000) may be written off against share premium account (*CA 1985, s 130*) – hence, the balance sheet of A.

B's balance sheet is virtually irrelevant. In the group accounts, it is the fair value of B's assets (£800,000) which are consolidated, not their book value. In the consolidated accounts, a price of £1,030,000 is compared to fair value of net assets of £800,000, to arrive at goodwill of £230,000. This should be capitalised and amortised under *FRS 10*.

29.13 The tax analysis of the transaction is fairly straightforward. The shareholders in B will have a capital gain based on gross disposal proceeds of £1,000,000. The base cost to A of the acquisition, for capital gains purposes, will be £1,020,000. The costs of share issue (written off against share premium) is not part of the cost of the asset. The £10,000 cost of raising loan moneys is allowable as a corporation tax deduction against income under the loan relationship rules. (Stamp duty is ignored in the example but, in real life, will be payable on the purchase price of £1,000,000.)

For cash, loan notes and shares

29.14 It is normal for an acquisition to combine the above three elements. A variation of *Example 29.5* is now considered.

Example 29.6
The facts are the same as in *Example 29.5*, except that the purchase price of company B is satisfied by:

Cash	£500,000
Loan Notes	£300,000
	£800,000

plus the issue of new shares in A which, on the day of completion, have the value of £200,000 (it is assumed that A is a quoted company, and the mid-market price at the close of business the previous day will be used).

In the event, the number of new £1 ordinary shares issued is 30,000. Because only £500,000 of actual cash is required, no further shares need be issued. (The £10,000 cost of the share issue in *Example 29.5* is avoided.) The cost of issuing the 30,000 × £1 shares is £2,000.

The individual and group balance sheets immediately after acquisition are:

	A £	B £	Group £
Investment in B	1,030,000	–	–
Goodwill	–	–	230,000
Other Net Assets	508,000	700,000	1,308,000
Loan Notes	(300,000)	–	(300,000)
	1,238,000	700,000	1,238,000
Share Capital	130,000	100,000	130,000
Share Premium	168,000	–	168,000
Profit and Loss	940,000	600,000	940,000
	1,238,000	700,000	1,238,000

29.15 The net assets of A are £508,000, being the £500,000 in *Example 29.5* plus the £10,000 cost saving on non-issue of 100,000 × £1 shares, less the £2,000 cost of issue of 30,000 × £1 shares. Although, in accounting terms, this is written off against the share premium on the issue of the 30,000 shares (200,000 – 30,000), it still has to be physically paid – hence the adjustment on bank balance (included in 'Other Net Assets').

29.16 The tax analysis of the above is almost identical to that in **29.13** above.

The main additional feature is the possibility of capital gains rollover under *TCGA 1992, s 135*. A clearance under *TCGA 1992, s 138* is essential.

29.17 On a practical note, it is likely that a vendor would want the loan note 'underwritten' by a clearing bank (or similar). If there is genuine risk in the loan note, it may be preferable to introduce terms into the document (such as expressing the note in foreign currency) to avoid the loan note being a qualifying corporate bond (see *TCGA 1992, s 117*). It is generally not attractive to have qualifying corporate bonds where there is risk (as there is no relief for any capital loss).

29.18 *Corporate Transactions – The Practice*

An underwritten loan note is attractive to a vendor because he gets an investment return on a gross investment. It is attractive to a purchaser (although, in security terms, the bank will regard it in much the same way as a loan) because the rate of interest on it is likely to be below its normal cost of capital. Typically, a rate of return equal to, say, base rate is negotiated, thereby giving some benefit to both buyer and seller.

ACQUISITION OF A 'HIVE DOWN' COMPANY

29.18 The following example illustrates the acquisition of a company into which a business and associated assets have recently been 'hived down'.

Example 29.7
Company A is in receivership. It carries on several trades, one of which is capable of trading successfully. The receiver causes a new company, B, to be formed as a 100% subsidiary of A, and he 'sells' the trade and assets of the potentially successful business from A to B, with proceeds left on loan account. The opening balance sheet of B is:

	£
Property	500,000
Net Current Assets	500,000
Owing to A	(999,900)
Net Assets	100
Share Capital	100

Shortly after, the receiver sells the entire share capital of B to Company C. That company pays £1.5 million in total, being £500,100 to acquire the shares, and the making of a loan of £999,900 to B (thus enabling B to discharge its debt to A).

Company C values the property at £750,000 and accepts that the net current assets are fairly stated at £500,000.

The separate and group balance sheets of B and C following acquisition are:

	B	C	Group
	£	£	£
Property	500,000	1,000,000	1,750,000
Investment in B	–	500,100	–
Goodwill	–	–	250,000
Net Current Assets	500,000	700,000	1,200,000
Loan from C	(999,900)	–	–
Loan to B	–	999,900	–
Net Assets	100	3,200,000	3,200,000
Share Capital	100	1,000	1,000
Reserves	–	3,199,000	3,199,000
	100	3,200,000	3,200,000

29.19 In accounting terms, the treatment is fairly straightforward. In total, C is expending £1.5 million, being the £500,100 to purchase the shares and £999,900 lent to B to discharge the debt to A. It is effectively acquiring assets with a book value of £1 million (£500,000 + £500,000), believing them to be worth £1.25 million (£750,000 + £500,000) and paying £1.5 million. Therefore, in the group accounts, prepared under fair value rules, it is acquiring assets of £1.25 million (£750,000 + £500,000) at a price of £1.5 million. The premium – or goodwill – is therefore £250,000.

29.20 The tax analysis is not complex but there are traps.

The 'hive down' of the trade by A to B ought not, in itself, to cause a problem. *ICTA 1988, ss 100, 343* and *TCGA 1992, s 171* apply. There should not be any VAT ramifications (transfer of a business as a going concern). If the trade hived down has a tax loss, then the solvency of A must be tested for the purposes of *ICTA 1988, s 343(4)*.

On the sale of B to C, a number of further considerations arise. A will suffer a capital gain on the disposal of the shares in B of £500,000, although it may be possible to argue that the true value of assets transferred is £1.5 million, even though only £1 million is payable (by B to A), and hence the effective consideration for the shares is £500,100. In practice, it rarely matters, because A is likely to have trading losses to offset the capital gain.

Other interesting points arise, though. Any losses hoping to be passed under *ICTA 1988, s 343* are only available providing B trades whilst still a subsidiary of A. Therefore, same day hive-downs and sell-ons should be avoided. Even if this pitfall (and the *s 343(4)* restriction) can be avoided, there is still the hurdle of *ICTA 1988, s 768* (the 'major change' provision) to overcome.

Even more alarming is the deemed disposal of chargeable assets by B on leaving the A group ('within six years') under *TCGA 1992, s 179*. B is deemed to suffer a capital gain on a notional sale of the property and the goodwill. The property gain could have been avoided by selling the property direct to

29.21 *Corporate Transactions – The Practice*

C by A (the gain would have arisen to A, but this could probably be covered by losses). It is more difficult in relation to goodwill as it is not easy to sell goodwill as a separate asset. Some components of goodwill, eg trade marks, copyrights, licences etc, may be separate assets.

So, from the tax viewpoint of C, the deal would have been better structured C had directly purchased: (1) the property for £750,000; (2) the licences, trade marks, copyrights etc for £250,000; and (3) at a cost of £100, the share capital in B, a company with £500,000 of net current assets, with a debt due to A of £499,900 (although stamp duty costs would have been increased).

DIVIDEND OUT OF PRE-ACQUISITION PROFITS

29.21 The following example illustrates how a dividend may be paid out of pre-acquisition profits.

Example 29.8
Company A is the subject of a management buy-out. The management team form a new company, B. They subscribe at par for 100,000 × £1 ordinary shares in B. A venture capitalist subscribes at £4 per share for 100,000 × £1 ordinary shares, and £1.5 million for 1.5 million × £1 preference shares (10% 'net' coupon).

The net book value of A's assets on acquisition is £3 million. It is considered that this is also the fair value of those assets. The purchase price of the entire share capital of A is £2 million. In other words, B has made a 'bargain purchase', in that it has acquired assets with a fair value of £3 million for £2 million. It has received a discount of £1 million. In most circumstances, a premium over the fair value of the assets acquired has to be paid (often referred to as a 'control premium') and positive goodwill arises. In this case, it is *negative* goodwill that arises. *FRS 6* requires this negative goodwill to be shown in the consolidated balance sheet alongside positive goodwill (but separately identified).

During the first 12 months after the buy-out, A breaks even. Just before year end, A pays a dividend (under group election) of £150,000 to B. B declares a dividend of £150,000 on the preference shares. The question to address is whether B has the legal capacity to pay the dividend to the holders of the preference shares; in other words, is the dividend received from a realised profit?.

The individual and group balance sheets of A and B are as below:

	A £	B £	Group £
Investment in A	–	2,000,000	–
Negative Goodwill			(1,000,000)
Other Assets	2,850,000	150,000	3,000,000
Dividend Payable	–	(150,000)	(150,000)
Net Assets	2,850,000	2,000,000	1,850,000

	A	B	Group
	£	£	£
Share Capital	500,000	1,700,000	1,700,000
Share Premium	–	300,000	300,000
Profit and Loss	2,350,000	–	(150,000)
	2,850,000	2,000,000	1,850,000

29.22 The group balance sheet looks odd: there is a negative balance on Profit and Loss, and yet a dividend is proposed. Dividends, however, are not paid by groups, but by individual companies. B has received a dividend of £150,000. This is a realised profit in the hands of A, but has been paid out of profits earned by A prior to the acquisition by B. Therefore, the question becomes whether or not the dividend received by B is realised, and therefore distributable by B.

The key guidance is given in para 16 of Appendix 1 to *FRS 6* 'Acquisitions and Mergers'. This paragraph states that, if a dividend is paid out of pre-acquisition profits, as in the example above, it should be applied to reduce the carrying value of the investment to the extent necessary to provide for a diminution in value of the investment in the accounts of the parent company. To the extent that this is not necessary, the amount received will be a realised profit (and hence distributable) in the hands of the parent company.

29.23 In this case, B is carrying the cost of the investment in A at £2 million and, at worst, the value of A's assets is £2.85 million (£3 million – £150,000). There is no need, therefore, to write down the investment, as long as the fair values attributed to the assets remain valid, and the dividend can be paid.

However, it should be noted that the circumstances set out in the example are rather unusual, in that B has paid £2 million for net assets with a fair value of £3 million, giving rise to negative goodwill (a 'bargain purchase') of £1 million. In most circumstances, a 'premium' is paid (such that positive goodwill arises), and it may be more difficult to argue that the value of the investment in the subsidiary has not been diminished by the payment of a dividend out of pre-acquisition reserves (ie out of the assets acquired).

FRS 6 requires the negative goodwill arising on the acquisition of A to be amortised to the profit and loss account over the periods expected to benefit.

PURCHASE OF OWN SHARES

Wholly out of distributable profits

29.24 In the next example, the purchase by a company of its own shares wholly out of distributable profits is examined.

29.25 *Corporate Transactions – The Practice*

Example 29.9
A company has 1,000 × £1 ordinary shares in issue. These were issued at £1.10 per share several years ago. The company is proposing to purchase 500 of its shares. It wishes to understand how its balance sheet will appear in three scenarios: (i) the purchase at a price of 80 pence per share, (ii) at £1.00 per share, and (iii) at £1.20 per share.

The existing balance sheet and its revised form in the three scenarios are:

	Original	Scenario (i)	Scenario (ii)	Scenario (iii)
	£	£	£	£
Net Assets	10,000	9,600	9,500	9,400
Share Capital	1,000	500	500	500
Share Premium	100	100	100	100
Capital Redemption Reserve	–	500	500	500
Profit and Loss	8,900	8,500	8,400	8,300
	10,000	9,600	9,500	9,400

29.25 In accounting terms, it can be seen that it matters very little whether the shares were originally issued at a premium, or whether they are being redeemed at a discount, premium, or par. The total amount of cash exiting the company is charged to distributable profits (in this case, assumed to equate to Profit and Loss). The nominal value of the shares purchased (and cancelled) is transferred to the capital redemption reserve.

29.26 The basic tax analysis is that the purchase of shares is a distribution for corporation tax purposes (*ICTA 1988, s 209(2)(b)*). The measure of the distribution is the redemption price (80 pence, £1 or £1.20) less the amount originally subscribed (ie £1.10). In certain circumstances, the receipt can be treated as a capital one (*ICTA 1988, s 219 et seq*).

Wholly out of distributable profits and the proceeds of a new issue

29.27

Example 29.10
The same company as in *Example 29.9* has determined to redeem the shares at £1.20 per share. It is issuing an additional 400 shares at £1.22 per share to help finance the acquisition.

The original and final balance sheets are:

	Original £	Final £
Net Assets	10,000	9,888
Share Capital	1,000	900
Share Premium	100	138
Capital Redemption Reserve	–	12
Profit and Loss	8,900	8,838
	10,000	9,888

Working (i) Proceeds of fresh issue   400 × 1.22 = 488
            Nominal value of shares redeemed   500 × 1 = 500
            Shortfall

Working (ii) Lower of: original premium on shares now purchased   12/50

            current balance on share premium account
            (including new shares to be issued)   188

            = £50

29.28 In accounting terms, this is complex and anomalous.

Under *CA 2006, s 687*, where the shares being purchased were originally issued at a premium, any premium payable on redemption may be paid out of the proceeds of a fresh issue, up to an amount equal to the lower of:

(a) the share premium on the shares being purchased; and

(b) the current balance on the company's share premium account (including share premium on the new shares being issued).

What this means is that, to the extent of the lower of (a) or (b), the premium on the redemption may be written off against share premium.

In the example above, therefore, the numbers can now be understood.

The original net assets (£10,000) are increased by the amount received on the new issue (£488) and reduced by the amount paid to purchase the old shares (£600), giving revised net assets of £9,888.

The nominal value of issued shares (£1,000) is increased by the new shares (£400) and reduced by the cancelled shares (£500), giving revised share capital of £900.

29.29 *Corporate Transactions – The Practice*

The premium on redemption is £100. The *CA 2006, s 687* calculation is at working (ii) above. This permits £50 to be written off against share premium, with the balance against distributable profits.

At working (i) above, the transfer to capital redemption reserve is computed under *CA 2006, s 733(3)*.

The revised balance on the Profit and Loss account is derived from the original £8,900, less £12 transferred to capital redemption reserve and £50 balance on the premium on redemption not capable of write-off to share premium account under *CA 2006, s 687*.

The anomaly is that the net effect of these adjustments has been a reduction of capital from £1,100 (£1,000 + £100) to £1,050 (£900 + £138 + £12). The objective of maintaining capital for the protection of creditors, therefore, has not been achieved.

CA 2006, s 687 is permissive and not obligatory. The £50 written off to share premium could have been written off to Profit and Loss. Many accountants would in fact do this.

29.29 The tax analysis is indifferent to the accounting complexities. The provisions mentioned in **29.26** above continue to apply.

Out of capital (at a discount)

29.30

Example 29.11
A private company, A, wishes to purchase 1,000 (in nominal value) of its issued ordinary £1 shares for £900. It proposes to issue 600 × £1 ordinary shares at par. Its distributable profits are only £200. The balance sheet before and after the redemption is:

	Before	After
	£	£
Net Assets	2,000	1,700
Share Capital	1,800	1,400
Capital Redemption Reserve	–	300
Profit and Loss	200	–
	2,000	1,700

Working	Purchase price	900
	Less distributable profits	(200)
	Less proceeds of shares issue	(600)
	Permissible capital payment	100

29.31 The net assets have fallen by £300, being the injection of the new share proceeds (£600) less the cash payment (of £900) on purchasing the shares to be redeemed.

The nominal value of the issued shares is reduced (by £1,000) in respect of the shares purchased, and increased (by £600) by virtue of the new share issue.

The difference between the permissible capital payment plus proceeds of share issue (£100 + £600) and the nominal value of shares purchased (£1,000) is £300, and is transferred to capital redemption reserve (see **28.13** above).

29.32 The tax analysis remains the same as in **29.26** above.

Out of capital (at a premium)

29.33

Example 29.12
A private company, B, wishes to purchase 1,000 (in nominal value) of its issued ordinary £1 shares for £1,100. It issues 850 × £1 new ordinary shares at par for the purpose. It has only £50 of distributable profits. Its balance sheet before and after the purchase is:

	Before	After
	£	£
Net Assets	2,000	1,750
Share Capital	1,500	1,350
Share Premium	450	400
Capital Redemption Reserve	–	–
Profit and Loss	50	
	2,000	1,750

29.34 *Corporate Transactions – The Practice*

Working	Purchase price	1,100
	Less distributable profits	(50)
	Less proceeds of share issue	(850)
	Permissible capital payment	200

29.34 The net assets have fallen by £250, being the injection of proceeds of new share issue (£850) less the purchase price of the shares being redeemed (£1,100).

The nominal value of the issued shares is reduced (by £1,000) in respect of the shares being purchased, and increased (by £850) in respect of the new shares issued.

The permissible capital payment (£200) plus the proceeds of new share issue (£850) exceed the nominal value of the shares being acquired. The excess of £50 is (as explained in **29.13** above) deducted from (in this case) the existing share premium account.

29.35 Once again, the tax analysis remains as explained in **29.26** above.

MERGER

29.36 The following example considers the individual and group accounts for a typical merger of two companies satisfying *CA 2006, s 612* and *FRS 6* tests for merger relief and merger accounting.

Example 29.13
Two companies, A and B, wish to merge. The merger is achieved by Company A offering the shareholders in Company B one new share in Company A for every two existing shares in B. The offer is accepted. The individual and group accounts just after merger are as below:

	A	B	Group
	£'000	£'000	£'000
Investment in B	100	–	–
Other Net Assets	1,100	800	1,900
Net Assets	1,200	800	1,900
Share Capital	200	200	200
Capital Reserve	–	–	100
Profit and Loss	1,000	600	1,600
	1,200	800	1,900

Corporate Transactions – The Practice **29.39**

29.37 In accounting terms, the transaction is quite simple.

Because of *CA 2006, s 612* merger relief, A is not required to create a share premium account when it issues the 100,000 new £1 ordinary shares in return for the acquisition of the 200,000 × £1 ordinary shares in B.

The group accounts do not need to reflect the fair values of the target company, B. The assets, liabilities and distributable profits are simply amalgamated.

There remains an imbalance, in that the 'cost' of the investment in B is £100,000, whereas the nominal value of the shares in B is £200,000. These 'cancel' but there is a 'spare' £100,000. The *Companies Act 2006* does not prescribe what is to be done with any consolidation difference arising. *FRS 6* merely provides that any differences (positive or negative) should be shown as a movement on other reserves in the consolidated statements. Most accountants would, therefore, include such positive balances in a capital reserve. If there is a negative balance, then it is normally written off against other reserves, usually against the most restrictive.

29.38 This is not a difficult transaction to analyse for tax purposes. The share swap ought to come within *TCGA 1992, s 135*, although stamp duty will be payable on the value given for the 200,000 × £1 shares in B (in this case, 100,000 × £1 ordinary shares in A). If the shareholders of A and B were identical, then the consideration might as well have been 1 × £1 ordinary share. This would have reduced the stamp duty to an infinitesimal amount. (Alternatively, if the shareholders in A and B are identical, stamp duty relief under *FA 1986, ss 75, 77* might be appropriate.)

DEMERGER OF TWO COMPANIES

Simple type

29.39 The following example considers a relatively straightforward demerger of two companies.

Example 29.14
Company X has two trading subsidiaries, Y and Z. The two shareholders in X get along well but they feel that Y and Z would be better able to prosper if they were not part of the same group. It is believed the shares in Y are worth £1 million and those in Z are worth £500,000. The draft balance sheets of X, Y and Z are:

29.40 *Corporate Transactions – The Practice*

	X £	Y £	Z £
Investment in Y	10,000	–	–
Investment in Z	20,000	–	–
Other Assets	70,000	500,000	400,000
Net Assets	100,000	500,000	400,000
Share Capital	10,000	10,000	20,000
Profit and Loss	90,000	490,000	380,000
	100,000	500,000	400,000

The following scheme is entered into:

(i) The shares in X are reorganised into A and B shares, with A shares carrying all the rights (to dividends, proceeds on liquidation etc) deriving from Company Y. Similarly for the B shares (which derive their value from Z) in relation to Company Z.

(ii) X's investment in Z is revalued to £500,000.

(iii) X declares a dividend *in specie* on its B shares, represented by the shares in Company Z.

(iv) The B shares of X are now worthless. X purchases the B shares for £1 (out of distributable profits).

The balance sheet of X at each of the above four points is:

	(i) £	(ii) £	(iii) £	(iv) £
Investment in Y	10,000	10,000	10,000	10,000
Investment in Z	20,000	500,000	–	–
Other Assets	70,000	70,000	70,000	69,999
Net Assets	100,000	580,000	80,000	79,999
A Share Capital	5,000	5,000	5,000	5,000
B Share Capital	5,000	5,000	5,000	–
Revaluation Reserve	–	480,000	–	–
Capital Redemption Reserve	–	–	–	5,000
Profit and Loss	90,000	90,000	70,000	69,999
	100,000	580,000	80,000	79,999

29.40 The net result of the above arrangement is that a demerger has been effected. The revaluation of the shares in Z at step (ii) is necessary to create the revaluation reserve from which the dividend can be paid. Normally, of course, a revaluation reserve is not a realised profit, but it may be used where it derives from the revaluation of an asset which is to be distributed *in specie* (*CA 2006, s 846*).

The purchase of the (now worthless) B shares is simply a tidying-up process (not necessary to achieve the demerger purpose). The capital redemption reserve is set up as explained in **29.24** *et seq* above.

29.41 In the first instance, the dividend *in specie* of the shares in Z is a distribution for tax purposes (*ICTA 1988, s 209(4)*). However, as the conditions for demerger relief appear to apply, this will be an exempt demerger under *ICTA 1988, s 213(2)*. By virtue of *TCGA 1992, s 192* the arrangements whereby the shareholders in X come to hold not only shares in X but also shares in Z are treated as a reorganisation of share capital for *TCGA 1992, s 126* purposes. Tax clearance is essential.

There is no exemption from stamp duty in respect of the transfer of shares in Z from X to the shareholders in X, but even more importantly, there is no exemption from capital gains tax on Company Z leaving the X group. This can be a considerable inconvenience, in practice, which often leads to the adoption of a more complex demerger path (see below).

More complex type

29.42 The following example considers the way of avoiding the exit capital gain described above.

Example 29.15
The facts are the same as in *Example 29.14*, except that the two shareholders in X (Mr Smith and Mr Jones) wish to go their separate ways. Additionally, they wish to avoid the exit capital gain on demerger and, as far as possible, reduce any stamp duty implications.

The following scheme is adopted:

(i)   The shares in X are reorganised into A and B shares, having the rights described in *Example 29.14*. Mr Smith takes the A shares, and Mr Jones takes the B shares.

(ii) X's investment in Z is revalued to £500,000.

(iii) Mr Jones now forms a new company, J. He subscribes £900 for 900 × £1 new ordinary shares in J.

(iv) X declares a dividend *in specie* on the B shares represented by the shareholding in Z. However, the shares in Z are not transferred to Mr Jones directly, but to the company J, which in consideration issues 100 additional new shares to Mr Jones.

(v)   X purchases the (now worthless) B shares.

29.43 *Corporate Transactions – The Practice*

The end result is that Mr Smith owns Company X which owns Company Y, and Mr Jones owns Company J which owns Company Z.

The balance sheet of Company J, before and after the receipt of the shares in Company Z, is:

	Before	After
	£	£
Net Assets	900	500,900
	900	500,900
Share Capital	900	1,000
Share Premium	–	499,900
	900	500,900

29.43 The accounting is straightforward. For X, it is the same as in *Example 29.14*. For J, it issues 100 new £1 shares in return for the receipt by it of the shares in Z which are worth £500,000. It is required (*CA 2006, s 610*) to create a share premium account of £499,900.

29.44 The distribution of the shares in Z remains an exempt distribution for tax purposes (*ICTA 1988, s 213(3)(b)(ii)*). In the first instance, the situation where Mr Smith comes to own all the shares in Company X, and Mr Jones comes to own all the shares in Company J, will not qualify as a reorganisation of share capital for *TCGA 1992, s 126* purposes. However, Statement of Practice SP5/85 by concession will allow the arrangement to be treated as a reorganisation or reconstruction, even though there is the change of company ownership as described. Moreover, under *TCGA 1992, s 139* the transfer of the Z shares to Company J is treated, for the purposes of capital gains, as having taken place on a no gain, no loss basis. The capital gain problem identified in *Example 29.14* has been solved.

Stamp duty remains in respect of the transfer of the Z shares to Company J. However, the consideration is *not* £500,000. What was given for those Z shares was 100 shares in Company J. That represents 10% of the issued share capital of Company J. Company J is worth, say, £500,900; therefore, the value of the consideration is £50,090 (at most). So, the subscription for 900 × £1 shares before the dividend *in specie* has substantially reduced the stamp duty.

A final word of warning is needed on the tax analysis. In the above example, Mr Smith appears to have effected a considerably better deal than Mr Jones. This raises questions as to whether the deal was genuinely at arm's length. If not, then inheritance tax and capital gains value-shifting considerations need to be borne in mind.

COMPARISON WITH INTERNATIONAL ACCOUNTING STANDARDS

29.45 *Example 29.8* shows a dividend being paid out of pre-acquisition profits. UK GAAP requires all distributions, whether out of pre-acquisition or post-acquisition profits, to be taken to the profit and loss account and, separately, consideration is given to whether the carrying value of the investment has been impaired as a result. If an impairment has occurred, the investment should be written down. *IAS 27* requires dividends out of pre-acquisition profits to be deducted from the cost of the investment.

29.46 *Example 29.13* covers merger accounting, which is not permitted under *IFRS 3*. Merger accounting is rarely seen in the UK because of the restrictive criteria for its use set out in *FRS 6*.

Chapter 30

Limited Liability Partnerships

30.1 Limited liability partnerships (LLPs) are governed by the *Limited Liability Partnerships Act 2000*, which came into effect on 6 April 2001. The Act is supplemented by the *Limited Liability Partnerships Regulations 2001 (SI 2001/1090)* (the '*LLP Regulations*'), and further supplemented by the *Limited Liability Partnerships (Accounts and Audit) (Application of Companies Act 2006) Regulations 2008 (SI 2008/1911)* (the '*LLP Accounting Regulations*').

The main difference between LLPs and conventional partnerships is that, in most circumstances, the liability of the individual 'members' of an LLP (equivalent to partners in a conventional partnership) is limited to the amounts they have invested in the LLP, whereas the partners in a conventional partnership have unlimited personal liability for all business debts and liabilities. In certain circumstances, individual members can be sued in their personal capacity, which reinstates unlimited liability for that individual.

LEGAL REQUIREMENTS

30.2 LLPs are subject to the *Companies Act 2006* and are, therefore, required to prepare financial statements that give a true and fair view. The *LLP Accounting Regulations* modify the *CA 2006* requirements to accommodate LLPs, but the provisions for small and medium-sized companies also apply to small and medium-sized LLPs. The thresholds introduced in 2006 for companies have application to LLPs also.

30.3 The regulations set out minimum reporting requirements, and refer to 'members' rather than 'partners'.

Modifications to the balance sheet requirements include two new headings: 'loans and other debts due to members' and 'members' other interests', which is further subdivided into members' capital, revaluation reserve, and other reserves.

30.4 The profit and loss account requirements provide for 'profit or loss for the financial year before members' remuneration and profit shares'. In addition, interest payable to members is not to be shown under the heading 'interest payable', the consequence being that all amounts due to members, irrespective of whether they are salaries, interest on capital or share of the profits of the LLP, are shown after this sub-total.

LLPs are not required to produce a 'directors' report' under *CA 2006* and the *LLP Regulations*. Copies of the accounts and auditor's report must be sent to members and others no later than the date on which they are actually delivered to the Registrar.

UK GAAP

30.5 The Consultative Committee of Accountancy Bodies (CCAB) issued a Statement of Recommended Practice (SORP) for LLPs in May 2002, which has been approved by the ASB, although the latter has no plans for an explicit standard dealing with LLPs. Following consultation, the final version of a revised SORP was approved by the ASB on 30 March 2006.

The SORP applies to LLPs incorporated in Great Britain that choose to report under UK GAAP rather than IFRS. The LLP SORP provides (at para 24) that the annual report of an LLP should consist of:

- the financial statements;
- a statement of members' responsibilities in relation to the production of financial statements;
- a report on the financial statements by a registered auditor, if required by the Regulations; and
- a report to the members.

30.6 The financial statements of an LLP that is not exempt under the small and medium-sized companies regulations comprise a profit and loss account, statement of total recognised gains and losses in accordance with *FRS 3*, a cash flow statement prepared in accordance with *FRS 1*, a balance sheet and notes to the financial statements.

30.7 The members' report is required to disclose the following information:

- the principal activities of the LLP and its subsidiary undertakings, indicating any significant changes during the year;
- an indication of the existence of any branches outside the UK;
- the identity of anyone who was a designated member during the year; and
- the policy of the LLP regarding members' drawings, and the subscription and repayment of amounts subscribed or otherwise contributed by members.

30.8 *Limited Liability Partnerships*

The SORP also requires an analysis of members' participation rights separately into equity and liability components, which will depend on the terms of the members' agreement, in accordance with *FRS 25* and *UITF 39*.

PAYMENTS TO MEMBERS

30.8 In relation to payments to members, the SORP distinguishes between non-discretionary amounts in respect of participation rights in the profits, and discretionary division of profits under equity participation rights. The former are to be presented as an expense within the profit and loss account, within the heading 'Members' remuneration charged as an expense'. The latter are debited directly to equity and not shown as an expense.

A table detailing the treatment of members' remuneration is given in para 47 of the LLP SORP and reproduced below:

Nature of element of a member's remuneration	Treat as:
Remuneration that is paid under an employment contract	Expense, described as 'Members' remuneration charged as an expense', and deducted after arriving at 'Profit for the financial year before members' remuneration and profit shares'
Other payments, arising from components of members' participation rights in the profits for the year that give rise to liabilities in accordance with *FRS 25* and *UITF 39*, such as mandatory interest payments.	
Automatic division of profits	
Any share of profits arising from a division of profits that is discretionary on the part of the LLP (ie where the decision to divide the profits is taken after the profits have been made).	Allocation of profit

Paragraph 52 of the SORP clarifies the position regarding loans and other debts due to members, noting that, although they are substantively liabilities of the LLP, they do not form part of the external financing and, as such, should be shown separately in the analysis of net debt required by *FRS 1* 'Cash Flow Statements'.

The members' report is also required by the SORP to disclose the overall policy in relation to members' drawings, including any transfer of members' interests from equity to debt, and vice versa.

RETIREMENT BENEFITS

30.9 *FRS 17* should be used to account for retirement benefits provided for employees of the LLP. In relation to retirement benefits of members,

Limited Liability Partnerships **30.13**

the LLP must analyse their contractual obligations between those giving rise to financial liabilities within the scope of *FRS 25*, and those giving rise to liabilities of uncertain timing and amount, thereby falling under *FRS 12* 'Provisions, Contingent Liabilities and Contingent Assets'.

Amounts recognised in respect of retirement benefits of current members should be charged to the profit and loss account. For post-retirement benefits, those in respect of current members and those in respect of former members should be shown separately, and the accounting policy note should disclose the LLP's policy in relation to post-retirement payments to members.

TAXATION

30.10 Where tax to be paid on member's remuneration is a personal liability of the members, it falls within 'Members' interests' in the balance sheet and should not appear in the profit and loss account.

If an LLP is subject to tax as a corporate entity in another jurisdiction, the tax liability should be recorded in the profit and loss account, and the related liability carried as a creditor in the balance sheet.

REVENUE RECOGNITION AND PROVISIONS

30.11 *SSAP 9*, together with Application Note G of *FRS 5* and *UITF Abstract 40*, applies to LLPs, as does *FRS 12* in relation to provisions and contingencies.

RELATED PARTIES

30.12 *FRS 8* applies to LLPs. An LLP that is under the control of another LLP, partnership or company or other entity will be a related party of that other entity. However, the fact that some members of an LLP are also members of another LLP does not of itself make the businesses related parties.

TAXATION CONSIDERATIONS

30.13 In the vast majority of cases, the tax consequences of operating a business as an LLP are the same as those applying to conventional partnerships, ie LLPs are transparent entities for tax purposes, notwithstanding that members have the benefit of limited liability. So, despite having the filing and other obligations associated with incorporation, LLP members are taxed on their respective shares of the profits, rather than the entity itself.

PART IV

CONCEPTUAL DEVELOPMENTS

Chapter 31

Accounting and Tax Profit – Background and Present Position

31.1 This chapter sets out the current position on the weight given to accountancy principles in the determination of taxable profits from trading.

BASIC TAX PRINCIPLES

31.2 Business profits are charged to income tax by *ITTOIA 2005, s 5* and corporation tax by *CTA 2009, s 35* which both state that tax shall be charged in respect of the 'profits of a trade'. Previously, *ICTA 1988, s 60* explained that the charge under the former Schedule D Case I would be on the 'full amount of the profits or gains'.

31.3 In the absence of a statutory definition of 'profit', many cases have come to court. In the early days, the accountancy profession was undeveloped and there was no codified basis of accounting corresponding to that described earlier in this book. Judges therefore took it upon themselves to apply their own gloss to the statutory words. It quickly became clear that 'annual' or 'full amount of' profits should mean 'profits determined on proper commercial principles'. (There are many variants of this expression, such as 'correct accountancy principles'. Nothing much hangs on the precise formulation of the words, except possibly a slight difference of nuance between the words 'principle' and 'practice'.) That, of course, begged the question as to what those principles were, so judge-made 'rules of thumb' evolved. One of these was the so-called rule that, for income tax purposes, 'neither a profit nor a loss should be anticipated'.

31.4 As the years passed, the accountancy profession became more ordered and sophisticated. Company law recognised and 'built in' accountancy standards. Judges, whilst retaining the ultimate power of decision-making, increasingly relied on accountants to 'advise' (or give evidence at hearings) as to what should constitute the proper way of accounting for particular transactions. The tax statutes increasingly drew on accountancy practice to determine taxable profits, particularly in relation to corporation tax.

31.5 *Accounting and Tax Profit – Background and Present Position*

THE PROBLEMS

31.5 Commercial life is dynamic, and accountancy principles have had to move with the times. This changing environment does not sit easily with the judicial process, which relies so much on the principle of precedent. Increasingly strained reinterpretations of early cases are needed to make any kind of logical sense. (Appendix A summarises and comments on some of the major cases of the past 100 years.) The debate about possible alignment of accounting and tax profits took off in the late 1990s and is not yet complete. The following is a summary of the direction the debate has taken so far.

Accounting Concepts and Revenue Law – Tax 18/97

31.6 In September 1997, the Tax Faculty of the ICAEW met with the then Inland Revenue, following which an agreed note of the meeting was published as a Guidance Note (Tax 18/97). The thrust was that the Tax Faculty was 'pushing' the Inland Revenue to say why there could not be a wholesale alignment of accounting and tax profits. This was resisted by the Inland Revenue for the following main reasons:

- Materiality concepts for tax and accounting were different.

- The Revenue believed that accounting standards were not exclusively or even primarily looking at the measure of profit, being more concerned with (materiality and) balance sheet issues.

- Some accounting standards (eg *FRS 5* – the 'substance over form' standard) called for finely balanced economic judgement, on which individual practitioners would often differ. The resultant uncertainties in the application of *FRS 5* militated against its use as a core feature of the tax system.

Tax Bulletin No 32

31.7 This was issued in December 1997 and specifically addressed (at page 485) the relationship between accountancy and taxable profits. Unsurprisingly, this restates the Revenue position, as articulated in Tax 18/97. It also confirms the continuing relevance of the so-called judge-made 'rules of thumb', as specifically illustrated in two contemporary cases before the Special Commissioners (*Meat Traders Limited v Cushing* [1997] SCD 245, SpC and *Herbert Smith v Honour* [1999] 72 TC 130 – see Appendix A).

Finance Act 1998, s 42

31.8 *FA 1998, s 42* states that, for the purposes of Schedule D Case I or II, the profits of a trade (etc) must be computed on an accounting basis which

Accounting and Tax Profit – Background and Present Position 31.8

gives a 'true and fair view', subject to any adjustment required or authorised by law. The object of this was to remove the option of the 'cash' basis for professional practices, but the wording was a little wider than that. It is quite curious. It referred to 'an accounting basis' in the singular, as though there were only one such basis to consider. It also introduces – without definition – the concept of a basis which gives a true and fair view of the profits. As the Revenue themselves recognised in Tax 18/97, modern accounting standards are more concerned with materiality and balance sheet issues. Much debate within the accountancy profession exists on the question of the primacy of the balance sheet over the profit and loss (or vice versa). In many circumstances, the more 'right' the balance sheet, the more 'wrong' becomes the profit and loss. So, compromise solutions need to be found. The concept of a free-standing 'true and fair profit and loss' is, therefore, quite odd. For periods of account beginning after 6 April 1999, the first step was to ensure that the accounts give a true and fair view. The second step (*FA 1998, s 42(2)*) required that adjustments be made to comply with tax rules. The move from determining profit from case law to explicitly using accounts, unless the law provided otherwise, was controversial at the time, and it was not long before the question of IFRS (IAS at the time) came to prominence. *Council Regulation (EC) 1606/2002* (the '*IAS Regulation*') required that consolidated group accounts of listed companies were to be drawn up in accordance with international accounting standards with effect from 1 January 2005. Also in 2002, a statutory definition of generally accepted accounting practice was introduced (*FA 2002, s 103* amending *FA 1998, s 42*), and a new *s 836A* was inserted into *ICTA 1988* which read as follows:

'(1) In the Tax Acts, unless the context otherwise requires, "generally accepted accounting practice"–

  (a) means generally accepted accounting practice with respect to accounts of UK companies that are intended to give a true and fair view, and

  (b) has the same meaning in relation to–

    (i) individuals,

    (ii) entities other than companies, and

    (iii) companies that are not UK companies,

  as it has in relation to UK companies.

(2) In subsection (1) "UK companies" means companies incorporated or formed under the law of a part of the United Kingdom.'

A further amendment was then made (*FA 2004, s 50*) which redefined GAAP to include both EC-adopted IAS and UK GAAP for periods beginning on or after 1 January 2005. Now the position is that, whenever a provision refers to GAAP, this includes a reference to IAS.

31.9 *Accounting and Tax Profit – Background and Present Position*

Tax Law Rewrite

31.9 The Tax Law Rewrite project has resulted in the abolition of Schedule D, for income tax by *ITTOIA 2005* and then for corporation tax by *CTA 2009* (in the interim, the old Schedule D continued to apply to companies), both of which now say:

> 'The profits of a trade must be calculated in accordance with generally accepted accounting practice, subject to any adjustment required or authorised by law ...' (*ITTOIA 2005, s 25; CTA 2009, s 46*).

31.10 Putting all these issues into the melting point, an attempt will now be made to summarise the current position.

THE ANALYSIS

31.11 Accounting principles are normally what determine taxable profits (subject to specific statute).

This has been confirmed by almost every relevant case in the last 100 years, and then, following much debate, enshrined in statute in 1998, with subsequent amendments to clarify the nature of GAAP. This may, however, be subject to 'rules of thumb' and continues to be resisted to some extent by HMRC, as demonstrated by the recent joined cases of *HMRC v William Grant and Sons Distillers Ltd* and *Small (Inspector of Taxes) v Mars UK Ltd*.

31.12 This applies, in theory, whether there is a capital/revenue problem or a timing issue in relation to income or expenditure, but in practice capital/revenue distinctions are harder to draw by relying solely on accountancy evidence.

Judges may be more reluctant to follow accountancy principles in capital/revenue cases, as there is a statute 'disallowing' capital expenditure. There is no accounting standard or accounting definition of capital expenditure, and so this is one area where the courts will intervene and treat as a matter of law, although allowing practical or business considerations to influence their decisions.

31.13 Accountancy principles are dynamic, and what constitutes a true and fair measure of company profit changes over time.

> 'As has often been pointed out, such principles are not static: they may be modified, refined and elaborated over time as circumstances change and accounting insights sharpen'. (*Gallagher v Jones* [1993] STC 555)

> 'Accountancy is not a static art'. (*Symons v Weeks*, 56 TC 630)

The ASB's Statement of Principles, published in 1999, states (at para 11):

'The true and fair view is, furthermore, a dynamic concept, because its content evolves in response to changes in, inter alia, accounting and business practice. This dynamism pervades the whole system of financial reporting, affecting the interpretation of every requirement and instigating and providing direction to the development of accounting practice.'

31.14 Accounting standards have become much more important and authoritative:

'The Court is slow to accept that accounts prepared in accordance with accepted principles of commercial accountancy are not adequate for tax purposes ...'. (*Johnston v Britannia Airways* [1994] STC 782)

HMRC's Business Income Manual states (at BIM31003):

'... if there are no relevant tax rules or principles which affect a particular case, correct accountancy principles will determine the amount of the taxable profit.'

31.15 The courts are reluctant to ignore accountancy evidence:

'[he] envisaged the possibility of a Court deciding that a prevailing system of commercial accounting did not correspond to the correct principles of commercial accounting. It is however observed that no case was cited to me, nor do I know of any, where a Court has in fact done that'. (*Symons v Weeks* 56 TC 630)

31.16 Where there is an unambiguous single correct accounting principle, that should determine the issue. There should be no room for 'rules of thumb' (eg no anticipation of profits or losses).

'Rules of thumb' are simply judges' early attempts at defining what proper accountancy principles should be. Once those principles are recognised and widely accepted, rules of thumb should become redundant.

31.17 Where there is no single unambiguous correct accountancy principle, then the courts may select that which is the better in the particular case. This implies that different accounts could be produced, each of which could be said to produce a true and fair view. In reaching their conclusion, the rules of thumb may assist.

This may arise because there is no authoritative pronouncement of accountancy principle (eg the capital/revenue divide) or where there are two different (but acceptable) ways of accounting.

This is confirmed in many cases, but is illustrated both in the *Willingale* and *Britannia Airways* cases.

31.18 Where there are two or more ways of accounting, the particular method adopted by the company will be strongly persuasive that that basis should be used for tax purposes.

31.19 *Accounting and Tax Profit – Background and Present Position*

31.19 Accounts may yet exhibit a true and fair view but not form the basis for determining taxable profits. This is because of the principle of 'materiality'.

In accounting terms, for a company with turnover of £10 million, with profits of £1 million, an error of £30,000 in valuing stock would not be material, and accounts containing that 'error' would still be regarded as being true and fair.

There is no developed concept of materiality in the sphere of tax.

This is illustrated in the *Britannia Airways* case, where the judge appeared not to take on board that, by comparing the variances (in estimates to final outcomes) against the reported level of profit, the company was effectively putting forward a materiality argument.

31.20 Broadly, the same principles apply to unincorporated businesses.

However, it should be noted that many of the recent legislative changes to specifically require reference to accounting practices do not apply to income tax. For example, the foreign exchange and loan relationship legislation, and research and development credits, only have application under corporation tax and not income tax.

Chapter 32

Future Developments

32.1 This edition of the book has been produced at a time of unprecedented turbulence in both the accountancy and tax spheres. It is no longer sufficient to be concerned with national developments; indeed, awareness of the influence of worldwide developments on local practices is now essential.

IFRS ADOPTION

32.2 The number of countries that have now adopted, or are planning to adopt, IFRS has created an unstoppable force. As of June 2009, 117 countries were using the system. It is important to note, however, that the development and adoption of IFRS is not just concerned with technical accounting changes. It also represents a transformation in cultural terms, bringing capital market reporting to some jurisdictions where it previously did not exist.

In 2007, KPMG published a report 'International Financial Reporting Standards: The Quest for a Global Language'. The report draws on commentaries from a number of key players in the UK accounting world. On the plus side, the commentators observe that there is greater comparability and more discussion taking place, for example in relation to financial instruments. On the other side, there are concerns about increased complexity, particularly that stemming from the disconnect between internal business operations and the use of fair values for external reporting.

In an address to the Economic and Monetary Affairs Committee, European Parliament, on 28 September 2009, Sir David Tweedie, Chairman of the IASB, stressed the IASB's response to the global financial crisis has been to work on a defined programme to address three specific issues, ie the application of fair value in illiquid markets, accounting for off balance sheet items, and disclosures relating to risk. The second of these is something the G20 has also expressed concern about.

CONVERGENCE

UK–IFRS

32.3 The ASB first published a discussion paper in March 2004, entitled 'UK Accounting Standards: A Strategy for convergence with IFRS'. In that

32.4 Future Developments

paper, a phased approach to convergence was mooted, such that new standards would be introduced to enhance existing UK financial requirements, to take effect from 2005 and 2006, and thereafter replacement of UK standards based on IFRS would proceed by step change. Respondents to the discussion paper were in favour of the phased approach and, in March 2005, the ASB published an exposure draft (ED) entitled 'Accounting Standard Setting in a changing environment: The Role of the Accounting Standards Board'. This statement of policy positioned the ASB as a valuable agent in the development of new accounting standards by the IASB. In addition to describing the envisaged role of the ASB, the document also reaffirmed the commitment to a phased approach to convergence. This was followed by an apparent change of heart by respondents, who, with some experience in preparing statements under IFRS, threw some doubt on the wisdom of the phased approach. A subsequent public meeting, hosted by the ASB in January 2006, discussed the possibility of a 'big bang' approach in preference to progressive convergence.

Following further work by the ASB, a press notice (PN 289) was issued in May 2006 outlining the Board's tentative proposals, specifically:

'1. All UK Public Quoted and other publicly accountable companies would be required to apply full IFRS, irrespective of turnover and whether they present group accounts or not. This would mean that approximately another 1,000 to 1,500 companies would be required to report under IFRS.

2. The use of the ASB's Financial Reporting Standard for Smaller Entities (FRSSE) ... would be extended beyond small companies to include medium-sized entities. This would mean that approximately another 30,000 companies would be able to use the FRSSE.

3. UK subsidiaries of group companies that apply full IFRS would also be required to apply full IFRS in respect of measurement and recognition, but with reduced disclosure requirements ... This would affect approximately 14,000 companies.

4. There has not yet been a decision on companies that do not fall within 1, 2 or 3 above. There are approximately 7,000 companies in this "gap" ...'

32.4 In 2007, the IASB published an ED of an IFRS for SMEs, and the ASB then published it for consultation regarding the potential implications for UK and Irish entities. The ASB deferred its decision on convergence pending feedback on this issue. Respondents were supportive of the IFRS for SMEs, but concerned about its appropriateness for micro entities, envisaging a residual need for FRSSE for these organisations.

In August 2009, the ASB issued a policy proposal consultation paper entitled 'The Future of UK GAAP', requesting comments by 1 February 2010. In the introduction, it is stated that '[t]he intention is to work under the IASB framework and to converge to the fullest extent possible consistent with the needs of UK entities'. The result will be that the existing body of UK GAAP effectively ceases to exist, although the ASB reserves the right to set UK GAAP in future.

The new proposals adopt a three-tier approach as follows:

Accounting Regime	Type/Nature of Entities
Tier 1	
EU Adopted IFRS	EU listed - consolidated
	AIM
	IEX (Irish Enterprise Exchange)
	Publicly accountable including publicly accountable 100% subsidiaries
Tier 2	
IFRS for SMEs	Non-Publicly Accountable Entities
Tier 3	
FRSSE	Small (as at present).

The benefits expected to flow from this approach are:

- simpler reporting arrangements that are proportionate to size and also accountability;
- using IFRS as a basis promotes consistency and reduced compliance burdens; and
- a follow on benefit arising from improved comparability and understanding is better access to capital markets and increased transparency.

One key differentiating feature is that of public accountability. The ASB recognises there are several possible ways of determining this, and states that an entity is considered to have public accountability if:

(i) its debt or equity instruments are traded in a public market or it is in the process of issuing such instruments for trading in a public market (ie a domestic or foreign stock exchange or an over-the-counter market, including local and regional markets); or

(ii) it is a deposit-taking entity and/or holds assets in a fiduciary capacity for a broad group of outsiders as one of its primary businesses. This is typically the case for banks, credit unions, insurance companies, securities broker/dealer, mutual funds or investment banks.

This notion of public accountability is not new and has been deployed by the *Companies Acts* and EU Directives. The ASB is looking at a more generic definition than that currently in law, so as to better match the financial reporting requirements to the stewardship and accountability obligations of the entity.

32.5 *Future Developments*

IASB–US GAAP Convergence

32.5 A parallel, but equally important, development is the convergence project between the IASB and the US Financial Accounting Standards Board (FASB). A Memorandum of Understanding was agreed in 2006 that described a programme aimed at improving accounting standards and achieving substantial convergence between IFRS and US GAAP. The Memorandum was updated in 2008 and, in November 2009, the two Boards issued a further statement outlining the steps for completion of the convergence work by 2011. The Securities and Exchange Commission, however, has set a conversion deadline of 2014.

One problem that faces non-US companies that use IFRS is the need to produce a reconciliation statement to US GAAP. This is something that both Boards recognise, but one of the barriers to its removal is the effective implementation of IFRS across companies and jurisdictions, which will take some time yet.

2011 is also the target year for convergence between IFRS and Japanese GAAP. The Japanese Business Accounting Council approved, in June 2009, a 'roadmap' for the adoption of IFRS in Japan. On 11 December 2009, Japan's Financial Services Agency announced regulatory changes that allow listed companies to prepare their consolidated financial statements using IFRS for fiscal years ending on or after 31 March 2010. In addition, from 31 March 2016, it will no longer be possible for Japanese listed companies to submit consolidated financial statements using US GAAP.

The September 2009 meeting of the G20 leaders reaffirmed the commitment to the development of converged accounting standards, and urged completion of the convergence project by June 2011.

EXTENSIBLE BUSINESS REPORTING LANGUAGE (XBRL)

32.6 eXtensible Business Reporting Language (XBRL) is an internet-based language for electronic communication of business and financial data that is an open-standard, licence-free system developed by an international consortium of approximately 450 companies, organisations and Government agencies. The basic premise is that every individual item of data is provided with an identifying 'tag', which then allows for sophisticated computer analysis, more efficient storage and data handling. It means that companies can use a common electronic language that is freely available, and allows for consistency of reporting between entities using it. It is suggested that companies using XBRL can save considerable costs, as well as being able to streamline their data collection processing for financial reporting purposes. A central database is used to store reporting data, rather than multiple databases each storing data and forwarding it to other systems, for example from the management accounting system to the tax return preparation system. For analysts of financial data, the use of a global internet-based system allows for analysis of more data more efficiently.

The IASB has developed an XBRL taxonomy, which is an 'electronic description and classification systems for the contents of financial statements and other business reporting documents'.

Company tax returns

32.7 In the UK, from 1 April 2011, all company tax returns must be filed online. In addition, companies must file accounts and computations in a set format, specifically inline eXtensible Business Reporting Language (iXBRL). While XML has been a standard code for some time, iXBRL is not yet in common use, and HMRC is the first major organisation to introduce it.

This new development stems from Lord Carter's 2006 review that recommended HMRC and Companies House provide a joint online filing facility as well as the adoption of iXBRL. The advantage is that companies will be able to make a single transmission over the internet for their company tax return and accounts. The Chartered Institute of Taxation has expressed concern over the timeline and the expected cost of the changeover for companies. HMRC have moved on the implementation of mandatory XBRL submissions ahead of Companies House, and arguably before the accounting software community is fully ready for the change.

COMMON CONSOLIDATED CORPORATE TAX BASE (CCCTB)

32.8 The progress towards global adoption of IFRS has also led to growing confidence in the prospect of adopting a CCCTB in Europe. The European Commission held a public consultation in 2003 concerning the use of IFRS as a possible starting point for a CCCTB and, in July 2004, a non-paper was issued for discussion, which led to the creation of a working group to move the idea of a CCCTB forward. Progress has been slow, however, and it seems unlikely that a new proposal will be released until well into 2010. The Czech Presidency of the EU postponed plans to progress the CCCTB, preferring to focus attention on the fight against tax evasion and avoidance.

SPECULATION ON FUTURE DEVELOPMENTS IN ACCOUNTING AND FINANCIAL REPORTING STANDARDS

32.9 A feature of the last few years has been a series of financial scandals and crises. A likely response is an increase in regulation of all aspects of financial markets and the institutional players in those markets, including those involved in financial reporting. This, coupled with the increasing complexity of commercial transactions, is likely to result in accounting standards of greater length and increasing technical complexity, with a greater emphasis on regulation via detailed rules rather than overriding principles, and extensive disclosure requirements. The IASB/FASB conversion project may well exacerbate this process.

32.9 Future Developments

The rapid changes experienced in the modern business environment are also likely to lead to more frequent amendments to standards, particularly via ad hoc pronouncements, placing a premium on maintaining up-to-date technical knowledge.

To a significant extent, the increasing technical complexity of financial reporting and accounting standards reflects growing demands for public accountability, a concept most applicable to larger and publicly traded entities. Critics query the value of the additional cost burden on smaller entities that are not publically traded, and this is likely to give impetus to the ASB's proposed multi-tier approach for UK GAAP, resulting in growing divergence between the published financial statements of listed and unlisted companies.

Some commentators attribute the recent economic crisis, at least partially, to the increasing use of fair values in accounting standards, particularly in the absence of an active and liquid market. It is arguable that this has increased the use of inherently subjective valuations in financial reporting. The need to resolve the conflict between the original and, arguably, primary objective of financial reporting – namely, to assist the shareholders to judge how well the directors have run the company on their behalf – and the desire to provide more current valuations in order to assist users of financial statements to make projections about likely future performance, may well give further impetus to the search for a conceptual framework for financial reporting.

APPENDICES

Appendix A

A Summary and Commentary on the Main Cases

Gresham Life Assurance Society v Styles (1890) 3 TC 185, HL

The company carried on a life assurance business and in that capacity paid out annuities (to beneficiaries of policies). The Revenue claimed that 'profits' for tax purposes meant 'gross profits' and the annuities should not be deducted in arriving at taxable profits.

There was no accounting evidence but it was argued for the company that the very nature of the business was to make a profit, being the difference between revenue receipts and expenses. There was no commercial logic to the disregarding of the annuities paid out in determining profit. Halsbury LJ said: 'the thing to be taxed is the amount of profits and gains. The word "profits" I think is to be understood in its natural and proper sense – in a sense in which no commercial man would misunderstand'. Consequently, the decision went in favour of the taxpayer company.

It does today, of course, seem preposterous to seek not to allow the deduction claimed. This early case, though, gives an indication that what is required is a proper commercial measure of profit.

Sun Insurance Office v Clark (1912) 6 TC 59, HL

This company offered fire insurance policies. Premiums were received in respect of cover designed to last several years. In its published accounts, it reserved 40% of its annual premiums as representing estimated losses on unexpired risks. The Revenue sought to disallow the reserve.

Before the Commissioners, an independent auditor gave evidence in respect of the propriety of the reserve.

The courts found for the company. Haldane LJ said:

> 'It is plain that the question of what is or is not profit or gain must primarily be one of fact to be ascertained by the tests applied in ordinary business. Questions of law can only arise when some express statutory direction applies and excludes ordinary commercial principles.'

Appendix A *A Summary and Commentary on the Main Cases*

This is an early case where the courts were influenced by the accountancy evidence given, and reinforces the interpretation given in the *Gresham* case to the imprecise words used in the statute. This approach thus entails looking first at the accountancy practice, then considering whether there was a rule of law that went against it.

JP Hall & Co Ltd v CIR (1921) 12 TC 382, CA

The company entered into what turned out to be profitable contracts just before the beginning of the First World War. Profits were made during the war years and were included in the company's accounts for those years. An Excess Profits Duty (at high rates) was levied on wartime profits, so the company attempted to argue that the profits should be charged to pre-war income tax (at low rates), on the grounds that that was when the contracts were entered into. Effectively, the company sought to argue that its accounts should be disregarded and profits treated as arising for tax purposes on the date the contracts were signed.

The company called its auditor to give evidence that the way the profits had been brought into profit in the accounts would be 'normal accounting practice', but he claimed that, had the accounts been prepared differently, and the profits taken in the earlier year, he would not have 'qualified the accounts'.

The company's claim was not successful. The courts held that it would not be normal commercial practice to bring profits into account in the year of contract, and using this method would be wrong.

The decision in this case was hardly surprising. It is difficult to see how any other decision, then or 90 years later, could be reached. The auditor's evidence was flimsy and, if anything, detrimental to the company's claim. However, as will be seen in the *Willingale* case, there is recent judicial support for disregarding a company's own accounts for tax purposes.

Edward Collins & Sons Ltd v CIR (1924) 12 TC 773, CS

The company had forward contracts to purchase raw materials. At the year end, world prices for such raw materials had fallen. Even though the company had not yet acquired or taken delivery of the materials, it was committed to paying the (higher) price. In preparing its year end accounts, there was included a provision for the 'loss', being the difference between the contract and the world price. The Revenue sought to disallow the provision because of the fact that the loss was contingent (it depended upon world prices at the time of acquisition, not the year end) and the lack of precision in its quantification.

Both parties to the appeal argued whether the accounting for the loss was proper or not, but neither called expert evidence in support. In the event, the court found for the Revenue. The *Sun Insurance Office* case was distinguished, for there, an independent accountant had given evidence of the propriety of the provision and that such provisions were normal in that particular business. There was no such evidence here. Clyde LP had the following to say:

A Summary and Commentary on the Main Cases **Appendix A**

'It is commonplace that subject as always to the observance of rules and general principles of the Income Taxes Acts, no particular method of computing profits is a part of the universal law. The Appellants are asking that a sum put to reserves out of profit, in view of an apprehended loss in the future, should be treated – contrary to the ordinary principles of commercial account taking – as a deduction from those profits.'

This case would undoubtedly be dealt with much differently today, although precisely the same issue – what is the correct way of accounting for the loss? – would arise. Expert accountants would be called and there would be a debate about *FRS 12* (provisions, contingent liabilities and assets).

Whimster & Co v CIR (1925) 12 TC 813, CS

This is a similar case to *Edward Collins* heard before the same judge. The report of the case suggests that the auditor was present but he did not give evidence. Not surprisingly, Clyde LP found for the Revenue following the precedent he set in the earlier case.

This case is mentioned because it was specifically referred to in *Gallagher v Jones*. Referring to the *Whimster* case, Sir Thomas Bingham MR commented: 'there appears to have been no evidence to suggest that the taxpayer's accounts complied with the ordinary principles of commercial accountancy …'.

Ryan v Asia Mill Ltd (1951) 32 TC 275, HL

Under wartime arrangements, all companies had to buy their cotton from the Cotton Controller. Such cotton was acquired by the company and invoiced to them at a price not itself capable of revision.

By a separate provision, there was a periodic evaluation of the overall stocks held by companies in comparison with known orders and a payment then fell due to or from the Controller. In the period in question, the company paid £55,087 under this provision to the Controller.

The company included an appropriate proportion of the £55,087 as part of the costs of closing stocks, yet sought to exclude that element in its tax computations. The Revenue called an expert accountant who confirmed that, in his opinion, the accounts had been properly prepared.

Whilst the High Court and the Court of Appeal found for the Revenue, the House of Lords was unanimous in finding for the company.

This is an unusual case, in that expert evidence was given, not challenged, yet did not carry the day at the end.

The main mistake made by the Revenue was not getting their expert accountant to say more (or, if he did say more, to ensure it was faithfully recorded by the Special Commissioners in the Stated Case).

As Lord Radcliffe said:

Appendix A A Summary and Commentary on the Main Cases

> 'It is not as if it were evidence that by settled principles of commercial accounting or the established general practice of accountants payments such as these arising under an agreement such as this are treated as part of the cost of stock in trade. If there were any such evidence, uncontradicted, it might well have been the Commissioners' duty to act on it, for if the law guides itself by the principles of accountancy as to the cost or market price, whichever be the lower, it must I think guide itself also by any of its principles which determine how cost is made up.'

In other words, had the accountant been able to say that these sort of arrangements were common, and the normal and accepted way of accounting would have been to include the sum in stock, that might have been conclusive. In effect, what he said (or appeared to have said) was along the lines that he had looked at the contract and formed his own opinion that it should be interpreted so as to bring a proportion of the £55,087 into stock. The House of Lords felt that the accountant was thereby expressing a legal interpretation of a set of documents and circumstances. They felt they were the better equipped to undertake this task than he. For reasons which are not important at this point, they felt that the arrangements had characteristics such as to exclude the necessity to include any part of the £55,087 in closing stocks for tax purposes – even though included in the accounts themselves.

Patrick v Broadstone Mills Ltd (1953) 35 TC 44, CA

This company was in the business of cotton spinning. Its accounts included stocks under the base stock (see Chapter 13) method rather than at the lower of cost or market value.

Expert accounting evidence was given for both sides. For the company, a leading accountant gave evidence that the base stock method was an accepted accounting basis for that industry, whilst conceding that it was not in universal use. He confirmed that he would not have qualified any accounts using the base stock method consistently.

For the Revenue, the Crown's accountancy adviser was of the opinion that the base stock method was being used less frequently, and produced a leaflet published by the accountancy bodies which stated that the base stock method should be limited in use, and that the preferred method was the lower of cost or market value. He also produced illustrative calculations to demonstrate distortions which could arise in using the base stock method.

Effectively, the courts had to choose whose evidence they preferred. On balance, they preferred that of the Revenue.

This case is interesting in that both sides effectively relied on expert evidence, and the courts were left to judge the relative merits of two accounting bases, both of which had some validity. It is also interesting to note that, in this instance, the courts were ahead of the accountancy profession. From the evidence, it is clear that the base stock method was on the way out, but it was not until *SSAP 9* – many years later – that it was formally denied the status of an acceptable accounting basis.

A Summary and Commentary on the Main Cases **Appendix A**

Owen v Southern Railway of Peru Ltd (1956) 36 TC 602, HL

The company ran a railway in Peru. Under local law, there was a potential liability to pay employees on leaving service, in some (but not all) circumstances. The amount payable depended on length of service and final salary. Its accounts included a deduction for the estimated future amounts it might have to pay out. The Revenue denied that the deduction was proper for tax purposes because the payment was contingent, and in any case not capable of precise calculation.

The company's auditor gave evidence that the making of the provision was proper and that, without it, he would have qualified the accounts.

The Special Commissioners in fact found for the company on the grounds that the method of accounting was in accordance with correct accounting practice. In the event, the courts found for the Revenue on the grounds that the claimed deductions did not represent an accurate discounted assessment of what it might ultimately have to pay; it was insufficiently precise for tax purposes.

The Special Commissioners accepted the company's accounting method as proper, and therefore allowed its appeal. The courts were in complete sympathy with this view. In fact, the leading judgment includes the statement that:

> '… I should view with dismay the assertion of legal theories as to the ascertainment of true annual profits which were in conflict with current accountancy practice and were not required by some special statutory provision of the Income Tax Acts.'

However, the evidence showed that there were flaws and inaccuracies in the method of computation adopted by the company in making its estimate. It is fairly clear that the courts were cautious not to give the green light to taxpayers to insert rough estimates of potential future liabilities into their accounts and thereby attract tax relief, so found against the taxpayer company. It should be noted that, what the courts took exception to was not that there was an inherent uncertainty in the amount to be provided, but that the company had not made the best effort to cope with the future unknowns. Indeed, the provision would not have met the requirement of the current *FRS 12*.

Duple Motor Bodies Ltd v Ostime (1961) 39 TC 537, HL

A long-established company prepared accounts, in which work in progress was valued only on a direct cost basis. No account was taken of indirect costs. The accounts had always been accepted by the Revenue until the year in question, at which time they alleged that, for tax purposes, the accounts should be adjusted to reflect a work in progress valuation incorporating indirect overheads also (the so-called 'on-cost' method).

Both sides produced expert independent accountants. They each confirmed that both accounting methods were accepted by the accountancy profession as correct accounting. The company claimed that the direct cost method was superior, but the independent accountant called on its behalf did concede that this would be a minority view of the accountancy profession. The Revenue's expert witness sought to show the flaws in the direct cost method.

Appendix A   *A Summary and Commentary on the Main Cases*

The courts held that the Revenue had not shown that the company's method of work in progress valuation was inconsistent with *ICTA 1988*, nor that it contravened accepted accounting practice. Therefore, the company succeeded in its appeal.

By modern standards, this is a case in which the taxpayer company should be regarded as fortunate. The evidence showed that there were (then) two acceptable methods, but that the on-cost method was superior to the direct cost method. The courts were being asked to select the more appropriate, but seemed to give considerable weight to the fact that the company itself considered the direct cost method more appropriate to its circumstances. Not every court by any means would have been so generously disposed to the taxpayer company, and the decision is difficult to reconcile with the *Willingale* case.

If heard today, the strong weight of accountancy evidence, backed by *SSAP 9*, would be that the direct cost method was unacceptable. It is difficult to see how the company could succeed today.

BSC Footwear Ltd v Ridgeway (1971) 47 TC 495, HL

The taxpayer company retailed fashion shoes. In its year end accounts, it valued its stock according to a formula which included in part an amount based on replacement cost discounted by the normal gross margin. For shoes which were going out of fashion, this could mean that their stock value was below original cost, even though they might still be expected to be sold at a (reduced) profit.

The Revenue argued that this basis was unacceptable and that the lower of cost or net realisable value should be substituted.

Both sides produced expert accountancy evidence.

The company's expert witness gave evidence on the different methods by which a company might account for stock, although he was forced to concede that the method adopted by the company could lead to the anticipation of a loss which ultimately might not – and probably would not – arise. The Revenue's expert asserted that a valuation below cost was wrong, as it anticipated a loss when none would occur. He thought this a 'cardinal principle of commercial accounting'.

The courts found for the Revenue. A number of important observations were made by the leading judge, Reid LJ:

> 'The company's method makes a considerable inroad upon the broadly accepted principle that neither expected future profits nor expected future losses are to be anticipated.'

> 'The application of the principles of commercial accounting is, however, subject to one well-established though non-statutory principle. Neither profit nor loss may be anticipated. A trader may have a contract in year one that is virtually certain to produce a large profit in year two. But he cannot be required to pay tax on that profit until it actually accrues.'

'It is well settled that ordinary principles of commercial accounting must be used except in so far as to any specific statutory provision requires otherwise.'

'If there is a uniform accounting practice, it should not be rejected without good reason.'

The court's decision in this case is not difficult to accept. There was evidence before the courts that there were two 'acceptable' methods of accounting, but clearly the one favoured by the company did cause distortions. Under modern principles, *SSAP 9* would not recognise the company's method as acceptable and, if reheard today, there is little doubt that the decision would go the same way.

The particularly interesting feature, though, lies in some of the judicial comments, particularly in relation to the statement that neither profit nor loss should be anticipated – the so-called 'rule of thumb'. Judicial comments of this nature are frequently quoted in support of argument without fully understanding their origin.

There is only one fundamental principle – profits should be determined on proper commercial lines. If there is more than one accepted commercial basis, that which the court prefers is to be adopted.

The 'principle' of not anticipating a profit or loss represents the earliest attempts by judges – in the absence of a well-established accountancy code – to lay down guidelines. As accountancy principles have developed, and greater sophistication has been applied, in some circumstances it is proper to anticipate profits and losses (indeed, in some circumstances it would be improper not to do so, and accounts not so doing would not satisfy the 'true and fair' criterion). The principles of commercial accountancy are not static and, to some extent, the 'rule of thumb' has become partially redundant. The decision in the *BSC* case was in fact reviewed in *Gallagher v Jones*. No weight was attached to the dicta concerning anticipation of profits or losses.

Odeon Associated Theatres Ltd v Jones (1971) 48 TC 257, CA

During the Second World War, the company bought cinemas. Because of wartime restrictions, these were not in a good state of repair, although evidence was given that this did not affect their purchase price. After the war, the cinemas were repaired. The Revenue argued that the dilapidations had accrued prior to ownership and should be capitalised effectively as part of the original cost. The taxpayer company claimed the expenditures as a normal revenue expense, charged against profit.

The Revenue produced no accounting evidence. The company produced expert evidence to the effect that the standard accounting practice in respect of deferred repairs was to charge that expenditure to profit and loss account.

The court found for the taxpayer company. A useful comment was made by Salmon LJ that, 'where, however, there is evidence which is accepted by the court as established, sound commercial accounting practice conflicting with no statute, that normally is the end of the matter'.

Appendix A *A Summary and Commentary on the Main Cases*

This is an important case showing the folly on the part of the Revenue in not calling their own expert witness, or discrediting the expert evidence given on behalf of the company. At the time, the Revenue were taken back by the weight given by the court to the accountancy evidence, and they speedily found another case (see below) in an attempt to restore the balance.

Heather v PE Consulting Group Ltd (1972) 48 TC 293, CA

A management consultancy company employed a high number of qualified professional staff. A major shareholder died, and staff became worried about a takeover. The workforce felt undermined, and the wellbeing of the company was threatened. The company, therefore, contributed funds to a trust formed for the purpose of giving staff a chance to acquire shares in the company and prevent an outsider gaining control.

The Revenue claimed that the expenses (in contributing to the trust) were not wholly and exclusively for the purposes of the trade, and also that each payment represented an instalment of a capital sum, and therefore on two grounds, no tax deduction was possible.

No accounting evidence was adduced for the Revenue, but the company did do so. Essentially, the expert accountant gave evidence that the normal accounting treatment was to charge such expenditure to revenue. As in the *Odeon* case, accountancy evidence given and not refuted was accepted by the court, so the company won its case.

This appears to be another defeat for the Revenue for almost the same reasons as in the *Odeon* case. However, several useful (from the Revenue point of view) dicta were 'teased' out of the judges. In particular, the Master of the Rolls said:

> 'it seems to me that the *Odeon* case does not add to or detract from the value of accountancy evidence. The courts have always been greatly assisted by the evidence of accountants. Their practice should be given due weight; but the courts have never regarded themselves as being bound by it. It would be wrong to do so. The question of what is capital and what is revenue is a question of law for the courts. They are not to be deflected from their true course by the evidence of accountants, however eminent.'

The Revenue were 'content' that, although having lost the particular case, they had 'undermined' the weight which taxpayers had been increasingly attaching to accountancy evidence. (However, see dicta in the *Symons* case.)

ECC Quarries Ltd v Watkis (1975) 51 TC 153, Ch D

The company were sand and gravel extractors. They incurred expense in an unsuccessful attempt to get planning permission on three sites for the extraction of minerals. They did this because existing sites were coming to the end of their useful lives and the new sites would be workable for around 30 years.

Independent accountancy evidence was given on behalf of the company that its treatment of the abortive expenditure – which was to write it off as a revenue expense – accorded with proper commercial principles. That evidence was not challenged by the Revenue.

The Special Commissioners and the High Court found for the Revenue in determining that the expenditure was on capital account, being in the nature of a single payment to secure an enduring benefit.

This is not an easy case to analyse. The judge felt that the distinction between capital and revenue expense was a matter of law, not of accountancy evidence. The problem with this is that the concepts of capital and revenue are accountancy in nature, so the argument is rather circular.

In the final few words of the judgment, there seemed to evolve a distinction between 'correct accountancy principles' (which were for the courts to determine) and 'correct accountancy practices' (which is what accountants 'do' and how matters appear in statutory accounts). Perhaps 30 years ago, such a distinction was more valid. The early standards (the SSAPs) referred to 'practices', the later standards (the FRSs) dropped the word 'practice', and the most recent development is the 'Statement of Principles'. Company law makers are also slightly hazy on this distinction. *CA 1985, Sch 5, para 10(1) (d)* alluded to 'generally accepted accounting principles or practices', whilst *CA 1985, s 262(3)* referred to 'such profit or losses of the company as fall to be treated as realised in accordance with principles generally accepted ...'.

Pearce v Woodall-Duckham Ltd (1978) 51 TC 271, CA

A company changed the 'basis' on which it valued work in progress. This produced a £579,874 difference between the closing work in progress value at end of the previous year, and the value at which the same work in progress was included as the opening balance at the beginning of the current year. In modern terms, this would be called a prior year adjustment and would not figure in the profit and loss account, but the company's accounts were prepared before *SSAP 6* (see Chapter 7), and the £579,874 was included in the profit and loss account and described as 'surplus arising from a change in accounting basis'. The Revenue claimed the £579,874 to be taxable in the year of change. The company claimed the £579,874 as not taxable, or if taxable then for earlier years, and not the current year. In fact, four accountants gave evidence – three for the company and one for the Revenue. There was a remarkable concurrence of view. They all agreed that the new basis was acceptable and that the surplus was 'revenue' in nature. As to whether the £579,874 should or should not be included in the profits of the business for the year, they differed, but for reasons which were not well articulated and which did not carry much weight either way with the courts.

In the event, the courts found for the Revenue using an analogy argument. They regarded the 'write-up' of work in progress at the beginning of the year (on the change of basis) as akin to the write-down of stock or work in progress (to net realisable value) (as a normal year-end adjustment), as mirror images which should be afforded a similar tax treatment.

Appendix A   *A Summary and Commentary on the Main Cases*

This case is interesting in that, if heard today, the £579,874 would be differently accounted for (under *FRS 3* – the successor to *SSAP 6*), and independent accountancy evidence of weight could be given. The decision may well have been different in these circumstances.

Willingale v International Commercial Bank Ltd (1978) 52 TC 242, HL

An international finance company purchased bills of exchange which it then held to maturity. In its accounts, it brought in a fraction of the ultimate profit on the bills, and this amount it called 'accrued interest'.

However, in its tax computations, the company sought to exclude this element of profit. The Revenue made assessments on the basis of including these accrued amounts. The company appealed.

The Revenue produced an accountant to give evidence. He stated that the company's accounts had been prepared on proper commercial principles and, therefore, that should determine the matter. For the company, its own auditor gave evidence that there were other acceptable methods of accounting for the matter, one of which involved the exclusion of the accrued element. Although the clearing banks used the accrued interest basis, he claimed the taxpayer company's business was different, and he would not have qualified the accounts had the accrued interest been excluded.

The courts found for the taxpayer company, appearing to be applying the 'rule of thumb' that neither profits nor losses should be anticipated. Indeed, Fraser LJ effectively confirmed this in stating:

> 'But the general rule is subject to the exception that where ordinary commercial principles run counter to the principles of Income Tax they must yield to the latter when computing profits or gains for tax purposes.'

This is a difficult case to reconcile and has been criticised. On reading the case, the principal factor appears to be the 'rule of thumb' that neither profits nor losses should be anticipated.

The rationale of the *Willingale* case was considered in the *Gallagher* case. It was emphasised that, in the *Willingale* case, there was evidence of two competing but (equally) acceptable accounting bases, and the courts selected the one they preferred. By implication, therefore, the 'rule of thumb' seems to live on in those circumstances in which commercial accounting practice does not give an unambiguous clear answer. The profits in question would be taxed today under the loan relationship rules.

Symons v Weeks and Others (1982) 56 TC 630, Ch D

A firm of architects entered into contracts in the standard form provided by the Royal Institute of British Architects (RIBA). These contracts provided for each contract to be subdivided into stages at which invoices could be raised. The accounting treatment was only to recognise profits when they were reasonably certain, and this usually meant towards the end of the contract

A Summary and Commentary on the Main Cases   **Appendix A**

life. Thus, although the firm received substantial payments at each stage of the contracts, they were not brought into profit until near completion of the contract itself.

The firm contended that its accounts had been drawn up on a proper commercial basis, but the Revenue argued that the progress payments should nevertheless be brought into profit and loss account as they fell due.

The firm produced an eminent independent accountant (later to become the President of the Institute of Chartered Accountants) who confirmed that the accounts had been properly prepared on the principles which were shortly after incorporated into *SSAP 9*, thereby being established as the proper basis of accounting. The Revenue did not realistically challenge this opinion. Because of the weight of the expert evidence, the court found in favour of the taxpayer firm.

This case is interesting because of the sub-plot. At an earlier time, the Revenue had refused the firm's request to submit accounts on a cash basis. Had they acceded to the request, the progress payments would have been brought into tax on receipt. Moreover, the firm had incorporated itself during 1975/76. The progress payments were argued to be pre-cessation receipts (not caught by the then post-cessation receipts legislation). If the payments on account were not taxed on receipt, they would fall out of the tax net completely.

There are two very useful comments in this case, both uttered by Warner LJ:

'Accountancy is not, however, a static art'.

'[he] envisaged the possibility of a court deciding that a *prevailing* system of commercial accounting did not correspond to the *correct* principles of commercial accounting. It is however observed that no case was cited to me, nor do I know of any, where a court has in fact done that'.

RTZ Oil & Gas Ltd v Effiss (1987) 61 TC 132, Ch D

An oil exploration company acquired tankers and a drilling rig to investigate and exploit an oil field. The contract required that, at completion, the company was required to return the rig and tankers to their original condition and dismantle the well head and other equipment. The company made a provision for the anticipated cost of the expenditure. This provision was attacked by the Revenue on several fronts, some of which were not pursued in the courts, others which the courts found unnecessary to consider.

The company relied upon the expert evidence of a leading accountant who confirmed the correctness of the provision. Unfortunately for the company, one of the Revenue's several arguments – that, even if the accounts were properly prepared on commercial principles, then nevertheless the provision was in respect of a capital expenditure – found favour with the court. On that ground, the court found for the Revenue.

This is not an easy case to rationalise. The accountancy evidence for the company was accepted, yet still the taxpayer lost on a distinction – capital/

Appendix A *A Summary and Commentary on the Main Cases*

revenue – which in essence is an accountancy concept. By providing for the whole of the eventual costs in one go, a challenge was, of course, invited under capital/revenue grounds. It is arguable that an alternative accounting policy, whereby a proportion of the estimated final reinstatement costs was charged to revenue each year during the life of the contract, could have been equally acceptable (slightly less prudent but closer to the matching principle) and would have assisted in defeating a capital/revenue argument.

Gallagher v Jones; Threlfall v Jones (1993) 66 TC 77, CA

These two cases – with almost identical facts – were heard together in 1993 and provide a comprehensive exposition of the place of accountancy principles and evidence in the taxation system at that time.

The taxpayers traded in the short-term hiring of narrowboats. In that capacity, they leased narrowboats. The leases provided for a large initial rental followed by monthly rentals for 17 months. Thereafter, additional annual rentals of £5 p.a. were payable for 21 years. The business accounts for the initial period of trading, from November 1989 to April 1990, included the full initial rent and 5 out of the 17 monthly rental payments. The accounts gave rise to a large loss, but the Inspector restricted the claim by spreading the total payable in the primary 18 months evenly over that period.

The taxpayers' case rested mainly on the so-called *Vallambrosa* principle (expenditure being deductible when incurred even if to secure a future benefit; *Vallambrosa Rubber Co Ltd v Farmer* (1910) 5 TC 529). The Revenue called expert accountancy evidence who quoted extensively from *SSAPs 2* and *21*(which dealt with finance leases before *FRS 12*). The Revenue's evidence was not challenged.

The Commissioners found for the Revenue, but the High Court reversed that decision. The appeal from the High Court was expedited and, shortly after, the Court of Appeal unanimously, and with seeming little doubt, found for the Revenue.

This is a most important case on many levels.

The taxpayers were not limited companies, yet arguments based on proper commercial principles, evidenced by *SSAPs 2* and *21*, were successful. Therefore, sole traders and partnerships do not have a defence that is not available to their incorporated counterparts.

The leading judgment contains a comprehensive review of many previous cases (including several of those analysed above), in which their true rationales are considered.

A particular point worthy of comment is that *Vallambrosa* should not be read as of universal application and does not lead to a principle of 'expenditure being deductible when incurred'. The expenditure in that company was ordinary ongoing maintenance on an existing asset. No accountancy evidence was given that the method of accounting did not conform with generally accepted practice.

A Summary and Commentary on the Main Cases   Appendix A

Sir Thomas Bingham MR stated:

> 'Subject to any express or implied statutory rule, of which there is none here, the ordinary way to ascertain the profits or losses of a business is to apply accepted principles of commercial accountancy. That is the purpose for which such principles are formulated. As has often been pointed out, such principles are not static; they may be modified, refined and elaborated over time as circumstances change and accounting insights sharpen. But so long as such principles remain current and generally accepted they provide the surest answer to the question which the legislation requires to be answered.'

R v CIR, ex parte S G Warburg & Co Ltd [1994] STC 518

'Warburgs' is a merchant bank. It has always valued its stocks (of investments) at the lower of cost or market value (LCM). In anticipation of changes brought about by the 'Big Bang', it changed its valuation to the mark to market (MTM) basis – essentially, this involved valuing its stock at market value. There was an uplift to opening stock of over £4m. The company argued that both bases were 'valid' and, on the basis of the then Revenue practice (SP/B5), the £4m opening uplift fell not to be taxed. The Inspector argued that the MTM basis was not a valid basis, so SP/B5 did not apply; therefore, tax would continue to be computed on the LCM basis. Oddly, on the company's basis, even after excluding the £4m uplift, the taxable profits of the year exceeded the profits which the Revenue computed on the LCM basis. In the correspondence between the Inspector and the company's tax advisers, the Inspector incorporated (what was later accepted by both sides to be) a manifestly wrong conclusion drawn from SP/B5.

Shortly after the Inspector's error, the company, without notice, applied for judicial review on the grounds that, in refusing to apply SP/B5, they, the Revenue, were exceeding their authority. The Revenue offered to have the substantive point – whether the MTM basis was 'valid' – heard by the Commissioners (or by way of stated case, the courts), and if MTM was determined to be valid, then SP/B5 would be applied. The company declined and the hearing for judicial review proceeded. Judicial review is not a tax concept, and Mr Justice Hidden is not noted for any previous tax work. The hearing lasted six days. It was held that the Revenue had not acted unreasonably. There was (at least) an argument that the MTM basis was not valid. The proper way to determine MTM's validity was before the Commissioners, not by way of judicial review. Just because, at any such hearing, the financial effect of the argument would be that the Revenue would push for a lower figure of tax profit than the company, it would not of itself render those proceedings a 'pantomime' (as the company claimed).

The case is interesting, but ultimately of little value except in relation to the process of judicial review. A judge, not versed in tax knowledge, attempted a statement of the relevant tax principles, but in the event, the details of these were not relevant.

It was fairly clear that the proper forum to determine the matter was before the Commissioners, that the company had latched onto an obvious error by the

Appendix A A Summary and Commentary on the Main Cases

Inspector, and attempted to use that as a springboard to mount a quick 'raid' to have the case determined in its favour.

Johnston v Britannia Airways Ltd [1994] STC 763

The company operated a fleet of aeroplanes. Engines required overhaul every 17,000 hours, which equated to between three and four years of use. On the basis of its experience of the cost of earlier overhauls, the company was able to estimate accurately the likely future cost of major overhauls. These likely future costs were accrued as revenue expenses in the account, on the basis of the number of hours flown each year. Several other airlines adopted this basis, although the practice was not universal, there being at least two other methods of accounting for such costs. British Airways, for example, made no provision but simply charged the cost of each overhaul as an expense when it was incurred.

For the company, substantial accountancy evidence was given, in particular by a member of the ASB, that the method of accounting complied with *SSAP 2* and was a proper commercial method of reflecting the position. For the Revenue, the Board's accounting adviser gave evidence that a 'better' method would be to (effectively) account in the BA way.

The Special Commissioners found for the company. Their view was upheld in the High Court.

This is a landmark case, from which many interesting points emerge.

There was evidence that there were several different ways of accounting for the expense of overhaul. The company had selected the one which was most suitable for its situation. This was accepted by the Commissioners as a fact. The courts could not interfere. The Revenue argument that (because there was an alternative accounting policy which would have had the effect of excluding any provision for the expense) the provision was not 'essential' (a dictum taken from the *Southern Railways* case) was dismissed:

> 'In my judgement, the use of the word "essential" in the context does not connote that the existence of any other accounting technique capable of adoption for tax purposes which makes no such provision is necessarily fatal to the adoption of an accepted accountancy technique that does make such a provision which is sufficiently reliable to present a true statement.'

The court was satisfied that the quantification of the provision was sufficiently accurate to satisfy the test in the *Southern Railways* case. In evidence, the company had demonstrated how the provisions measured up to what the eventual costs had been and had demonstrated that the estimates had rarely been out by much. The variances had also been related to the level of the company's pre-tax profits. This appears to have been a materiality point, and does not seem to have played a big part in the debate – indeed, it is not clear if the point was properly perceived – 'I must confess to having some difficulty in seeing what the significance of the correlation is ...' (p 784).

A Summary and Commentary on the Main Cases   **Appendix A**

Finally, a useful quote:

> 'The Court is slow to accept that accounts prepared in accordance with accepted principles of commercial accountancy are not adequate for tax purposes as a true statement of the taxpayer's profits for the relevant period.'

Meat Traders Ltd v Cushing [1997] SCD 245, SpC

A supplier of processed meats made a provision of £850,000 in respect of 'future operating losses' foreseen in relation to continued trade with one customer. The provision was made because, after year end, the company had run a credit check on the customer and the credit agency had suggested a £50,000 limit. The actual indebtedness at year end was £900,000. The excess was provided in the profit and loss. The directors had explained that they had continued to trade with that customer, and permitted the indebtedness to grow, because the alternative would have been the loss of turnover, and consequent loss of jobs. In fact, by the time the accounts were finalised, the debt had been repaid. In the following year, the provision was written back to profit and loss.

The company's auditor gave expert accountancy evidence as did the Inland Revenue's accountancy adviser. The Special Commissioner preferred the evidence of the Inland Revenue's expert. He said that the provision was permissible but did not represent best practice. Best practice would have been to make no provision but to append a note to the accounts.

However, the fact that the provision did not offend accounting standards did not get the company home. The Commissioners relied on the principle that neither a profit nor a loss should be anticipated. That is precisely what the provision purported to do, but this was not acceptable for tax purposes.

This is an interesting case. Had the taxpayer's argument been a little stronger – for example, if the debt had got bigger and ultimately proved problematic or if heavier weight expert evidence had more convincingly argued that best practice would have been to provide for the credit risk – then the decision could have been closer. As it was, the facts were weak, thus enabling the Commissioners to use the familiar non-anticipation of profit rule.

Herbert Smith v Honour (1999) 72 TC 130

A firm of solicitors vacated its leased premises to move into new accommodation. It was advised that it would not be able to sub-let its old premises because of the poor state of the letting market. Consequently, the firm made a charge against its current year profits of all the rent which it would be due to pay on the old premises, up to the expiry of the lease more than 10 years hence.

Evidence was given that, in circumstances of this sort, there was no uniformity within the accounting profession on how the 'accruals basis' should be applied, albeit the Special Commissioners did concede that the principle of 'prudence' would require the immediate charge to profit and loss. The Special Commissioners held that the 'no anticipation of profit or loss' rule

Appendix A   *A Summary and Commentary on the Main Cases*

for tax purposes overrode the prudence concept, and in the absence of a definitive accounting practice as to the application of the 'accruals' concept to circumstances like this, the application of this tax rule would prohibit immediate tax deduction. In the High Court, the firm's appeal was allowed, on the basis that there was no rule of law against anticipating liabilities.

The Revenue accepted the decision and subsequently announced, in a press release dated 20 July 1999, their acceptance of *FRS 12* for future years.

Tapemaze Ltd v Melluish (2000) 73 TC 167

This case was concerned with a company that carried on a business of hiring assets and received payments in advance. The question at issue was whether advance payments retained following the sale of a business were taxable as profits of the trade. According to the HMRC Manual (BIM31001), the Revenue's adviser accountant said:

> 'The accounting treatment, accordingly, answers the question when the £5,189,609 should be brought into account: it was proper in accounting terms to bring that income into account for the year ended 31 July 1994. It is not for an accountant, however, to answer the question of law as to whether or not it is trading income, that is, whether that income of £5,189,609 arose to Tapemaze for that year from any trade.'

This decision underscores the complexity of the relationship between accounting and tax profits, such that it is not always possible to just 'follow the accounts'. The correct accountancy treatment was clearly explained, but here, for tax purposes, another question arose, ie whether the profit shown in the accounts arose from the trade.

HMRC v William Grant and Sons Distillers Ltd and Small (Inspector of Taxes) v Mars UK Ltd [2007] UKHL 15

This case involved the tax treatment of depreciation where it is taken to be part of the cost of trading stock. Until 2007, the view taken by HMRC was that depreciation relating to trading stock should be added back in the year in which the relevant stock was manufactured. Following the decision in the Hong Kong case of *Secan Limited v CIR* (2000) 74 TC 1, HMRC issued a statement (*Tax Bulletin No 59*) confirming this approach. The House of Lords in this combined appeal, however, took a different view, which HMRC now accepts (see BIM33190). Lord Hoffmann made the following statement:

> 'The costs of stocks which remain unsold at the year end are not deducted for the purposes of computing the profits for the year, but are carried forward to be matched against revenue from their sale in future years.'

Both of the companies in this case had prepared their accounts in accordance with *SSAP 9* and, accordingly, distinguished between depreciation in fixed assets relating to the production of goods that were sold during the year, and

A Summary and Commentary on the Main Cases **Appendix A**

that relating to unsold stock. Expert accountancy evidence for both sides agreed that this was in accordance with the standards and further gave a true and fair view.

As a result of this decision, the requirement for capital expenditure to be added back does not apply to the depreciation that is attributable to unsold stock. It will be deducted in computing the profit in the year in which the stock is subsequently sold, and that is the year in which it should be added back. The decision of the House of Lords came as a relief to some commentators, who saw the HMRC stance on this, and the support of HMRC in earlier appeals, as potentially eroding the progress that has been made in recent years to align accounting and tax profits.

Appendix B

Further Reading

ACCOUNTING TEXTBOOKS AND MATERIALS

A range of accounting textbooks exists, from very basic texts aimed at diploma or undergraduate level students, through to more complex volumes dealing with the complexities of the accounting rules at a much higher level. The coverage of these texts varies in terms of how they deal with international standards, and increasingly IFRS are given prominence, in some cases to the exclusion of UK GAAP. Some useful titles are as follows:

- Dyson, John, *Accounting for Non-Accounting Students*, 7th edition, Financial Times/Prentice Hall, 2007
- Wood, Frank and Sangster, Alan, *Frank Wood Business Accounting Vol 1*, 11th Edition, Financial Times/Prentice Hall, 2008
- Mclaney, Eddie and Attrill, Peter *Accounting: An Introduction*, 4th edition, Financial Times/Prentice Hall, 2007.

In addition, a number of large accounting firms produce impressively large tomes dealing with the intricacies of accountancy practice and are valuable resources, frequently more up to date than student textbooks. Examples of publications available from the Big Four accounting firms include:

Deloitte UK

In addition to hardback volumes of UK GAAP and iGAAP, published by LexisNexis, Deloitte UK also produces an iGAAP quarterly newsletter that includes articles on recent developments as well as interviews with key players in the accounting world.

Ernst & Young

IFRS Outlook: a monthly newsletter http://www.ey.com/GL/en/Issues/Governance-and-reporting/IFRS/Publications

International GAAP® 2010, published by John Wiley

KPMG

Financial Reporting Update, periodical newsletter outlining current issues and developments.

PricewaterhouseCoopers

A practical guide to IFRS 2009. This 48-page guide provides a high-level outline of the key requirements of new IFRS standards and interpretations that came into effect in 2009, in question and answer format.

Useful websites

Companies Act

The Department for Business Innovation and Skills is a good place to find links to the Companies Act and associated materials, including conversion tables showing the origins of CA 2006 provisions and destinations of CA 1985 provisions:

http://www.berr.gov.uk/whatwedo/businesslaw/co-act-2006/index.html

Similar links and latest news is available on the Companies House website:

http://www.companieshouse.gov.uk/companiesAct/companiesAct.shtml

IFRS

The IASB website provides access to the latest developments in the production and promulgation of IFRS:

http://www.iasb.org/Home.htm

UK GAAP

For information regarding UK GAAP developments, see the Accounting Standards Board website, which is part of the Financial Reporting Council:

http://www.frc.org.uk/asb/

HMRC

Her Majesty's Revenue and Customs have an *Accounting and Tax Group* which meets regularly to discuss developments in the relationship between accounting rules and tax law. The minutes of meetings are available on HMRC's website:

http://www.hmrc.gov.uk/consultations/atg-mins-070419.htm

The HMRC Manuals contain relatively up-to-date discussions of specific issues where the accounting rules are used in tax computations, for example the Business Income Manual and Corporate Finance Manual:

http://www.hmrc.gov.uk/thelibrary/manuals-a-z.htm

Academic research

Ashby, L. (2007) 'International Financial Reporting Standards and their impact on tax' in *Taxline Tax planning 2007/08* Lagerberg, F. and Moore, J. (eds), London: Institute of Chartered Accountants in England and Wales.

Appendix B *Further Reading*

De Zilva, A. (2003) 'The Alignment of Tax and Financial Accounting Rules: Is it Feasible?', *Australian Tax Forum* Vol 18, pp 265–284.

Freedman, J. (1993) 'Ordinary Principles of Commercial Accounting – Clear Guidance or a Mystery Tour?', *British Tax Review*, pp 468–478.

Freedman J (1995) 'Defining Taxable Profits in a Changing Accounting Environment', *British Tax Review,* pp 434–444.

Freedman, J. (2004a) 'Aligning Taxable Profits and Accounting Profits: Accounting Standards, legislators and judges', *eJournal of Tax Research* Vol 2 No 1, pp 71–99.

Freedman, J. (2004b) 'Accounting Standards: A Panacea?' *Tax Journal* Issue 761, 2

Green, S. (1995) 'Accounting Standards and Tax Law: Complexity, Dynamism and Divergence', *British Tax Review* pp 445–456.

ICAEW Tax Faculty and the CBI (2003) TAXREP 27/03 'The Implications of Adoption of International Financial Reporting Standards (IFRS) for the UK tax system: a discussion paper', London: The Institute of Chartered Accountants in England and Wales.

Macdonald, G. (2003) '*IRC v John Lewis Properties PLC*: Cutting the Gordian Knot of 'Income or Capital', *British Tax Review*, pp 203–207.

Macdonald, G. and Martin, D. (2004a) 'Tax and Accounting: a response to the 2003 consultation document on corporation tax reform', The Institute for Fiscal Studies TLRC Discussion Paper No. 4.

Macdonald, G. and Martin, D. (2004b) 'Aligning Tax and Accounting Profits The Need to Review Current Legislation', The Institute for Fiscal Studies TLRC Discussion Paper No. 5.

McMahon, F. and Weetman, P. (1997) 'Commercial Accounting Principles: Questions of fact and questions of tax law', *British Tax Review* pp 6–18.

Nobes, C. (2003) *A Conceptual Framework for taxable income of businesses, and how to apply it under IFRS*, London: Certified Accountants Educational Trust.

Schön, W. (2005) The Odd Couple: A Common Future for Financial and Tax Accounting? *Tax Law Review*, Vol 58, pp 111–136.

Vander-Wolk, J. (2002) 'Thoughts on the Use of Accounting Principles to Determine Taxable Income: A Side Effect of Globalisation?' *Asia Pacific Journal of Taxation*, Vol 6 No 3, pp 80–83.

Whittington, G. (1995) 'Tax Policy and Accounting Standards', *British Tax Review* pp 452–456.

Wilson, A. (2001) 'Financial Reporting and Taxation: Marriage is out of the Question', *British Tax Review* pp 86–91.

Index

[*All references are to paragraph numbers*]

10% corridor approach
  pension valuations, and, 19.8
Accountancy bodies
  limited liability companies, and, 2.9
Accounting
  Accounting Standards Board, 4.1
  balance sheet, 3.8–3.27
  EC Regulation 1606/2002, 4.3–4.8
  'entity' convention, 3.3–3.7
  FRS, 4.1
  IAS, 4.2
  IFRS, 4.2
  International Accounting Standards
      Board, 4.2
  introduction, 3.1–3.2
  principles
    accounting bases, 5.7
    alternative accounting rules,
        5.9–5.21
    capital/revenue expenditure,
        5.26–5.30
    developments, 5.24
    FRS 18, 5.22–5.23
    historical cost accounting, 5.8
    introduction, 5.1–5.3
    legal requirements, 5.4–5.6
    materiality, 5.25
    revenue, 5.31–5.37
  profit and loss account, 3.28–3.33
  ratios, 3.34–3.40
  SSAP, 4.1
  standards, 4.1–4.13
  UK GAAP
    balance sheet, 3.8–3.27
    'entity' convention, 3.3–3.7
    profit and loss account, 3.28–3.33
    ratios, 3.34–3.40
Accounting bases
  generally, 5.7
Accounting for tax
  comparison with IAS 12, 22.19–22.20
  corporation tax
    current tax (FRS 16), 22.6
    deferred tax (FRS 19), 22.7–22.18

Accounting for tax – *contd*
  corporation tax – *contd*
    introduction, 22.5
    current tax (FRS 16), 22.6
    deferred tax (FRS 19)
      decision to provide, 22.14
      deferred assets, 22.16
      disclosures, 22.18
      discounting, 22.17
      generally, 22.7–22.11
      liability method of quantification,
          22.13
      non-monetary assets, 22.15
      revaluations, 22.15
      timing differences, 22.12
    introduction, 22.1
  taxation, 22.21
  VAT (SSAP 5)
    comparison with IAS 18, 22.19
    generally, 22.2–22.4
Accounting policies
  consolidated accounts, and, 23.21
Accounting principles
  accounting bases, 5.7
  alternative accounting rules, 5.9–5.21
  capital/revenue expenditure,
      5.26–5.30
  developments, 5.24
  FRS 18, 5.22–5.23
  groups, and
    FRS 2, 23.10–23.24
    FRS 9, 23.25–23.32
  historical cost accounting, 5.8
  introduction, 5.1–5.3
  legal requirements, 5.4–5.6
  materiality, 5.25
  revenue, 5.31–5.37
Accounting records
  limited liability companies, and, 2.11
Accounting standards
  generally, 4.1–4.13
Accounting Standards Board
  accounting principles, and, 5.2
  generally, 4.1

Index

Accruals
  accounting principles, and, 5.5
Acquisition of assets on finance (SSAP 21)
  cars, 17.32
  comparison with IAS 17, 17.28
  definitions
    fair value, 17.14
    finance lease, 17.10
    interest rate implicit in a lease, 17.13
    introduction, 17.8
    lease, 17.9
    lease term, 17.12
    operating lease, 17.11
  disclosures, 17.23
  fair value, 17.14
  finance leases
    generally, 17.10
    taxation, 17.31
  generally, 17.4–17.7
  hire purchase
    generally, 17.2
    taxation, 17.29
  interest rate implicit in a lease, 17.13
  introduction, 17.1–17.3
  lease, 17.9
  lease term, 17.12
  lessees, 17.15–17.19
  lessors, 17.20–17.22
  long funding leases, 17.33
  operating leases
    generally, 17.11
    taxation, 17.30
  operation of standard
    lessees, 17.15–17.19
    lessors, 17.20–17.22
  problem areas, 17.24–17.27
  taxation
    car finance, 17.32
    finance leases, 17.31
    hire purchase, 17.29
    long funding leases, 17.33
    operating leases, 17.30
Acquisition of hive down company
  generally, 29.18–29.20
Acquisition of subsidiary
  generally, 29.11–29.17
Acquisitions
  accounting, 28.27–28.29
  consolidated accounts, and, 23.23
Alternative accounting rules
  generally, 5.9–5.10
  revaluation reserve, 5.11–5.18
  tangible fixed assets, and, 15.6

Amortisation
  goodwill and intangible assets, and, 20.4
Applied research
  research and development expenditure, and, 26.5
Assets
  And see **Tangible fixed assets**
  acquisition on finance, and
    comparison with IAS 17, 17.28
    disclosures, 17.23
    generally, 17.4–17.14
    introduction, 17.1–17.3
    lessees, 17.15–17.19
    lessors, 17.20–17.22
    problem areas, 17.24–17.27
    taxation, 17.29–17.33
  reporting the substance of transactions, and
    control, 6.7
    generally, 6.4
    identification, 6.10
    offset, 6.13
    recognition, 6.10
Associates and joint ventures (FRS 9)
  comparison with IAS 28, 23.34
  comparison with IAS 31, 23.35
  equity accounting, 23.27
  gross equity method, 23.28–23.32
  introduction, 23.25–23.26
Attributable profit
  long-term contracts, and, 14.3–14.6
Audit report
  limited liability companies, and, 2.17
Balance sheet
  generally, 3.8–3.27
  limited liability partnerships, and, 30.3
Base stock
  stocks, and, 13.9
'Big bath' provisions
  provisions and contingencies, and, 18.2
Bill and hold arrangements
  revenue recognition, and, 12.3
Bonuses
  post-balance sheet events, and, 8.11
Business bought for resale
  goodwill and intangible assets, and, 25.13
Called-up share capital
  generally, 28.4–28.7
Capital-based grants
  generally, 21.5
  no repayment, 21.11
  repayment, 21.12

Index

Capital expenditure
generally, 5.26–5.30
Capital gains
depreciation, and, 16.19
Capital redemption reserve
generally, 28.13
Capitalisation of finance costs
depreciation, and, 16.19
Capitalised interest
cash-flow statements, and 11.6
Cars
lease finance, and, 17.32
Cash flow statements (FRS 1)
capitalised interest, 11.6
comparison with IAS 7, 11.8
example, 11.4
format, 11.3
generally, 11.2–11.4
introduction, 11.1
material non-cash transactions, 11.7
smaller entities, and, 10.6
tax items, 11.5
taxation, 11.9
City Code on Take-overs and Mergers
limited liability companies, and, 2.22
Close family
related parties, and, 9.5
Combined Code
limited liability companies, and, 2.23
Common Consolidated Corporate Tax Base (CCCTB)
generally, 32.8
Companies
accountancy bodies, 2.20
audit report, 2.17
City Code on Take-overs and Mergers, and, 2.22
classification by activity, 2.9
classification by size, 2.7–2.8
classification by status, 2.4–2.6
Combined Code, 2.23
directors' accounting responsibilities, 2.10
directors' report, 2.16
dormant companies, 2.9
financial year, 2.14
format of accounts, 2.12–2.13
formation, 2.3
introduction, 2.2
investment companies, 2.9
keeping and maintaining accounting records, 2.11
large companies, 2.7
laying and delivering accounts, 2.18

Companies – *contd*
medium-sized companies, 2.7
non-limited companies, 2.24
Senior Accounting Officer appointments, 2.19
small companies, 2.7
Stock Exchange, and, 2.21
true and fair view, 2.15
Company law requirements
groups, and
generally, 23.2
parent companies, 23.3–23.9
investment properties, and, 16.15
lease finance, and, 17.2
related parties, and, 9.1
research and development expenditure, and, 26.11
smaller entities, and, 10.1–10.3
stocks, and, 13.12–13.15
tangible fixed assets, and
alternative valuation basis, 15.7
finance costs, 15.4
initial measurement, 15.2
Complex assets
depreciation, and, 16.7
Consignment stock
And see **Stocks**
reporting substance of transactions, and, 6.9
Consistency
accounting principles, and, 5.5
Consolidated accounts (FRS 2)
examples
accounting policies, 23.21
acquisitions, 23.23
basic consolidation, 23.15–23.17
disposals, 23.24
inter-company dividends, 23.20
inter-company loans, 23.19
inter-company trading (unrealised profits), 23.18
introduction, 23.10
minority interests, 23.22
foreign currency translation, and
closing rate/net investment method, 24.12–24.13
generally, 24.10–24.11
matching, 24.15
quasi-equity, 24.14
introduction, 23.10
objectives, 23.11–23.12
preparation, 23.13–23.14
Construction contracts
long-term contracts, and, 14.9

335

Index

Contingencies (FRS 12)
  assets, 18.17
  'big bath' provisions, and, 18.2
  comparison with IAS 37, 18.18
  introduction, 18.1–18.4
  liabilities, 18.14–18.16
  taxation, 18.19–18.20
  timing, and, 5.31
Control of asset
  substance over form, and, 6.7
Conversion costs
  stocks, and, 13.4–13.6
Convertible debt instruments
  comparison with international
    standards, 27.8
  FRED 3, 27.1
  FRS 4, 27.4
  FRS 13, 27.5
  FRS 25
    comparison with IAS 32, 27.8
    generally, 27.2–27.3
  FRS 26
    comparison with IAS 39, 27.8
    generally, 27.6
  FRS 29
    comparison with IFRS 7, 27.8
    generally, 27.7
  introduction, 27.1
  meaning, 27.1
  summary, 27.18
  taxation
    derivative contracts, 27.17
    generally, 27.9–27.10
    indirect issues, 27.11
    loan relationships, 27.14–27.15
    non-lending relationships, 27.16
    recent developments, 27.12–27.13
  types, 27.1
Corporate transactions
  acquisition accounting, 28.27–28.29
  acquisition of assets, 29.6–29.8
  acquisition of hive down company,
    29.18–29.20
  acquisition of subsidiary, 29.11–29.17
  called-up share capital, 28.4–28.7
  capital redemption reserve, 28.13
  demerger of two companies
    generally, 28.48
    more complex type. 29.42–29.44
    simple type, 29.39–29.41
  distributable profits, 28.19–28.26
  dividend out of pre-acquisition profits
    comparison with IAS 27, 29.45
    generally, 29.21–29.23

Corporate transactions – *contd*
  financial assistance, 28.49
  incorporation of sole trader business,
    29.9–29.10
  introduction, 28.1
  limited liability, 28.2
  merger accounting
    comparison with IFRS 3, 29.46
    group accounts, 28.35–28.38
    individual companies, 28.31–28.34
    introduction, 28.30
    practice, in, 29.36–29.38
  own shares reserve, 28.14
  practical issues
    acquisition of assets, 29.6–29.8
    acquisition of hive down company,
      29.18–29.20
    acquisition of subsidiary,
      29.11–29.17
    comparison with IAS, 29.45–29.46
    demerger of two companies,
      29.39–29.44
    dividend out of pre-acquisition
      profits, 29.21–29.23
    incorporation of sole trader
      business, 29.9–29.10
    introduction, 29.1
    merger, 29.36–29.38
    purchase of own shares,
      29.24–29.35
    reorganisation, 29.2–29.5
  profit and loss account, 28.18
  purchase of own shares
    financial assistance, 28.49
    generally, 28.39–28.47
    out of capital at discount,
      29.30–29.32
    out of capital at premium,
      29.33–29.35
    wholly out of distributable profits,
      29.24–29.26
    wholly out of distributable profits
      and proceeds of new issue,
      29.27–29.29
  redenomination reserve, 28.12
  reorganisation, 29.2–29.5
  reserves
    called-up share capital, 28.4–28.7
    capital redemption reserve, 28.13
    introduction, 28.3
    other, 28.16–28.17
    own shares reserve, 28.14
    profit and loss account, 28.18
    redenomination reserve, 28.12

Index

Corporate transactions – *contd*
reserves – *contd*
reserves provided for by articles of association, 28.15
revaluation reserve, 28.11
share premium account, 28.8–28.10
reserves provided for by articles of association, 28.15
revaluation reserve, 28.11
share premium account, 28.8–28.10
Corporation tax, accounting for
current tax (FRS 16), 22.6
deferred tax (FRS 19)
decision to provide, 22.14
deferred assets, 22.16
disclosures, 22.18
discounting, 22.17
generally, 22.7–22.11
liability method of quantification, 22.13
non-monetary assets, 22.15
revaluations, 22.15
timing differences, 22.12
introduction, 22.5
Cost of acquisition
goodwill and intangible assets, and, 25.12
determination of fair value
Costs
stocks, and
calculating related costs, 13.9
generally, 13.4–13.6
methods of costing, 13.7
relating costs to contracts, 13.8
Current assets
See also **Stocks**
historical cost accounting, and, 5.8
Current cost accounting
generally, 5.9–5.10
revaluation reserve, 5.11–5.18
Current ratio
generally, 3.36
Current tax (FRS 16)
accounting for tax, and, 22.6
'Cut-off'
stocks, and, 13.1
Debtors' collection period
ratios, and, 3.36
Deferred tax (FRS 19)
decision to provide, 22.14
deferred assets, 22.16
depreciation, and, 16.19
disclosures, 22.18
discounting, 22.17

Deferred tax (FRS 19) – *contd*
generally, 22.7–22.11
liability method of quantification, 22.13
non-monetary assets, 22.15
revaluations, 22.15
timing differences, 22.12
Defined benefit schemes
pensions, and, 19.3
Defined contribution schemes
pensions, and, 19.3
Demerger of two companies
generally, 28.48
more complex type. 29.42–29.44
simple type, 29.39–29.41
Depreciation (FRS 15)
complex assets, 16.7
computation methods
introduction, 16.3
other, 16.6
reducing balance, 16.5
straight line, 16.4
disclosures, 16.12
disposal of revalued property, 16.11
generally, 16.2
introduction, 16.1
investment properties (SSAP 19)
company law requirements, 16.15
introduction, 16.13–16.14
leased properties, and, 16.16–16.17
optional depreciation, 16.16
redesignation of property, 16.18
output of asset method, 16.6
permanent diminution in value
disposal of revalued property, 16.11
generally, 16.10
reducing balance method, 16.5
revaluations, 16.8–16.9
straight line method, 16.4
taxation, 16.19
usage of asset method, 16.6
Derivatives
comparison with international standards, 27.8
FRED 3, 27.1
FRS 4, 27.4
FRS 13, 27.5
FRS 25
comparison with IAS 32, 27.8
generally, 27.2–27.3
FRS 26
comparison with IAS 39, 27.8
generally, 27.6

Index

Derivatives – *contd*
  FRS 29
    comparison with IFRS 7, 27.8
    generally, 27.7
    introduction, 27.1
    meaning, 27.1
    summary, 27.18
    taxation
      derivative contracts, 27.17
      generally, 27.9–27.10
      indirect issues, 27.11
      loan relationships, 27.14–27.15
      non-lending relationships, 27.16
      recent developments, 27.12–27.13
    types, 27.1
Development work
  And see **Research and development expenditure**
  generally, 26.6
Directors' accounting responsibilities
  limited liability companies, and, 2.10
Directors' emoluments
  post-balance sheet events, and, 8.11
Directors' loan accounts
  post-balance sheet events, and, 8.11–8.12
Directors' reports
  limited liability companies, and, 2.16
  limited liability partnerships, and, 30.4
Disclosures
  deferred tax, and, 22.18
  depreciation, and, 16.12
  extraordinary and exceptional items, 7.20
  historical cost profits, 7.15–7.17
  lease finance, and, 17.23
  prior period adjustments, 7.21–7.25
  profit and loss account, 7.13–7.14
  recognised gains and losses, 7.18
  related parties, and
    control, 9.8
    exemptions, 9.9
    introduction, 9.8
    transactions and balances, 9.8
  reporting financial performance, and
    extraordinary and exceptional items, 7.20
    historical cost profits, 7.15–7.17
    prior period adjustments, 7.21–7.25
    profit and loss account, 7.13–7.14
    recognised gains and losses, 7.18
    shareholders' funds and reserves, 7.19

Disclosures – *contd*
    reporting substance of transactions, and, 6.14
    research and development expenditure, and, 26.10
    shareholders' funds and reserves, 7.19
    stocks, and, 13.11
Discounted selling price
  stocks, and, 13.9
Discounting (FRS 16)
  accounting for tax, 22.6
Disposal of revalued property
  depreciation, and, 16.11
Disposals
  consolidated accounts, and, 23.24
Distributable profits
  generally, 28.19–28.26
  substance over form, and, 6.16
Dividend cover
  ratios, and, 3.38
Dividend yield
  ratios, and, 3.38
Dividend out of pre-acquisition profits
  comparison with IAS 27, 29.45
  generally, 29.21–29.23
Dormant companies
  generally, 2.9
Earnings per share (FRS 22)
  background, 7.2
  generally, 7.28–7.34
  introduction, 7.28
  P/E ratio, 7.29
  taxation, 7.35
Earnouts
  goodwill and intangible assets, and, 25.12
EC Regulation 1606/2002
  generally, 4.3–4.8
Employee share ownership plans (FRS 20)
  comparison with IAS 19 and IFRS 2, 20.7
  FRS 5, and, 20.2
  generally, 20.4–20.6
  introduction, 20.1
  taxation, 20.8
  UITF 13, and, 20.3–20.4
  UK GAAP, 20.2–20.6
'Entity' convention
  generally, 3.3–3.7
'Equity recognition' approach
  pension valuations, and, 19.8

Index

ESOPs (FRS 20)
comparison with IAS 19 and IFRS 2, 20.7
FRS 5, and, 20.2
generally, 20.4–20.6
introduction, 20.1
taxation, 20.8
UITF 13, and, 20.3–20.4
UK GAAP, 20.2–20.6
eXtensible Business Reporting Language (XBRL)
company tax returns, 32.7
generally, 32.6
Extraordinary and exceptional items
reporting financial performance, and, 7.20
Factoring of debts
reporting substance of transactions, and, 6.9
Fair value (FRS 7)
assets and liabilities, 25.10
business bought for resale, 25.13
cost of acquisition, 25.12
determination
  accounting treatment, 25.15–25.19
  distributable profits, 25.17–25.19
  generally, 25.14
  negative goodwill, 25.16
  positive goodwill and intangibles, 25.15
  realised profits, 25.17–25.19
introduction, 25.9
lease finance, and, 17.14
valuation basis, 25.11
Finance costs
tangible fixed assets, and, 15.4
Finance leases
And see **Lease finance**
depreciation, and, 16.19
generally, 17.10
taxation, 17.31
Financial assistance
generally, 28.49
Financial instruments
comparison with international standards, 27.8
FRED 3, 27.1
FRS 4, 27.4
FRS 13, 27.5
FRS 25
  comparison with IAS 32, 27.8
  generally, 27.2–27.3
FRS 26
  comparison with IAS 39, 27.8

Financial instruments – *contd*
FRS 26 – *contd*
  generally, 27.6
FRS 29
  comparison with IFRS 7, 27.8
  generally, 27.7
introduction, 27.1
meaning, 27.1
summary, 27.18
taxation
  derivative contracts, 27.17
  generally, 27.9–27.10
  indirect issues, 27.11
  loan relationships, 27.14–27.15
  non-lending relationships, 27.16
  recent developments, 27.12–27.13
types, 27.1
Financial Reporting Review Panel (FRRP)
relationship with HMRC, 1.9
Financial Reporting Standard for Smaller Entities (FRSSE)
generally, 10.5–10.7
IASB view, and, 10.8–10.9
introduction, 10.1–10.4
Financial Reporting Standards (FRS)
generally, 4.1
Financial year
limited liability companies, and, 2.14
Foreign currency translation (SSAP 20/FRS 23)
comparison with IAS 21, 24.17–24.18
examples, 24.27–24.33
FRS 23, 24.16
group consolidated accounts
  closing rate/net investment method, 24.12–24.13
  generally, 24.10–24.11
  matching, 24.15
  quasi-equity, 24.14
individual companies
  buying and selling assets, 24.4
  introduction, 24.3
  long-term monetary items, 24.8
  matched long-term borrowings, 24.9
  realisation of monetary assets and liabilities, 24.7
  year end adjustments, 24.5–24.6
introduction, 24.1
SSAP 20
  group consolidated accounts, 24.10–24.15
  individual companies, 24.3–24.9
  introduction, 24.2

Index

Foreign currency translation (SSAP 20/FRS 23) – *contd*
 taxation
  basic proposition, 24.24
  deferral of unrealised gains, 24.26
  intermediate system, 24.21
  introduction, 24.19
  matching, 24.25
  new system, 24.20
  old system, 24.22–24.23
'Foreseeable future'
 accounting principles, and, 5.5
Foreseeable losses
 long-term contracts, and, 14.4–14.6
Format of accounts
 generally, 2.12
 IAS, under, 2.13
Framework for the Preparation and Presentation of Financial Statements
 generally, 5.3
FRED 3
 financial instruments, and, 27.1
FRED 10
 cash flow statements, and, 11.1
FRED 12
 goodwill and intangible assets, and, 25.1
FRS 1 (cash flow statements)
 capitalised interest, 11.6
 comparison with IAS 7, 11.8
 example, 11.4
 format, 11.3
 generally, 11.2–11.4
 introduction, 11.1
 material non-cash transactions, 11.7
 tax items, 11.5
 taxation, 11.9
FRS 2 (consolidated accounts)
 examples
  accounting policies, 23.21
  acquisitions, 23.23
  basic consolidation, 23.15–23.17
  disposals, 23.24
  inter-company dividends, 23.20
  inter-company loans, 23.19
  inter-company trading (unrealised profits), 23.18
  introduction, 23.10
  minority interests, 23.22
 introduction, 23.10
 objectives, 23.11–23.12
 preparation, 23.13–23.14

FRS 3 (reporting financial performance)
 background, 7.2
 comparison with IAS 1 and IAS 8, 7.26
 disclosures
  extraordinary and exceptional items, 7.20
  historical cost profits, 7.15–7.17
  prior period adjustments, 7.21–7.25
  profit and loss account, 7.13–7.14
  recognised gains and losses, 7.18
  shareholders' funds and reserves, 7.19
 extraordinary and exceptional items, 7.20
 generally, 7.12
 historical cost profits, 7.15–7.17
 introduction, 7.11
 prior period adjustments, 7.21–7.25
 profit and loss account, 7.13–7.14
 recognised gains and losses, 7.18
 shareholders' funds and reserves, 7.19
 taxation, 7.27
FRS 4 (financial instruments)
 generally, 27.4
FRS 5 (reporting the substance of transactions)
 Application Notes
  introduction, 6.9
  revenue recognition, 12.2–12.3
 assets
  control, 6.7
  generally, 6.4
  identification, 6.10
  offset, 6.13
  recognition, 6.10
 background, 6.1
 basic concepts
  assets, 6.4
  control of asset, 6.7
  introduction, 6.3
  liabilities, 6.5
  recognition, 6.8
  risk, 6.6
 control of asset, 6.7
 disclosure, 6.14
 distributable profits, 6.16
 employee share ownership plans, and, 20.2
 generally, 6.2
 identifying assets and liabilities, 6.10
 international standards, 6.17
 introduction, 6.1

Index

FRS 5 (reporting the substance of transactions) – *contd*
liabilities
  generally, 6.5
  identification, 6.10
  offset, 6.13
  recognition, 6.10
linked presentation, 6.11–6.12
methodology, 6.10–6.14
offset of assets and liabilities, 6.13
profit recognition, 6.15
recognition
  assets and liabilities, 6.10
  generally, 6.8
revenue recognition, and, 12.2–12.3
risk, 6.6
share-based payments, and, 20.2
taxation
  introduction, 6.18
  Ramsay principle, 6.20–6.22
  statutory construction, 6.19
transactions in previously recognised assets, 6.10

FRS 8 (related parties)
close family, 9.5
comparison with IAS 24, 9.10
disclosures
  control, 9.8
  exemptions, 9.9
  introduction, 9.8
  transactions and balances, 9.8
generally, 9.2
introduction, 9.1
key management, 9.6
meaning, 9.3–9.4
taxation, 9.11–9.13
transactions, 9.7

FRS 9 (associates and joint ventures)
comparison with IAS 28, 23.34
comparison with IAS 31, 23.35
equity accounting, 23.27
gross equity method, 23.28–23.32
introduction, 23.25–23.26

FRS 10 (goodwill)
amortisation, 20.4
business bought for resale, 25.13
comparison with IAS 38, 25.20
cost of acquisition, 25.12
determination of fair value
  accounting treatment, 25.15–25.19
  distributable profits, 25.17–25.19
  generally, 25.14
  negative goodwill, 25.16

FRS 10 (goodwill) – *contd*
determination of fair value – *contd*
  positive goodwill and intangibles, 25.15
  realised profits, 25.17–25.19
earnouts, and, 25.12
fair value (FRS 7)
  assets and liabilities, 25.10
  business bought for resale, 25.13
  cost of acquisition, 25.12
  determination, 25.14–25.19
  introduction, 25.9
  valuation basis, 25.11
FRED 12, 25.1
generally, 25.2
impairment reviews, 25.5
initial recognition, 25.3
introduction, 25.1
negative goodwill, 25.7
regime of 2002, 25.22
revaluation, 25.6
SSAP 22, 25.1
taxation, 25.21
transitional rules, 25.8
valuation basis, 25.11

FRS 11 (impairment of fixed assets and goodwill)
generally, 15.8–15.9
introduction, 15.2

FRS 12 (provisions and contingencies)
'big bath' provisions, and, 18.2
comparison with IAS 37, 18.18
contingent assets, 18.17
contingent liabilities, 18.14–18.16
introduction, 18.1–18.4
provisions
  definitions, 18.6
  generally, 18.5–18.13
taxation, 18.19–18.20
timing, and, 5.31

FRS 13 (financial instruments)
generally, 27.5

FRS 15 (tangible fixed assets)
alternative valuation bases, 15.6–15.7
comparison with IAS 16, 15.12
depreciation
  And see **Depreciation**
  complex assets, 16.7
  computation methods, 16.3–16.6
  disclosures, 16.12
  generally, 16.2
  introduction, 16.1
  permanent diminution in value, 16.10–16.11

Index

FRS 15 (tangible fixed assets) – *contd*
  depreciation – *contd*
    revaluations, 16.8–16.9
    taxation, 16.19
  finance costs, 15.4
  impairment, 15.8–15.9
  initial measurement, 15.2
  introduction, 15.1
  investment properties (SSAP 19)
    company law requirements, 16.15
    introduction, 16.13–16.14
    leased properties, and, 16.16–16.17
    optional depreciation, 16.16
    overview, 15.11
    redesignation of property, 16.18
  non-impairment gains and losses, 15.10
  start-up costs, 15.3
  subsequent expenditure, 15.5
FRS 16 (accounting for current tax)
  generally, 22.6
FRS 17 (pensions)
  comparison with IAS 19, 19.8
  defined benefit schemes, 19.3
  defined contribution schemes, 19.3
  generally, 19.5–19.7
  introduction, 19.1–19.3
  objective of standard, 19.5
  SSAP 24, and, 19.4
  taxation, 19.9
  valuation of assets and liabilities, 19.6
FRS 18 (accounting policies)
  generally, 5.22–5.23
  introduction, 5.3
FRS 19 (deferred tax)
  decision to provide, 22.14
  deferred assets, 22.16
  disclosures, 22.18
  discounting, 22.17
  generally, 22.7–22.11
  liability method of quantification, 22.13
  non-monetary assets, 22.15
  revaluations, 22.15
  timing differences, 22.12
FRS 20 (share-based payment)
  comparison with IAS 19 and IFRS 2, 20.7
  FRS 5, and, 20.2
  generally, 20.4–20.6
  introduction, 20.1
  taxation, 20.8
  UITF 13, and, 20.3–20.4
  UK GAAP, 20.2–20.6

FRS 21 (post-balance sheet events)
  comparison with IAS 10, 8.9
  directors' emoluments, 8.11
  directors' loan accounts, 8.11–8.12
  extended debate with HMRC, 8.13
  generally, 8.2–8.8
  introduction, 8.1
  taxation, 8.10–8.12
FRS 22 (earnings per share)
  background, 7.2
  generally, 7.28–7.34
  introduction, 7.28
  P/E ratio, 7.29
  taxation, 7.35
FRS 23 (foreign currency translation)
  comparison with IAS 21, 24.17–24.18
  examples, 24.27–24.33
  generally, 24.16
  introduction, 24.1
  taxation, 24.19–24.26
FRS 25 (financial instruments)
  comparison with IAS 32, 27.8
  generally, 27.2–27.3
FRS 26 (financial instruments)
  comparison with IAS 39, 27.8
  generally, 27.6
FRS 29 (financial instruments)
  comparison with IFRS 7, 27.8
  generally, 27.7
FRSSE
  generally, 10.5–10.7
  IASB view, and, 10.8–10.9
  introduction, 10.1–10.4
Gearing
  ratios, and, 3.37
Generally accepted accounting principles (GAAP)
  background, 1.9
  balance sheet, 3.8–3.27
  'entity' convention, 3.3–3.7
  profit and loss account, 3.28–3.33
  ratios, 3.34–3.40
Going concern
  accounting principles, and, 5.5
Goodwill (FRS 10)
  amortisation, 20.4
  business bought for resale, 25.13
  comparison with IAS 38, 25.20
  cost of acquisition, 25.12
  determination of fair value
    accounting treatment, 25.15–25.19
    distributable profits, 25.17–25.19
    generally, 25.14
    negative goodwill, 25.16

Index

Goodwill (FRS 10) – *contd*
  determination of fair value – *contd*
    positive goodwill and intangibles, 25.15
    realised profits, 25.17–25.19
  earnouts, and, 25.12
  fair value (FRS 7)
    assets and liabilities, 25.10
    business bought for resale, 25.13
    cost of acquisition, 25.12
    determination, 25.14–25.19
    introduction, 25.9
    valuation basis, 25.11
  FRED 12, 25.1
  generally, 25.2
  impairment reviews, 25.5
  initial recognition, 25.3
  introduction, 25.1
  negative goodwill, 25.7
  regime of 2002, 25.22
  revaluation, 25.6
  SSAP 22, 25.1
  taxation, 25.21
  transitional rules, 25.8
  valuation basis, 25.11
Government grants (SSAP 4)
  capital-based grants
    generally, 21.5
    no repayment, 21.11
    repayment, 21.12
  comparison with IAS 20, 21.7
  concepts, 21.3
  generally, 21.2
  introduction, 21.1
  repayments, 21.6
  revenue-based grants
    generally, 21.4
    relating to current year, 21.9
    relating to expenditure over several years, 21.10
  taxation, 21.8–21.12
Gross equity method
  associates and joint ventures, and, 23.28–23.32
Gross profit margin
  ratios, and, 3.35
Groups
  accounting principles
    FRS 2, 23.10–23.24
    FRS 9, 23.25–23.32
  associates and joint ventures (FRS 9)
    comparison with IAS 28, 23.34
    comparison with IAS 31, 23.35
    equity accounting, 23.27

Groups – *contd*
  associates and joint ventures (FRS 9) – *contd*
    gross equity method, 23.28–23.32
    introduction, 23.25–23.26
  consolidated accounts (FRS 2)
    accounting policies, 23.21
    acquisitions, 23.23
    basic consolidation, 23.15–23.17
    comparison with IAS 27, 23.33
    disposals, 23.24
    examples, 23.15–23.24
    inter-company dividends, 23.30
    inter-company loans, 23.19
    inter-company trading (unrealised profits), 23.18
    introduction, 23.10
    minority interests, 23.33
    objectives, 23.11–23.12
    preparation, 23.13–23.14
  corporate law, 23.2
  introduction, 23.1
  joint ventures (FRS 9)
    comparison with IAS 31, 23.35
    equity accounting, 23.27
    gross equity method, 23.28–23.32
    introduction, 23.25–23.26
  parent companies, 23.3–23.9
  taxation, 23.36–23.42
Hire purchase
  And see **Lease finance**
  generally, 17.2
  taxation, 17.29
Historical cost accounting
  generally, 5.8
  reporting financial performance, and, 7.15–7.17
IAS (International accounting standards)
  format of accounts, 2.13
  generally, 4.2
  meaning, 4.4
IAS 1
  reporting financial performance, and, 7.26
IAS 2
  stocks, and, 13.16
IAS 7
  cash-flow statements, and, 11.8
IAS 8
  reporting financial performance, and, 7.26
IAS 10
  post-balance sheet events, and, 8.9

Index

IAS 11
   long-term contracts, and, 14.9
IAS 14
   segmental reporting, and, 7.8
IAS 16
   tangible fixed assets, and, 15.12
IAS 17
   lease finance, and, 17.28
IAS 18
   accounting for VAT, and, 22.19
   revenue recognition, and, 12.5
IAS 19
   pensions, and, 19.8
   share-based payments, and, 20.7
IAS 20
   government grants, and, 21.7
IAS 24
   related parties, and, 9.10
IAS 27
   dividend out of pre-acquisition profits, and, 29.45
IAS 28
   associates, and, 23.34
IAS 31
   joint ventures, and, 23.35
IAS 32
   financial instruments, and, 27.8
IAS 37
   provisions and contingencies, and, 18.18
IAS 38
   goodwill and intangible assets, and, 25.20
   research and development expenditure, and, 26.12
IAS 39
   financial instruments, and, 27.8
IAS Regulation (EC) 1606/2002
   generally, 4.3–4.8
IASB (International Accounting Standards Board)
   convergence with US standards, 32.5
   generally, 4.2
   smaller entities, and, 10.8–10.9
IFRS (International Financial Reporting Standards)
   convergence with UK standards, 32.3–32.4
   future adoption, 32.2
   generally, 4.2
IFRS for Private Entities
   smaller entities, and, 10.8–10.9
IFRS 2
   employee share ownership plans, and, 20.7
IFRS 3
   merger accounting, and, 29.46
IFRS 7
   financial instruments, and, 27.8
Impairment
   tangible fixed assets, and, 15.8–15.9
Impairment reviews
   goodwill and intangible assets, and, 25.5
Incorporation of sole trader business
   generally, 29.9–29.10
Initial measurement
   tangible fixed assets, and, 15.2
Intangible assets (FRS 10)
   amortisation, 20.4
   business bought for resale, 25.13
   comparison with IAS 38, 25.20
   cost of acquisition, 25.12
   determination of fair value
      accounting treatment, 25.15–25.19
      distributable profits, 25.17–25.19
      generally, 25.14
      negative goodwill, 25.16
      positive goodwill and intangibles, 25.15
      realised profits, 25.17–25.19
   earnouts, and, 25.12
   fair value (FRS 7)
      assets and liabilities, 25.10
      business bought for resale, 25.13
      cost of acquisition, 25.12
      determination, 25.14–25.19
      introduction, 25.9
      valuation basis, 25.11
   FRED 12, 25.1
   generally, 25.2
   impairment reviews, 25.5
   initial recognition, 25.3
   introduction, 25.1
   negative goodwill, 25.7
   regime of 2002, 25.22
   revaluation, 25.6
   SSAP 22, 25.1
   taxation, 25.21
   transitional rules, 25.8
   valuation basis, 25.11
Inter-company dividends
   consolidated accounts, and, 23.20
Inter-company loans
   consolidated accounts, and, 23.19
Inter-company trading
   consolidated accounts, and, 23.18
Interest cover
   ratios, and, 3.37

Index

International accounting standards (IAS)
format of accounts, 2.13
generally, 4.2
meaning, 4.4
International Accounting Standards Board (IASB)
convergence with US standards, 32.5
generally, 4.2
smaller entities, and, 10.8–10.9
International Financial Reporting Standards (IFRS)
convergence with UK standards, 32.3–32.4
future adoption, 32.2
generally, 4.2
International standards
substance over form, and, 6.17
Investment companies
generally, 2.9
Investment properties (SSAP 19)
company law requirements, 16.15
introduction, 16.13–16.14
leased properties, and, 16.16–16.17
optional depreciation, 16.16
overview, 15.11
redesignation of property, 16.18
Investors' ratios
generally, 3.38–3.40
Joint ventures (FRS 9)
comparison with IAS 31, 23.35
equity accounting, 23.27
gross equity method, 23.28–23.32
introduction, 23.25–23.26
Keeping and maintaining accounting records
limited liability companies, and, 2.11
Key management
related parties, and, 9.6
Large companies
generally, 2.7
Last in, first out (LIFO)
stocks, and, 13.9
Laying and delivering accounts
limited liability companies, and, 2.18
Lease finance (SSAP 21)
cars, 17.32
comparison with IAS 17, 17.28
definitions
fair value, 17.14
finance lease, 17.10
interest rate implicit in a lease, 17.13
introduction, 17.8

Lease finance (SSAP 21) – *contd*
definitions – *contd*
lease, 17.9
lease term, 17.12
operating lease, 17.11
disclosures, 17.23
fair value, 17.14
finance leases
generally, 17.10
taxation, 17.31
generally, 17.4–17.7
hire purchase
generally, 17.2
taxation, 17.29
interest rate implicit in a lease, 17.13
introduction, 17.1–17.3
lease, 17.9
lease term, 17.12
lessees, 17.15–17.19
lessors, 17.20–17.22
long funding leases, 17.33
operating leases
generally, 17.11
taxation, 17.30
operation of standard
lessees, 17.15–17.19
lessors, 17.20–17.22
problem areas, 17.24–17.27
taxation
car finance, 17.32
finance leases, 17.31
hire purchase, 17.29
long funding leases, 17.33
operating leases, 17.30
Legal framework
dormant companies, 2.9
introduction, 2.1
investment companies, 2.9
large companies, 2.7
limited liability companies
accountancy bodies, 2.20
audit report, 2.17
City Code on Take-overs and Mergers, and, 2.22
classification by activity, 2.9
classification by size, 2.7–2.8
classification by status, 2.4–2.6
Combined Code, 2.23
directors' accounting responsibilities, 2.10
directors' report, 2.16
financial year, 2.14
format of accounts, 2.12–2.13
formation, 2.3

345

Index

Legal framework – *contd*
  limited liability companies – *contd*
    introduction, 2.2
    keeping and maintaining accounting records, 2.11
    laying and delivering accounts, 2.18
    Senior Accounting Officer appointments, 2.19
    Stock Exchange, and, 2.21
    true and fair view, 2.15
  medium-sized companies, 2.7
  non-limited companies, 2.24
  small companies, 2.7
  summary, 2.25
Lessees
  lease finance, and, 17.15–17.19
Lessors
  lease finance, and, 17.20–17.22
Liabilities
  substance over form, and
    generally, 6.5
    identification, 6.10
    offset, 6.13
    recognition, 6.10
Limited liability
  generally, 28.2
Limited liability companies
  accountancy bodies, 2.20
  audit report, 2.17
  City Code on Take-overs and Mergers, and, 2.22
  classification by activity, 2.9
  classification by size, 2.7–2.8
  classification by status, 2.4–2.6
  Combined Code, 2.23
  directors' accounting responsibilities, 2.10
  directors' report, 2.16
  dormant companies, 2.9
  financial year, 2.14
  format of accounts, 2.12–2.13
  formation, 2.3
  introduction, 2.2
  investment companies, 2.9
  keeping and maintaining accounting records, 2.11
  large companies, 2.7
  laying and delivering accounts, 2.18
  medium-sized companies, 2.7
  non-limited companies, 2.24
  Senior Accounting Officer appointments, 2.19
  small companies, 2.7
  Stock Exchange, and, 2.21

Limited liability companies – *contd*
  true and fair view, 2.15
Limited liability partnerships
  balance sheet, 30.3
  introduction, 30.1
  legal requirements, 30.2–30.4
  payments to members, 30.8
  profit and loss account, 30.4
  provisions, 30.11
  related parties, 30.12
  retirement benefits, 30.9–30.10
  revenue recognition, 30.11
  SORP, 30.5
  taxation, 30.13
  UK GAAP, 30.5–30.7
Linked presentation
  substance over form, and, 6.11–6.12
Linking of contractual arrangements
  revenue recognition, and, 12.3
Liquidity
  ratios, and, 3.36
Loan accounts
  post-balance sheet events, and, 8.11–8.12
Loan transfers
  reporting substance of transactions, and, 6.9
Long funding leases
  lease finance, and, 17.33
Long-term contracts (SSAP 9)
  attributable profit, 14.3–14.6
  comparison with IAS 11, 14.9
  foreseeable losses, 14.4–14.6
  introduction, 14.1–14.2
  meaning, 14.1
  payments on account, 14.7–14.8
  revenue recognition, and, 12.3
  taxation, 14.10
Long term gearing
  ratios, and, 3.37
Maintaining accounting records
  limited liability companies, and, 2.11
Matching
  foreign currency translation, and
    group consolidated accounts, 24.15
    individual companies, 24.9
    taxation, 24.25
  lease finance, and, 17.15
  Statement of Principles for Financial Reporting, and, 5.24
  stocks, and, 13.2
Materiality
  generally, 5.25

Measurement
  Statement of Principles for Financial
    Reporting, and, 5.24
Medium-sized companies
  generally, 2.7
Merger accounting
  comparison with IFRS 3, 29.46
  group accounts, 28.35–28.38
  individual companies, 28.31–28.34
  introduction, 28.30
  practice, in, 29.36–29.38
Minority interests
  consolidated accounts, and, 23.22
Negative goodwill
  goodwill and intangible assets, and, 25.7
Net assets per share
  ratios, and, 3.38
Net realisable value
  historical cost accounting, and, 5.8
  stocks, and, 13.10
'No off-set principle'
  accounting principles, and, 5.5
Non-limited companies
  generally, 2.24
Offset of assets and liabilities
  substance over form, and, 6.13
Operating leases
  And see **Lease finance**
  generally, 17.11
  taxation, 17.30
Output of asset
  depreciation, and, 16.6
Own shares reserve
  generally, 28.14
Parent companies
  groups, and, 23.3–23.9
Payments on account
  long-term contracts, and, 14.7–14.8
P/E ratio
  earnings per share, and, 7.29
Pensions (FRS 17)
  comparison with IAS 19, 19.8
  defined benefit schemes, 19.3
  defined contribution schemes, 19.3
  generally, 19.5–19.7
  introduction, 19.1–19.3
  objective of standard, 19.5
  SSAP 24, and, 19.4
  taxation, 19.9
  valuation of assets and liabilities, 19.6
Permanent diminution in value
  depreciation, and, 16.10–16.11

Post-balance sheet events (FRS 21)
  comparison with IAS 10, 8.9
  directors' emoluments, 8.11
  directors' loan accounts, 8.11–8.12
  extended debate with HMRC, 8.13
  generally, 8.2–8.8
  introduction, 8.1
  taxation, 8.10–8.12
Presentational standards
  earnings per share
    background, 7.2
    FRS 22, 7.28–7.34
    introduction, 7.28
    P/E ratio, 7.29
    taxation, 7.35
  introduction, 7.1–7.2
  reporting financial performance
    background, 7.2
    comparison with IAS 1 and IAS 8, 7.26
    disclosures, 7.13–7.25
    extraordinary and exceptional items, 7.20
    FRS 3, 7.12–7.25
    historical cost profits, 7.15–7.17
    introduction, 7.11
    prior period adjustments, 7.21–7.25
    profit and loss account, 7.13–7.14
    recognised gains and losses, 7.18
    shareholders' funds and reserves, 7.19
    taxation, 7.27
  segmental reporting
    background, 7.2
    comparison with IAS 14, 7.8
    introduction, 7.3
    reportable segments, 7.5–7.7
    scope of standard, 7.4
    SSAP 25, 7.4–7.7
    taxation, 7.9–7.10
Price/earnings ratio
  generally, 3.38
Prior period adjustments
  reporting financial performance, and, 7.21–7.25
Private Finance Initiative
  reporting substance of transactions, and, 6.9
Profit and loss account
  corporate transactions, and, 28.18
  generally, 3.28–3.33
  limited liability partnerships, and, 30.4
  reporting financial performance, and, 7.13–7.14

Index

Profit margin on sales
ratios, and, 3.35
Profit per accounts
generally, 1.1
Profit recognition
substance over form, and, 6.15
Profitability
ratios, and, 3.34–3.35
Provisions (FRS 12)
'big bath' provisions, and, 18.2
comparison with IAS 37, 18.18
definitions, 18.6
generally, 18.5–18.13
introduction, 18.1–18.4
limited liability partnerships, and, 30.11
taxation, 18.19–18.20
timing, and, 5.31
Prudence
accounting principles, and, 5.5
stocks, and, 13.2
Purchase costs
stocks, and, 13.4–13.6
Purchase of own shares
financial assistance, 28.49
generally, 28.39–28.47
out of capital at discount, 29.30–29.32
out of capital at premium, 29.33–29.35
wholly out of distributable profits, 29.24–29.26
wholly out of distributable profits and proceeds of new issue, 29.27–29.29
Pure research
research and development expenditure, and, 26.4
Quick ratio
generally, 3.36
***Ramsay* principle**
substance over form, and, 6.20–6.22
Ratios
current ratio, 3.36
debtors' collection period, 3.36
dividend cover, 3.38
dividend yield, 3.38
gearing, as to, 3.37
generally, 3.34
gross profit margin, 3.35
interest cover, 3.37
investors, for, 3.38–3.40
liquidity, as to, 3.36
long term gearing, 3.37
met assets per share, 3.38

Ratios – *contd*
price/earnings ratio, 3.38
profit margin on sales, 3.35
profitability, as to, 3.34–3.35
quick ratio, 3.36
return on capital employed, 3.35
stock turnover, 3.36
total gearing, 3.37
Recognised gains and losses
reporting financial performance, and, 7.18
Recognition
reporting substance of transactions, and
assets and liabilities, 6.10
generally, 6.8
profit, 6.15
Statement of Principles for Financial Reporting, and, 5.24
Redenomination reserve
generally, 28.12
Reducing balance method
depreciation, and, 16.5
Related parties (FRS 8)
close family, 9.5
comparison with IAS 24, 9.10
definition
close family, 9.5
generally, 9.4
introduction, 9.3
key management, 9.6
disclosures
control, 9.8
exemptions, 9.9
introduction, 9.8
transactions and balances, 9.8
generally, 9.2
introduction, 9.1
key management, 9.6
limited liability partnerships, and, 30.12
meaning, 9.3–9.4
taxation, 9.11–9.13
transactions, 9.7
Reorganisation
generally, 29.2–29.5
Repayments
government grants, and, 21.6
Replacement cost
stocks, and, 13.9
Reporting financial performance (FRS 3)
background, 7.2
comparison with IAS 1 and IAS 8, 7.26

348

Index

Reporting financial performance (FRS 3) – *contd*
disclosures
  extraordinary and exceptional items, 7.20
  historical cost profits, 7.15–7.17
  prior period adjustments, 7.21–7.25
  profit and loss account, 7.13–7.14
  recognised gains and losses, 7.18
  shareholders' funds and reserves, 7.19
extraordinary and exceptional items, 7.20
generally, 7.12
historical cost profits, 7.15–7.17
introduction, 7.11
prior period adjustments, 7.21–7.25
profit and loss account, 7.13–7.14
recognised gains and losses, 7.18
shareholders' funds and reserves, 7.19
taxation, 7.27

Reporting the substance of transactions (FRS 5)
Application Notes
  introduction, 6.9
  revenue recognition, 12.2–12.3
assets
  control, 6.7
  generally, 6.4
  identification, 6.10
  offset, 6.13
  recognition, 6.10
background, 6.1
basic concepts
  assets, 6.4
  control of asset, 6.7
  introduction, 6.3
  liabilities, 6.5
  recognition, 6.8
  risk, 6.6
control of asset, 6.7
disclosure, 6.14
distributable profits, 6.16
generally, 6.2
identifying assets and liabilities, 6.10
international standards, 6.17
introduction, 6.1
liabilities
  generally, 6.5
  identification, 6.10
  offset, 6.13
  recognition, 6.10
linked presentation, 6.11–6.12
methodology, 6.10–6.14

Reporting the substance of transactions (FRS 5) – *contd*
offset of assets and liabilities, 6.13
profit recognition, 6.15
recognition
  assets and liabilities, 6.10
  generally, 6.8
revenue recognition, and, 12.2–12.3
risk, 6.6
taxation
  introduction, 6.18
  Ramsay principle, 6.20–6.22
  statutory construction, 6.19
transactions in previously recognised assets, 6.10

Research and development expenditure (SSAP 13)
accounting treatment, 26.7–26.9
applied research, 26.5
basic research, 26.4
company law requirements, 26.11
comparison with IAS 38, 26.12
definitions
  applied research, 26.5
  basic research, 26.4
  development, 26.6
  introduction, 26.3
  pure research, 26.4
development, 26.6
disclosures, 26.10
generally, 26.2
introduction, 26.1
pure research, 26.4
taxation, 26.13

Reserves
called-up share capital, 28.4–28.7
capital redemption reserve, 28.13
introduction, 28.3
other, 28.16–28.17
own shares reserve, 28.14
profit and loss account, 28.18
redenomination reserve, 28.12
reserves provided for by articles of association, 28.15
revaluation reserve, 28.11
share premium account, 28.8–28.10

Retirement benefits
limited liability partnerships, and, 30.9–30.10

Return on capital employed
ratios, and, 3.35

Revaluation reserve
generally, 5.11–5.18
introduction, 28.11

349

Index

Revaluations
  depreciation, and, 16.8–16.9
  goodwill and intangible assets, and, 25.6
Revenue
  See also **Revenue recognition**
  distinction from capital, 5.26–5.30
  expenses, 5.34–5.37
  sales, 5.32–5.33
  timing, 5.31–5.37
Revenue-based grants
  generally, 21.4
  relating to current year, 21.9
  relating to expenditure over several years, 21.10
Revenue recognition
  FRS 5, App Note G, 12.2–12.3
  IAS 18, 12.5
  introduction, 12.1
  limited liability partnerships, and, 30.11
  overview, 6.9
  taxation, 12.6–12.7
  UITF 40, 12.4
Risk
  substance over form, and, 6.6
Sale and repurchase agreements
  reporting substance of transactions, and, 6.9
Sale with rights of return
  revenue recognition, and, 12.3
Securitised assets
  reporting substance of transactions, and, 6.9
Segmental reporting (SSAP 25)
  background, 7.2
  comparison with IAS 14, 7.8
  introduction, 7.3
  reportable segments, 7.5–7.7
  scope of standard, 7.4
  taxation, 7.9–7.10
Senior Accounting Officer appointments
  limited liability companies, and, 2.19
Separation of contractual arrangements
  revenue recognition, and, 12.3
Share-based payment (FRS 20)
  comparison with IAS 19 and IFRS 2, 20.7
  FRS 5, and, 20.2
  generally, 20.4–20.6
  introduction, 20.1
  taxation, 20.8
  UITF 13, and, 20.3–20.4

Share-based payment (FRS 20) – *contd*
  UK GAAP, 20.2–20.6
Share premium account
  generally, 28.8–28.10
Shareholders' funds and reserves
  reporting financial performance, and, 7.19
Small companies
  generally, 2.7
Smaller entities (FRSSE)
  generally, 10.5–10.7
  IASB view, and, 10.8–10.9
  introduction, 10.1–10.4
SSAP 1 (associated companies)
  generally, 5.3
  groups, and, 23.25
SSAP 2 (disclosure of accounting policies)
  generally, 5.3
SSAP 3 (earnings per share)
  generally, 7.2
SSAP 4 (government grants)
  capital-based grants
    generally, 21.5
    no repayment, 21.11
    repayment, 21.12
  comparison with IAS 20, 21.7
  concepts, 21.3
  generally, 21.2
  introduction, 21.1
  repayments, 21.6
  revenue-based grants
    generally, 21.4
    relating to current year, 21.9
    relating to expenditure over several years, 21.10
  taxation, 21.8–21.12
SSAP 5 (taxation)
  comparison with IAS 18, 22.19
  generally, 22.2–22.4
SSAP 6 (extraordinary and prior year items)
  generally, 7.2
SSAP 8 (taxation under the imputation system)
  generally, 22.6
SSAP 9 (long-term contracts)
  attributable profit, 14.3–14.6
  comparison with IAS 11, 14.9
  foreseeable losses, 14.4–14.6
  introduction, 14.1–14.2
  meaning, 14.1
  payments on account, 14.7–14.8
  taxation, 14.10

Index

SSAP 9 (stocks)
  base stock, 13.9
  company law requirements, 13.12–13.15
  comparison with IAS 2, 13.16
  conversion costs, 13.4–13.6
  costs
    calculating related costs, 13.9
    generally, 13.4–13.6
    methods of costing, 13.7
    relating costs to contracts, 13.8
  'cut-off', 13.1
  definition, 13.3
  disclosures, 13.11
  discounted selling price, 13.9
  first in, first out (FIFO), 13.9
  generally, 13.2
  introduction, 13.1
  last in, first out (LIFO), 13.9
  net realisable value, 13.10
  purchase costs, 13.4–13.6
  replacement cost, 13.9
  taxation, 13.17–13.18
SSAP 10 (statement of source and application of funds)
  generally, 11.1
SSAP 13 (research and development expenditure)
  accounting treatment, 26.7–26.9
  applied research, 26.5
  basic research, 26.4
  company law requirements, 26.11
  comparison with IAS 38, 26.12
  definitions
    applied research, 26.5
    basic research, 26.4
    development, 26.6
    introduction, 26.3
    pure research, 26.4
  development, 26.6
  disclosures, 26.10
  generally, 26.2
  introduction, 26.1
  pure research, 26.4
  taxation, 26.13
SSAP 14 (group accounts)
  generally, 22.6
SSAP 15 (accounting for deferred tax)
  generally, 22.7
SSAP 17 (post-balance sheet events)
  generally, 8.1
SSAP 19 (investment properties)
  company law requirements, 16.15
  introduction, 16.13–16.14

SSAP 19 (investment properties) – *contd*
  leased properties, and, 16.16–16.17
  optional depreciation, 16.16
  overview, 15.11
  redesignation of property, 16.18
SSAP 20 (foreign currency translation)
  comparison with IAS 21, 24.17–24.18
  examples, 24.27–24.33
  generally, 24.2
  group consolidated accounts
    closing rate/net investment method, 24.12–24.13
    generally, 24.10–24.11
    matching, 24.15
    quasi-equity, 24.14
  individual companies
    buying and selling assets, 24.4
    introduction, 24.3
    long-term monetary items, 24.8
    matched long-term borrowings, 24.9
    realisation of monetary assets and liabilities, 24.7
    year end adjustments, 24.5–24.6
  introduction, 24.1
  taxation
    basic proposition, 24.24
    deferral of unrealised gains, 24.26
    intermediate system, 24.21
    introduction, 24.19
    matching, 24.25
    new system, 24.20
    old system, 24.22–24.23
SSAP 21 (leased assets)
  background, 1.4–1.8
  cars, 17.32
  comparison with IAS 17, 17.28
  definitions
    fair value, 17.14
    finance lease, 17.10
    interest rate implicit in a lease, 17.13
    introduction, 17.8
    lease, 17.9
    lease term, 17.12
    operating lease, 17.11
  disclosures, 17.23
  fair value, 17.14
  finance leases
    generally, 17.10
    taxation, 17.31
  generally, 17.4–17.7

351

Index

SSAP 21 (leased assets) – *contd*
  hire purchase
    generally, 17.2
    taxation, 17.29
  interest rate implicit in a lease, 17.13
  introduction, 17.1–17.3
  lease, 17.9
  lease term, 17.12
  lessees, 17.15–17.19
  lessors, 17.20–17.22
  long funding leases, 17.33
  operating leases
    generally, 17.11
    taxation, 17.30
  operation of standard
    lessees, 17.15–17.19
    lessors, 17.20–17.22
  problem areas, 17.24–17.27
  taxation
    car finance, 17.32
    finance leases, 17.31
    hire purchase, 17.29
    long funding leases, 17.33
    operating leases, 17.30
SSAP 22 (goodwill and intangible assets)
  generally, 25.1
SSAP 24 (pensions)
  generally, 19.4
SSAP 25 (segmental reporting)
  background, 7.2
  comparison with IAS 14, 7.8
  introduction, 7.3
  reportable segments, 7.5–7.7
  scope, 7.4
  taxation, 7.9–7.10
Start-up costs
  tangible fixed assets, and, 15.3
Statement of Changes in Equity
  generally, 7.26
Statement of Principles for Financial Reporting
  generally, 5.24
  introduction, 5.3
Statement of Total Recognised Gains and Losses (STRGL)
  generally, 7.12
  smaller entities, and, 10.6
Statements of Recommended Practice (SORP)
  limited liability partnerships, and, 30.5
Statements of Standard Accounting Practice (SSAP)
  generally, 5.2
  introduction, 4.1

Stock Exchange
  limited liability companies, and, 2.21
Stock turnover
  ratios, and, 3.36
Stocks (SSAP 9)
  base stock, 13.9
  company law requirements, 13.12–13.15
  comparison with IAS 2, 13.16
  conversion costs, 13.4–13.6
  costs
    calculating related costs, 13.9
    generally, 13.4–13.6
    methods of costing, 13.7
    relating costs to contracts, 13.8
  'cut-off', 13.1
  definition, 13.3
  disclosures, 13.11
  discounted selling price, 13.9
  first in, first out (FIFO), 13.9
  generally, 13.2
  introduction, 13.1
  last in, first out (LIFO), 13.9
  net realisable value, 13.10
  purchase costs, 13.4–13.6
  replacement cost, 13.9
  taxation, 13.17–13.18
Straight line method
  depreciation, and, 16.4
STRGL
  generally, 7.12
Subsequent expenditure
  tangible fixed assets, and, 15.5
Substance over form
  Application Notes
    introduction, 6.9
    revenue recognition, 12.2–12.3
  assets
    control, 6.7
    generally, 6.4
    identification, 6.10
    offset, 6.13
    recognition, 6.10
  background, 6.1
  basic concepts
    assets, 6.4
    control of asset, 6.7
    introduction, 6.3
    liabilities, 6.5
    recognition, 6.8
    risk, 6.6
  control of asset, 6.7
  disclosure, 6.14
  distributable profits, 6.16

352

Substance over form – *contd*
  FRS 5
    application, 6.9
    basic concepts, 6.3–6.8
    distributable profits, 6.16
    generally, 6.2
    international standards, 6.17
    methodology, 6.10–6.14
    profit recognition, 6.15
    taxation, 6.18–6.22
  identifying assets and liabilities, 6.10
  international standards, 6.17
  introduction, 6.1
  liabilities
    generally, 6.5
    identification, 6.10
    offset, 6.13
    recognition, 6.10
  linked presentation, 6.11–6.12
  methodology, 6.10–6.14
  offset of assets and liabilities, 6.13
  profit recognition, 6.15
  recognition
    assets and liabilities, 6.10
    generally, 6.8
  revenue recognition, and, 12.2–12.3
  risk, 6.6
  smaller entities, and, 10.6
  taxation
    introduction, 6.18
    Ramsay principle, 6.20–6.22
    statutory construction, 6.19
  transactions in previously recognised assets, 6.10

Tangible fixed assets (FRS 15)
  alternative valuation bases, 15.6–15.7
  comparison with IAS 16, 15.12
  finance costs, 15.4
  impairment, 15.8–15.9
  initial measurement, 15.2
  introduction, 15.1
  investment properties, 15.11
  non-impairment gains and losses, 15.10
  start-up costs, 15.3
  subsequent expenditure, 15.5

Taxation
  cash-flow statements, and, 11.9
  contingencies, and, 18.19–18.20
  depreciation, and, 16.19
  earnings per share, and, 7.35
  employee share ownership plans, and, 20.8

Taxation – *contd*
  financial instruments, and
    derivative contracts, 27.17
    generally, 27.9–27.10
    indirect issues, 27.11
    loan relationships, 27.14–27.15
    non-lending relationships, 27.16
    recent developments, 27.12–27.13
  foreign currency translation, and
    basic proposition, 24.24
    deferral of unrealised gains, 24.26
    intermediate system, 24.21
    introduction, 24.19
    matching, 24.25
    new system, 24.20
    old system, 24.22–24.23
  goodwill and intangible assets, and, 25.21
  government grants, and
    capital-based grants, 21.11–21.12
    generally, 21.8
    revenue-based grants, 21.9–21.10
  groups, and, 23.36–23.42
  lease finance, and
    car finance, 17.32
    finance leases, 17.31
    hire purchase, 17.29
    long funding leases, 17.33
    operating leases, 17.30
  limited liability partnerships, and, 30.13
  long-term contracts, and, 14.10
  pensions, and, 19.9
  post-balance sheet events, and
    directors' emoluments, 8.11
    directors' loan accounts, 8.11–8.12
    introduction, 8.10
  provisions, and, 18.19–18.20
  related parties, and, 9.11–9.13
  reporting financial performance, and, 7.27
  research and development expenditure, and, 26.13
  revenue recognition, and, 12.6–12.7
  segmental reporting, and, 7.9–7.10
  share-based payments, and, 20.8
  stocks, and, 13.17–13.18
  substance over form, and
    introduction, 6.18
    Ramsay principle, 6.20–6.22
    statutory construction, 6.19
  work in progress, and, 13.17–13.18

Timing
  generally 5.31

Index

Timing – *contd*
    expenses, 5.34–5.37
    sales, 5.32–5.33
Total gearing
    ratios, and, 3.37
True and fair view
    background, 1.9
    limited liability companies, and, 2.15
Turnover
    And see **Revenue recognition**
    principal or agent, as, 12.3
UITF 13 (employee stock ownership plan trusts)
    generally, 20.3–20.4
UITF 17 (employee share schemes)
    generally, 20.3–20.4
UITF 40 (revenue recognition)
    generally, 12.4
    taxation, 12.7
    timing, and, 5.32
UK GAAP
    balance sheet, 3.8–3.27
    differences from international standards, 4.11
    employee share ownership plans, and, 20.2–20.6
    'entity' convention, 3.3–3.7
    generally, 4.3–4.13
    IAS Regulation, and, 4.6
    limited liability partnerships, and, 30.5–30.7
    profit and loss account, 3.28–3.33
    ratios, 3.34–3.40
Unrealised profits
    consolidated accounts, and, 23.18

Use of asset
    depreciation, and, 16.6
Valuation
    depreciation, and, 16.19
    goodwill and intangible assets, and, 25.11
    pensions, and, 19.6
VAT, accounting for (SSAP 5)
    cash flow statements, and, 11.5
    comparison with IAS 18, 22.19
    generally, 22.2–22.4
    groups, and, 23.40
Work in progress (SSAP 9)
    base stock, 13.9
    company law requirements, 13.12–13.15
    comparison with IAS 2, 13.16
    conversion costs, 13.4–13.6
    costs
        calculating related costs, 13.9
        generally, 13.4–13.6
        methods of costing, 13.7
        relating costs to contracts, 13.8
    'cut-off', 13.1
    definition, 13.3
    disclosures, 13.11
    discounted selling price, 13.9
    first in, first out (FIFO), 13.9
    generally, 13.2
    introduction, 13.1
    last in, first out (LIFO), 13.9
    net realisable value, 13.10
    purchase costs, 13.4–13.6
    replacement cost, 13.9
    taxation, 13.17–13.18